The Elementary School Subjects

Books by Luella Cole

BACKGROUND FOR COLLEGE TEACHING

THE ELEMENTARY SCHOOL SUBJECTS

IMPROVEMENT OF READING

PSYCHOLOGY OF ADOLESCENCE
Revised Edition

PSYCHOLOGY OF THE ELEMENTARY SCHOOL SUBJECTS

TEACHING IN THE ELEMENTARY SCHOOL

STUDENTS' GUIDE TO EFFICIENT STUDY
Third Edition (with J. M. Ferguson)

The
ELEMENTARY SCHOOL
SUBJECTS

by

LUELLA COLE

RINEHART & COMPANY, INC.

Publishers   *New York*

To

the Memory of

Helena M. Cole

Preface

The core of academic work in elementary school consists of reading, simple arithmetic, spelling, handwriting, geography, and the beginnings of English composition and history. These subjects are necessary in all walks of life, are basic for work beyond the sixth grade, and are not too difficult for children to master. Throughout the last forty years extensive research in each of these subjects has been focused on objectives, the social and academic value of each subject in the curriculum, the content of work for each grade, the abilities and interests of elementary school children, methods of learning, types of errors, and methods of teaching. So much material on all these aspects has been accumulated that the teacher in training encounters an embarrassment of riches. Yet she should be informed as to the major results of all this work in order that she may make her teaching as effective as possible.

For clarity in presentation the text has been divided into three main sections, dealing respectively with reading, writing, and arithmetic. The material on reading includes the special problems presented by assignments in geography and history. Handwriting, spelling, and composition have been included under the general topic of writing, since each contributes to written work and since all three should be closely integrated with one another. The third section contains material on the fundamental processes and on problem solving in arithmetic. Each major section deals with such important phases of the subject as learning, motivation, difficulty, readiness, and remedial work.

While some students who use this text will already have had work in standardized tests and in educational psychology, others will not, and these are likely to lack the vocabulary necessary for studying this book. To help equalize differences in preparation and to serve as a review if needed, I have prepared in an appendix a brief explanation of such special terms drawn from testing as I have used in this book. This material may be assigned to the whole class, to individual members, or not at all, according to need.

In an earlier text,[1] which this book displaces, each chapter concluded with a brief section entitled "Precepts for the Teacher." In this new book I have listed the precepts but once, illustrating them with examples from several subjects and placing the material in Appendix II, where it can be used by those who desire it and easily avoided by those who do not.

Suggestions for further reading appear at the end of each main division. Most of the books listed parallel this text in a general way, but some give extensive discussion of topics that I have considered only briefly. These references are mainly for undergraduates, who should certainly do a good deal of collateral reading. Moreover, throughout the text, in footnotes intended primarily for the instructor and advanced students, I have listed titles that should serve to bring the student into contact with the literature on a given problem. If he starts with the references given here, he will find in them many more which will enable him to pursue a topic as far as he wishes. These references, incidentally, do not cover the literature after March 1, 1945. In addition to the list of books found at the end of each main division there is a series of exercises and projects based on the main points of the preceding chapters.

Throughout the book it has been my intention to present only such facts as may, by their usefulness in and application to the daily work of the classroom, contribute directly to an increase of teaching efficiency. To these facts I have tried to give life and reality whenever possible by means of case studies, exercises, illustrations, or accounts of specific experiments.

LUELLA COLE

Berkeley, California
January, 1946

---

[1] *Psychology of the Elementary School Subjects,* Farrar & Rinehart, Inc., 1934, 330 pp.

Contents

CONTENTS

PART III: ARITHMETIC

List of Figures

List of Tables

Part I · READING

SENSORY EQUIPMENT AND EYE MOVEMENTS

GENERAL AND TECHNICAL VOCABULARY

COMPREHENSION, ESPECIALLY IN THE SOCIAL SCIENCES

INTEREST, TASTE, AND DYNAMICS

THE DIFFICULTY OF READING MATTER

READING READINESS

REMEDIAL WORK IN READING

READING

READING is a highly synthetic process. It requires simultaneous func-tioning of eye and articulatory muscles, recognition of separate words and phrases, immediate memory for what has just been read, remote memories based on the reader's earlier experiences, interest in the reading matter, and a sufficient degree of intelligence to understand what is read. If everything functions perfectly, comprehension follows, but the various elements are all so dependent upon each other that trouble at any point at once lowers the degree of comprehension and may quite destroy it. If a person accustomed to looking at every word on a line is so hurried that he looks only at every third word, he gets little if any meaning; or if he is accustomed to whisper words to himself but tries to suppress this habit, he finds his comprehension to be less than usual. Let enough unfamiliar words be introduced, and he derives no meaning at all. If the reading matter concerns unfamiliar activities, the reader may make almost no sense out of it even though he knows the separate words. And who has not experienced difficulty in understanding a selection in which he has no spark of interest or for which he lacks either the necessary background or the native ability? Comprehension takes place only when all these elements work together, and a failure to comprehend may be due to any malfunctioning of one or more of them. For a child, such a highly synthetic process often fails to "click." His eyes are not yet mature and have not yet been trained for accurate and economical fixating; his memory span is short; he has little ex-perience in the light of which meaning can be interpreted; the reading matter is often uninteresting to him; he finds dozens of new words every day; and the reading matter he is given is sometimes too hard for his stage of development. It is not surprising that his comprehension is not always adequate for his needs.

It does not seem desirable to go into the question of what the exact psychological nature of the reading process may be. Not much is known about it, and what is known does not seem to contribute a great deal to solving the problem of teaching children to read. It would appear more profitable to consider in some detail the various conditions that have an effect upon reading ability. There are so many of these factors that some grouping of them appears to be needed. Naturally, all of them function simultaneously during any act of reading, but it is not possible to discuss all of them simultaneously. The various factors will, therefore, be considered in order, but the reader should not forget that each element is a part of a whole rather than an independent entity that functions in isolation. The successive chapters in this section on reading will deal: (1) with the nature and extent of eye defects, the frequency of defects in hearing and speech, eye dominance, laterality, the effect of these factors upon reading, the nature of eye movements, and vocalization; (2) with the development of general and technical vocabularies and the problem of phonics; (3) with the development of comprehension, especially in the reading of the social sciences; (4) with the interests of children in different types of material; (5) with the measurement of reading difficulty; (6) with the readiness of children to begin the task of reading; and (7) with the recent developments in remedial reading.

I · Sensory Equipment and Eye Movements

A child needs normal eyes, ears, and speech if he is to learn how to read by ordinary classroom methods and without resort to such compensations as are necessary when the senses are defective. Even with normal sensory equipment a child may fail to hit upon a proper coordination of his receptive and reacting mechanisms. He may begin his efforts to read when his eyes, nervous system, motor control, and speech are all too immature for the demands made upon them. For an understanding of the reading process, a student must first understand the physical basis upon which the process rests. Although a normal sensory, neural, and muscular equipment will not automatically guarantee success in learning to read, any serious defect in the physical basis is likely to cause difficulty, even though bright children often find a way to compensate for their defects, without help from adults.

A. SENSORY EQUIPMENT

1. Defects of Vision: The per cent of children who have defects of vision has been found by different investigators [1] to be somewhere between 25 and 75 per cent of the groups tested, the figure depending presumably upon the thoroughness of the examination, the degree to which the pupils were a selected group, and the examiner's standard of just how

[1] See, for instance, G. E. Berner and D. E. Berner, "Reading Difficulties in Children," *Archives of Ophthalmology,* 20: 829–838, 1938; E. A. Betts and A. S. Austin, "Seeing Problems of School Children," *Ophthalmic Weekly,* 31: 1151–1153, 1181–1183, 1209–1211, 1265–1268, 1293–1295, 1321–1323, 1407–1409, 1431–1437, 1461–1464, 1940; 32: 5–6, 33–37, 102–103, 147–152, 158–160, 173–177, 201–202, 257–259, 285–286, 313–314, 369–371, 1941; and 33: 425–428, 1942; F. W. Brock, "Fusion Disturbances in Binocular Vision," *Optometric Weekly,* 34: 207–209, 269–70, 297, 319, 1943; M. M. Gillett, "Reading Deficiencies and Vision," *Research Quarterly of the American Association of Health and Physical Education,* 13: 178–184, 1942; G. E. Park and C. Burri, "Eye Maturation and Reading Difficulties," *Journal of Educational Psychology,* 34: 535–546, 1943.

much deviation was to be considered abnormal. A sample study gives the following figures concerning the per cent of elementary school pupils in a random sampling who showed defects. Vision was perfectly normal for only 27 pupils in the 225 tested.

TABLE 1

Incidence of Visual Defects [2]

(Kindergarten—Grade 6)

	Per Cent
Visual acuity below normal *	43
Squint	4
Inadequate fusion of images from the two eyes	26
Inadequate perception of depth	49
Nearsightedness	13
Farsightedness	46
In need of glasses	30

*The highly technical words used in the original table have been omitted and less special terms are used in their place.

The most frequent defects among elementary school children, as shown by all studies combined, are farsightedness, lack of fusion for such small objects as letters or words, inadequate accommodation or convergence after a few minutes of reading, astigmatism, muscular imbalance at reading distance, lowered visual acuity, and nearsightedness.[3] Any of these defects may cause difficulty in reading, although none does so inevitably. Farsightedness is a normal condition of young children, and the condition often continues till the entrance to school. For instance, out of one group of 183 pupils, 80 were farsighted. In this same group, 37 were astigmatic in one or both eyes, 23 did not have complete fusion, and 23 showed muscular imbalance, but only 4 were nearsighted.[4] Approximately this distribution of defects is typical of children at the time of their entrance to the first grade.

In some cases, there are physical symptoms such as redness or swelling or watering of the eyes whenever a child tries to read. The eyelids may become swollen or inflamed, or the pupil may constantly rub his eyes. Children with such reactions are lucky because the symptoms lead

[2] Park and Burri, *op. cit.* Used by permission of the publishers.

[3] Farsightedness and nearsightedness are caused by the shape of the eyeball. Astigmatism comes from a defect in the lens or cornea of the eye.

[4] E. A. Betts, *The Prevention and Correction of Reading Difficulties,* Row, Peterson and Company, Evanston, Illinois, 1936, 402 pp.

to a speedy remedying of the underlying defect. Some children show other physical reactions, especially dizziness and nausea after a few minutes of visual effort. Sometimes children complain of pain in their eyes, but more often they do not. Occasionally a pupil says that there are spots before his eyes or that the words jump around on the page or that the print is not clear. Even those who never complain show their defects indirectly by various reactions that are of a nature to protect their eyes against strain. The protective nature is obvious when a child puts his head down in his arms on the desk or covers his eyes with his hands or brings the book up to the end of his nose. Less obvious is the purposeful inattention of the pupil who holds his book properly but looks through the book at the horizon. His teacher is likely to think him stupid, although he is merely being intelligent. Other pupils scowl or hold their heads at an odd angle or make great effort to keep away from light. Some react to eyestrain by becoming irritable, restless, and—if pushed far enough—rebellious, and disorderly. But by far the commonest symptoms, however, are an avoidance of reading whenever possible, a substitution of ears for eyes, a development of sundry neat methods of distracting the teacher whenever she asks for evidence of reading, a dependence upon the prompting of friends, and a blank refusal to so much as attempt reading when avoidance fails and the teacher refuses to be distracted. A quiet but firm resistance plus a moderate amount of ingenuity has permitted many a child to escape reading and thereby to conceal the visual defects which, if corrected, would have made reading a pleasant instead of a painful task.

Typical behavior of some non-readers with visual disabilities are presented below in order to make clearer the nature of the protective reactions just described.

Herbert was a beautiful illustration of the reactions made by an intelligent child to a serious reading difficulty. His fifth grade teacher reported that he read practically nothing, although he seemed very bright and alert, and that he was failing or almost failing in every subject. Previous teachers had had similar experiences, and his fourth grade teacher had failed him in reading. In the early grades, the teachers had never been quite sure whether he really read or just was very clever in picking up things by ear. Herbert admitted to me that most of what he learned he got by listening, remembering, and guessing. The boy impressed me as nervous and overstrained. When I tested his oral reading, his performance was highly revealing. He read fluently for two or three lines, then badly for two or three more, and then not at all. He merely looked up from his book and began to talk in a most engaging manner. At the end of perhaps five minutes, he again began to read, was again fluent, then stumbling, and then conversational for another five minutes. I let the examination continue for a half-hour, during which he made five excellent starts, only to run down after a few lines. At no time did he display any resistance; he merely substituted conversation for reading and tried to be so interesting that I would not notice his meagre progress in the book. I explained to Herbert that he had been able to keep up with his class until recently because he learned quickly, listened carefully, and remembered what he heard, but that now the other children were learning so much through reading that he could no longer compensate by listening. And I assured him that the situation would get worse rather than better in subsequent years unless he began to read in longer snatches than a few lines. Herbert was concerned over his poor standing in school and bewildered by it, but he could give no explanation. Nor could he tell me why he stopped reading so quickly, when the initial lines showed him to be so fluent. To relieve the tension I arranged for Herbert to remain in the remedial reading room each morning and to try to pass only those subjects that came during the afternoon—geography, music, art, oral English, and handwriting. The next semester he was to take the subjects given in the morning session in the fifth grade, spend the afternoon in the sixth, and the following summer make up enough arithmetic, reading, spelling, and composition to catch up with his class. In this way, Herbert could spread out the work of the following two semesters over enough time to let him relax a little. Herbert was eager to plunge into reading drill at once, but he was still too overstrained for concentrated work, so for two or three days he drew pictures on the blackboard, ran errands for me, slept, and wandered about the playground in the sunshine. Among other things he had a complete physical examination and a session with the oculist. The former found him underweight and overanxious while the latter located the boy's basic defect—his extreme farsightedness. It was not, however, sufficient to give Herbert glasses and turn him loose, because he had built up an elaborate set of reactions behind which his defect had long lain concealed. If Herbert had been a stupid child he would have persisted long enough in his efforts to read to give him pain in his eyes, but he was much too bright for that. Perhaps he once read long enough to develop pain, but before he had been in school six weeks he had begun to substitute ears for eyes. In the early grades he was successful enough to establish his avoiding reactions permanently. Herbert had never complained of pain because he had never read long enough at once to have any. Being bright, he avoided what had presumably once hurt him. This avoidance behavior had been going on so long that it was hard to remedy. Although Herbert's eyestrain no longer existed, his inability to apply himself did. I did not want to resort to pressure because Herbert had had too much of that already. Finally, I hit upon the plan of making Herbert my assistant and

without checking the accuracy of the statement, we concluded that Wilbur was well started on the road to success in reading. He was promoted the following June and each semester thereafter, until now he has reached the Grade V-B. Meanwhile, he has been transferred to another public school where his records in reading have justified our conclusions that poor vision was the cause of his difficulty.[6]

The very first step to be taken in teaching reading is to be sure that a child's eyes function well enough to make reading a pleasure. It should be emphasized that nearsightedness by itself is the least important visual defect, because it can be compensated for by bringing the book closer to the eye. Farsightedness, astigmatism, and lack of perfect muscular balance are far more serious, partly because they are harder to recognize and partly because a child cannot easily compensate for his defect. The mechanics of the reading process proceed smoothly only when eyes are normal or are so corrected as to function normally.

2. **Eye Dominance and Laterality:** The average person would certainly assume that he normally looked at a page of type with both eyes. Some people do, but many people prefer one eye to the other and do most of their reading with it. In extreme cases, the unused eye actually deteriorates. Eye preference is linked in the nervous system to hand preference, or laterality. An individual who is wholly "right-sided" reads with his right eye, uses his right hand, takes off with his right foot when he jumps, and has no unusual difficulty in learning to speak or write. It is for this type of person that the world is arranged, but although he is the predominant type he is not the only one. There is also the completely reversed individual who uses his left eye, hand, and foot in preference to his right. If the "southpaw" is not disturbed, he usually learns to speak normally, although he may have trouble in both reading and writing because he tends to reverse his directions. The right-eyed and right-handed child begins at the left end of a word or line of print because he sees them more clearly than the other end, and he proceeds easily from left to right. The left-eyed and left-handed child tends to look at the right end of a word or line and to progress from right to left. If books were printed especially for him, the words would appear in a reversed order from right to left, and he would learn to read as easily as anyone else. Unfortunately, he has to learn to reverse his already-reversed tendencies and proceed from left to right. During the process he usually

[6] Condensed from B. Leland, "Wilbur," *Journal of Educational Research,* 16: 132–135, 1927. Used by permission of the *Journal.*

sees *b* as *d, q* as *g, was* as *saw, on* as *no, god* as *dog,* and so on. To be
sure, all small children also show some of these reversals because they
cannot always focus their immature eyes correctly or control the wan-
derings of their immature attention, but right-handed children emerge
from their confusion within a year after entrance to school, whereas
left-handed ones are less likely to do so. The latter also have a tendency
to mirror writing. That is, they start on the side of the sheet away from
their hand, just as right-handed children do, slant their script in the
opposite direction, and write backward in the following manner:

FIGURE 1: Mirror Writing

Since they can read in the same direction, they do not see why the
teacher regards their product as illegible.

The world is hard enough for a left-handed child, but in the matter
of reading he is better off than the child with mixed dominance. Such
children are right-eyed but left-handed, or else left-eyed but right-
handed. The inborn connections between eyes and hands suffer from
interference since each eye is already linked preferentially to the hand on
the same side. Some children who have a mixed dominance manage
to solve their own problems of coordination, but this group produces an
unusual proportion of children with defective speech, poor reading habits,
and badly controlled handwriting.

When one examines good and poor readers in a school, one is likely
to find that the best readers are predominantly right-eyed and right-
handed while the poor readers are either left-eyed and right-handed or
of the reverse mixed dominance.[7] These same two groups may produce
many stutterers and stammerers.

[7] See, for instance, H. R. Crosland, "Superior Elementary School Readers Contrasted
with Inferior Readers," *Journal of Educational Research,* 32: 410–427, 1939. On the subjects of handedness, eye dominance, and reversals, see, E. A. Betts, "Reversals in Reading," *Visual Digest,* 4: 38–45, 1940; G. Hildreth, "Bilateral Manual Performance, Eye
Dominance, and Reading Achievement," *Child Development,* 11: 311–317, 1940; G.
Hildreth, "Reversals in Reading and Writing," *Journal of Educational Psychology,* 25:
1–20, 1934; A. Phillips, "Relation of Left-Handedness to Reversals in Reading," *Elementary English Review,* 11: 97–98, 1934; G. Spache, "Eye Preference, Visual Acuity, and
Reading Ability," *Elementary School Journal,* 43: 539–543, 1943; M. E. Smukler, "Mirror
Writing in School Children," *Pennsylvania Medical Journal,* 43: 21, 1939; C. A. Selzer,
"Lateral Dominance and Visual Fusion," *Harvard Monographs in Education,* No. 12, 1933,
119 pp.; I. S. Wile, "Eye Dominance: Its Nature and Treatment," *Archives of Ophthalmology,* 28: 780–790, 1942; P. A. Witty and D. Kopel, "Sinistral and Mixed Manual-

3. Relation of Eye Defects to Reading Ability: The effect of inadequate eyesight upon reading is not as immediate as one might suppose. Apparently some children manage to read in spite of visual difficulty, either because they compensate in some way for their defect or because they want to read so badly that they accept the eyestrain as a concomitant circumstance. This attitude is especially noticeable among children with severe defects who keep right on learning to read at any cost. If an investigator studies the visual efficiency of good and poor readers of the same age and intelligence, he sometimes finds little or no difference between the two groups.[8] Other investigators have found fairly reliable differences in visual efficiency between good and poor readers, and a few have discovered a rather large proportion of visual defects in children whose reading deficiencies were severe.[9] In one case 51 out of 100 children who could hardly read at all showed visual defects, while only 23 of 100 good readers showed similar handicaps. In another instance, 59 per cent, or 654 of 1,109 poor readers had defects; of these 654 children, 71 per cent, or 464, improved in reading after their visual defects were corrected.[10] Figures from a third investigation appear in Table 2. The nature of the defects is given at the left, while the two columns show the per cent of children in each group having each defect. Failure of coordination, poor fusion, muscular imbalance, and far-

Ocular Behavior in Reading Disability," *Journal of Educational Psychology,* 27: 119–134, 1936; F. T. Wilson and C. W. Fleming, "Reversals in Reading and Writing Made by Children in the Kindergarten and Primary Grades," *Journal of Genetic Psychology,* 53: 3–31, 1938. For a test see L. Teegarten, "Tests for the Tendency to Reversals in Reading," *Journal of Educational Research,* 27: 81–97, 1933.

[8] See, for instance, L. E. Bird, "A Study of Certain Visual Characteristics of High and Low Achievers in Reading," *Pennsylvania State College Studies in Education,* No. 22, pp. 9–10, 1940; B. Clark, "Binocular Anomalies and Reading Ability," *American Journal of Ophthalmology,* 23: 885–892, 1940; M. T. Eberl, "Summarization, Criticism, and Explanation of Data Pertaining to the Relation of Visual Disorders to Reading Disability," *American Journal of Ophthalmology,* 18: 537–549, 1941; V. Ilg and L. F. Davis, "Parallel Development and Visual Skills," *Optometric Weekly,* 34: 647–649, 675–680, 1943; N. D. Rizzo, "Studies in Visual and Auditory Memory Span, with Special Reference to Reading Disability," *Journal of Experimental Education,* 8: 208–244, 1939.

[9] See, for instance, W. F. Dearborn and I. H. Anderson, "Aniseikonia as Related to Disability in Reading," *Journal of Experimental Psychology,* 23: 559–577, 1938; T. H. Eames, "A Comparison of the Ocular Characteristics of Unselected and Reading Disability Groups," *Journal of Educational Research,* 25: 211–215, 1932; and 29: 1–5, 1935; G. E. Park and C. Burri, "The Effect of Eye Abnormalities on Reading Difficulty," *Journal of Educational Psychology,* 34: 420–430, 1943; and "The Relationship of Various Eye Conditions and Reading Achievement," *ibid.,* pp. 290–299; F. O. Schwartz, "Ocular Factors in Poor Reading," *American Journal of Ophthalmology,* 23: 535–539, 1940; G. Spache, "The Role of Visual Factors in Spelling and Reading Disabilities," *American Journal of Orthopsychiatry,* 10: 229–239, 1940; G. W. Wagner, "Maturation of Certain Visual Functions and the Relationship between These Factors and Success in Reading and Arithmetic," *Psychological Monographs,* 48, No. 3: 108–146, 1937.

[10] Dearborn and Anderson, *op. cit.* and Schwartz, *op. cit.*

sightedness occur much oftener among the poor readers and probably contribute to their inefficiency.

TABLE 2

Eye Defects of Poor and Normal Readers [11]

Defect	Poor Readers	Normal Readers
Lack of coordination of eyes at reading distance	69	22
Farsightedness	53	28
Anomalies of eyedness	51	39
Mixed dominance	49	30
Inadequate fusion	44	18
Astigmatism	30	44
Anomalies of handedness	14	12
Nearsightedness	3	7
Number of cases	100	143

Other investigators compared the scores made on a reading test with the proportion of children having defective eyesight, with results as shown in Table 3.

TABLE 3

Vision and Reading Proficiency [12]

Reading Test Scores in Points	Per Cent of 228 Pupils with Below-Average Vision
110—156	17
100—109	23
90— 99	19
80— 89	16
70— 79	33
60— 69	64
50— 59	74
0— 49	90

There were some pupils with defective vision in the four highest scoring groups, about 19 per cent. In the fifth group, the per cent increases, then

[11] Eames, *op. cit.* Used by permission of the publisher.
[12] Park and Burri, *op. cit.* Used by permission of the publisher.

almost doubles itself, and thereafter increases twice more until, in the group making the lowest scores in reading, there were 90 per cent with less than average eyesight. These results suggest varying degrees of relationship between vision and reading.

Investigators do not, however, agree among themselves as to the extent of this relationship. Until they do, one is perhaps justified in choosing a middle path and concluding that visual inefficiency is probably somewhat more common among poor readers than among good and that it is therefore one cause of poor reading, even though it is rarely the only cause. What differentiates the poor reader from the good is possibly not so much his defects as his failure to adjust to them or to overcome them.

4. **Defects of Hearing and of Speech:** Failure to hear adequately or to pronounce words correctly has an influence upon a child's ability to learn reading, because his visual image of a word is normally reinforced by its sound as his teacher speaks it aloud and by his own pronunciation. Few people learn by visual cues alone. The percentage of hearing defects among school children varies from one investigation to another because investigators use different standards as to what constitutes impaired hearing, but it seems probable that at least 10 per cent of the school population shows some loss of hearing and that a much larger per cent—given in one study as 40—shows a failure to hear the entire range of tones.[13] Some children who seem to hear well enough in general cannot distinguish between the sounds of *m* and *n,* or *p* and *b,* or *s* and *z*. Both spelling and reading are affected by failure to hear clearly. In addition to finding actual loss of hearing, one group of investigators reported that three fourths of the children had nasolaryngeal conditions that would, if not cured, be likely to cause deafness sooner or later.

Partially deaf children show their defect in their behavior and speech. They do not hear what is said to them when their back is toward the speaker, and they stare at the speaker's face when they are turned toward him. They mispronounce even the commonest words in conversation, saying, for instance, *He is vary streng* for *He is very strong*. They make an abnormal number of errors in spelling, often omitting entire syllables, such as *unstand* for *understand* or *bofly* for *butterfly*. They grasp oral

[13] See, for example, A. Ciocco and C. E. Palmer, "The Hearing of School Children," *Monographs of the Society for Research in Child Development,* Vol. 6, No. 3, 1941, 77 pp.; S. R. Guild *et al.,* "Impaired Hearing in School Children," *Laryngoscope,* 50: 731–746, 1940 (1,365 children, ages 8–14); J. Rohr, "Report of a Hearing Survey Project," *American Annals of the Deaf,* 87: 155–172, 1942 (37,818 cases).

directions accompanied by gestures, but fail to grasp the words by themselves. They substitute one number or letter for another when they write from dictation—5 for *4* or *hin* for *hen*. Sometimes a child hears the teacher but not other children, or vice versa, because he is deaf for certain tones, and sometimes he sings on only one note. Such reactions should lead a teacher to suspect blurred hearing and to send the child to the school doctor for investigation.[14]

The effect of speech defects upon reading is somewhat indirect. For instance, if a child knows the sounds of *w* and *r* when he hears them but nevertheless pronounces *run* as if the *r* were a *w,* he will expect it to appear as *wun* and may not recognize its true form. Failure to pronounce words correctly may also operate to prevent the enlargement of vocabulary because a child does not recognize the sounds he himself makes. Defects in speech are not as serious as those in vision or hearing, but they are often factors in retarding a child's progress in reading.[15] Incidentally, it has been noted by a number of investigators that left-handedness is a good deal more common among stammerers and stutterers than it is in the general population. The effect of stammering upon oral reading is, of course, greater than upon silent.

Not all people who have visual, auditory, or speaking defects become poor readers. Nearly half of them do succeed in learning, and some become superior readers. Presumably they have made some adjustment by means of which they have avoided the most serious results of their handicap. If a child is known to have a defect, however, his teacher should try to have it remedied, even if at the moment it is not interfering with progress.

B. REDUCING EYESTRAIN

Children frequently have to read material that is not well printed, and they do not always have adequate light. If a child is eager enough to read he will overcome such obstacles as glare from the paper, blurred type, dim light, or crowded lines, but such unnecessary features take their toll from normal eyes and increase the inefficiency of defective eyes. On page 17 are two samples of print, one that is hard to read and one

[14] See, for instance, W. B. Koehler, "Word Deaf Children," *Elementary School Journal,* 43: 273–281, 1943.

[15] See, for example, F. P. Gaines, "Interrelation of Speech and Reading Disabilities," *Elementary School Journal,* 41: 605–613, 1941; M. R. Kennedy, "Speech Defects," *Journal of Pediatrics,* 21: 421–427, 1942; M. A. Moss, "The Effect of Speech Defects on Second Grade Reading Achievement," *Quarterly Journal of Speech,* 24: 642–654, 1938.

that is easy. In the latter case the print is large enough, there is great contrast between the black letters and the white background, there is no glare, the edges of the letters are clear cut, and there is no crowding either within or between the lines.[16] In the sample of poorly printed

When Gray Owl learned what many hunt
their guns and traps , he was dearly shoe
ger be a trapper. So he cleared the wood
built. Then he and his wife started to t
a road beside their door. They studied t
mush as they could. Once, when the mother
of a whole family of young beavers. The
about the camp as if they were puppies. /
more and more time in the pond, but frequ
be fed. As Grey Owl went about in his ca
into it. After greeting him with wiggles
...y to bite through the cords of his pack,
food he always carried about for them.

One winter when we Mountain Crows had traveled to the mouth of the Yellowstone to visit our kin of the River band, we had wonderful sport. It was such fun to go coasting downhill on a buffalo rib toboggan. Then we would spin tops on the smooth ice. Each boy tried to upset his neighbor's with his own, and when he succeeded, he would cry, "I have knocked you out!" I was a good player, but one day I came home crying because my fine new top was stolen. Another time, a bigger boy cheated, knocking out my wooden top with a heavy stone, and it was all my mother could do to comfort me.

FIGURE 2: Hard and Easy Print to Read

material, the print is so blurred and indistinct as to be almost unreadable. One can decipher it but not read it. This sample is taken from a series of mimeographed exercises used by a fourth-grade teacher. One needs to be especially careful with homemade materials because they are

[16] For discussion of proper print and allied topics, see, M. Luckiesh and F. K. Moss, *Reading as a Visual Task*, D. Van Nostrand Company, 1942, 428 pp.

especially likely to be below the standards for legibility. Since there is adequate information as to what physical qualities a book ought to have, it seems rather inexcusable that pupils should be asked to read material that will damage their eyes.

Sometimes teachers unintentionally put on the blackboard words or other materials that are hard to read. The two most important points to be considered are the amount of glare and degree of contrast between the writing and its background. The blackboard should have a very dull and very black surface, and the teacher should make the whitest possible marks on it.[17] Narrow, fine, dim lines are likely to cause eyestrain. It is best to avoid the necessity of reading from the blackboard whenever possible, unless the children are allowed to go to the board and stand in front of the written material.

Teachers should, of course, seat children with defects of vision or hearing so that their defects will interfere as little as may be with the apprehension of instructions or explanations. This point seems obvious, but it is sometimes overlooked. Special allowances and permissions—to go to the blackboard as needed, to copy from a neighbor's paper, to write answers instead of stammering through a verbal response, and so on— are also desirable for defective children who are sufficiently mature to use rather than abuse their special dispensations.

C. EYE MOVEMENTS AND VOCALIZATION

Even excellent eyes may move so inaccurately and inefficiently that the reader obtains little meaning from his efforts. In recent years there have been numerous investigations [18] into the nature of eye movements under all sorts of reading conditions and by persons of all ages and degrees of efficiency in reading, until it is now possible to say how the eyes should move in order to get the best results and at what grade or age most children are able to achieve these correct movements.

It is not entirely clear whether inaccurate and clumsy movements are the cause of poor reading or merely a symptom of it. Some investigators assume that the comprehension of meaningful units of thought

---

[17] See W. G. Darley and L. S. Ickis, "A Study of Blackboard Visibility," *The Illuminating Engineer*, 35: 431–443, 1940.

[18] See I. H. Anderson, "Study in the Eye Movements of Good and Poor Readers," *Psychological Monographs*, 48, No. 3: 1–35, 1937; G. T. Buswell, "Fundamental Reading Habits," *Supplementary Educational Monographs*, No. 21, University of Chicago Press, 1922, 150 pp., and "How Adults Read," *ibid.*, No. 45, 1937, 154 pp.; E. A. Taylor, *Controlled Reading*, University of Chicago Press, 1937, 367 pp.

is dependent upon correct movements of the eyes. They therefore recommend direct training of the eyes, on the assumption that comprehension will follow just as soon as the eyes are able to see whole phrases at a time. Others believe that the training should be directed toward increasing comprehension. According to this interpretation of the matter, a child's eyes will automatically move correctly if his reading material is easy enough and interesting enough. The truth probably is that the different elements which go into the reading process are so intimately connected with one another that an improvement in one produces an improvement in the others also. Probably both sides are therefore right.[19] In any case, a teacher needs to understand the nature of eye movements since they are intimately related to comprehension.

1. **Eye Movements:** The efficiency with which an individual's eyes move during the process of reading is reflected in five different but inter-related measurements. (1) As a child's eyes move across a line of print they stop from time to time; it is during these pauses, or fixations, that reading is done. The first measure of efficiency in eye movement is the number of fixations per line of print. The fewer pauses, the more efficient the reading. (2) As long as reading is progressing normally, the eyes move toward the right from the beginning of a line to the end, but sometimes the reader loses his place or becomes confused as to the meaning and his eyes move back across the same line from right to left. The movements in the reverse direction are called regressions. A second measure is the number of regressions per line. (3) At the end of every line the eyes must make a long jump from right to left in order to start on the next line. This movement is not counted as a regression but is termed a return sweep. The third measure concerns the accuracy of these return sweeps. (4) Although the pause made by the eyes at a single fixation is extremely short, it is measurable in twenty fifths of a second. The fourth measure is the average length of the fixations. (5) A comparison of the number of fixations per line and the length of the line shows how many spaces the eye saw at a single pause. The width of the space within which the letters seen lie is called the reading span. The last measurement is the width of this span.

19 See, for example, W. F. Dearborn and I. H. Anderson, "A New Method of Teaching Phrasing and for Increasing the Size of Reading Fixations," *Psychological Record,* 1: 459–475, 1937; W. Kottmeyer, "On the Theory of Controlling Eye Movements in Reading," *School and Society,* 52: 496–498, 1940; D. H. Russell, "Note on a New Theory about Visual Functions and Reading Disabilities," *Journal of Educational Psychology,* 34: 115–120, 1943; M. A. Tinker, "Role of Eye Movements in Diagnosis and Remedial Treatment of Reading," *School and Society,* 39: 147–148, 1933.

Just below is shown a record of the eye movements of an adult who was reading to himself.[20] As he read, his eye movements were photographed. The words he read are printed as they appeared in the book. The small, upright lines show the points at which his eyes made a fixation. Above the lines are numbers which show the order in which the fixations were made. This adult's eyes moved across each line without regressions, as shown by the order of the numbers from one to five.

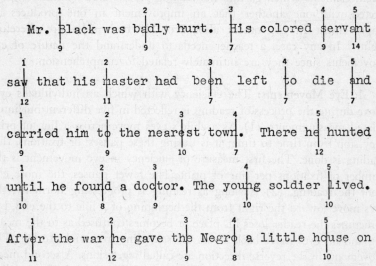

FIGURE 3: Record of the Eye Movements of an Average Adult Silent Reader

This reader made his first pause in each line about three spaces in from the left end, and he hit this point so accurately that he never had to make a regression to correct himself. Under each fixation line is a figure showing how many twenty fifths of a second the reader's eyes paused at that point—9, 9, 7, 9, and 14 twenty fifths for the first line, and so on. The total reading time for the five lines was 9.5 seconds. The number of spaces in a line, divided by the number of fixations, gives a rough [20a] measure of the width of the reading span. For this reader, the span was ten spaces wide. The spaces between the words count in the span as well as the letters.

[20] From page 60 of Buswell, *op. cit.* Used by permission of the publisher.

[20a] Rough, because one cannot know how much was seen to the left of the line's first letter or to the right of the line's last letter.

For these particular lines of reading matter the five measurements noted above are as follows:

(1) Average fixations per line 5.0
(2) Average regressions per line 0.0
(3) Number of inaccurate return sweeps 0.0
(4) Total reading time (seconds) 9.2
(5) Average width of span (spaces) 10.0

This record was made by an average adult reader. There are only a few fixations per line, no regressions, great accuracy in the return sweeps, relatively short fixations, and a moderately wide reading span. These are the characteristics of all good, silent readers. Study of the chart reveals one further point. The eyes move with rhythm; that is, once the reader gets under way the pauses occur at approximately the same points

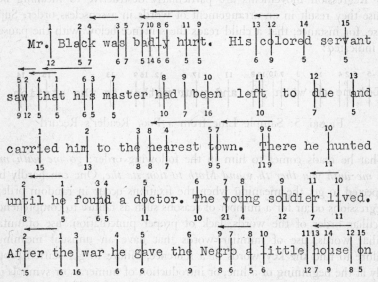

FIGURE 4: Record of the Eye Movements of a Poor Adult Silent Reader

in the line. As in any muscular activity, the achievement of rhythm has a marked advantage both in avoiding strain and in making the processes go forward automatically.

By way of contrast Figure 4 [21] shows the record of the eye move-

—— [21] Buswell, *op. cit.*, page 59. Used by permission of the publisher.

ments of a poor adult reader. It can be seen at once that the fixations are more numerous, that they do not occur in a proper sequence, and that they lack rhythm. The summary for this figure appears below:

(1) Average fixations per line 12.6
(2) Average regressions per line 2.8
(3) Number of inaccurate return sweeps 3.0
(4) Total reading time (seconds) 21.0
(5) Average width of span (spaces) 4.0

This adult showed over twice as many fixations as the other and a span less than half as wide. He had almost three regressions per line and failed to hit the beginning of a new line accurately after three of his four return sweeps. He shows no rhythm. His characteristics are those of all poor readers at all ages.

Regression movements are particularly destructive to meaning because they result in an arrangement of words in a senseless order. Suppose, for instance, that a child reads the sentence below with the pauses as indicated:

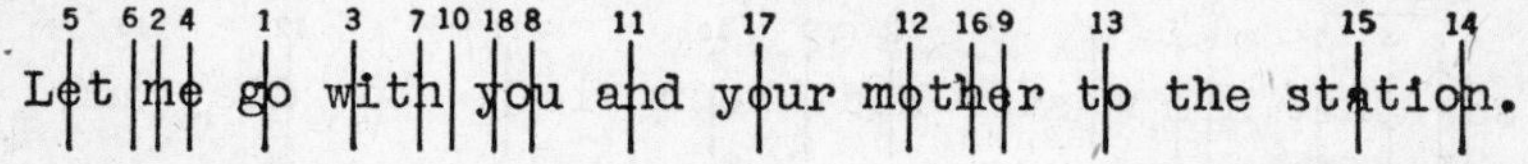

FIGURE 5: Sample Line from a Poor Reader's Record

What he reads comes to him in the following order: *go me with me let me with you ther th y and Moth to tion sta the.* One can hardly be expected to get the meaning when the fixations occur in random order. Regressions occur for a number of reasons such as failure to comprehend, peculiar order of the words, lack of proper punctuation, use of unfamiliar words, use of familiar words that have an unusual meaning, failure to find the key words of a sentence, failure to get started properly at the beginning of a line, or introduction of numerals or symbols of any kind.[22] A few regressive movements per page occur in almost anyone's reading and are not sufficient to interfere appreciably with comprehension, but an average of several regressions per line causes a decreased and confused meaning.

The difference between good and poor reading is by no means a function of age. Many children develop efficient eye movements in the

[22] E. Bayle, "The Nature and Causes of Regressive Movements in Reading," *Journal of Experimental Psychology,* 11: 16–36, 1942.

primary grades. Figures 6 and 7 [23] contrast the records of two second grade children. As can be seen, the eye movements of the good reader are nearly as good as those of the adult whose record appeared in Figure 3. The child averaged 6.5 fixations per line, had no regressions on half the lines and averaged .9 of a regression per line. He hit the

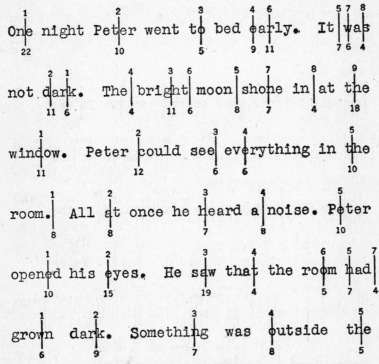

FIGURE 6: Record of the Eye Movements of a Good Silent Reader in the Second Grade

beginning of four lines accurately and missed one. His span was 6.8 spaces wide. The third, fourth, and sixth lines were read at an adult level of five pauses and no regressions. His total reading time was 13.08 seconds.[24] The inefficient child made a record worse than that of the inefficient adult, but the two records show the same features, only the

[23] C. R. Stone, *Better Primary Reading,* Webster Publishing Company, St. Louis, 1936, 536 pp. (From pp. 148–149.) Used by permission of the publisher.

[24] Because of the many fixations, the length of each has been omitted from the record, in the interests of clearness.

child's inefficiency is more marked. He used from 8 to 39 pauses per
line, with an average of 20.7, and had an average of 8.7 regressions. He
did not even approximately hit the beginning of any line. On the fifth
line his eyes moved forward 19 times and backward 20 times. His span
was 2.6 spaces wide. As compared with the good reader of the same

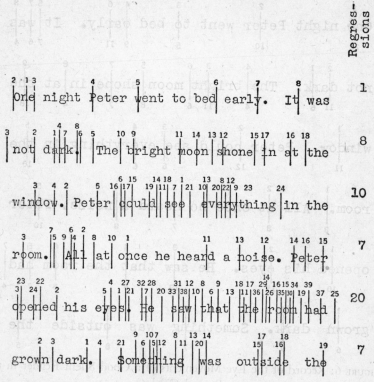

FIGURE 7: Record of the Eye Movements of a Poor Silent Reader in the
Second Grade

grade, he used more than three times as many fixations and over nine
times as many regressions. His span is less than half as wide. His total
reading time was 41.2 seconds—over three times as long as the good
reader's. One finds the same contrast at all levels of development.

The records already shown are derived from photographs and are
presented schematically, so as to show what words were being read.
Actual photographs of eye movements look quite different. Copies of two

Pupil A

Pupil B

FIGURE 8: Actual Photographs of Eye Movements of
Two Readers

records appear in Figure 8.[25] The line at the left on Pupil A's record shows the path taken by the left eye and that at the right the path of the right eye. The fixations are shown by the vertical black lines, their length being the length of the fixation. A movement to the right or left along the line of print appears as a horizontal line. Pupil A began with a fixation a little too far to the right and made a regression at once. There is another very slight regression at the beginning of the third line. For the first line, after the regression, Pupil A had four fixations. Then she made a return sweep, shown by the long horizontal line at the bottom of the "flight of stairs." For the second line she needed four pauses, for the third she took five, and so on. The record of Pupil B shows his movements for only two lines of print, because he needed as much time to read two lines as pupil A did to read ten. At the start of the first line he made a regression, then two tiny forward movements, then a tiny regression, then a long fixation, followed by a period of vacillation before the next forward movement. Pupil A read at the rate of 372 words a minute, while Pupil B's rate was only 20 words a minute. In the course of getting through 100 words he took nearly 300 fixations and made 125 regressions.

The typical development in eye movements from Grade 1 through college is indicated by the diagram in Figure 9.[26] The amount of film used for these records held only two lines for the average first grader, almost four lines for the average fifth grade child, and over seven lines for the typical college student. The averages for the number of fixations and regressions appear in Table 4. The first grade pupils averaged 190

TABLE 4

Norms for Eye Movements [27]

Grade	1	2	3	4	5	6	7	HS	College
Fixations per 100 words	190	150	137	115	100	98	95	88	70
Regressions per 100 words	40	32	30	25	20	16	15	13	8

fixations and 40 regressions for each 100 words they read. Gradually, the averages become smaller until, in college, they are 70 and 8, respectively.

---

[25] From pp. 112–113 of Taylor, *op. cit.* Used by permission of the publisher.
[26] Taylor, *op. cit.*, p. 128. Used by permission of the publisher.
[27] *Ibid.*, p. 126. Used by permission of the publisher.

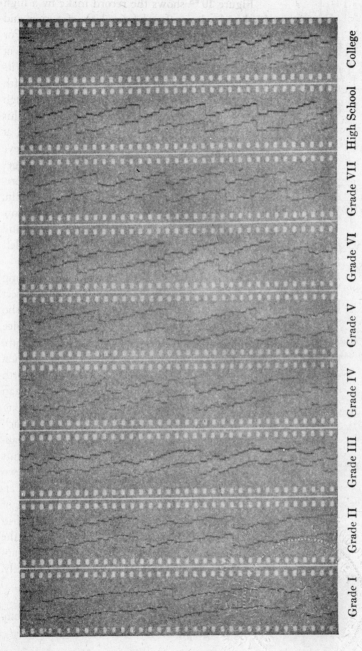

Grade I   Grade II   Grade III   Grade IV   Grade V   Grade VI   Grade VII   High School   College

FIGURE 9: Average Eye Movements from Grade I through College

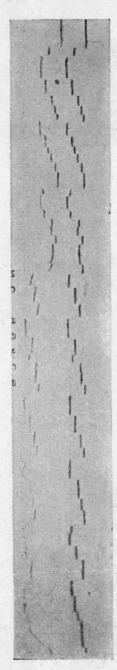

Figure 10 [28] shows the record make by a high school girl who suffered from lack of fusion and therefore used only one eye much of the time. For the first two lines her eyes moved together, but at the end of the third line her left eye began its failure to stay with the right. The fourth and fifth lines were evidently read with both eyes, although the right was doing most of the work. From this point on, the fusion became less and less, until, at the end, the girl was reading with her right eye only and presumably disregarding the images furnished by her left eye. She thus avoided blurring and confusion but at the cost of eyestrain. Unless this difficulty is corrected it will grow worse, because the used eye will become more and more proficient through practice while the left deteriorates through disuse.

The mechanical habits that underlie reading are important, not in themselves, but in their effect upon both comprehension and speed. A pupil who uses four fixations per line will cover ground twice as fast as a pupil using eight of similar length. The increase in rate of reading that occurs when the number of pauses decreases is in itself worth while, but an excess of fixation does more than merely retard the rate of progress. Pauses beyond four or five per line break the text up into such small fragments as to render it practically meaningless. The wider the span is, the larger the units of meaning. An excess of pauses operates in two further ways to lessen the degree of meaning attained. It makes reading so slow that the end of an average reading assignment is a long way off in time from the beginning—so far off that the chances of the entire lesson's becoming an organized whole are considerably diminished. Finally,

[28] *Ibid.*, p. 121. Used by permission of the publisher.

FIGURE 10: Lack of Fusion as Revealed by Photograph of Eye Movements

inaccurate and clumsy eye movements require a child to keep most of his attention on the mere mechanics of the reading procedure and leave him little energy to devote to comprehension. As in all learning, one must master elementary habits so thoroughly that they function automatically before one can use them in complex situations. The achieving of correct eye movements is therefore desirable at the earliest possible moment, not as an end in itself, but as a first and absolutely essential step in developing comprehension.

2. **Vocalization:** All reading, no matter how "silent" it may seem, is accompanied by some degree of vocalizing, but the degree should be as slight as possible. The term "vocalizing" refers to any movement of the lips, tongue, or other parts of the vocal apparatus. It varies all the way from the complete pronunciation of every word to tiny vibrations of the vocal cords such as occur in good silent reading. Regardless of the method by which a small child learns to read, he will usually vocalize considerably at first. The pronouncing of words to oneself is a common way of getting acquainted with them. It is a small child's main technique for recognizing words, because he is more familiar with their sound from hearing them in speech than with their appearance. However, as children learn to recognize more and more words easily, they usually drop off the audible pronunciation.

In estimating the vocalizing of a pupil it is possible to distinguish five degrees of seriousness, as listed below:

(1) Loud whispering of almost every word.
(2) Faint whispering of many words.
(3) Pronounced lip movement but no sound.
(4) Faint (or no) lip movement, no sound, but sufficient vibration of the vocal cords to be felt by the fingers on the throat.
(5) No sound, no lip movement, no movement in the throat perceptible to the fingers.

To be sure, some movement remains and can be registered by a delicate instrument, but it is insufficient to be felt by the fingers. The good reader of any age achieves this final stage. It is desirable that vocalization be eliminated as soon as possible. It slows down the rate markedly because words can be enunciated by the vocal apparatus not more than half as rapidly as they can be read by the eyes alone. It prevents, in direct proportion to its seriousness, the development of correct eye movements and fosters the habits of excessive fixation and frequent regression. Thus, if pupils are asked to read two passages of known equal difficulty, one without any inner speech and one with pronunciation to themselves of each word, the former method is must faster than the latter.[29] The unit of pronunciation is a single syllable because one can make only one sound at a time, but a syllable is not a unit of meaning. Consequently, the persistence of vocalizing tends to keep the eyes from seeing such a phrase as *my little brother* as a whole because it consists of too many speech units. Further, vocalization is distracting to the attention both of the reader and of children sitting near him. By causing slow and piece-meal reading and by intruding itself into the reader's focus of attention, vocalization interferes with comprehension.

The vocalizer is not hard to find in a schoolroom because he makes a noise. The effort being put forth by the vocalizer was probably once necessary, but most pupils can dispense with their inner speech as they grow older. One brief history of a heavy vocalizer appears below:

Edward was a foreign boy in the sixth grade and had been in this country three years. His speech was almost without accent, but his speaking vocabulary was small. His reading vocabulary turned out to be large and his comprehension excellent. He had a real interest in words and liked to pick them out or look up their meanings in the dictionary. No one had to urge Edward to read, but his rate was slow, his progress laborious, and his vocalizing very strong indeed. He enunciated almost every word in a stage whisper. The remedy I applied is simple, if unconventional. I first selected some interesting stories that were well within his vocabulary. He was to read these stories to himself for an hour a day in the remedial reading room and chew gum vigorously all the time he was reading. No one can whisper and chew gum at the same time. Since the stories were easy, I put a little pressure on him to hurry through them. Edward took a book home with him most days and continued the treatment during the evening. Within a week the heavy whispering was gone except for an occasionally difficult word, and within a month Edward was reading easily and without vocalization. All I had to do then was to break him of the gum-chewing habit!

3. **Phrase Reading:** It is important that a child should read by phrases rather than by isolated words or syllables. The eyes can easily take in the words printed on a width of fifteen to twenty or even more spaces. That is, a pupil can see at one fixation such phrases as *in a little while* (17 spaces), *long, long ago* (14 spaces), or *behind the fence*

[29] F. M. Beers and C. Bird, "Maximum and Minimum Inner Speech in Reading," *Journal of Applied Psychology*, 17: 182–187, 1933.

(16 spaces). Reading by phrases is rapid and it leads to good comprehension. In fact, the longer the span, the better the meaning. A wide span is dependent, however, upon the establishment of correct eye movements and the suppression of vocalization.

There are various ways in which children can be trained to have a wide span, and consequently require fewer fixations. The first step is to convince them that the eye can see several words at once; even college students will rarely believe this without demonstration. For a simple experiment, a teacher can make up a series of flash cards [30] each containing such groups of words as *see me, open the door,* or *where are you going?* The teacher holds up a card, but keeps it hidden by a blank piece of cardboard; then, at a signal, she moves the cardboard —not the card—and at once replaces it, thus exposing what is on the card for one tenth to one fifth of a second. This exposure gives time for just one look. By use of such cards the children convince themselves that their eyes will see two or three words at once. After this demonstration the teacher can explain to the pupils that looking at every second or third word of a line is sufficient to see all the words, provided the words are simple and familiar.

A phrase not only has more meaning than the isolated words composing it, but often has a meaning of its own that is not merely the sum total of its parts. Thus, in the sentence, "She has her hands full today," the idiom used must be taken as a whole; the phrase does not mean that the lady has something in her hands, but rather that she is busy. The phrase has, therefore, a meaning that is independent of the words composing it. First grade children rarely read by phrases, partly because primer type is so big, but word-by-word reading should end and phrase reading should begin in the second grade if possible because reading by phrases is an essential step in achieving adequate comprehension.

4. **Speed:** The speed at which one reads is dependent upon the number of fixations and regressions per line, the degree of vocalization, and the extent to which the reader groups words into phrases. Rapid reading is emphatically not hurried or forced reading. It depends not upon going beyond one's normal rate but upon acquiring a normal rate that is rapid. As soon as a child forces himself to hurry, his habits degenerate and his comprehension approaches zero. Rapid reading is a matter of efficiency, not pressure. Some teachers have not understood clearly the difference between reading rapidly and reading hurriedly. Perhaps they have been

[30] See pp. 172–173.

told at some time that rapid readers are also good readers and have deduced from this fact that the way to make a slow reader into a fast one is to hurry him. The result of such treatment is tension and distress of mind, not improvement in reading. The pressure for speed makes any visual defects worse and often produces nervous disorders.[31]

On the other hand, if a child's fundamental habits are good and if he has sufficient maturity, his rate can be increased without loss of comprehension or overstrain. Most people could read faster than they do. The curve in Figure 11 [32] shows the development in rate of reading

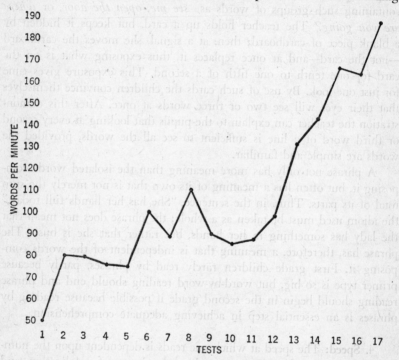

FIGURE 11: Development of Reading Rate in an Individual

by one child during a few weeks' emphasis upon speed. The child had an average of 50 words a minute at the start and 190 at the end. The increase permitted him to cover material almost four times as fast as he had earlier been able to do.

[31] See, for instance, F. D. McCluskey, "Oral Reading," *Nation's Schools,* No. 4, 30: 14–15, 1942.

[32] Stone, *op. cit.,* p. 503. Used by permission of the publisher.

Individual pupils often make surprising gains in speed during a few weeks of intensive training. The following case studies show a record of changes in rate. It should be noted that comprehension was improved, as well as speed.

A.P. was a ten-year-old child in the fourth grade. His general average for all work was only fair, while his reading was reported as poor. His rate was 73 words per minute on a test for which the fourth-grade norm is 160 words. His comprehension was equally low. A.P.'s parents were foreign born and he heard little, if any, English at home. This boy showed an average of 11.7 fixations and 2.4 regressions per line, and an average duration of 13.1 fiftieths of a second. The remedial training he received was given for a half-hour daily over a period of seven weeks. At the end of this time he showed only 7.8 fixations and 1.0 regression per line, with an average duration of 13.0 fiftieths of a second. His scores on the Courtis test revealed more than a doubling of his earlier rate and comprehension.

L.C. was the fastest and best reader in his fifth-grade room. He showed no evidence of any defect in the mechanics. His initial Courtis scores gave him a speed of almost eighth-grade level and a perfect record in comprehension. His average fixations and regressions per line were 5 and 0.3 respectively. It would seem as if this boy were reading as well as he could. At the end of seven weeks' training, however, his rate had increased to 395 words per minute—a good speed for an adult—while his comprehension was 97 per cent. His total understanding was actually greater than before, because on the first test he answered all of 47 questions correctly while on the second he answered 62 out of 64 correctly. His fixations per line had been reduced to 3.5 and his regressions to 0.2.

M.C. was a twelve-year-old pupil in the seventh grade. She had the reputation of being a hopelessly slow and careful reader. She was, in fact, the typical, slow, word-for-word reader. She not only fixated each word once but many of them several times. Such simple words as *is, to, no, from, and, they* required two or more fixations. Her initial Courtis rate score was 170 words a minute—a score just halfway between the fourth- and fifth-grade norms. Her comprehension of the little she read was perfect. She averaged 8.4 fixations and 2.5 regressions per line, with a duration of 10.3 fiftieths of a second. She was overcautious, meticulous, and dawdling. She showed a slow, plodding, leisurely mode of procedure which is probably the result of either a lack of interest or a superfluous amount of oral reading. At the end of the training period M.C. had reduced her fixations to 6.5 per line and her regressions to 1.6. The duration remained the same. On her final Courtis test she read at a rate of 368 words per minute—a speed nearly normal for her grade—and a comprehension of 96 per cent of the material she read. Her total understanding was enormously improved. On the first test she got 28 answers right out of 28, but on the last, 65 answers right out of 67.[33]

It is probable that increases in speed during elementary school are due primarily to growth and only incidentally to teaching. A child of ten reads faster than a child of eight chiefly because he has had an additional two years of bodily development and experiences. That childhood increases are due mostly to growth is proved by the gains of various groups of children who did not have any instruction in reading over a period of years. Such groups sometimes gain more than reading norms indicate as average, suggesting that some methods of teaching may operate to decrease speed.

The rate of reading is usually determined by having children read a given passage and timing them to find out how many words were read per minute. The norms are simply the average or median score per grade for large groups of children. Norms from two investigations appear in Table 5.

TABLE 5

Norms for Speed in Reading [34]

Grades	Words per Minute	Words per Minute
3	95	115
4	153	168
5	189	190
6	215	200

These norms show a consistent rise from grade to grade. They cannot, however, be used in general, because speed is to a great extent a function of the difficulty of the material being read. For a harder selection than those on which these norms are based, the averages would be too high, and they would be too low if the material were substantially easier. The only reading matter to which they apply is the selection read by the pupils whose scores were used in calculating the norms. They are included to show the increase in rate from grade to grade as measured by two typical selections.

Speed is important for purely practical reasons, but it is not essential. Comprehension is. Usually the two go hand in hand, but if one of

<hr>

[33] These three studies are from J. A. O'Brien, *Silent Reading,* The Macmillan Company, 1921, 289 pp. From pp. 246–247, 252, 262. Used by permission of the publisher.
   [34] From the *Pressey Diagnostic Reading Tests: Speed,* Public School Publishing Company, Bloomington, Ill., and from Taylor, *op. cit.,* p. 126.

them has to be sacrificed, it should be the rate. A teacher has to use judgment as to the amount of pressure for speed each child can comfortably stand. A few pupils will remain deliberate because slowness is part of their nature. If they are going as fast as they can without becoming tense and if they are understanding what they read, they should be let alone. Speed is a highly individual matter, and a teacher cannot afford to push children beyond their normal limits. Pupils in the same grade may read at widely different rates but with equal comprehension.[35]

5. Oral versus Silent Reading: Some teachers in all elementary school grades use oral reading a good deal more than others do. As a method of instruction oral reading has its advantages and disadvantages, although the latter probably outweigh the former. Oral reading does not have a high utility value because it is almost exclusively a "school" technique; 99 per cent of all extraschool reading at any age is silent. As a means of helping pupils to read better silently it is not of much value because the habits underlying oral reading are quite different from those for silent reading, as will be seen presently. There is, therefore, some question as to when children should read aloud and how much, if at all.

Three recent studies have shown the negative relationship between oral and silent reading,[36] although the authors have been inclined to stress what positive relations there are between the two. The results in Figure 12 [37] tell the story. The four sections of the figure give averages for four measures of reading: the duration of the fixations, the width of the span, the number of regressions, and the rate of progress. In all cases there is comparison between oral and silent reading for poor, average, and good readers. The average length of fixation for the readers of all types when reading orally was longer than when reading silently. The span was wider for silent than for oral reading, the regressions were more numerous when the pupils read aloud, and the rate was more rapid when they read to themselves. The difference in efficiency between the two types of reading increased with the degree of skillfulness, as is shown by the relative heights of each pair of columns. All four meas-

[35] See J. B. Stroud and M. Henderson, "Rate of Reading and Learning by Reading," *Journal of Educational Psychology,* 34: 193–205, 1943.
[36] D. E. Swanson, "Common Elements in Silent and Oral Reading," *Psychological Monographs,* No. 3, 48: 36–60, 1937; I. H. Anderson and D. E. Swanson, "Common Factors in Eye-Movement in Silent and Oral Reading," *ibid.,* pp. 61–69; G. Fairbanks, "The Relation between Eye-Movements and Voice in the Oral Reading of Good and Poor Silent Readers," *ibid.,* pp. 78–107.
[37] Swanson, *op. cit.* Used by permission of the publisher.

urements show this relationship. The better the reader, the greater the contrast between his two performances.

The oral reader is slow because he must retard his eyes in order to keep them from getting ahead of his voice, because his eyes can read words faster than his vocal apparatus can pronounce them. If the oral

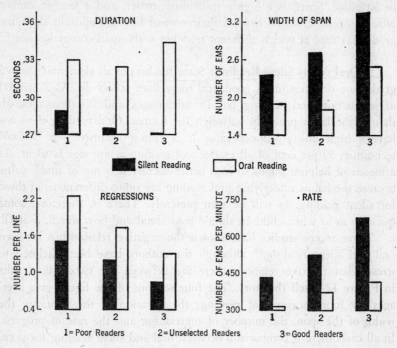

FIGURE 12: Comparison of Silent and Oral Reading

reader's eyes stayed exactly with his voice, he would have as many fixations as there were syllables on a line, because the unit of pronunciation is a syllable. Since the eyes almost inevitably move too fast, the reader must occasionally bring them back to the word he is pronouncing—thus causing a regression. Figure 13 [38] shows in diagrammatic form the relation of voice and eyes during the oral reading of four lines of type. At the point at which this excerpt begins, the reader's voice was just saying the word *but* in the top line, while his eyes had already moved on to the following line of type and were looking at the word *brought,* the

[38] G. T. Buswell, "Oral Reading: An Experimental Study of the Eye-Voice Span." *Supplementary Educational Monographs,* No. 17, 1920, 106 pp. This figure from page 90 is used by permission of the publisher.

sixth word ahead of that being spoken. The reader's eyes moved on to the end of *brought* while he said *it*. Then they paused on the word *under* long enough for the voice to say *must be more,* thus finishing the top line. The eyes made their fourth pause when the voice was silent between words. While the eyes were looking at the right end of the line in fixations 5, 6, and 7, the voice was just starting to speak the same line the eyes were just finishing. Throughout the selections, the voice

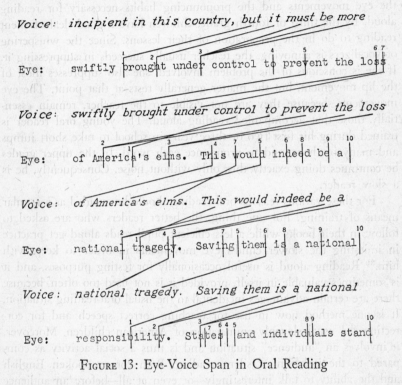

FIGURE 13: Eye-Voice Span in Oral Reading

is reading the left half of a line when the eyes are on the right half, and the right half when the eyes have already moved on to the left half of the following line. The first line showed no regressions, but the second and fourth lines have two each and the third line, three. After each period the reader stopped so long that his eyes had time to make three or four fixations. The eyes move so fast that they frequently get too far ahead of the voice and have to look back again. The movements are by no means as efficient as those shown earlier for good silent readers.

In the first half year of school, a pupil's fixations are so numerous and the focusing of his eyes is so inaccurate that his silent reading is generally no more rapid than his oral. Moreover, he has a tendency to vocalize words—that is, to pronounce them—whether reading aloud or to himself. The initial stages of reading are, therefore, more or less oral, no matter how the children are taught. By the second grade, however, the eyes can already move nearly twice as fast as the voice. If the children continue to receive intensive drill in oral reading, they develop the eye movements and the pronouncing habits necessary for reading aloud. By the third or fourth grade, children have a good deal of silent reading to do in the preparation of their lessons. Since the whispering of vocalizers is annoying, the teacher usually succeeds in suppressing it. If she is conscious of the problem involved, she also suppresses most of the lip movement, but the matter generally rests at that point. The eye movements, because they are not visible to the teacher, remain essentially those that accompanied reading aloud. The young oral reader is trained during his first two or three years in school to take short jumps and many of them, and to pronounce each word. In the upper grades he continues doing exactly this, only without noise. Consequently, he is a slow reader.

For these various reasons oral reading should be avoided as a regular means of training. For one thing, the better readers who are asked to follow in their books while a less efficient pupil reads aloud get practice in imitating the slower child's eye movements in order to keep with him.[39] Reading aloud is useful occasionally for testing purposes, and it is sometimes valuable in itself, provided it is not used too often, because there are certain advantages incidental to the usual oral-reading situation. It is one method now in use for teaching correct speech and for correcting the usual slovenly enunciation of American children. Moreover, it involves an "audience" situation and is thus a social activity as compared to the isolation of silent reading. Both correct spoken English and the ability to talk interestingly—or even at all—before an audience are of social value. However, the writer has doubts that oral reading is the most effective means for bringing about these desired ends. There seems little that could not be accomplished better by means of oral composition. A child can read a story to himself and then tell it to other children, referring to his book now and then if he so desires. By this technique he is using his eyes but not his voice to read, and his voice but not his eyes to address his friends, thus avoiding the develop-

[39] L. C. Gilbert, "Effect on Silent Reading of Attempting to Follow Oral Reading," *Elementary School Journal*, 40: 614–621, 1940.

ment of eye-voice habits that may later operate to prevent the normal accretions of speed with age.

D. SUMMARY

The process of reading rests upon an adequate development of the senses, especially vision. Throughout the grades a proportion of the children have eyes so defective as to make reading difficult, and in the lowest grades the farsighted children sometimes outnumber those with normal eyesight. Mild defects of vision and hearing are important in proportion as the teaching emphasizes visual or auditory learning.

Eye movements show a gradual maturing during elementary school. Children at first make many fixations and many regressions, but the number of both is reduced from grade to grade. Some pupils acquire almost adult eye movements while they are still in the primary grades. Speed, correct movements, width of span, and phrase reading are all intimately related. The good reader at all ages differs from the poor one in that he has a wide span, reads by phrases, and covers material rapidly, without pressure or hurrying. The basic habits that underlie oral and silent reading respectively are of a sufficiently contradictory nature as to make training in the one inhibit rather than facilitate growth in the other.

II · General and Technical Vocabulary

[...]

From time to time the writer has acted as a consulting psychologist
to whom teachers sent children who were making little or no progress
in reading. Two out of every five were unable to read simply because
they did not know enough words, and for no other reason, while inadequate vocabulary was a contributing cause in almost every case. In
all probability, an inadequate vocabulary is the greatest single cause for
failure to read with comprehension, in either general or technical fields.
There are many reasons why an individual child may fail to learn
words—poor eyesight, frequent absences from school, too much guessing
at meanings, too little study of words in isolation, exposure to too many
new words for any to be well learned, lack of phonics, a feeling that
the separate words are unimportant, an emotional resistance to reading,
indifference to or fear of new words, a conviction of failure and inferiority—but the effect is the same whatever the cause. Teachers sometimes
feel that if they can interest the children in the thought development of
a story the word meanings will take care of themselves. As a means of
teaching rapid assimilative reading, this emphasis upon interest and
comprehension is excellent, but as a means of building vocabulary it is
inadequate. When a child reads he sees only the general outline of words
and pays little attention to details. This slighting of the individual word
helps in bringing about phrase reading, but it may prevent the learning
of new terms because the single words are not seen clearly. The best
way for most people to acquire a new word is to separate it from its
context and study it in isolation. Naturally, not all reading should become word study, as it would if vocabulary were overemphasized. Reading and word study are two different but supplementary activities, the
former for deriving meaning from connected reading matter in which
most of the words are familiar and the latter for enlarging the vocabulary by the study of unfamiliar words, preferably out of context.

A. GENERAL VOCABULARY

In all of the numerous analyses of reading vocabulary,[1] at all levels, one point has stood out clearly: there is a central core of words that make up the bulk of all reading matter. For instance, 9 words are repeated so often that they constitute 25 per cent of all words in written material; 69 words constitute 50 per cent, and 732 make up 75 per cent. As soon as one gets beyond this central core, the frequency of use for the remaining thousands of words in the language diminishes rapidly.

Perhaps the simplest way to illustrate the comparative frequency of words is to give a few sample words from each thousand of the Thorndike Word Book, in which the 20,000 most commonly used words are listed:

TABLE 6
Examples from the Thorndike Word List

First Thousand
   First 500:   came, can, child, corn, color
   Second 500: cake, catch, cent, cloud, cook

[1] See, for instance, B. R. Buckingham and E. W. Dolch, *Combined Word List,* Ginn and Company, 1936, 185 pp.; H. A. Curtis, "Wide Reading for Beginners," *Journal of Educational Research,* 32: 255–262, 1938; E. W. Dolch, "Basic Sight Vocabulary," *Elementary School Journal,* 36: 456–460, 1936; S. E. Daw, "A Controlled Vocabulary for the Middle Grades," *University of Pittsburgh Bulletin,* No. 3, 37: 76–83, 1941; D. D. Durrell and H. B. Sullivan, "Vocabulary Instruction in the Intermediate Grades," *Elementary English Review,* 15: 138–145, 160, 1938; D. D. Durrell, "A Vocabulary for Corrective Reading," *Elementary English Review,* 11: 106–109, 1934; A. I. Gates, *Reading Vocabulary for the Primary Grades,* Bureau of Publications, Teachers College, Columbia University, 1935; W. G. Hayward and N. M. Ordway, "Vocabularies of Recently Published Preprimers," *Elementary School Journal,* 37: 608–617, 1937; G. Hildreth, "All in Favor of a Low Vocabulary," *Elementary School Journal,* 43: 462–470, 1943; J. A. Hockett, "The Vocabularies and Contents of Elementary School Readers," *California State Department of Education Bulletin,* No. 3, Sacramento, 1938; J. A. Hockett and D. P. Neeley, "A Comparison of the Vocabulary of 33 Primers," *Elementary School Journal,* 37: 190–202, 1936; J. A. Hockett and N. G. Neeley, "The Vocabulary of 28 First Grade Readers," *ibid.,* pp. 344–352, 1937; M. D. Horn, "The 1003 Words Most Frequently Used by Kindergarten Children," *Childhood Education,* 3: 50–52, 1927; R. G. Langston, "A Core Vocabulary for Preprimer Reading," *Elementary School Journal,* 41: 766–773, 1941; G. E. Rickard, "The Recognition Vocabulary of Primary Pupils," *Journal of Educational Research,* 29: 281–291, 1935; M. Rudisill, "Selection of Preprimers and Primers—a Vocabulary Analysis," *Elementary School Journal,* 38: 683–693, 767–775, 1938; G. Spache, "A Minimum Reading-Spelling Vocabulary for Remedial Work," *Journal of Educational Research,* 33: 161–174, 1939; and "New Trends in Primary Grade Readers," *Elementary School Journal,* 42: 283–290, 1941; C. R. Stone, *Stone's Graded Vocabulary for Primary Reading,* Webster Publishing Company, St. Louis, 1941, 29 pp.; C. R. Stone, "The Vocabulary of Twenty Preprimers," *Elementary School Journal,* 41: 423–429, 1941, and "The Second Grade Reading Vocabulary," *Elementary School Journal,* 35: 359–367, 1935; E. L. Thorndike, *Teachers Word Book,* Bureau of Publications, Teachers College, Columbia University, 1931, 182 pp.; H. E. Wheeler and E. Stowell, "A First Grade Vocabulary Study," *Elementary School Journal,* 31: 52–60, 1930; L. R. Wheeler, "The Study of the Relative Difficulty of Primary Reading Vocabulary," *Journal of Genetic Psychology,* 52: 183–201, 1938.

Second Thousand
    First 500:   camp, carriage, charm, comfort, curtain
    Second 500: cave, central, chest, citizen, crew
Third Thousand
    First 500:   charity, cellar, climate, conclude, crime
    Second 500: cabin, cannon, cedar, conquest, cordial
Fourth Thousand
    First 500:   chatter, clever, comparison, contend, crust
    Second 500: campaign, clip, corrupt, crimson, cuckoo
Fifth Thousand
    First 500:   chant, clause, comedy, coral, critic
    Second 500: clove, coil, commonwealth, crackle, cylinder
Sixth Thousand: capacious, chafe, cleft, commune, cram
Seventh Thousand: cadence, cherubim, cope, cubic, chanticleer
Eighth Thousand: chastise, clamorous, compassionate, combat, credulous
Ninth Thousand: cambric, coincidence, colon, conscientious, curd
Tenth Thousand: chiffon, cocoon, component, corroborate, crucifix
Eleventh Thousand: cartilage, chaplain, clinic, concise,. curate
Twelfth Thousand: candor, circumscribe, collateral, cower, cutlass
Thirteenth Thousand: calumny, centrifugal, chandelier, clarion, contingency
Fourteenth Thousand: carnage, chalice, concubine, corrugate, custodian
Fifteenth Thousand: chronology, circumvent, commissary, coquetry, cozen
Sixteenth Thousand: cameo, cerebral, chimerical, concomitant, cursory
Seventeenth Thousand: catalpa, chicory, colossus, creole, cruse
Eighteenth Thousand: cairn, caudal, chaffinch, chromatic, creel
Nineteenth Thousand: capstan, cerement, cockerel, cosine, cuneiform
Twentieth Thousand: candelabrum, cogency, confabulate, cynosure, cusp

The words in the first five hundred are so common as to be repeated
many times in a single book. Those in the second five hundred and in
the second and third thousand are also common, though not as constantly used as the first five hundred. Words from the fourth and fifth
thousand, while not unusual, are distinctly less common than the
previous samples. From the sixth to the tenth thousand, the words seem
to change only slowly from more to less frequent, but those in the
eleventh to the fourteenth thousand are distinctly unusual words. From
the fifteenth thousand on, the words are rarer and rarer. There are
probably some in the last two thousand that are beyond the limit of
the reader's vocabulary. For elementary school reading, the mastery
of the first five thousand words is the main task, plus such further
words as are necessary for understanding arithmetic, geography, history, elementary science, and English composition. This number of

words is well within the ability of the average pupil, as shown by the norms to be presented later.

1. Size of Vocabulary: The usual way of estimating the total size of vocabulary is to select, from either the Thorndike Word List or a standard dictionary, a given number of words at random. If the Thorndike list is used, one may take 10 words from each thousand; from a dictionary one takes the first word on perhaps every twentieth page. These words are then made into a test. Usually the pupil is given four or five possible definitions of each word, from which he selects the one he thinks is best. If a pupil gets 72 words right out of the 100 taken from the Thorndike list, his vocabulary is estimated at 7,200 words, since each word on the test stands for 100 words of similar frequency on the list. If the dictionary test gives 100 words selected on the basis of one per 20 pages and if a pupil makes a score of 72, his vocabulary is estimated at 72 times the average number of words on 20 pages of the dictionary from which the selection was made. The results from such estimates are rough and are not always in agreement since the Thorndike list contains only 20,000 words and the dictionaries contain many times that number. Results from three typical investigations are given in Table 7.

TABLE 7

Sample Norms for General Vocabulary [2]

	Pressey	Terman	Smith
Grade 1	620		
Grade 2	1,220		3,400
Grade 3	2,500		4,100
Grade 4	3,600	4,500	4,550
Grade 5	4,500	5,400	4,900
Grade 6	5,400	6,300	5,200
Grade 7	6,100	7,200	5,550
Grade 8	7,100	8,100	5,900
Grade 9	7,800	9,000	6,450

[2] S. L. Pressey, *Diagnostic Reading Tests: Vocabulary,* Public School Publishing Company, Bloomington, Ill.; M. K. Smith, "Measurement of the Size of General English Vocabulary through the Elementary Grades," *Genetic Psychology Monographs,* 24: 313–345, 1941; L. M. Terman, "The Vocabulary Tests as Measures of Intelligence," *Journal of Educational Psychology,* 9: 452–456, 1918. See also I. Gansl, "Vocabulary: Its Measurement and Growth," *Archives of Psychology,* No. 236, 1939, 52 pp.

The differences in these estimates are probably due to differences in the selection of the words. One is based upon the Thorndike list, the other two upon different dictionaries.

The number of words, counting derivatives, that the average child knows well enough to recognize is much larger than has been supposed. In a recent study, in which knowledge of all the basic (167,000) and derivative (204,000) words in a standard dictionary was sampled, the average college graduate's score indicated that he could recognize the meaning of 157,000 words (61,000 basic and 96,000 derivatives) and could even use 153,000 of them correctly in illustrative sentences.[3]

Any one of the vocabulary estimates given above is more than adequate for the number of essential words needed, according to numerous analyses of basic readers, although the entire load of words may be beyond the estimates. In one study the teacher will find eight lists of fundamental words, each list containing those needed for a given level in reading. The list is based upon analysis of 21 pre-primers, 21 first grade readers, and 21 second grade readers, all published between 1931 and 1941. The levels of difficulty are as follows:

TABLE 8

Size and Classification of a Fundamental Vocabulary [4]

	New Words	Cumulative Total
Levels I and II: Most Important Words for Beginning Reading	150	150
Level III: Easy Primer Material	100	250
Level IV: First Primer and Easy First Reader	150	400
Level V: Difficult First Reader Material	210	610
Level VI: Easy Second Reader Material	350	960
Level VII: Difficult Second Reader Material	485	1,445
Level VIII: Easy Third Reader Material	555	2,000

These words are eventually more or less mastered by school pupils as shown in Figure 14.[5] The good readers learn them rapidly, the average readers eventually, and even the laggards learn nearly half of them by the end of elementary school.

Another quite short list of essential vocabulary containing only 119

[3] R. H. Seashore, "Further Data on the Measurement of General-English Vocabulary," *Psychological Bulletin*, 36: 525, 1939.
[4] Stone, *Better Primary Reading, op. cit.*, pp. 61–130.
[5] Stone, *Better Primary Reading, op. cit.*, p. 60. Used by permission of the publisher.

words, arranged from easiest to hardest, gives the beginning teacher information concerning the best words to begin with and the expected difficulty of each. The easiest word, *to,* was learned by all but one first

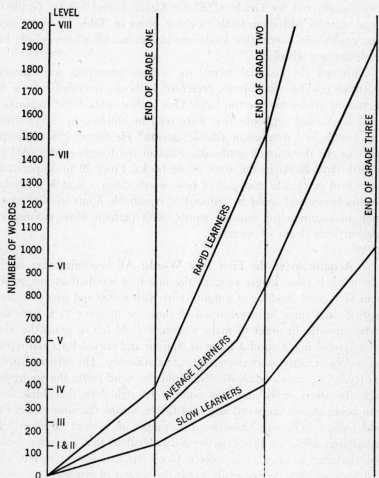

FIGURE 14: Mastery of Fundamental Vocabulary

grade child, while the hardest, *train,* was missed by 121 out of 207.[6] In still another study, 79 words made up two thirds of all the words used in several pre-primers.[7]

[6] Rickard, *op. cit.*
[7] Langston, *op. cit.*

One of the numerous studies of basic vocabulary gives lists of words for the intermediate grades.[8] The selection is based upon analysis of 18 to 20 books for each grade. The words in the resulting core vocabularies number 691 for Grade 4, 525 for Grade 5, and 849 for Grade 6. If one were to add these totals to those given in Table 8 for the first three grades, the cumulative totals would become 4,065 basic words for the elementary school.

Although the essential terms are not too numerous for mastery, the entire reading vocabularies presented in books intended for use in the various grades may be too large. One author studied the vocabulary of 101 books and textbooks that were read by children in the intermediate grades in a number of school systems.[9] He found 4,381 different words in the third grade textbooks, 7,264 in the fourth grade, 9,423 in the fifth, and 10,546 in the sixth grade books. From 20 to 30 per cent of the load per grade consisted of new words. Such a load is undoubtedly too heavy and could be reduced to reasonable limits by the substitution of common for unusual words, with perhaps some sacrifice of style but little if any of meaning.

2. Acquisition of the First Few Words: All beginnings are likely to be hard. It takes longer to learn the first fifty words than any subsequent fifty, partly because of unfamiliarity with words and partly because the first ones must be overlearned if they are to serve as a basis for further growth. In order to make a start, a child has to grasp the idea that a symbol made up of a series of straight and curved lines can represent an object, activity, characteristic, or relationship. The writer remembers trying to teach a feeble-minded child the word *table;* the youngster knew the word orally and was familiar enough with the object, but upon being shown the word and told that it meant the same object the child replied, "Oh no! Those are just marks on a sheet of paper." It proved impossible for this defective to understand that a written word could be used in place of an object. Until children have a mental age of at least six they do not easily grasp the notion of symbols.

The acquisition of the first four or five hundred words consists of the substitution of a written symbol for words well known when heard orally. The initial procedure is simple. The teacher puts a word on the board, telling the children what it is; they repeat it, study it, and tell what it means. They listen to the teacher's voice, look at the word, say

[8] Durrell and Sullivan, *op. cit.*
[9] Dow, *op. cit.*

it themselves, and use it in sentences. This process continues until a small nucleus of words has been memorized. Then some simple sentences using these words may be read by the children. With this basis to build on, the teacher presents such new words as occur in each successive day's reading lesson. The acquiring of the first words consists, essentially, in sheer memorizing. No amount of interesting stories will substitute adequately for the labor of learning a basic group of words until recognition is spontaneous.

In the more progressive schools teachers usually approach the reading less directly than by putting words on the blackboard. The basic vocabulary is presented by means of directed play activities, and the children learn the words incidentally. This indirect method is not only pleasanter as far as the child is concerned, but it seems to produce a larger vocabulary than the more traditional methods.[10] Not every teacher, however, can use activities constructively. In inexpert hands, the children are likely to learn less than by more formal methods.

The exact number of words to be thus learned, one by one, is not the same from one set of readers to another. Although modern pre-primers and primers are supposedly based upon either the Thorndike or the Gates lists, some of them still contain too many different words for efficient learning in the early stages. For example, an analysis of 10 pre-primers yielded a total of 241 words.[11] The number of repetitions for these 241 was as follows:

The commonest 72 words were used 9,047 times and constituted 76 per cent of the total.

The next group of 72 words were used 2,033 times and constituted 17 per cent of the total.

The remaining 97 words were used 834 times and constituted 7 per cent of the total.

The first 72 words constituted the core for these 10 beginning readers. The 97 words of the third group could probably have been omitted, or words from the preceding 144 substituted for them without too much loss of interest and certainly with a considerable gain in ease of reading.

Pre-primers and primers vary a good deal in the demands they make upon the pupil. They differ from each other in length, in the number of different words used, in the number of repetitions per word,

10 Wheeler, *op. cit.*
11 Curtis, *op. cit.*

and in the type and number of concepts in the reading matter. Data
from a few samples appear in Table 9.

TABLE 9

Differences among Primers and Pre-Primers [12]

Primer	Pages in Primer	Total Words	Number of Different Words	Per Cent of One-Line Sentences	Average Repetition of First 500 Words
A	52	1,207	66	93	13.9
B	32	188	48	100	12.0
C	35	695	106	84	5.0
D	39	575	36	100	14.3
E	68	1,591	58	—	13.0
F	50	1,251	42	—	30.0

Pre-primer A contained over six times as many words as Pre-primer
B, but had only 18 more different words. It contained some sentences
that were more than a line long. Throughout the book there was
much repetition. Pre-primer C contained more than twice as many different words as B and three times as many as D. It repeated words less
than half as often as the other books. It was the hardest of the four,
since it had the largest vocabulary, gave the least repetition, and introduced from two to three times as many new words as any other book
on the list. Pre-primer D was the easiest, although it was longer than
B or C and had over three times as many words as B. Pre-primer E
was long, but not especially hard, while F was conspicuous for having
few different words that were repeated for an average of 30 times.

The concepts contained in reading matter also present difficulties
to the youthful reader. For instance, many words have more than one
meaning or pronunciation and are therefore difficult both to learn and
to use. The word *row* is a case in point, so also the word *bed,* since it
may be used for flowers as well as for people! The English language is
especially productive of words with two or more meanings, since most
nouns can be used as verbs also. One can *rake* a lawn, have a *rake,*
or even be a *rake;* one can *swim* or take a *swim;* one can *fly,* kill a
fly, cast a *fly,* or button a *fly.* A *reader* may be both the person who is
reading and the thing being read. English is so full of common words
with multiple meanings that a writer of primary readers cannot avoid

[12] Stone, *Better Primary Reading, op. cit.,* p. 308. The last two items are from "The
Vocabulary of Twenty Preprimers," *op. cit.* Used by permission of the publishers.

using some of them. In one analysis of pre-primers and primers, there were from 6 to 23 such words in the former and from 29 to 63 in the latter.[13]

Both the number and the type of concepts vary from one reader to another. In the study just quoted the pre-primers contained 61 to 111 different concepts and the primers 270 to 408. A few sample differences between two supposedly parallel books are listed from another excellent and most detailed study. The results appear in Table 10 on the next page. Reader B uses the names of four times as many colors, twice as many items of food or types of dishes, but requires comprehension of less than half as many common activities. Also, though not shown here, Reader A needed 116 different concepts and experiences as background, whereas Reader B needed only 70. There are not a great many duplicates in the two series.

The vocabulary used in a pre-primer or primer is usually listed in the back of the book. It is always small, but usually not small enough because the authors have introduced a number of words that are used only once or twice and are therefore probably so underlearned as to be forgotten by many of the pupils. The published lists are also of value to the teacher, especially the Gates and Stone lists. By examining both the vocabularies in her pre-primers and the various lists described in this section, a teacher can arrive at a very satisfactory list of words to be used at the beginning of a child's reading experience. The advantages of a small and concentrated vocabulary are that children can begin to read sentences and little stories almost at once, they need less help from their teacher because there are few if any new words, they do not develop a sense of failure in their early efforts because they are not asked to learn more words than they can remember, and they enjoy reading from the very beginning.[14]

A final point in regard to these first words is that they must be overlearned—learned beyond any possibility of forgetting. This need may bring about drill *ad nauseam* for the teacher, but a core of words thus permanently memorized is essential as a basis for further acquisitions. The first reading books now allow for sufficient repetition for the average or bright child, but for the dull child even more drill is required. If, after completing one pre-primer, he still stumbles over some of the words, he should read another pre-primer and another until the vocabu-

[13] R. I. Sims, "Concept Analysis of Primers and Pre-primers," *Elementary English Review*, 15: 302–305, 1938.
[14] Hildreth, *op. cit.*

TABLE 10

The Conceptual Load of Two Readers [15]

Concepts Demanded by:

Reader A		Reader B	
A. Colors		**A. Colors**	
pink		brown	yellow
white		white	black
		red	blue
		green	grey
B. Food and Dishes		**B. Food and Dishes**	
oranges		milk	knife
eggs		chicken	fork
toast		cakes	glass
milk		cup	sugar bowl
birthday cake		plate	cream
ice cream		spoon	saucer
			teapot
C. Sounds		**C. Sounds**	
bow-wow		mew	
meow		bow-wow	
baa-aa-aa		choo-choo	
choo-choo		cock-a-doodle-do	
		peep	

D. Activities		**D. Activities**	
Jane plays with kitty	Dog may come to birthday party	read a book	
Jane played house	Ride on scooter	play with a ball	
Jane played with her doll	Go with left foot on scooter	open the door	
Come to breakfast	Stop scooter with foot	sit down	
Children played with:	Stay with me	call a dog or cat	
doll	Sailing a boat	put doll to bed	
cat	Dog asleep in sand	sit by the fire	
dog	Boat was carried far away	mother calls children	
goat	Wake up	eat breakfast	
wagon	Bring back my boat	play doll house	
Ride in a wagon	Carry water to garden	pull horse	
Went to a picnic	Get weeds out of garden	ride a horse	
Play in the sand	Get up early	play school	
Make a house in the sand	Go to work early	run into house	
Run in the sand	Sit down to rest	read a letter	
Ran after Jack	Play the organ	rooster walks erect	
Had dinner at the picnic	Play on the sea-saw	hop	
Play ball with the dog	You go away up on the sea-saw	girl dances up and down	
Throw the ball	Have a circus		
Run after the ball	Run around and around		
Dig in the sand with a spade	Come out (on stage)		
Fill pail with sand	Put blocks on floor		
Jane makes cakes in the sand	Be still		
Bring sand to Jane	Fall over in the mud		
Make birthday cake in the sand			
Make candles			

[15] C. E. Mannwiller, "Differences in Emphasis on Experiences and Concepts in Readers," *Pittsburgh Schools*, 13: 65–98, 1939. Used by permission of the publisher.

lary used is his permanent possession. Nothing is gained by hurrying a child at this stage; twenty words learned beyond any possibility of forgetting are better than a hundred that are half learned and about which the child still has to guess.

The difficulty in teaching at this early level is not so much with the amount of work to be done as with the individual deficiencies of the pupils. One teacher of the writer's acquaintance has a good solution to this problem. Before she uses a given primer or reader she prepares some slips of paper, each containing a single word from the list at the end of the book. She makes from three to five duplicate slips for each word, then sorts the slips into an alphabetical series. As the regular reading period progresses, one child may fail to know the word *sheep,* another slips up on *has,* another confuses *what* and *that,* and so on. As each error is made, she not only corrects it, but selects from the pack of slips the one containing the unrecognized word (or the two containing a pair of confused words) and gives the slip to the child. At the time nothing else is said, but at the end of the lesson each child collects what slips he has received and studies them, asking the teacher for the meaning of any word he still does not recognize. The slips remain in his possession till the next day when, at the beginning of the hour, each child reads his slips to the class. The children soon learn that they are responsible for learning the particular words they missed. The slips are then returned to the teacher's desk. More than half the slips made out for one reader are immediately transferable to another, so that such a pack of slips once started is easy to keep up to date. By this simple device each child can study each day only those words that he did not know.

3. Phonics: When a nucleus of the simplest and commonest words has been acquired it is time to use some other method besides visual presentation, pronunciation, and memorizing. In the high first or low second grade the teacher usually introduces work in phonics. For instance, the children already know the word *and;* using this as a basis, the teacher proceeds to teach *sand, land, band, hand.* Or, with *in* as a basis, she builds up *ink, pin, fin, tin, win, sin, pink, think, sink.* If a child has been learning words by memorizing at the rate of two a day, he can learn related words at the rate of at least five a day. Children enjoy such play with words, provided the game is not kept up too long. A variation of the above procedure is to work on series of words often confused, such as:

that	which	has	very
this	where	have	every
the	when	had	ever
them	while		even
they	who		
those	why	do	
these	what	did	always
there	whom	done	almost
then	whose	does	also

Such series have the merit of forcing a child to look all the way through a word in order to distinguish it from its mates. This need helps to disabuse children of the idea that a word can be guessed from its initial sound alone. When one reads, a glance at the initial letters and outline of a word is usually enough, but when the word is just being acquired, such a cursory observation is insufficient.

As children learn the phonograms, they learn the sounds of the consonants and of the common blends such as *th, ch, sh, tr, br, wr,* and *wh.* The objective in such work should be to give children a few guides to pronunciation in places where they will be of assistance rather than to give a systematic course on phonetics. English is, of course, a highly unphonetic language. Its words contain unpronounced letters, the same letters spell different sounds in different words, and the same sound may be spelled in a number of ways. The vowel sounds not only vary greatly in their spelling, but they change into short *u's* whenever they occur in an unaccented syllable. For instance, such a word as *department* is actually pronounced *dupartmunt* even in the best circles; and *alliance* becomes *ulliunce.* In American speech it is very hard, indeed, to retain the quality of a short vowel in an unaccented syllable. Because of these fundamental characteristics of the language, it is not worth while to overemphasize phonics or to use a purely phonetic approach. However, children can pronounce many of the new words they encounter if they can give the consonant sounds correctly and if they can break up the words so as to discover recognizable elements. Thus, if a child can see in the unfamiliar word *bold* his familiar friend *old* and if he knows the consonant sounds, he can acquire the new word by pronouncing it.

The extent to which phonics are to be taught has been a moot question for many years. A recent investigation based upon the reports of 627 primary teachers showed that most teachers used more or less phonetic analysis. Some of the typical reactions to questions about the most commonly used devices are given in Table 11.

TABLE 11

Practices of Teachers in the Use of Phonics [16]

	Per Cent of Teachers			
	Grade 1	Grade 2	Grade 3	All Grades
1. With respect to phonetic training I: c) follow well-defined practices which, however, can hardly be called a system*	62	67	64	64
2. With regard to devices for teaching phonetic analysis I: b) have a rather large number that I have found useful	31	36	31	33
c) have only a few that seem to be of value	44	49	52	48
4. I give instruction in phonetic analysis: a) to the class as a whole	55	61	50	56
5. With regard to scheduling time for teaching phonetics I: a) set aside a period every day apart from reading for such instruction	37	36	24	32
b) occasionally have a separate period	30	33	32	31
c) give the training incidentally in the regular reading period	31	30	44	35
6. One form of "ear" training consists in giving children sounds and having them put the sounds together to make words. I do this: b) frequently	27	32	40	33
c) occasionally	32	33	35	33
7. Another kind of ear training is to have some child make the separate sounds and then have some other child pronounce the whole word. I do this: b) frequently	12	16	18	15
c) occasionally	23	28	39	30
d) never, or almost never	57	53	39	50
8. With respect to the separate consonant sounds I teach children: a) all of them	57	57	45	53
b) about 2/3rds of them	12	19	19	16
9. With respect to consonant blends (*tr*, *bl*, *st*, etc.) I teach children: b) all the common ones	37	51	50	46
c) only a few of the commonest	38	22	20	27
10. With respect to the separate vowel sounds I teach children: b) the commonest sounds of all the vowels	41	54	50	48

[16] W. A. Brownell, "Current Practices with Respect to Phonetic Analysis in the Primary Grades," *Elementary School Journal*, 42: 195–206, 1941. Used by permission of the publisher.

    * Only those answers appear that were selected by a considerable number of teachers. There were four or five possible answers to each question.

TABLE 11—*Continued*

	Per Cent of Teachers			
	Grade 1	Grade 2	Grade 3	All Grades
11. With respect to suffixes (*-ed, -tion,* etc.) I teach children:				
c) just a few of the commonest	64	52	37	51
12. With regard to the prefixes (*con, in,* etc.) I teach children:				
c) just a few of the commonest	39	51	45	45
a) none at all, as such	46	19	8	25
13. With respect to phonograms I teach:				
b) all the common ones	35	48	43	42
c) only a few	27	16	29	25
14. In respect to "sound families" I have my pupils:				
a) identify all words possible by this device	25	37	33	31
b) note sound resemblances of a large number of words	45	45	50	47
c) know only a few sound families	21	11	11	15
15. With respect to blending the component sounds I provide:				
b) a rather large amount of drill	27	18	42	32
c) only occasional practice	37	47	41	41
17. I provide practice on phonograms and families by means of flash cards and rapid blackboard exercises:				
b) very often	36	40	37	37
c) seldom	23	21	28	24
d) never, or almost never	24	21	20	22
18. I review the lessons taught in phonics by sounding familiar words, phonograms, etc.;				
b) frequently	48	61	57	55
c) rarely	22	14	25	20
19. I require the sounding of the individual letters or combinations in new words encountered in reading:				
c) not for all words but only as needed	61	74	76	70
20. With respect to rules for pronunciation I:				
c) point out the facts but require no formulation or memorization	36	51	68	51
d) pay no attention at all to them	54	40	21	39
22. I use rhymes and rhyming as a means of teaching words:				
c) somewhat	41	33	42	39
d) not at all	26	39	35	33
23. When a word is mispronounced I advise the child *first* to:				
b) try to get the pronunciation by noting sound resemblances to familiar words	40	40	46	42
c) try to get the pronunciation from the probable meaning of the word in context	26	23	19	23

TABLE 11—*Continued*

	Per Cent of Teachers			
	Grade 1	Grade 2	Grade 3	Ail Grades
24. When new words appear in reading I advise the child *first* to:				
a) sound the word by syllables or other sound elements	50	.45	41	45
b) try to find sound resemblances to familiar words	21	32	38	30
28. With regard to sound units in new words I:				
a) train children to be on the alert for such units	47	57	53	52
b) permit them to use these units if they find them	36	34	35	34
29. In my opinion children in the second term of Grade 1 should receive phonetic training:				
b) as soon as they have a sight vocabulary of 50 to 100 words	53	49	56	53
c) whenever and only whenever needed	42	40	32	38
Number of Teachers	198	175	173	546

The above list gives an idea of what current practice is in regard to the use of phonics. It does not, of course, tell what it should be. On this point there is a variety of opinion but not enough proof to be definitive.

Some evidence exists to show that the teaching of phonics is not necessary and may have a negative effect upon the rate of reading. One investigation brought out the fact that phonics were best for teaching vocabulary but that the look-and-say method was somewhat better for teaching children to read sentences and much better for helping them get meaning from whole paragraphs.[17] If, however, one compares a wholly phonic approach to reading, a wholly nonphonic approach, and a method that is basically visual but brings in some degree of phonic training in an incidental way, the third method is the best, the nonphonic next, and the formal phonic the poorest in all phases of reading. The children who had no phonics at all learned to read, but those who

[17] H. L. Tate, "The Influence of Phonics on Silent Reading in Grade One," *Elementary School Journal*, 37: 752–763, 1937.

See also S. C. Garrison and M. T. Heard, "An Experimental Study of the Value of Phonetics," *Peabody Journal of Education*, 9: 9–14, 1931; A. I. Gates, "Studies of Phonetic Training in Beginning Reading," *Journal of Educational Psychology*, 18: 217–226, 1927; R. M. Mosher and S. M. Newhall, "Phonic versus Look-and-Say Training in Beginning Reading," *Journal of Educational Psychology*, 21: 500–506, 1930; E. K. Sexton and J. S. Herron, "The Newark Phonics Experiment," *Elementary School Journal*, 27: 690–701, 1928; H. L. Tate, T. M. Herbert, and J. K. Zeman, "Nonphonic Primary Reading," *Elementary School Journal*, 40: 529–537, 1940.

were given incidental work in phonics had larger vocabularies and slightly better comprehension. In another instance, the group of pupils receiving the most emphasis upon phonics showed better pronunciation and better oral reading than the group having the least drill, but the latter group read faster. A quite recent and carefully controlled experiment [18] contains data that suggest a greater value for phonics than has sometimes been found by other investigators. The children who were given phonetic analysis and drill scored very reliably higher on tests of phonetics, as might have been expected, than pupils who had learned to read by sight methods. In addition, however, the training transferred to word study sufficiently to give them great superiority over the control classes in both word pronunciation and vocabulary. Their silent reading scores varied from being the same as those of the control group to being slightly better. In oral reading they made fewer errors and their eye-voice span was larger, but they read a great deal more slowly.

Although children can learn to read by visual means alone, the sounding out of words does seem to be helpful. Moreover, ignorance of the sounds is a characteristic of certain types of poor readers. For example, in one group of 194 children, 58 per cent could not sound individual consonants, nor could they blend a series of sounds—such as *s, l, ee, p*—into a word when the individual letters were sounded for them by another person.[19] Out of 112 third grade children who scored low in reading, 19 per cent were unable to sound any letters at all, from 4 to 12 per cent did not recognize the capital forms of letters, 37 to 51 per cent were unable to sound common blends. Other children who have been sent to psychologists as poor readers have proved to be defective only in their knowledge of sounds and have learned to read through phonetic drill.[20] The boy described below was such a child:

Donald was in the sixth grade although his teacher knew well enough that his reading ability was inadequate for keeping up with his lessons. He got some meaning out of what he read, but not enough, and he did better in the content subjects than his work in reading would lead one to expect. It did not take long to determine that Donald's chief trouble was lack of vocabulary. He not only tested at third grade level on vocabulary tests, but

[18] D. C. Agnew, *The Effect of Varied Amounts of Phonetic Drill on Primary Reading,* Duke University Press, Durham, 1939, 50 pp.

[19] K. B. Hester, "A Study of Phonetic Difficulties in Reading," *Elementary School Journal,* 43: 171–173, 1942.

[20] J. Tiffin and M. McKinnis, "Phonic Ability," *School and Society,* 51: 190–192, 1940. See also A. Bennett, "The Analysis of Errors in Word Recognition Made by Retarded Readers," *Journal of Educational Psychology,* 33: 25–38, 1942.

whenever he came to a long or unfamiliar word I could see his eyes skip over it. On the other hand his recognition of technical words in geography and arithmetic was up to sixth grade level. When I asked him to read a passage aloud, the nature of his difficulty was at once apparent, because he had no idea of how to pronounce any word that he did not instantly recognize. He did not know that letters had sounds or that long words could be broken into syllables. The technical words he knew because his teachers had carefully dissected them for him and taught them to him orally. In fact, he knew only such words as had at one time or another been specifically taught him. He had no technique for mastering a new word by himself. His former teachers had done a good job of teaching him to read by eye alone, but this method was not adequate for normal advancement above the primary grades. I gave Donald a short but intensive course in phonics, at the end of which, since he had a rather good speaking vocabulary, he was able to identify most of the words in his books as soon as he pronounced them. I watched him at intervals for over a year to make sure that he did not begin to vocalize words he already knew—a result that a course in phonics often has. He did pronounce many unnecessary words for a while but by the end of six months he was again reading visually and reserving his sounding of words for those that were new to him.

Of recent years it has been suggested that phonetic drill might be of more value if it were concentrated upon syllables instead of phonograms. Suppose, for instance, that a child knows the phonograms *-ess, -ound, -one,* and *-ill.* He may not, however, be able to find them in the words *soundless* and *millstone,* because phonograms begin with vowels and most syllables begin with consonants. Moreover, many phonograms are useful mainly for the recognition of monosyllabic words. The teaching of the commonest syllables does not seem to be a solution of the problem, either. One investigator[21] analyzed the syllables found in 14,000 running words taken from sample passages in arithmetic, history, and geography texts. There were 8,509 syllables, but less than 12 per cent contained phonograms as they are usually taught. Even when all variations were counted and the most liberal interpretation was given, a knowledge of phonograms would contribute to the pronunciation of only 39 per cent of the syllables. Of the 8,509 syllables there were 1,255 different ones. The 101 most common ones were included in only a small proportion of the entire 14,000 words. The commonest, *-ing,* for instance, occurred in only 135 words, and most of

21 E. W. Dolch, "Phonics or Polysyllables?" *Elementary English Review,* 15: 120–124, 1938, and "Sight Syllables versus Letter Phonics," *Elementary School Journal,* 41: 38–42, 1940; A. G. Gunderson, "Simplified Phonics," *Elementary School Journal,* 39: 593–603, 1939.

the 101 in less than 10 words. It would hardly be feasible to teach children how to pronounce 1,255 different syllables, especially since even this number does not presumably represent the total in existence among frequently used words.

These facts do not mean that no phonograms should be taught but that the teacher should not expect an automatic transference from them to the pronunciation of syllables. The whole question of phonics is still under discussion. However, it would seem that drill in phonics is rather essential for some children, though perhaps not for others. Those pupils who have good visual acuity and good visual memory can and do learn without phonetic drill, but if vision is blurred or memory confused, it seems necessary to reinforce the visual presentation of words by auditory stimuli.

4. Methods of Developing Vocabulary: [22] One of the earliest forms of vocabulary drill consists of an arrangement by means of which children can drill themselves in phonograms. A useful form for this instructional material is illustrated below.

FIGURE 15: Book of Phonograms

What the pupil does is to sound the consonant on the first small page at the left with the phonogram, which is always kept visible. Then he turns over to the second page of the little booklet and sounds this new consonant, or combination of consonants, with the phonogram. He continues through the pages of the booklet until he has sounded all of the words. Then he goes back to the beginning and does it over again. Over 100 such booklets can be made. When a pupil thinks he can sound each word in a booklet, he takes it back to the teacher's desk and gets another. Even as early as the second grade, pupils can drill themselves in this way. If desired, they can work in pairs and check each other. Naturally, not every word is sounded correctly, but most of them will be; the pupil's vocabulary consequently grows. Children

[22] See also the relevant section in the chapter entitled Remedial Work in Reading.

enjoy this exercise and will give themselves constant drill without any special urging. The most useful phonograms are listed below.

TABLE 12
List of Phonograms [23]

ab	ang	eal	est	ine	og	ow
ack	ank	eam	et	ing	oil	own
ad	ap	eat	ew	ink	oke	oy
ade	ape	eck		ip	one	
ag	ar	ed	ice	ipe	ong	ub
aid	are	ee	ick	ire	ook	uck
ail	ash	eed	id	ist	ool	ug
ain	ass	eek	ide	it	op	um
air	at	eel	ift	itch	ope	ump
ake	atch	een	ig	ite	ore	un
ale	ate	eep	igh	ive	orn	unch
all	ave	eet	ight		ose	ung
am	aw	ell	ile	oad	oss	unt
ame	awl	en	ill	oat	ot	ush
amp	ay	ench	im	ob	ote	ust
an		end	ime	ock	ought	ut
and	each	ent	in	od	ound	
ane	eak	ess	ind	oe	out	y

As children progress through the grades they can add to their vocabularies by learning to recognize the commonest of the prefixes and suffixes. Approximately a fourth of all words on the Thorndike list have prefixes, and of these 82 per cent are compounded with one of 15.[24] A child could, therefore, be helped in his recognition of over 4,000 of the commonest 20,000 words by knowing the meaning of the following 15 prefixes:

TABLE 13
List of Prefixes with Their Commonest Meaning and the Number of Words in the Thorndike List in Which Each Prefix Occurs

Prefix	Number of Words	Prefix	Number of Words
ab- (from)	98	ex- (out)	286
ad- (to)	433	in- (into)	336
be- (by)	111	in- (not)	317
com- (with)	500	pre- (before)	127
de- (from)	282	pro- (in front of)	146
dis- (apart)	299	re- (back)	457
en- (in)	182	sub- (under)	112
		un- (not)	378

[23] The writer is indebted to Miss Minnie McKean of Haight School, Alameda, California, for both this list and the arrangement for drill shown in Figure 15.

[24] R. G. Stauffer, "A Study of Prefixes in the Thorndike List to Establish a List of Prefixes That Should Be Taught in the Elementary School," *Journal of Educational Research*, 35: 453–458, 1942.

If a teacher wishes she may vitalize this list of prefixes into an interesting game for children in the sixth grade. She simply writes, one to a card, the prefixes listed above. Below each item she writes two or three familiar words illustrating the use of the prefix. On the back of the card she writes the meaning of the word element being studied, plus meanings for the sample words if she wishes. The two sides of a sample card appear below:

```
        un = not
     untrue = not true

  What do these words mean?

  unhealthy      untried
  unreal         unable
  untrained      uninjured
  unaided        unworn
```

```
                Answers
  unhealthy = not healthy
  unreal    = not real
  untrained = not trained
  unaided   = not aided
  untried   = not tried
  unable    = not able
  uninjured = not injured
  unworn    = not worn
```

FIGURE 16: Front and Reverse of a Sample Card for Drill with Prefixes

The pupil studies the cards, observes the examples, and learns the meanings. These exercises form a short and definite unit of work, because only a limited number of prefixes are worth learning.

A similar list of suffixes can be used to help children acquire new words.[25] There are usually several meanings for each suffix, only the commonest of which need be taught. For elementary school children, it

TABLE 14

List of Suffixes

-able (-ible)	-er	-ive
-age	-ent	-less
-al (-ial)	-ful	-like
-an (-ian)	-ion (-tion or -ation)	-ment
-ance (-ence)	-ic	-ness
-ant	-ical	-or
-ary	-ish	-ous
-ate	-ity (-ty)	-ure
		-y

is probably sufficient that each type of suffix be recognized as such, without specifications as to the exact shade of meaning given by each.

[25] E. L. Thorndike, "The Teaching of English Suffixes," *Teachers College Contributions to Education*, No. 847, 1941, 82 pp

Pupils should, however, learn to recognize these common units within words, so that they may be aided in pronouncing and understanding new words. A teacher can construct practice cards similar to those already shown for the prefixes.

Children begin to read a considerable number of new polysyllables about the time they reach the fourth grade, and they have to learn how such words are pronounced, since most of them will not be pronounced for them by the teacher. They need, therefore, some assistance in breaking words into syllables and pronouncing them. Such practice results in significant growth in vocabulary and prevents the plateau that sometimes appears when children first encounter unfamiliar long words.[26]

There are numerous games that can be played with the dictionary as soon as the pupils are old enough to use one. A teacher can, for instance, give a group of pupils a certain number of words, supply each with a dictionary, start them all at the same time, and see how many can get from the dictionary the correct spelling, pronunciation, and meaning of each term. A time limit may be set or not, as desired. Another dictionary game is to give pupils a single word and ask them to find as many synonyms as possible. For example, if the original word is *beautiful,* they will find, upon looking it up in the dictionary, various synonyms such as *lovely, gorgeous, pretty,* and so on. They then look up each of these synonyms and find still more, until they have a long list of words that could be used as equivalents. Naturally one cannot use dictionary drills too frequently, but an occasional game of either of these types is profitable.

Simplified dictionaries for use as low as the sixth grade have appeared during the past decade.[27] It is advisable to use these if possible since children have great difficulty in finding their way through a large dictionary. Moreover, the definitions have been rewritten so as to avoid the use of unfamiliar and difficult words.

Several interesting methods for increasing vocabulary have been suggested by one author.[28] Not all can be used at all levels, but teachers can find in the lists helpful hints for drills, especially if these can be arranged as games.

[26] See, for instance, R. W. House, "The Effect of a Program of Initial Instruction on the Pronunciation Skills at the Fourth Grade Level as Evidenced by Skills' Growth," *Journal of Experimental Education,* 10: 54–56, 1941.

[27] *Thorndike-Century Junior Dictionary,* Scott, Foresman & Company, 1935, 970 pp., and *Winston Simplified Dictionary,* John C. Winston Company, Philadelphia, 1937, 630 pp.

[28] M. I. Addy, "Development of a Meaning Vocabulary in the Intermediate Grades," *Elementary English Review,* 18: 22–26, 30, 1941.

TABLE 15

Methods of Increasing Vocabulary

Direct Teaching	Good Exercises
1. Study of word as to appearance, sound, and meaning	1. Memorizing of short poems with good vocabulary
2. Seeing relation to known words	2. Conversation lessons on topics involving new words
3. Finding dictionary definition	3. Selection of best descriptive words in a series
4. Etymology of word	
5. Finding synonyms or antonyms	4. Finding adjectives or adverbs for describing things or actions
6. Analyzing for prefix, stem, and suffix	
7. Finding derivatives or parallels of word	5. Supplying correct word to complete sentences.

The direct teaching of vocabulary, especially when it is individualized, has definite and often immediate results in growth and mastery of words. Two case studies from different school levels illustrate the nature of the results when training is individual and intensive.

In September, 1925, James was thirteen years old and in the sixth grade. His home conditions were excellent. At the age of six James had spent a month in the first grade. Early in the semester, he had an attack of influenza which kept him in a delicate state of health, so he was withdrawn from school for the year. In the meantime his father died, and the following year the family moved to the Far West where James attended school for a year. The next year the boy was sent to a private school for a while and then transferred to a parochial school. Here he was at first in the second grade but was soon promoted to the third on account of his age, size, and general ability—although he was at the time deficient in reading. The following year he entered the fourth grade, where he began to feel his reading handicap because he was not able to prepare lessons in the content subjects. His mother helped him somewhat by reading aloud, so that he was always prepared reasonably well. He was unable to take a written test, however, because he could not read the questions nor spell well enough to answer them when they were read out loud to him.

When James was in the second half of the fifth grade he could not read primer material. The next year he was kept in the same grade for a month and then promoted because he was above standard in all subjects except reading and spelling. At this time systematic remedial work was started. A preliminary study by means of both formal and informal tests showed that James did not know enough words. He was also very sensitive about his deficiency. Once he had told his mother that he was praying to God, not for skill in reading, but to know why he could not gain that skill and be like everyone else. James obviously wanted to read badly enough but when the remedial work was actually begun he showed a real dread of his daily twenty minutes' period of individual instruction. His teacher tried to interest him in books, but failed. Even ten minutes of work seemed to be more than he could stand at once. Gradually, however, he lost his fear and began to gain a little confidence. The first steps in this child's progress were extremely slow, owing to his nearly complete emotional blocking. The training he received consisted almost exclusively of word drill, with some work in phonics. By the end of six months James was reading easily in fifth-grade books. At this time his test scores on a silent reading test showed a score in speed average for the sixth grade and a comprehension score between the sixth and seventh grades. A year later James was able to prepare his lessons unaided.

Melvin was sent to a remedial teacher for individual work because he could not read the material in the low second-grade books. No formal test was given, but it was at once evident that he had an inadequate vocabulary. Each day he came for fifteen minutes' instruction. The work began with the oral reading of a primer. Each day the teacher wrote down on separate cards the words Melvin did not know. When eight or ten such cards had accumulated, the reading was stopped, and Melvin was taught the words he had missed. Then the material was reread. Melvin took the cards back to his room with him and studied them at intervals during the day. On the next day these words were reviewed. Any that he did not at once recognize were returned to him. The others were filed. After about three weeks the instructor used the first five minutes of the period for phonetic work with word-families. Presently she gave Melvin two or three blank cards every day and asked him to find unknown words in his regular reading in class. Most days he brought back words he had copied from his class books. These were added to the collection. At the end of six weeks, the oral reading was discontinued and the whole time was spent on word study. The teacher got a copy of the reader Melvin was using in class and prepared a list of terms that he was likely not to know. During the training time Melvin pronounced and then learned these words. He soon became very proud of his rapidly growing file and would go voluntarily before school and run through part or all of his collection. Daily he brought more and more words for identification. Gradually practice exercises were introduced, any new words being treated as before. At the end of the semester Melvin had learned no less than 462 words. When this number is added to the 150 or so that he knew at the beginning, his total vocabulary had increased to at least 600 words—which is about normal for high first-grade children. Actually he must have known more because he scored in the first ten in the class on the Gates tests used by his room teacher at the end of the semester. No other remedial treatment beyond that described was given.[29]

[29] Sister Mary Grace, "Diagnosis and Treatment of Problem Cases in Reading," *Catholic Educational Review*, 25: 392–412, 1927. Used by permission of the *Review*.

In the sixth grade, and perhaps earlier, a teacher can begin to shift the burden for growth in vocabulary from herself to the individual child. In the last analysis, both strength and weakness in word knowledge are highly individual, and the training in vocabulary is likely to be effective in relation to the degree of its individualization. The procedure suggested below is simple and leads to good results.

The teacher first supplies each child with twenty-five or thirty slips of paper. If she can obtain 3 by 5 inch library cards and cut them in half, these small cards are better than paper slips because they can be handled more easily. She then instructs the pupils to copy each unknown word out of the books they read, writing one word on each card. The cards should be in readiness whenever the pupil is reading anything, no matter what the subject matter of the book may be. Since almost all the words thus recorded will be within a child's understanding as soon as they are pronounced, the teacher should let the pupils get together from time to time in groups of three, in which each one shows the others the words he does not know. Most of the words that have been collected by all three in a group will be recognized by one child or another. Any remaining words may be looked up in the dictionary if the children are old enough or may be handed to the teacher for her to explain. After the words are identified, each pupil goes through his own cards, saying over to himself each word he can remember. The cards containing those words that he can now identify he puts in one pile; the words that he cannot remember he puts in another. The three children in each group now pick up the cards containing words whose meaning they have forgotten and again identify these words for each other. Then each pupil reads through his own cards, once more arranging the words into two piles—those he now knows and those he has not yet learned. This procedure should continue until the pile of unknown words has disappeared.

The frequency of periods devoted to this individualized vocabulary drill should depend upon how rapidly the cards accumulate. Most children cannot handle more than twenty-five cards at once in this way. When the pupils have between twenty and thirty, the teacher should use the reading period for this drill. The cards used at one period are to be kept for a while and reviewed two or three times during the next month. When a pupil can go through a collection of cards easily, fluently, and accurately, he throws them away. Usually, one period a week of word study, carried on in this highly individualistic manner, will develop an adequate reading vocabulary for any intelligent child.

In the first place, he knows which words to study. In the second place, he gets a chance to concentrate on those words and no others. In the third place, he is taught the meaning by his own classmates, who are always more effective motivators than an older person. And finally, he can see his own progress. If, for instance, he starts a week with seventeen unknown words and if at the end of that time he has learned fifteen of them, he knows he is progressing. Every week each child has as his objective the learning of the words he has collected, and at the end of each week he knows just how close to that objective he has come. As a matter of fact, most children will get out their packages of cards and run through them whenever they have a few minutes of leisure. This procedure seems to give them a sense of mastery and, as a consequence, a feeling of great personal satisfaction. Learning words ceases to be monotonous and becomes interesting. Of course, not every child learns every word he has thus selected, but even if he learns half of them his vocabulary will grow considerably faster than by group methods of construction.

It will be noticed that the responsibility both for selecting the words and for learning them is put upon the child rather than the teacher. Her job is to remind him of this responsibility from time to time by providing him with cards, encouraging him to use them, and setting aside periods for study. She can also help him with definitions when no one in his group recognizes a given word. The responsibility, however, rests essentially on the pupil. This is exactly where it must rest, if vocabulary is to be acquired. No one else can tell a child which words in a story he does not know, but he can list them for himself. No one else can take the responsibility for finding out the meanings, because each child in a room of forty has a different list, and no teacher can teach forty lists simultaneously. Finally, no one can learn the words except the pupil himself. The whole business is thoroughly individualistic.

5. Experiments in the Teaching of Vocabulary: That training in vocabulary produces results has been proved by a number of experiments.[30] In practically all instances direct teaching of vocabulary was

[30] See, for example, Addy, *op. cit.;* P. W. Birch, *Retrieving the Retarded Reader, with Special Reference to Vocabulary,* Public School Publishing Company, Bloomington, Ill., 1940, 24 pp.; M. L. Bradley, L. A. Cahill, and H. L. Tate, "Acquisition of Reading Vocabulary," *Elementary English Review,* 18: 19–21, 32, 1941; H. M. Garvin, "Vocabulary Enrichment at Various Grade Levels," *Twentieth Yearbook of the Department of Elementary School Principals,* pp. 307–313, 1941; W. S. Gray and E. Holmes, "Development of Meaning Vocabulary in Reading," *Publications of the Laboratory School of the University*

found to be superior to incidental teaching or to wide reading without teaching of vocabulary. In a typical experiment,[31] 60 fourth grade children were grouped in one control and two experiment groups, equated for mental age, IQ, and initial knowledge of 100 words that had been selected as the material of the experiment. In the experimental classes the teacher taught specifically 65 of the 100 words, taught another 15 incidentally but without emphasis, and did not teach the remaining 20. After two months, the original test was repeated. The two experimental groups had gained 31 per cent over the control group on the words specifically taught, 25 per cent on those incidentally taught, and only 1 per cent on those not discussed at all. In other words, vocabulary will not grow without training, but with direct training it will grow rapidly.

In another experiment an elementary school teacher, working under the writer's supervision with a class of 26 poor readers in the fourth and fifth grades, used a variety of drills in general vocabulary. Before the training began, these pupils took a vocabulary test based on the *Teachers' Word Book* in which they showed an average general vocabulary of 1,600 words. These pupils were in the remedial reading class for the first fifty minutes of each school day. Their work was in large measure individualized. The experiment started so late in the year that it could run for only seven weeks. At the end of this time a second vocabulary test was given. The result showed an average vocabulary of 2,500 words. This increase is equal to slightly less than a year's gain by usual classwork. The teacher did not know what words would be used for the final testing, and there was no way by which she could have found out since the tests were not even constructed until the day before they were given. The gain is therefore due to the training procedures and not to any drill by the teacher on the particular words that would appear on the final test.

B. TECHNICAL VOCABULARY IN THE SOCIAL SCIENCES

In elementary school the subjects for which a technical vocabulary is necessary are arithmetic, geography, history, English composition, and a little science. For all these subjects, the fundamental vocabulary

of *Chicago*, No. 6, pp. 29–34, 1938; E. Holmes, "Vocabulary Instruction in Reading," *Elementary English Review*, 11: 103–105, 110, 1934.
    [31] Gray and Holmes, *op. ci.*

is already known, although the exact proportion of it needed in elementary school is not always quite clear. Since the special words in arithmetic are so necessary for the reading of verbal problems, the list of terms will be presented in Chapter XVII. The few words needed for English composition have also been postponed to the relevant chapter. The work in science is very elementary, it does not require an extensive vocabulary, and until more work has been done in determining what data is to be presented in elementary school and until the books have been rewritten in an easy enough form for children to read them with comprehension, it will not be possible to present a properly authenticated vocabulary in either science or hygiene for these early levels. During the summer of 1944 the writer analyzed the vocabulary load of a half dozen of the most widely used texts in elementary science for use in Grades 3 or 4. The easiest book would have been of appropriate difficulty for the high fifth or low sixth grades, one other was not too difficult for the high sixth, but the others had a vocabulary burden which equaled that of junior high school books. It does not seem worth while to present a vocabulary list derived from such texts because it would contain too many hard words quite inappropriate for use with children. The material of the present section will deal, therefore, with the two social sciences, history and geography.

1. **Special Vocabulary in Geography:** The essential words in any subject are determined by much the same methods already described for general vocabulary. A specific example may, however, make the points clearer. An investigation from the field of geography has been selected as an example. In this study fourteen different textbooks were analyzed to determine which special words a pupil would be likely to encounter. The procedure consisted in having different people read these textbooks, keeping a record of the number of times each special term occurred. The occurrences of each term for all fourteen textbooks were then added together and divided by the total number of books, so as to obtain a measure of the average frequency per book. The total number of different special terms found in these books was 2,962.[32] The frequencies varied from words that were found only once in the entire

[32] This number resulted from combining four pieces of research: E. L. Baxter, *A Comparative Study of the Vocabulary Employed in the Four Most Used Elementary Geographies*, Research Department, Ohio State Teachers Association, 1924; E. R. Gabler, "A Geography Vocabulary Study," *Journal of Geography,* 33: 104–108, 1923; L. C. Pressey, "The Fundamental Special Vocabulary of Geography," *Journal of Geography,* 33: 78–81, 1923; *Word Frequency Lists.* To be found in file G, Bureau of Educational Research, Ohio State University.

5,000 pages (approximately) to others that occurred over 600 times per book—or about three times on every two pages. Obviously, all of these terms could not be of equal importance to the reader. A word occurring only once in 5,000 pages does not usually contribute enough to the meaning to be worth knowing,[33] so far as geography is concerned, while a word that appears constantly must be learned if the reading matter is to be understood. The analysis of these texts provided merely a measure of frequency, not of importance, although importance and frequency are closely related.

To obtain a measure of importance for teaching, the entire list of 2,962 terms was submitted to many teachers of geography in elementary, junior high, and high school. Each teacher was asked to mark each word with a number, according to the following plan: If she thought a term so important that she could not teach without it, she marked it "3." If she thought it important but not absolutely essential, she marked it "2." If she thought it of some value but not really important, she marked it "1." If she thought it of no use in teaching, she marked it "0." These ratings of importance varied just as widely as the frequencies from the previous investigation. Some words were marked with a "3" by every teacher, while others were marked consistently with a "0."

The investigator had at this point, for each word, measures of frequency and of importance for teaching. Each word was therefore studied in the light of these two criteria. First the words that occurred less than 28 times in all textbooks put together—that is, on an average of not more than twice per book—were eliminated. Those for which the average rating by teachers was between 0 and 1.9 were also crossed off the list. The number of terms left was only 352, or approximately 12 per cent of the original number. Since children begin to read geography in about the third grade and continue the study through the eighth it should certainly be possible for them to learn 352 words. They would need to learn something less than fifty words a year, or about one word a week.

The essential technical vocabulary has now been determined for thirteen different school subjects,[34] but the only ones of interest to the elementary school teacher are arithmetic, English composition, geography, and history. These vocabularies vary in length from 96 to 520

---

[33] Once in a while a very rare word is essential.

[34] L. Cole, *The Teacher's Handbook of Technical Vocabulary*, Public School Publishing Company, Bloomington, Ill., 1940, 128 pp.

words. If the teacher herself knows what is absolutely essential, the first step has been taken toward a mastery by the pupils of these terms, because she is more likely to emphasize the essentials if she knows what they are than if she does not! Such knowledge by the teacher will not, however, eliminate the necessity of an individual attack upon the problem by each student.

The list for geography is given below:

TABLE 16

List of Technical Terms in Geography

	Thorndike Rating †			Thorndike Rating †
A. Animals, Plants, Minerals, Fuels, and Soils		21. grain		1b
		22. grapes		2a
1. camel	4b	23. oats		3a
2. cod	4b	24. olives		3a
3. hog	3b	25. potatoes		2a
4. llama	15	26. rice		3a
5. oyster	4a	27. rubber		3a
6. poultry	4a	28. rye		4b
7. reindeer	5b	29. spice		3b
8. salmon	6	30. tea		2a
9. seal	2b	31. tobacco		3a
10. whale	6	32. vegetables		2b
		33. wheat		1b
11. alfalfa	7			
12. barley	4a	34. clay		2b
13. cereal	8	35. coal		1b
14. cocoa	7	36. copper		2b
15. cocoanut	6	37. coral		5a
16. coffee	2a	38. deposit		3b
17. corn	1a	39. diamond		2a
18. cotton	2a	40. fuel		3b
19. flour	2a	41. gas		3a
20. fruit	1b	42. gasoline		5b

† The number in this column tells in which thousand each word occurs. In the first five thousand, *a* is used for those words in the lower half and *b* for those in the upper half. Thus *camel* has a rating of *4b,* which shows it to be in the less frequent 500 of the fourth thousand. Parentheses around the number mean that a word owes its frequency to one or more nontechnical meanings. For instance, Word 83—*hide*—is among the commonest 500, but not in its technical sense.

TABLE 16—*Continued*

A. Animals, Plants, Minerals, Fuels, and Soils —*Cont.*	*Thorndike Rating*		*Thorndike Rating*
43. granite	5b	78. cattle	2a
44. gravel	5b	79. dairy	3b
45. iron	1b	80. flock	2b
46. ivory	3b	81. grazing	3b
47. lava	9	82. herd	2b
48. lead	(1a)	83. hide	(1a)
49. limestone	7	84. leather	2a
50. marble	2b	85. livestock	15
51. metal	2b	86. ranch	7
52. mineral	4b	87. wool	2a
53. mud	2b	*88. business	1b
54. oil	2a	89. cloth	1b
55. ore	10	*90. commerce	2b
56. petroleum	6	91. demand	1b
57. quarry	5a	*92. export	5b
58. salt	1b	93. factory	3a
59. silver	1a	*94. goods	(1a)
60. soil	1b	*95. import	3b
61. steel	2a	*96. industry	2a
62. tin	3a	97. machinery	3b
63. turpentine	7	*98. manufacture	2b
		99. market	1b
B. Economic Life		100. mills	1b
64. acre	2b	101. mine	(1a)
*65. agriculture	3a	*102. production	5a
*66. crops	2a	*103. raw materials	
67. cultivate	3a	104. silk	1b
68. fertilizer	6	105. supply	1b
69. harvest	2a	106. textile	10
70. irrigation	7	*107. trade	1b
71. orchard	2b		
*72. plantation	5a	108. caravan	6
73. produce	2a	109. cargo	4b
74. raise	(1a)	*110. discovery	3
75. vineyard	6	111. dock	4a
76. wine	2a	*112. expedition	4a
77. yield	2a	*113. explore	4b
		114. freight	3a

* Asterisk means duplication with history list.

TABLE 16—*Continued*

	Thorndike Rating		Thorndike Rating
B. Economic Life—*Cont.*		*150. century	2b
*115. highway	4a	*151. colony	2b
116. journey	1b	152. country	1a
117. railroad	2a	*153. domestic	3a
*118. railway	3b	*154. foreign	2a
119. route	3a	*155. government	1b
120. shipping	4	156. internal	5b
121. steamship	6	*157. invention	3b
122. telegraph	4a	*158. local	3a
123. telephone	3a	*159. modern	2b
124. traffic	4a	*160. nation	1b
*125. transportation	4b	*161. province	2b
126. travel	1b	*162. republic	3b
127. vessel	2a	*163. rural	3b
*128. voyage	3a	*164. state	(1a)
129. wharf	8	*165. territory	3a
		166. village	1b
*130. civilized	6		
131. fisheries	11	**D. Physical Geography**	
*132. frontier	6	a. Divisions of the Earth	
*133. immigrant	7	167. area	3a
*134. inhabitant	5a	168. belt	(2b)
135. language	2a	169. border	2a
136. migrate	9	*170. boundary	3b
*137. native	2a	171. center	1b
138. nomad	9	172. circumference	8
139. occupation	3b	*173. continent	3a
*140. pioneer	5b	174. district	2b
*141. population	3a	175. earth	1a
142. primitive	7	176. globe	3a
*143. race	(1b)	177. hemisphere	6
144. savage	2b	178. location	4b
*145. settlement	3a	179. map	2a
146. shelter	2a	180. planet	4b
147. tribe	1b	181. region	2a
		182. section	2b
History		183. sphere	3b
*148. ancient	2a	184. surface	2b
*149. capital	2b	185. zone	3a

TABLE 16—*Continued*

	Thorndike Rating		*Thorndike Rating*
D. Physical Geography—*Cont.*		220. flood	2b
b. Measurement of the Earth's Surface		221. geyser	12
		222. glacier	12
186. altitude	6	223. gulf	2b
187. antarctic	11	224. harbor	2b
188. arctic	5b	225. iceberg	7
189. axis	6	226. ice sheet	
190. compass	2b	227. mouth	(1b)
191. direction	2a	228. narrows	(1b)
192. distance	1b	229. navigable	6
193. east	1a	230. ocean	1b
194. elevation	6	231. outlet	4b
195. equator	6	232. port	2a
196. horizon	4b	233. rapids	(1b)
197. latitude	7	234. reservoir	8
198. level	2a	235. seepage	20
199. longitude	7	236. sound	(1a)
200. meridian	6	237. source	3a
201. navigation	7	238. spring	(1a)
202. north	1a	239. strait	(3b)
203. point	(1a)	240. stream	1b
204. pole	2a	241. tide	2b
205. prime meridian		242. tributary	4a
206. rotate	9	243. waterfall	5a
207. sea level		244. waterpower	. 8
208. south	1a	245. waterway	10
209. tropics	6		
210. west	1b	d. Land Formations	
		246. barrier	5b
c. Water and Structures Built on or near the Water		247. beach	2b
		248. bottom land	
211. basin	(3b)	249. canyon	10
212. bay	1b	250. cape	(3a)
213. breakwater	12	251. chain	(1b)
214. canal	3a	252. cliff	3a
215. channel	3b	253. coast	1a
216. current	2b	254. coastal	12
217. dam	4a	255. crater	13
218. dike	12	256. delta	6
219. drainage	8	257. desert	2a

TABLE 16—*Continued*

	Thorndike Rating		*Thorndike Rating*
D. Physical Geography		294. timber	4a
d. Land Formations—*Cont.*		**f. Descriptive Words**	
258. divide	(1b)	295. abundant	3b
259. eruption	9	296. arid	11
260. highlands	4b	297. barren	3b
261. island	1b	298. bleak	6
262. isthmus	3a	299. dense	4a
263. lowlands	5b	300. extinct	7
264. mainland	8	301. fertile	4a
265. marsh	5a	302. frigid	9
266. meadow	2a	303. rugged	5a
267. mountain	1a	304. shallow	3b
268. oasis	7	305. stagnant	7
269. pasture	2b	306. steep	2b
270. peak	4b	307. temperate	3b
271. peninsula	5a	308. torrid	8
272. plain	(1a)	309. tropical	2b
273. plateau	5a		
274. prairie	5b	**E. Weather**	
275. range	(2a)	310. annual	12
276. reef	7	311. atmosphere	5b
277. ridge	3a	312. barometer	15
278. seaport	6	313. blizzard	11
279. seashore	8	314. breeze	3a
280. slope	2b	315. climate	3a
281. steppes	10	316. cyclone	14
282. summit	5a	317. dew	2b
283. swamp	4a	318. drought	8
284. tundra	20	319. earthquake	4b
285. uplands	8	320. fog	4a
286. valley	1b	321. freeze	2b
287. volcano	7	322. frost	2a
288. wasteland		323. hail	2b
		324. "high"	(1a)
e. Trees		325. humidity	9
289. evergreens	7	326. hurricane	8
290. forest	1b	327. "low"	(1a)
291. jungle	9	328. mist	3a
292. lumber	2a	329. lightning	3a
293. pulp	7	330. moisture	4b

TABLE 16—Continued

	Thorndike Rating			Thorndike Rating
E. Weather—Cont.		342. vapor		3a
331. pressure	5a	343. weather		1b
332. prevailing	(3b)			
333. rainfall	6	344. conservation		7
334. season	1b	345. decay		3a
335. shower	2b	346. deforestation		
336. storm	1b	347. erosion		10
337. temperature	3b	*348. natural resources		
338. thermometer	5b	349. reclamation		13
339. tornado	11	350. rot		6
340. trade wind		351. vegetation		7
341. typhoon	16	352. weathering		(1a)

In this list for geography there are 48 words that appear on the history list also. The number of words seems large when seen as a whole, but the load is not especially heavy because it can be spread out over many years. The heaviest burden comes in the fourth and fifth grades when the children are beginning the subject. The words for which the Thorndike rating is enclosed in parentheses are especially tricky because the common meaning may prevent the learning of the technical. The words *mine, race, belt, point, mouth* or *plain* are common enough, but not as a *coal mine,* the *Negro race,* the *corn belt,* a *compass point,* a *river's mouth,* or a *central plain.* Children may find such words confusing, not because they do not know them, but because they do.

Two investigations[35] have traced recognition of certain terms in geography from Grade 4 through either Grade 7 or Grade 12. One investigator first selected 135 words from a number of previous studies and constructed an objective test for measuring comprehension of these terms. The mastery in the fourth was 52 words, and the growth was approximately 10 words per year, with a median of 84 in the seventh grade. The growth in the different terms came from several sources —increase in the number of meanings for words used in several senses, increase in general information, increase through the substitution of basic for associated meanings, increase through the development of

[35] T. J. Eskridge, Jr., "Growth in Understanding of Geographical Terms in Grades 4 through 7," *Duke University Studies in Education,* No. 4, 1939, 68 pp., and L. C. Pressey, "A Study in the Learning of the Fundamental Special Vocabulary of History," pp. 155–218 in A. C. Krey and T. L. Kelly *Tests and Measurements in the Social Sciences,* Charles Scribner's Sons, 1934, 635 pp.

comprehensive meanings, and decrease of certain errors due to confusion of words having similar sounds and to the application of general
literary meanings for those that are technical. The author emphasizes
the negative transfer which occurs from the everyday meanings of
such words as *belt, center,* or *possessions* to their technical meanings.
These words are of the same type as those enclosed by parentheses in
the list given above. The second investigator made a similar study of

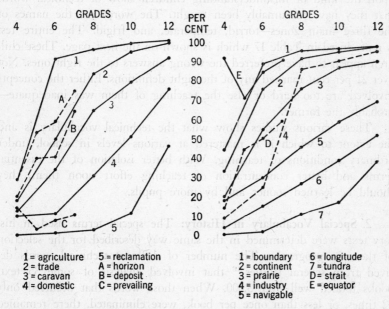

1 = agriculture   5 = reclamation
2 = trade   A = horizon
3 = caravan   B = deposit
4 = domestic   C = prevailing

1 = boundary   6 = longitude
2 = continent   7 = tundra
3 = prairie   D = strait
4 = industry   E = equator
5 = navigable

FIGURE 17: Learning Curves for Geographical Terms

both historical and geographical terms from Grade 4 through Grade 12.
A few sample words from both studies appear in Figure 17. Only two
of these words show a mastery of 90 per cent or more in the sixth
grade, and several do not show a 90 per cent mastery even at the end
of high school.

The curves are of sundry shapes. The words *agriculture, trade,*
boundary, prairie, and *continent* show a rapid rise and high final
achievement. The curves for *caravan,* and *navigable,* and *longitude* are
almost straight lines, while those for *domestic, reclamation,* and *tundra*
show a slow start and subsequent more rapid rise. *Industry* has a shape
all its own. Three of the five shorter curves, for *strait, deposit,* and

horizon, show consistent gains as far as they go, but those for *prevailing* and *equator* have a curious shape. Both words had just been taught in Grade 4 when the test was given, and the fourth grade scored high in consequence. By the fifth grade, however, enough pupils had forgotten the meaning of these words to produce a drop in the curve. In later grades the loss was made up.

One detailed study of only three words in geography throws light upon the kind of misunderstanding children show of technical words that they have presumably been taught. The words are the names of the three main zones—torrid, temperate, and frigid. The entire test is reproduced in Table 17 which is shown on the next page. These children appear to have preferred the wrong answers to the right ones. Not over 21 per cent marked any of the right definitions. Either the concepts involved are too hard or else the teaching of them was inadequate—probably the former.

These various studies show what the technical vocabulary is and the extent to which it is mastered at various levels in school, under ordinary conditions of teaching. With better isolation of the essential terms and better concentration of teaching effort upon them, they should be learned sooner and by more pupils.

2. **Special Vocabulary in History:** The special terms used in history texts were determined in the same way described for the selection of those in geography. The number of different technical words derived from several studies [36] that involved analysis of some 35 textbooks totaled well over 3,000. When those words that occurred only 22 times, or less than once per book, were eliminated, there remained 1,444 which were rated by approximately 50 teachers. By the use of the ratings for both frequency and importance, it was possible to select 431 words as essential. Not all these terms, however, need to be learned in elementary school. By comparison of the words found in elementary school texts and of the ratings made by elementary school

---

[36] A. S. Barr and C. W. Gifford, "Vocabulary of American History in Senior High School Textbooks in American History," *Journal of Educational Research,* 20: 103–121, 1930; R. Brown, "Vocabularies of History and History Textbooks," *Eighth Yearbook of the Department of Elementary School Principals,* pp. 408–411, 1931; M. G. Kelty, "The Special Vocabulary of History," *Normal Instructor and Primary Plans,* 29: 48, 1928; L. C. Pressey and S. L. Pressey, "Determination of a Minimum Vocabulary in American History," *Educational Method,* 12: 205–211, 1933; L. C. Pressey, *Vocabulary Lists in Fifteen School Subjects: History,* Public School Publishing Company, 1924; O. W. Stephenson and W. R. McGhee, "Vocabulary Common to Civics and American History," *Journal of Educational Research,* 22: 55–58, 1930; J. L. Ward, "The Vocabulary of a History Text," *Education,* 56: 359–361, 1936.

TABLE 17

Misunderstandings of Three Technical Terms [37]

Definitions	Per Cent of 1,110 Children in Grades 6, 7, & 8 Checking Each Answer †
Torrid Zone	
1. The zone in which every place has the noonday sun directly overhead all year	15
2. The zone in which snow never falls anywhere	28
3. The zone in which the days are always longer than the nights	19
4. The zone which includes all parts of the entire earth's surface where the sun is at any time directly overhead	19
5. The zone in which every place is always hot	30
Temperate Zones	
1. The zones in which the weather is always temperate	15
2. The zones which are never so hot as the torrid zone and never so cold as the frigid zones	46
3. The zones in which the sun appears daily but yet never mounts to a vertical position	21
4. The zones in which the weather is generally very mild: never very hot or very cold for long	21
5. The zones in which rain falls in moderate amounts in all seasons	5
Frigid Zones	
1. The zones in which the land is covered with ice all year	14
2. The zones which at some time of the year have 24 hours or more of continuous daylight	15
3. The zones throughout which there are 6 months of continuous day and six months of continuous night	25
4. The zones in which the temperature is always cold	28
5. The zones in which no green vegetation grows anywhere	11

[37] A. Atchison, "Torrid, Temperate, and Frigid Zones—Sources of Error in Children's Thinking," *32nd Yearbook of the National Society for the Study of Education*, 1933, pp. 483–485. The list from page 484 is used by permission of the publisher.

† The numbers do not add up to 100 because some children checked two answers and some omitted answers.

teachers it was possible to select the following 150 terms as necessary below the junior high school level.

TABLE 18

List of Technical Terms in Elementary School History

abolish	crime	illegal	navy	session
*agriculture	*crops	*immigrant	neutral	*settlement
alien		*import	nominate	siege
alliance	declaration	independence	Negro	slavery
allies	delegate	*industry		*state
amendment	democratic	*inhabitant	patriotism	strike
*ancient	development	international	peace	supreme court
annex	discovery	interstate	period	surrender
appoint	domestic	intolerance	persecution	
armistice		invasion	petition	tax
army	education	*invention	*pioneer	*territory
	election		*plantation	testimony
battle	employee	judge	*population	town
boundary	employer	jury	*prairie	*trade
	enemy	justice	president	*transportation
campaign	enforce		*production	treason
candidate	equality	labor		treasury
*capital	*expedition	law	*race	treaty
*century	*explore	legal	*raw material	troops
citizen	*export	legislature	rebellion	
city		liberty	recruit	unemployment
*civilized	federal	*local	reform	union
*colony	fleet		*region	
*commerce	*foreign	majority	repeal	verdict
community	freedom	*manufacture	representative	veto
competition	*frontier	military	*republic	vice-president
congress		*modern	republican	*village
conquer	*government		revolution	volunteer
constitution	governor	*nation	rights	vote
*continent		nationality	*rural	*voyage
convention	*highway	*native		
convict	House of	naturalize	*section	war
*country	Representa-	*natural re-	senate	welfare
court	tives	sources	senator	witness

* Asterisk means duplication with geography list.

Many more technical words than those just listed appear in the reading usually assigned in elementary school, but the situation is improving steadily because the writers of school materials are constantly reducing the vocabulary and deleting the topics that are beyond childish comprehension. The typical situation in the past is shown by the analysis of a single text in American history. Of 1,097 different special terms found in this one book, 695—or 63 per cent—appeared only once or twice.

TABLE 19

Frequency of Technical Terms in a Single Text

Number of Occurrences	Number of Terms
300—600	10
250—299	3
200—249	0
150—199	6
100—149	1
90—99	0
80—89	3
60—79	3
40—59	7
30—39	3
20—29	11
15—19	6
11—14	29
9—10	39
7—8	47
5—6	72
4	70
3	92
2	306
1	389
TOTAL	1,097

Only 82 words, 17 per cent of the total, occurred 10 times or more. In all probability the author of the text could have omitted or used easier substitutes for most of the 695 terms appearing once or twice. This change would have reduced the load nearly two thirds.

Most of the vocabulary burden comes from hundreds of unusual technical or literary words used so seldom that a pupil does not get enough practice to learn them. In this particular book, the vocabulary is spread out so thinly that few terms are likely to be acquired permanently. Moreover, the inclusion of many hard words of low frequency obscures the really important terms, and both teacher and pupil are likely to be confused as to what the essential words are. The first step toward an efficient mastery is the determination by research of what is and what is not important. Eventually the writers of texts will produce better books, but in the meantime a list of essentials will help everyone to concentrate upon what is most needed.

In Figure 18 some results are presented from a study that traced the learning of 346 concepts in social science from the fourth grade through the twelfth.[38] In this investigation the terms had already been selected, in the manner above described, as being essential. The results were expressed in terms of the per cent of children in each grade who were able to recognize the meaning of each technical term. The chil-

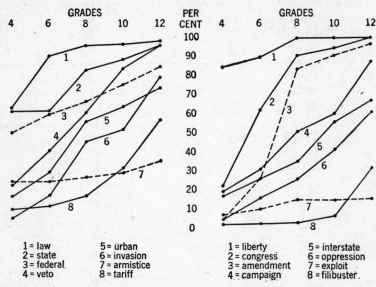

1 = law	5 = urban	1 = liberty	5 = interstate
2 = state	6 = invasion	2 = congress	6 = oppression
3 = federal	7 = armistice	3 = amendment	7 = exploit
4 = veto	8 = tariff	4 = campaign	8 = filibuster

FIGURE 18: Learning Curves for Historical Terms

dren did not write their definitions; they merely picked out the correct one. The test required, therefore, about the same degree of understanding that would be necessary if the children were reading these terms in a textbook.

The words *law, state,* and *liberty* were already known by over 60 per cent in the fourth grade. These three curves are, therefore, merely the tops of learning curves which have their beginnings in the first three grades. Mastery of these words was not complete, however, until the twelfth grade. Recognition of *federal* also started high but grew slowly. The word *amendment* started in the fourth grade as practically unknown. Year by year more children acquired meaning for this word until, in the twelfth grade, 95 per cent could recognize the correct defi-

[38] Pressey, *op. cit.,* p. 74.

nition. *Congress* showed a rapid initial rise and then a slower growth. The curves for *veto, urban, campaign, invasion, interstate,* and *oppression* had fairly regular growth rates but showed varying degrees of final mastery. The results for *tariff* and *filibuster* produced concave shapes, while *armistice* and *exploit* show an improvement from Grade 4 to Grade 12 of less than 10 per cent.

The mastery in Grade 6 of the 150 historical terms selected for the elementary school vocabulary is shown in Table 20. This degree of mastery may seem so low as to suggest that the vocabulary be made smaller in order that it might be better learned. One must remember,

TABLE 20

Mastery of the 150 Words in Elementary School History

Per Cent of Mastery	Number of Terms
100	1
95—99	6
90—94	5
85—89	8
80—84	8
75—79	7
70—74	12
65—69	8
60—64	21
55—59	10
50—54	17
45—49	8
40—44	11
35—39	7
30—34	8
25—29	5
20—24	3
15—19	4
10—14	1
TOTAL	150

however, that these words have been snowed under by hundreds of others of less importance and that teaching effort has been spread very thin over a much larger number. If pupils could concentrate on this small number of words, the learning would presumably be much higher.

Vocabulary appears to be one of the greatest difficulties facing the pupil when he tries to read his texts in history. Some, if not most, of the blame lies with the text rather than with either the pupils or the teachers. For instance, two teachers asked their 300 seventh and eighth grade pupils to list on slips of paper, one word to a slip, any new words they found as they read their assignments. The slips containing unfamiliar words finally totaled 3,733, of which almost half were words beyond the commonest 10,000 in the Thorndike list.[39] Certainly such books are too hard. To be sure, some new words should appear or vocabulary will not grow, but when there are too many, the pupil is too bewildered to learn as many as he would have learned had there been fewer of them.

Many teachers do not realize how completely lacking in technical vocabulary some pupils are. An example may emphasize this point.

Mabel was a bright child who had a fixed idea that she could not learn to solve problems in arithmetic. She could do good work as long as she stuck to the operations by themselves, but even the shortest verbal problem threw her into a state of disorganization. Mabel was asked to read a few problems aloud. At once the nature of her difficulty appeared. She did not recognize most of the special words. Her teacher had given her no work in phonics, and she was quite unable to pronounce a word she did not recognize. Mabel was given ten minutes of individual work in phonics every day. After about three weeks the special terms in arithmetic were introduced as training materials. In three months' time Mabel was no longer afraid of problems, and a year later she stood among the first ten pupils in her grade on a test of problem-solving. No other remedial treatment than that described above was used.

A student in first-year chemistry stayed after class one day and asked his instructor to give him extra help in understanding this law: "the volume of a gas is inversely proportional to its density." The instructor tried to explain, but without success. After some time he did what he should have done in the first place. He asked the student to define the terms being used. To his amazement he found that the boy had "volume" confused with its meaning as a book, thought that "gas" meant what is used in a stove, and had omitted the phrase "inversely proportional" because he had not the foggiest notion of its meaning. "Density" he defined only as "thickness." It is not surprising

[39] U. W. Leavell and G. E. Hollister, "Social Studies' Vocabulary Difficulty in the Upper Grades," *Peabody Journal of Education,* 12: 287–293, 1935.

that the law was hard for him to grasp, although he had carefully memorized it and had studied it until he was dizzy from reading and rereading the paragraphs above and below it.

Any experienced teacher can duplicate such instances. The significance is not always appreciated, however. The first and sometimes only explanation that occurs to the teacher is that the child is stupid. Lack of technical vocabulary often means only that a pupil has not yet been adequately informed. He can learn although he has not done so.

3. **The Teaching of Technical Vocabulary:** Experiments in the building of special vocabularies at the elementary school level are rare, presumably because general vocabulary is a greater problem in these early grades. The examples of experiments have to be taken, for the most part, from junior high or high school, but there is no reason to suppose that similar concentration upon vocabulary in elementary school would not be equally effective. In two instances [40] the direct teaching of even 100 terms increased not only the vocabulary of the pupils but their comprehension of history as well. Another teacher carried on a most successful experiment in plane geometry in high school.[41] In her class there were 46 pupils with IQ's ranging from 87 to 169. In September these students took an objective test which measured comprehension of 121 mathematical concepts necessary for work in the subject. The average score was 56, with a range from 26 to 101. The teacher of this class had prepared a dictionary of a type to be described presently. Each student was told which terms he had missed and was given opportunity to study them. From time to time, at intervals of about 6 weeks, the pupils tested themselves or each other. The next February the teacher repeated the original test. The scores now averaged 105.5 with a range from 86 to 121—a perfect score. The lowest score in February coincided with the third from the highest in September. The study of unknown words continued. After another 6 weeks had passed, the teacher gave the original test once again. The average was 119, with scores running from 106 to 121. A condensed form of the September and March distributions appears in Table 21.

[40] H. K. Newburn, "Vocabulary Drill in American History," *University of Iowa Studies in Education*, 9, No. 3: 9–30, 1934, and W. R. Phipps, "An Experimental Study in Developing History Reading Ability with Sixth Grade Pupils through the Development of an Active History Vocabulary," *Journal of Experimental Education*, 7: 19–23, 1938 or *Johns Hopkins University Studies in Education*, No. 28, 1940, 73 pp.

[41] N. M. Hastings, "A Study of the Use of a Glossary and a Series of Objective Tests as a Means of Eliminating the Vocabulary Difficulty of Plane Geometry," Master's Thesis, Ohio State University, 1932, 178 pp.

TABLE 21

Mastery of a Technical Vocabulary

Test	26–35	36–45	46–55	56–65	66–75	76–85	86–95	96–105	106–115	116–121	Median	Number of Pupils
September	3	10	9	9	6	5	3	1			56	46
March									12	34	119	46

The standing of the entire group had risen greatly. Even more conspicuous is the marked narrowing of the range. As in all diagnostic work, the chief effect showed at the lower end of the distribution—precisely where it is most needed. These students more than doubled their original mastery of technical vocabulary in this subject.

For adequate individual study of technical vocabulary the teacher needs the following equipment: (1) for her own use a list of the essential words in the subject being taught; (2) duplicate copies of this list for each student; (3) an objective test that is "keyed" to the list; and (4) a home-made dictionary. The procedure in using this equipment is straightforward and simple.

The teacher may construct her own list or she can buy one that is based on years of research carried on by many different people. Thus, the high school teacher of a foreign language can obtain a list containing a total of ninety-six terms, of which forty-six have already been encountered in elementary work in written English. She has, then, forty-six words to review and fifty new ones to teach. Since pupils of this age can handle a test fifty items long in one period, she can find out at the end of the first two days which terms, of those that he will soon need to know, each pupil recognizes. In other subjects, it may be desirable to administer the test in several sections, either because there are so many items or because the subject matter naturally falls into divisions, before each of which a brief test can be given.

The test items should always be keyed to the list. That is, Item 16 should measure comprehension of Word 16 on the list; Item 40 should test Word 40, and so on. When a teacher scores a pupil's test she does not need to mark the blank at all; she marks the corresponding items on the pupil's copy of the fundamental list. The diagnosis a student receives is this list which shows him the entire number of terms necessary to the subject with a mark against each word he did not know. His learning task consists of finding meanings for these marked words.

Since the most severe problems of technical vocabulary do not begin until junior high school, the children are old enough to guide their own remedial work. In the upper grades of elementary school they can drill themselves under the teacher's guidance. Once the teacher has isolated for each pupil the words he does not know, she should give him definite assignments for learning the missing words and should check him to make certain that he does so. The children may use an ordinary dictionary, but the task of searching for meanings is greatly simplified if a teacher constructs a "dictionary" of her own. She first numbers library cards to correspond with the numbers of the words on the list. Then she writes, on each card, the appropriate word and some sort of explanation—definition, illustration, graphical representation, or whatever may seem best for making the meaning clear. The pupils consult this dictionary as they need to do so in order to master the fundamental vocabulary. This set of definitions, once constructed, is a permanent acquisition.

At whatever intervals seem desirable the teacher repeats the original test—or a duplicate form of it. Each pupil keeps his checked list beside him and should answer *only those items testing recognition of words he missed on the preceding test.* When the teacher scores this second test, she need not mark the blanks. Instead, on each pupil's list, she should draw a line through the check mark in front of words missed on the first test but known on the second. The student's task is then to learn what terms still remain.

By this method, a pupil always knows what words he needs and how many of them he can recognize. He knows how he can get meanings for unfamiliar words. And he can always tell, by looking at his checked list, how much progress he has made and how much work remains to be done. Such a situation motivates a child to reach his clearly recognized goal. Vocabulary drill is, for both teacher and pupil, relatively hard work, although a plan like the one described above relieves most of the monotony. As pointed out earlier, there is no easy road to the learning of any language. There are, however, so many things in schoolwork that are made interesting and exciting for the learner that a little hard work, properly motivated, should do no harm.

C. SUMMARY

Vocabulary may be either general or technical. In elementary school the children concentrate for the most part upon mastery of the basic general vocabulary needed for reading at all, but they do make a beginning in the acquisition of a special vocabulary in geography, history, and arithmetic. While the special terms are not numerous, they are essential to the reading of assignments.

The first words are taught one by one, usually through a largely visual presentation. By the second or third year, if not earlier, most teachers supplement the visual approach by the use of phonics and word study. It would appear that this supplementation is needed if the pupils are to sound out new words for themselves.

Both general and technical vocabulary may be enlarged. No indirect method seems to work as well as the direct teaching of those words that the children need to know. Especially within the relatively narrow limits of a technical vocabulary is progress rapid when the teacher emphasizes the words and arranges for the pupils to diagnose and correct their own shortcomings.

III · Comprehension, Especially in the Social Sciences

As children progress through elementary school they have to do more and more reading, much of it in the content subjects. The reading class itself gradually develops into a class in elementary literature, and in other courses as well, reading has become a tool for the extraction of meaning from the printed page. Children need to use what skill they have developed to read problems in arithmetic, descriptions and expositions in geography, narratives and expository matter in history and hygiene, and expositions and problems in science. The content subjects make certain demands upon reading skill—sometimes demands that the reading of stories does not equip children to meet. The list given in Table 22 shows what some of these demands are.

TABLE 22
The Reading Demands of the Content Subjects [1]

I. Needs in reading history or geography

   A. Interpretation of directions, often mimeographed, designed for guidance in studying; reading such directions from note-book, when already written from dictation.

   B. Recognition and interpretation of the problem about which the unit is organized.

   C. Location of reference material; using guides to references, using indices, skimming to determine relevancy of a reference.

[1] Condensed from pp. 207–208, 225–226, and 247–248 of J. M. McCallister, *Remedial and Corrective Instruction in Reading,* D. Appleton-Century Company, 1936, 300 pp. Used by permission of the publisher. See also J. M. McAllister, "Determining the Types of Reading in Studying Content Subjects," *School Review,* 40: 115–123, 1932; M. Snedaker and E. Horn, "Reading in the Various Fields of the Curriculum," *Thirty-sixth Yearbook of the National Society for the Study of Education,* Part I, 1937, pp. 133–184; *Seventeenth Yearbook of the Department of Elementary School Principals Association,* Chapter 5, "Study Reading in the Content Fields," pp. 368–386, 1938; G. A. Yoakum, "The Improvement of Reading in the Middle Grades," *Education,* 56: 1–6, 1935.

D. Interpretation of reference material: mastery of discussion in textbook, formulating judgment of all materials read, finding answers to questions, learning to spell new technical words, associating maps or diagrams with the discussion about them.

E. Association of reference material with the problem of the unit; discrimination between relevant and irrelevant, between facts of major and minor importance.

F. Preparation and presentation of reports: note-taking, reviewing notes to organize them, reading notes while making oral report, reading especially telling passages orally to class, proof-reading reports for errors of content or English.

II. Needs in reading mathematics

A. Interpretation of descriptive materials, reading discussion in textbook, application of already-learned principles to new materials, interpretation of mathematical figures, association of descriptions with figures, formulae, or exercises.

B. Comprehension of illustrative exercises: analysis and solution, interpretation of directions for performing new processes and of formulae needed in exercises, following directions for constructing figures, association of directions with figures or formulae—new or already known —and with tables, recognition of familiar or new principles or processes needed in exercises, comparison of two or more figures to note similarities or differences.

C. Interpretation of mathematical exercises designed to give practice in applying principles or processes, reading technical words and symbols, analyzing the problem to determine what is to be found and what processes are to be used, interpretation of exercise in light of principles and processes already known and selection of those applicable, interpretation of directions for solving problems, association of directions with figures, formulae, or tables, reading, comparing, and analyzing geometrical figures; preparing, copying numerals for, and proof-reading solution.

I. Needs in reading science material

A. Interpretation and execution of study directions, often mimeographed; reading directions concerning forms of written work or activities in studying.

B. Interpretation of directions for exercises: learning technical words, comparing directions or explanations with illustrations, recognizing the purpose of an exercise and selecting procedure when two or more alternatives are present.

C. Interpretation of instructional materials: reading and re-reading textbook and other references; locating references, applying directions for study to them, and formulating questions about them; understanding units of measure; associating explanations in books with experiments performed or observed; comparing data from two or more sources; interpreting explanatory figures, comparing them, and associating them with discussions about them; reading tables and selecting pertinent facts from them; classifying facts, observing relationships between them, and formulating conclusions on the basis of facts; applying known principles of science to the interpretation of new materials.

D. Associating instructional materials with problems: discriminating between relevant and irrelevant.

E. Preparing written reports: selecting title, applying directions regarding form, organizing materials for presentation, preparing outlines, copying figures or drawings, proof-reading to detect errors either in content or in English.

From this list one can see that the demands made upon children by the content subjects are numerous and highly specialized. Pupils often need experience and drill in these various special types of reading,[2] before they are able to read assignments efficiently.

A. COMPREHENSION OF GENERAL READING MATTER

1. **Factors in Comprehension:** The ability to comprehend what is read is the one objective of reading, to which everything else is supplementary. If efficient eye movements and a large vocabulary did not contribute to a high degree of comprehension they would hardly be worth considering. They are important because children with clumsy mechanics or restricted vocabularies do not understand what they read. Moreover, an increase in a child's efficiency along either of these lines results in a higher degree of comprehension. An illustration of this fact is narrated below:

The writer was once asked to work with about fifteen children in a low fourth-grade class, to analyze their eye movements, and to give remedial work in mechanics where needed. She saw the children individually every other day for six weeks. The drill given was concerned exclusively with lessening the number of fixations, avoiding regressions, increasing the span, and decreasing the degree of vocalization. As a sort of general precaution, she gave tests in speed and comprehension at the beginning and end of the

2 See the "Work-type Reading Lessons" on locating materials, using dictionaries and appendices, organizing materials, reading graphs, tables and maps, by H. Prehm, *Thirty-sixth Yearbook of the National Society for the Study of Education,* Part I, pp. 164–182, 1937.

training period to the entire class, using duplicate forms of a standard test. The trained children gained nearly two years in speed, while the untrained members of the class made a gain of about two months. The really surprising thing, however, was a gain of well over a year in comprehension, although no drill had been given along this line. Not all this remarkable gain was due to the covering of a greater amount of reading matter in the time allowed by the test. The papers of the second test were re-scored by being graded only up to a point corresponding with the distance each child had read on his first test; it was then clear that a gain of nearly half a year had been made in the comprehension of the same amount of material of the same degree of difficulty. Although the training was devoted wholly to remedying deficiencies of mechanics, there was a substantial improvement in comprehension.[3]

Comprehension is a complex activity, to which many factors contribute. It is a centrally controlled process—that is, it is a function of the mind. It makes little difference whether the material to be understood is presented orally or visually, although most people prefer a visual presentation.[4] It does not, however, operate in a vacuum, but is highly dependent upon a number of factors, such as the type of material being read and the past experiences of the individual who is reading. It is not the same thing as general intelligence, although the two are related, for if they were the same, one's comprehension would not vary from one type of subject matter to another. One recent investigation furnishes a good illustration of this point.[5] A group of 205 college students read passages in geology, art, history (two passages), and general fiction. The students were scored for speed during the first few minutes of reading and were then allowed to finish each passage and show their comprehension by answering questions. Their rate of reading was not affected as much by the differences in subject matter as by their understanding. Their comprehension scores on the two passages in history correlated .98, but between fiction and geology, the coefficient was only .59, while those between either history or fiction and art or geology were all low, one as low as .17. Presumably these students did not change in intelligence from one reading to the next, but they did vary greatly in comprehension.

Assuming that a child's mechanical habits are reasonably good and

---

[3] L. C. Pressey, "Specific Elements Making for Proficiency in Silent Reading When General Intelligence Is Constant," *School and Society,* 24: 589–592, 1926.

[4] R. P. Larsen and D. D. Feder, "Common and Differential Factors in Reading and Hearing Comprehension," *Journal of Educational Psychology,* 31: 241–252, 1940.

[5] F. P. Robinson and P. Hall, "Studies of Higher-Level Reading Abilities," *Journal of Educational Psychology,* 32: 241–252, 1941.

that his vocabulary is reasonably adequate, his comprehension of a given selection depends upon his background of information and knowledge, his general intelligence, his purpose in reading, and the keenness of his interest. Comprehension is therefore not a uniform mental capacity but is conditioned by sundry factors. Because it is so easily influenced, a teacher can hope to improve it by supplying material that is interesting and intelligible in terms of the child's development and background, and by giving him as many guides as possible for finding meaning.

What is sometimes called the "depth" of comprehension is dependent almost wholly upon maturity and experience. Not much can be done about it in elementary school. For instance, the average child does not even see a moral in more than an occasional fable until he is twelve, despite the fact that such interpretations do not require great depth of understanding. Most children do not have the faintest suspicion that there is more than meets the eye in such books as *Pilgrim's Progress, Gulliver's Travels,* or *Alice in Wonderland;* in fact, it is only a rare child who has sufficient understanding of life or depth of comprehension to find the last book amusing or ridiculous. What is meant by depth of understanding may be illustrated by the responses of about one hundred college juniors to the reading of *Seventeen.* About thirty of them (being still very young) were made indignant at the way the older people in the book mistreated and misunderstood the poor suffering hero. All but one of the remaining number (being just out of their own silly adolescence) were enormously amused at the absurd behavior shown by the hero. The remaining student replied that the book was on the surface a comedy but was really a tragedy of the inability of one generation to understand either the one above or the one below, that this cruel misunderstanding had always existed and always would. Here are three different "depths" of comprehension. All members of the group understood the events in the story since all were well over the threshold of comprehension. The difference in interpretation is one of maturity. The school cannot teach depth; it can point out its existence for those who can see it, and it can do its share to give richness to the child's life.

Comprehension is affected also by the purpose for which the reading is being done. If one expects a thorough and important examination on a chapter in a text, one reads with greater comprehension than usual. A student who is reading to find illustrations of a general theory attends only to what is relevant, and his comprehension is uneven because he remembers what he was looking for but either forgets or never comprehends points that did not concern him. Any specific purpose generally results in an uneven degree of comprehension of the material as a whole. Reading for enjoyment lowers comprehension of whatever parts are not enjoyed but leads to heightened attention and subsequent retention of the parts that were especially appealing. Perhaps the lowest form of adult comprehension is illustrated in the attention paid to stories read to put the reader to sleep! The temporary understanding may be good enough, but the purpose of reading prevents concentration, and stories may be so completely forgotten that the same books are read a second time without recollection of the first reading until the denouement is reached, and sometimes not then. The purpose in reading is often referred to as the reader's "mental set." In general, the more purposeful the intention, the higher the degree of comprehension.

2. Errors in Comprehension: Anyone who reads at all sometimes misunderstands what he reads, and children are even more likely to do so than adults. There are numerous reasons why misunderstandings occur. A few of these are illustrated in the following paragraphs.

    a. Addition or expansion of facts: Instead of sticking to the text in such a sentence as, "The Indians attacked the fort where the white men had barricaded themselves," the child interpolates some items from previous passages of a similar nature and reads, "The Indians attacked at dawn and scalped the white men and their families in the fort where they were barricaded."

    b. Meaning of one item underpotent: Instead of reading, "If the foreigner learns to speak English well, he usually adapts himself quickly to American ways," he reads, "The foreigner adapts himself quickly to American ways." The conditional clause is not potent enough to modify the meaning as it should.

    c. Overpotency of one element: This error occurs especially if one element is more dramatic than the others, or if a pupil does not know the answer to a question, or if he does not read quite far enough. "The submarine sank four ships, but the crews managed to escape," may become "The submarine sank four ships and their crews." Or, the question, "What inventions have been especially important in their influence upon farming and transportation?" may be read without "farming" or "transportation" if the pupil does not know part of the answer.

    d. Attachment of wrong meaning to a key word: "The mechanic has a great deal of specific knowledge" is read as "The mechanic knows a lot of difficult things" because the reader does not know the meaning of the word "specific."

e. Transference to the wrong position of elements that are correct in themselves: "If you want to keep your dress clean, stay out of the garden," may be read as, "If you stay out of the garden you will keep your dress clean."

f. Failure to sense meaning of connectives: This error is quite common, especially if one reads a bit too quickly. Sentences such as "My sister came in, but my brother had already gone" or "The kitchen keeps warm because we have a coal stove" become "My sister came in and my brother went out" and "The kitchen keeps warm and we have a coal stove." Usually "and" is the substituted connective because it is better known than any other.[6]

When children make mistakes in comprehension such as those enumerated above, the teacher should try to show them the source of their misapprehension. A blanket direction to "read more carefully" is not sufficient because it does not call attention to the reasons that have produced the errors.

One good but somewhat complicated way of analyzing comprehension to determine errors in thinking has recently been suggested.[7] The pupil reads a given amount of material and then has an oral interview with the examiner, who questions him. Unbeknown to the pupil, the entire conversation is recorded through hidden microphones. This method, though time-consuming, solves the chief difficulty in using an oral report—its lack of permanence. Before deciding just how well a pupil has understood and just what his errors are due to, the examiner can play over the record as many times as he desires. This method records the hesitations and inflections of the voice that often reveal degrees of comprehension more accurately than a written test can do.

Children make mistakes in comprehension partly from shortcomings and handicaps within themselves, partly from lack of experience, and partly from faults inherent in the reading matter. A list of a few such contributing elements is given in Table 23. With so many possible sources of interference with comprehension, it is surprising that children manage to get as much meaning as they do from their assignments. Of course, the difficulties arising from the reading matter could be eliminated, but those that come from immaturity and inexperience are not likely to disappear.

[6] Errors of these types and others are discussed by E. L. Thorndike, "The Understanding of Sentences: A Study of Errors in Reading," *Elementary School Journal*, 18: 98–114, 1917, and "Improving Ability to Read," *Teachers College Record*, 36: 1–19, 125–144, 229–241, 1934.

[7] J. C. Dewey, "A Technique for Investigating Reading Comprehension," *School and Society*, 39: 276, 1934.

TABLE 23

Sources of Failure to Comprehend [8]

I. Reading Difficulties Growing Out of a Pupil's Method of Attack

    1. Omission of parts of major importance

    2. Inability to use references or to find references to use

    3. Copying of material from text, without interpreting it

    4. Use of previous knowledge instead of assigned passages in reacting to reading matter

    5. Misinterpretation caused by lack of precise reading

    6. Failure to understand because of superficial reading

    7. Failure to understand because of overlooking a significant word or expression

    8. Failure to understand because of failure to read punctuation

    9. Skimming of what should have been read intensively

    10. Failure to solve problems because of failure to read illustrative examples, solutions, or formulae

    11. Mechanical following of directions without gaining understanding of process

    12. Careless reading of table or figure

    13. Fear of attacking new words

    14. Inability to retain what is read

    15. Inability to use index, table of contents, or dictionary

II. Reading Difficulties Caused by Inability to Recognize Relationships

    16. Failure to recognize relation of reference materials to text or to problem

    17. Failure to discriminate between relevant and irrelevant materials

    18. Failure to recognize the relative values shown between the general problem and specific points of importance

    19. Inability to associate descriptive material with accompanying figure or to use it in solving a problem

    20. Inability to distinguish likenesses and differences in closely related concepts

    21. Inability to distinguish between relative values shown by substitution of details for points of major importance

    22. Formulation of conclusions not justified by facts at hand

    23. Inability to recognize relationship between a known series of facts and problems based upon those facts

    24. Inability to distinguish between fact and mere improbability

[8] Based upon J. M. McAllister, "Reading Difficulties in Studying the Content Subjects," *Elementary School Journal,* 31: 191–201, 1930, and Yoakum, *op. cit.* Used by permission of the publisher.

III. Reading Difficulties Arising from Lack of Knowledge of Subject Matter

    25. Failure to understand material because of failure to grasp preceding concepts

    26. Failure to interpret an exercise because of failure to understand the necessary processes

    27. Inability to understand an exercise because of an inability to comprehend basic facts involved

    28. Inability to interpret and execute directions

    29. Failure to read figure for lack of understanding of essential scientific principles

IV. Reading Difficulties Arising from Deficiencies of Vocabulary

    30. Misunderstanding of material because of ignorance of word meanings

    31. Misunderstanding of material because of ignorance of symbol, formula, mathematical expression, or abbreviation

V. Reading Difficulties Arising from Inaccuracies

    32. Misunderstanding of an essential point because of inaccuracy in interpreting references

    33. Misreading of technical words

    34. Misreading of directions

VI. Reading Difficulties Arising from Lack of Clearness in Directions Given to Pupils

    35. Poor arrangement

    36. Confusion caused by more than one possible interpretation

3. **Improving Comprehension:** Both by her daily assignments and by use of special exercises a teacher can improve comprehension. One simple exercise consists in finding the main idea of a paragraph. The children are asked to read a given paragraph and then state the main idea in their own words. At first, many of them can only quote one of the sentences in the paragraph, but presently they come to see that a paragraph has a central theme that is usually not specifically expressed in any single sentence. This type of drill becomes essentially a search for ideas and, as such, helps to emphasize the notion that one reads the words of a story only to obtain the ideas; the duller children especially tend to think that reading the words is the end of the performance. Another exercise consists in giving pupils a question, assigning some pages of reading matter, and asking them to cull from these pages all the facts bearing on the question. They are to find only the answer to the question

and omit irrelevant items. A third type of drill consists in asking for simple inferences, such as the main characteristics of some person in a story who is never directly described but about whom there is considerable indirect evidence. A somewhat more difficult type of exercise can be introduced in about the fifth grade—the appreciation of relationships among ideas. This kind of exercise is especially needed to help children read expository material. An exposition differs from a narrative in that its ideas are definitely integrated, related, and organized; and the mechanics of deriving the meaning involve an understanding of the outline or structure which the author has created. Naturally, any complex system of outlining is too difficult for children of this age, but a beginning can be made in grasping organized ideas.

For instance, one child upon finishing a three-page article about keeping water pure wrote the following statement:

Water should be pure because—
    It prevents many diseases
    It tastes better
    People will drink more of it and less of other drinks

Water can be made pure—
    By filtering
    By putting chemicals in it
    By boiling it

Water is especially likely to be impure—
    In wells
    In brooks
    In stagnant pools

This child had been given some guidance in making similar informal outlines. The effect of the training is easy to see; he has a grasp of the interrelationship of ideas in the passage. It should be noted that the use of some such informal outline provides a child with an instrument for study and analysis. By using it he learns how writers have put their ideas together, and he has a means for expressing his understanding of these relationships.

One series of suggestions should be especially helpful to teachers. The activities all emphasize meaning, sometimes of a short passage and sometimes of longer units of thought.

TABLE 24
Lessons for Teaching Comprehension [9]

I. Analysis

A. Reading to Get the Principal Idea

Lesson type 1: Matching questions to answering paragraphs.
Lesson type 2: Answering key questions by reading paragraphs.
Lesson type 3: Matching titles or headings to paragraphs.
Lesson type 4: Giving a name to paragraphs.
Lesson type 5: Improving paragraph headings.
Lesson type 6: Finding key sentences in paragraphs.
Lesson type 7: Recognizing the climax of a story.
Lesson type 8: Taking running notes.
Lesson type A:* Crossing out irrelevant sentences from a paragraph.

B. Recognizing the Relation of Ideas to Each Other

Lesson type 9: Anticipating content of a chapter.
Lesson type 10: Arranging ideas in proper order.
Lesson type 11: Classifying or grouping ideas.
Lesson type 12: Grouping paragraphs around a main point.
Lesson type 13: Locating subordinate or supporting points.
Lesson type 14: Completing a skeleton outline.
Lesson type 15: Making an outline.
Lesson type B: Finding points to prove or disprove a given statement.
Lesson type C: Arranging an outline when items are presented in random order:
Lesson type D: Predicting ideas of a textbook chapter from its headings.
Lesson type E: Finding illustrations of general principles.

II. Synthesis

Lesson type 16: Reproduction from an outline or from notes.
Lesson type 17: Securing material in answer to a problem.
Lesson type 18: Summarizing.
Lesson type F: Combining material from several sources on a given topic.

* The lessons indicated by letters are the author's additions to the original list.

All these procedures emphasize comprehension and lead pupils to look for, to rearrange, and to react to the ideas contained in their reading

[9] B. Goodykoonz, "Teaching Pupils to Organize What They Read," *Elementary English Review*, 7: 87–90, 1930. Quoted by permission of the *Journal.*

matter. In general, any type of exercise or assignment which emphasizes reading for meaning will result in the development of comprehension. Once a child knows what sort of thing to look for, he is likely to find it. The trouble with much reading in school is that the pupils are not looking for anything.

Before pupils can do reference reading intelligently they have to learn how to sort out the relevant from the irrelevant. Naturally, no one would expect school children to become expert in making such differentiations, but unless they make a beginning, they will waste a great deal too much time with irrelevancies. Suppose, for instance, that a teacher asks a group of fourth grade children to prepare a little talk for their classmates, to tell them briefly what sort of climate a dozen or more important sections of the world have. The ideas involved are not beyond the children's comprehension, but in order to locate them, they must know how to disregard the many pages in the geography on numerous subjects not pertaining to climate. The ability not to read is almost as important as the ability to do so.[10]

In all teaching which is devoted to the development of comprehension there is one basic principle. *Children will find meaning in what they read only if they are looking for it.* Conversely, the most common reason for failure to find meaning is the habit many children have of plodding along without expecting any. The teacher, through her type of assignment, inevitably develops or discourages this bad habit. For example, if a pupil is told to read the next five pages and is given no guidance whatever in what he may find there, he usually just plods, and his comprehension is more likely than not to be low. If he is told to read the next five pages and remember as much as he can of what he reads, his comprehension will be better. If he is told to read the next five pages and find out, for example, why most natural harbors have large cities on their banks, he will understand still more. If he is asked to read this selection and not only to find the necessary explanation but also to explain any exceptions, his comprehension will be improved even further. In other words, the more meaning the child is asked to get from a given assignment, the more he will obtain.

This basic principle of looking actively for meaning works out in different ways at different levels. When the first grade teacher is presenting individual words she can emphasize their meaning quite as much as their appearance. She can, for instance, put on the board a number

---

[10] See, for instance, R. Gans, "A Study of Critical Reading Comprehension in the Intermediate Grades," *Teachers College Contributions to Education*, No. 811, 1940, 135 pp.

of verbal commands, such as *jump, stand up, sit down, walk, lie down, turn around,* and so forth. The pupil called upon not only tells what the word is but acts out its meaning; in fact, he may do the latter without the former. As a technique for teaching nouns, a teacher may ask the pupils to match words with objects or pictures of objects. Such a procedure stresses the meaning of the word as much as its form. Any simple relating of a story or acting out of its events also stresses content. In the later grades the teacher can raise the level of comprehension if she never gives any assignment without providing clues as to what a pupil should find. Thus, for example, he may be asked to find the main ideas of a story or to note some particular type of detail. He may be given a set of questions to be answered by his reading. He may be asked to draw inferences of various sorts, to find in his reading matter arguments for or against a given conclusion, to write out what he thinks are good test questions, or to make simple outlines of what he has read. All these techniques emphasize meaning.

On the ground that a pupil should dig out the facts for himself, some teachers object to furnishing pupils with this kind of assistance. The process of digging out meaning for oneself without guidance is a characteristically adult performance. Elementary school children are certainly not mature enough for it. The reading matter they meet in their daily work is almost certain to be too hard for them to understand without help. Teachers frequently give their pupils a series of questions, answers to which they are supposed to find. Unfortunately, the questions are sometimes carelessly worded and poorly selected, and therefore furnish little guidance to comprehension. If, for instance, a child is given a half-dozen questions, each dealing with some trifling detail and each answerable by one or two words, he naturally gets the idea that reading consists of hunting around for minutiae that have no particular importance. The questions must be well selected and adequate. They need not be numerous and—although some of them will naturally involve consideration of details—they should necessitate a grasping of the main points in the assignment being read. If two or three properly formulated questions are provided, they will require comprehension of all the ideas in a selection before they are answered. Anyone who disapproves of these aids to understanding should make sure that the fault does not lie with her own questions.

Finally, teachers should be sure to make some kind of check upon any reading that is done. A child who has read a special book may tell the story to the rest of the class. Another pupil may build a model of some sort, illustrating what he has read. A third may prefer to write a summary, while a fourth turns in an outline. No formal test is necessary, but a teacher should always ask a pupil to give some evidence of comprehension, especially of the type of material generally classified as "outside reading." In the elementary school there is relatively little reading of this type, although even as low as the third grade some children do extra reading at home. As a child advances through school the amount of reading he does outside the class increases. The comprehension of this reading will always be better if the pupil knows the teacher will make a check upon it. Some teachers are certain to object to this idea because they feel that a child should read for the love of reading and not because his comprehension will sooner or later be measured. The question is not one of morals or of emotional attitude. It is rather a matter of reading aimlessly as compared to reading with a purpose. Books that are read without definite purpose are soon forgotten.

B. COMPREHENSION IN THE SOCIAL SCIENCES

In elementary schools the children use their reading skills, outside the reading period itself, chiefly in preparing their lessons in geography and history. There is also a little work in hygiene and elementary science and frequent reading of arithmetic problems. The skills needed for problem reading are, however, different from those used in reading a book, and the situation is complicated by the necessity of reading numbers and symbols as well as words. Reading of this type will therefore be discussed in a later chapter that deals with problem solving.

1. **Factors Interfering with Comprehension:** The reading of history and geography may be complicated by at least four factors:[11] the presence of many technical words, the organization of ideas into an exposition instead of a narrative, the relative difficulty and unfamiliarity of

[11] Much of the material in this section comes from A. M. Ayer, "Some Difficulties in Elementary School History," *Teachers College Contributions to Education,* No. 212, 1926, 70 pp.; J. C. Dewey, "A Case Study of Reading Comprehension Difficulties in American History," *University of Iowa Studies in Education,* No. 1, 10: 26–54, 1935; W. F. Grunizer, "Some Difficulties Children Encounter in the Reading of Historical Material," *University of Pittsburgh Bulletin,* No. 3, 27: 274–275, 1941; A. Hanthorn, "History and Geography in the Upper Elementary Grades," *American Childhood,* 18: 10–12, 1933; M. G. Kelty, "Reading the Materials of the Social Sciences in the Middle Grades," *Elementary School Journal,* 39: 337–351, 1939; J. M. Lacey, "Social Studies Concepts of Children in the First Three Grades," *Teachers College Contributions to Education,* No. 548, 1932, 89 pp.; H. Meltzer, "Children's Social Concepts," *ibid.,* No. 192, 1925, 110 pp.

many ideas, and sometimes the use of an unnecessarily involved style by the textbook writer.

Inability to understand was analyzed in one case [12] by means of personal interviews with pupils. The errors in comprehension thus determined are similar in nature to those already discussed for general reading matter. Pupils may misinterpret a passage from a history text because they cannot suppress some previous item of information which, while true, has no relevancy to the material. The passage reminds them of something they know and they interpret it in terms of their irrelevant knowledge—after the fashion of the student who is asked on a quiz to list the difficulties in learning to read but is reminded by the word *difficulties* of material he has recently studied and proceeds to list difficulties in learning arithmetic, of which the first one is poor reading ability. Such a student is not able to suppress the tenuous but recent connections that lead to an irrelevant answer. Other pupils fail to understand a passage because they omit some of the modifying elements in the sentences they have read. Thus, they read, "Except for Neanderthal man, this race has the largest known skull" and either fail to see the initial phrase or else simply disregard it and read the sentence as "This race has the largest known skull." Pupils are especially likely to make this sort of error if what they omit makes the reading matter agree better with their preconceived prejudices. In a group of people reading such a sentence as "The Negro children scored lower than the whites, but one must remember that the test was intended for urban populations and that the Negro children were from rural backgrounds," the prejudiced ones may never get beyond the comma or may disregard the second half of the sentence, even if they read it. Among children, perhaps the most common reason for misunderstanding is their tendency to give back verbatim what they read without trying to make sense out of it. This reaction is commonest among highly verbal children who are asked to read or learn something that is too difficult for them. They rattle off the words and hope for the best without even trying to understand. For instance, one small child who recited, with apparent comprehension, the "What is so rare as a day in June" selection, which ends with the words "in the nice ear of Nature which song is the best?" surprised her mother no little by announcing firmly, "People sometimes have big ears, but Nature's ears are nice." The more difficult a selection is to understand, the more children will take refuge in sheer verbalism.

[12] Dewey, *op. cit.*

A study of history and geography books for use in the intermediate grades reveals such passages as those given below:

Franklin was seventy-eight years old when he returned from his last European sojourn, and his name was venerated in England and France as well as in America. Everybody spoke of him as one of the greatest Americans, one of the founders of the American republic, and its most distinguished scientist and diplomat.

It was a vastness that appealed to Webster. And this dominating force in his nature explains his idea of nationality and his opposition to States Rights. He was too large in his views of life to limit himself to his State at the expense of his country. To him the Union stood first and the State second, and to make the Union great and strong became the ruling passion of his life.[13]

Both these passages are too hard for children. One can analyze the difficulties as being due to the use of literary embellishments, of abstract ideas (with the abstract words for expressing them), and of difficult sentence structure. The first passage contains two technical words (*diplomat, republic*), while the second passage contains five (*nationality, States Rights, country, union, opposition*). However, these are lost in the literary spate of words and probably contribute little to the difficulty of the passages. These two paragraphs, with several others, were submitted to numbers of children in the fifth, sixth, seventh, and eighth grades. The children were asked to write in their own words the gist of each passage. A few typical samples for the two above passages were as follows:

1. Franklin was a European boy and knew France as well as America.
2. He was famous.
3. It meant he was a very good man and a kind man
4. If Franklin didn't go to France he would have lost the world war so Franklin was helpful to win the world war.

1. Webster was too large to view himself as a state expense.
2. He was faithful to his country.
3. Webster was a very good man in the war and good everywhere else. It was great that plead of Webster. And that increasing power in his ways. It tells his thoughts of different people and his ways against the rights of the state. He was big in the seeings of life, to give himself to the state at the cost of America.

[13] Ayer, *op. cit.* Used by permission of the publisher.

For the most part these answers either make a general and harmless statement—sometimes one for which there is no basis in the selection—or else consist of gibberish. Until textbooks abandon such passages as those quoted above, the comprehension of children is likely to remain low.

As already mentioned in the previous chapter the basic difficulty of reading expositions consists in finding the organization of ideas. An exposition does not run on and on like a narrative; it has clearly defined topics, the relationship of which is stated, and the numerous details under a given topic are logically arranged so as to bring out certain central ideas. To be sure, history texts embody some passages of a purely narrative or descriptive character, but they also contain more or less exposition. In a geography, the presentation is largely expository, with the addition of some descriptive passages. Children encounter great difficulty with expositions, perhaps because they try to translate them into narratives, only to find them sadly lacking in chronology. A teacher must show children the manner in which an exposition organizes a large number of details and so presents them as to show their interrelations and to lead up to central ideas.

Any kind of drill that will help children to understand this type of writing, usually first encountered in the fourth grade, should be used.[14] Exercises in finding the main idea of paragraphs, the use of questions as guides to help children in looking for the important facts, and the making of a simple outline are invaluable aids.[15] In one investigation several hundred fifth grade children were divided into groups on the basis of their scores on several reading tests, their age, and their standing on a test of historical information. One half of these children studied their reading assignments as usual, while the other half were shown how to make summaries and then were required to use summarizing as a technique in their daily preparation of lessons. This difference in study methods resulted in increased mastery of the subject matter on the part of the latter group, as shown by the test scores for experimental and nonexperimental groups at the end of twelve weeks. In addition to attaining a better understanding, the trained children had been equipped with a technique for making a distinction between the important and the unimportant. Both the summary and the outline are well worth teaching, not only as a means of improving comprehension

[14] See C. O. Newlun, "Teaching Children to Summarize in Fifth Grade History," *Teachers College Contributions to Education,* No. 404, 1930, 75 pp.

[15] For some sample exercises see pp. 176–180.

of the current geography or history text but also as a permanent equipment to be used in extracting meaning from an exposition.

Any attempt to go into the past in time or the distance in space requires a constructive imagination such as few children possess. Even with the aid of many pictures and stories in addition to textbook material, children in a warm climate have a most inadequate and inaccurate picture of an Eskimo's daily life, his problems of housing and food supply, his social relations, or his physical environment. Much more hazy are a child's ideas concerning the causes of the Revolutionary War. He may greatly enjoy reading about either Eskimos or early patriots, but in spite of his best efforts, matters alien to his own world are likely to remain merely words in a book. He can and does, of course, thoroughly learn the words; but conversations with a child will usually reveal the most curious misconceptions.

The writer recalls three examples of her own childish misunderstandings. In each case she had faithfully learned what was in the book, but was at a loss to understand it. The first trouble arose when she read that in Australia there were thousands of sheep but that the country was so large that, in spite of the number, there was only one sheep for every twenty square miles of country. To her this statement meant that all of Australia was fenced off into twenty-mile-square units, in each of which grazed one solitary sheep. For years she wondered why someone did not think of collecting these lonely sheep into herds. On another page in her geography there was a description of a gang plow, accompanied by a statement that it could be used only on level ground with few or no stones. A lifetime up until then spent in hilly, stony New England led to a lasting wonderment as to why anyone should invent so complicated a machine when it obviously could not be used; this feeling persisted until a trip to the Middle West brought actual observation of a new type of country. In a history text the writer was presented with the information that a tax on tea precipitated a war with England, but until her adult years she could never see why people did not simply drink coffee, cocoa, or soft drinks instead of tea and have peace instead of war. Somehow a cup of tea did not seem important enough to justify the ensuing bloody battles and privations—and no one she knew except her grandmother drank tea, anyway.

In all the above examples the failure to understand resulted from an interpretation of what was read in terms of the reader's own limited environment. No child's environment and personal experiences are sufficient to furnish an adequate background for a considerable proportion of the ideas presented to him in the average textbook in either geography or history. To be sure, children have imaginations that are vivid, but they also are likely to be fantastic and governed by little appreciation of life's realities. This sort of misunderstanding is a fundamental characteristic of childhood, and only growth can cure it. Children will eventually acquire wider experiences, both actual and imaginative, but by the time they have done so they are no longer children and no longer in elementary school. In the social sciences, especially, one finds the usual type of subject matter difficult, if not impossible, of comprehension by the child at his stage of experiential and intellectual development. When children are forced into such reading they usually make one of four adjustments: they do what they can to translate the words of their books into their own experiences, making innumerable errors in the process; they become convinced that all social sciences are unintelligible and develop an intense dislike for these subjects; they learn the words without even trying to understand the ideas; or, if they are very sensible, they isolate what they can understand and dismiss the remainder. None of these adjustments makes for a high degree of comprehension.

Undertaking mental journeys in time or space is a typically adult proceeding. A child has some chance of understanding what is going on about him, but much less chance of comprehending conditions at a distance. Thus, many a child can give a reasonably coherent statement concerning the reasons for the outbreak of World War II, the present-day conditions that cause strikes, the effect of motion pictures on children's thinking, or the reasons for the re-elections of Roosevelt. On such points a child has his own observation and his recollection of adult discussions to build upon, and he therefore has a basis for understanding something from the material he reads. There is nothing he is less prepared to understand than the actual reasons for the discovery of America —the subject with which opening paragraphs in American history used to deal. No child and few adults have a real understanding of the general expansion in many fields of knowledge during the thirteenth, fourteenth, and fifteenth centuries, of which the discovery of America is only one bit of evidence. A teacher who forces her pupils to read one thousand words about the reasons for the Missouri Compromise, for instance, will receive back from the children perhaps seventy-five words out of the total—and not much except words. From a psychological standpoint, history would be easier to understand if it began with a survey of the present and then worked backward in time in an effort to discover the reasons for current developments. The present is complicated but observable; the past is equally complicated and unobservable. The usual presentation of history requires a child to work from the unknown and directly unknowable past toward the present—a procedure that is difficult if not impossible for childish mentalities. Because of this basic situation, the child's comprehension of typical reading materials in history is likely to remain low.

The content of the average geography text has less intrinsic difficulty because many passages deal with relatively simple and objective facts. Moreover, pictures, diagrams, and models are available as aids to comprehension. Second grade children may, for instance, build a model Dutch town, or make a scrapbook of pictures showing different food products raised in a given country or section, or see a motion picture of life in a Zulu village. These visual aids are numerous for geography because so much of the material is concerned with features in the physical environment, products of various kinds, and material culture. History, on the other hand, takes place mostly in men's minds and hearts, and the pictorial material is therefore limited in both amount and usefulness. One may, for example, show children a picture of the Parisian mob storming the Bastille in 1792, but the picture cannot show why this action took place or what results it had, and history is concerned with causes and effects, of which no picture is possible.

Certain characteristics of reading matter make it hard to understand, especially by those with immature minds and only partially developed habits of reading. Unfortunately, much reading matter that is used in the social sciences has many characteristics that make it difficult. Teachers can help children to acquire the special skills they need for reading their lessons in history and geography if they prepare the pupils for the coming assignments by giving specific training that will eliminate some of these difficulties altogether and reduce the seriousness of others.

2. **Improvement of Comprehension in the Social Sciences:** It has already been pointed out [16] that direct teaching of technical vocabulary brings about an increase in the level of comprehension. The understanding of history or geography may be further improved by giving pupils one or two leading questions as to what they are to look for. The best time to produce these questions is before the reading is begun, not after it is finished.[17] A teacher need have no fear that the pupils will merely

---

[16] See p. 84.

[17] J. N. Washburne, "The Use of Questions in Social Science Material," *Journal of Educational Psychology* 20: 321–359, 1929. See also E. Benzler, "Making Reading Functional in the Social Sciences," *Seventeenth Yearbook of the Department of Elementary*

hunt out the answers to the questions and neglect everything else. Actually, all parts of an assignment seem to be understood better if there are questions that cover parts of it. The questions should be as general as possible, within the limits of childish comprehension. If, for instance, a teacher asks, "Why is the camel the most valuable animal to those living in desert country?" she will find that the children will acquire the basic facts relating to deserts in their effort to answer the question, and without consciously trying to learn them.

Another recent suggestion is the establishment of a pre-textbook period of preparation for those who need it. This experiment was carried out in several fourth grade classes, in which under normal circumstances the pupils would begin to read a text in history.[18] After the groups of 368 control and 381 experimental pupils had been equated for intelligence, initial ability to read history, and knowledge of historical facts, the experimental classes were given an introductory period of some weeks, during which their teachers tried to prepare them specifically for the reading task before them. The pupils in the control classes plunged at once into reading assignments in the text.

The pre-textbook training consisted primarily of three elements—oral presentation of historical stories to the pupils, expression by the children of what they understood, and gradual transfer to the reading of the same type of material. The teachers began by telling a story aloud and then giving some of the details. They used pictures and took the children to museums in an effort to give reality to the story. The children reacted by expressing the story in their own words, answering questions about it, dramatizing sections of it, and making posters or other pictures as illustrations. They also worked at vocabulary exercises and practiced using the words of history to express their ideas. As the pupils became familiar with the ideas and the vocabulary they began to read historical stories for themselves, to write brief compositions on points that interested them, and to answer in writing a number of questions that would lead them to interpret what they had read.

After their introductory period the pupils of the experimental classes began to read their texts. All children in both types of class were tested after three months and again after six months of history. The pupils in the lowest third of the experimental class profited greatly

School Principals, 1938, pp. 372–375; D. Curtis, "Reading as It Functions in Fifth-Grade Geography," *ibid.,* pp. 376-378.

[18] M. T. Wiederfeld, "An Experimental Study in Developing History Reading Readiness with Fourth Grade Children," *Johns Hopkins University Studies in Education,* No. 31, 1942, 80 pp.

by the pre-text training and outscored their partners in the control group. Those in the middle third made a better start and were superior to the middle third of the control pupils after three months but were on a level with them after six months. The upper third of both classes did equally well, irrespective of method.

The conclusions from this experiment seem to be that if children are ready to read history, as the brighter ones were, they might as well begin; but if they are not yet mature enough in their reading skills, they are greatly helped by a transitional period, during which they acquire some of the words they will need, get acquainted with the kind of ideas they will meet, and learn how to express themselves in appropriate language. It is always the lower end of the class that has the real difficulty with reading the text. If these children could be introduced to it gradually, it is probable that many serious problems could be avoided.

Another effort to determine readiness, this time for work in geography, has resulted in a list of desirable characteristics in either the pupils or the environment. The list was compiled from a much longer one by the votes of 196 competent teachers of geography as to the usefulness of each trait for work in this subject.

TABLE 25

Elements Contributing to Readiness for Geography [19]

	Per Cent of Teachers Marking Each Element
A. Characteristics and Abilities of Children	
1. An inquiring attitude toward things seen in pictures and not understood	98
2. An interest in simple stories containing travel elements	96
3. Ability to indicate the four cardinal points	92
4. Interest in people of other nationalities	92
5. Reading ability within one grade of present placement	90
6. Ability to identify landscape features seen in the locality	86
7. Interest in the weather	86
8. Realization that one's own type of life is not universal	86

[19] G. Whipple, "Elements in Geography Readiness," *Elementary School Journal,* 42: 256–267, 1942. From p. 258. Used by permission of the *Journal.*

   9. Ability to find a place in the neighborhood by following directions   85

  10. Realization that one has seen only a small part of the
world   84

  11. Ability to look at pictures reflectively   84

  12. Interest in realistic stories of animals   82

  13. Desire to travel and learn about other people   82

  14. Interest in cause and effect and in how things have
become as they are   79

  15. Sense of human interdependence   75

  16. Interest in camping and hiking   68

B. Experiences of Children

  17. Experience in seeing men at work in different
industries   94

  18. Familiarity with the countryside surrounding a city   92

  19. Familiarity with the means of transportation that
children commonly enjoy   92

  20. Familiarity with the services that supply food, cloth-
ing, and shelter   89

  21. Familiarity with the means of communication that
children commonly enjoy   85

  22. Experience in visiting zoos   85

  23. Familiarity with public parks in the city   79

  24. Experience in visiting the circus   78

  25. Experience in looking down on areas from a mountain or a high building   66

C. Features of the Locality

  26. Seasonal variations of the locality   88

  27. Variety in the work carried on in the community   87

  28. Variety of vegetation type in the locality   79

  29. Varied racial elements in the community   73

  30. Variety of relief or contour features in the locality   70

  31. Proximity of the locality to bodies of water   67

  32. Variety of languages spoken in the community   61

The task of reading geography books is easy in proportion as children have these characteristics and experiences. Some of the desirable
traits can be developed, especially through activities. Children who lack
most of the characteristics listed in the first section of Table 25 and most
of the experiences listed in the second can be expected to have diffi-

culty in reading their geography lessons and will probably profit by a postponement of the subject until they are more nearly ready for it.

C. SUMMARY

Comprehension improves as children grow older, acquire better methods of reading, develop more maturity of intellect and emotion, and have a greater wealth of experience in the light of which they can interpret what they read. The teacher's contribution to this process consists mainly in giving children things to read that will be stimulating to growth and in helping them to find meaning in the material. Children have an excellent defense mechanism against excessive demands upon their comprehension—they just learn the words and omit the meaning. This verbalism can easily become a habit if teachers do not help children to find meaning in what they read at all levels.

Reading in the content fields makes great demands upon comprehension, indeed too-great demands. Even with the simplified materials now available, elementary school children have somewhat defective understanding of what they read because they lack the necessary experiences. Their direct knowledge of environment is limited to whatever localities they happen to have lived in, and their knowledge of human nature to whatever people they happen to have known. Neither is likely to be adequate for the reading of geography or history. It is therefore most desirable that pupils should be helped as much as possible by visual aids to comprehension.

IV • Interest, Taste, and Dynamics

It has always been clear to teachers that interest in reading is of utmost importance as a motivating force. Research in this field has therefore been concentrated in discovering what reading interests children have in different grades or at different ages, and in compiling book lists upon the basis, in part at least, of these interests. Investigations have covered not only interests in reading but also those in nonschool activities, in order that reading matter might be selected in terms of as many spontaneous childish enthusiasms as possible. Of late years some efforts have been made to study and develop reading taste. Naturally, interest is not the only motive for reading, but it is among the best. Its presence will not solve all problems in reading, but it will help keep the child at work until his increasing maturity plus his teacher's instruction can bring about a high level of reading ability.

There are, of course, certain general motives, such as a desire to please the teacher or the parents, a general desire to be admired as a success, or an interest in learning for the sake of obtaining a feeling of mastery, that are equally applicable to all subject matter. These, while powerful enough, will be taken for granted, and this section devoted to the particular interests and drives that will lead to effort in reading.

In general, children like to read, although it is not at the very top of their list of interests. The radio and the motion picture come first, perhaps because they involve less effort; next comes reading of the "funnies," and then the reading of books, magazines, and newspapers.[1] For girls reading is more popular than for boys, most of whom prefer

[1] See, for example, I. Young, "A Preliminary Survey of Interests and Preferences of Primary Children in Motion Pictures, Comic Strips, and Radio Programs, as Related to Grade, Sex, and Intellectual Differences," *Kansas State Teachers College at Emporia Bulletin of Information,* Vol. 22, No. 9, 1942, 40 pp.; H. M. Bell, *Youth Tell Their Story,* American Council on Education, 1938, 273 pp.

games of almost all kinds to reading. Usually, the brighter children are, the better they like to read and the more time they spend doing so.

A. CHILDREN'S INTERESTS IN READING

A number of investigators have asked children of different ages what they liked and why. From these and related studies, one can de-

TABLE 26

Children's Reading Interests [2]

First Study			Second Study			
	Rank Order				Rank Order by Grades	
Reasons	Boys	Girls	Reasons	4	5	6
1. The story was about the life of children	4	8	1. The story was about exciting adventure	1	1	1
2. The story was a make-believe story	12	2	2. It was funny	2	2	4
3. It was about animals	5.5	12	3. It was interesting	4	3	2
4. It tells about things	9	11	4. It was about animals	3	4	6.5
5. It tells about other lands	11	6.5	5. It was about the old days	5.5	6	6.5
6. It was a made-up story about exciting things	2	1	6. It was about children	9	6	4
7. It was a true story of things that people have done	3	6.5	7. It was a fairy tale	5.5	9	11
8. It was about styles and kinds of story writing	10	9	8. It was about brave deeds	7.5	6	11
9. It was a story that tells how things look	13	13	9. It was about kind deeds	7.5	9	8.5
10. It was a story that tells how we should act and what we should do	5.5	4	10. It was a mystery story	12	11.5	4
11. It tells about things that happen to you every day	7.5	3	11. It was about nature	10.5	9	8.5
12. It tells about things people do in their spare time	7.5	10	12. It was about life in other lands	10.5	11.5	11
13. It tells about games	1	5				

duce what the characteristics are that appeal to boys and girls of different ages. Three sample studies [3] give typical results as to what elements

[2] Hockett, *op. cit.* and Humphreys, *op. cit.*

[3] J. A. Hockett and K. M. Forry, "Interests in Reading Expressed by Pupils in Grades 3 through 7," *Twelfth Yearbook of the California Association of Elementary School*

in stories call forth interest. The reasons for liking stories, as given in two studies, appear in Table 26.

The 387 boys in the first study liked books about games best, exciting fiction next, and true stories third; they disliked descriptions, make-believe stories, and tales of other lands. The 424 girls put the exciting fiction first, make-believe stories next, and stories of everyday happenings third; they disliked descriptions, animal stories, and books that tell about things. The children in the second study showed, as they grew older, some loss of interest in animals and fairy tales and an increase of interest in mystery novels, stories about children, and books about nature. With age, interest becomes a more important motive and humor seems less stimulating, but excitement is recognized at all three levels as a necessary ingredient.

The third study [4] is a report of the reactions shown by 2,891 children between the ages of 9 and 16, of whom 1,583 were in Grades 4, 5, or 6. These children marked a questionnaire that included such items as:

Yes No ? 1. *Lonesome Laddie Finds a Friend*
How a stray dog found a new master and showed his true love.

Yes No ? 8. *Is There a Doctor in the House?*
The doctor's everyday life. His exciting battle against accidents and sickness. His disappointments and rewards.

Yes No ? 49. *Meredith Hall*
How Jean, the shy, lonesome new girl, won a place at Meredith Hall by defending her roommate against the school tattletale.

Principals, pp. 89–95, 1940; P. Humphreys, "The Reading Interests and Abilities of 600 Children in the Intermediate Grades," *Twentieth Yearbook of the Department of Elementary School Principals,* 10: 421–428, 1941; R. L. Thorndike, *Children's Reading Interests: A Study Based on a Fictitious, Annotated Titles' Questionnaire,* Bureau of Publications, Teachers College, Columbia University, 1941, 48 pp. These materials are quoted by permission of the various publishers.

See also A. I. Gates, C. Peardon, and I. Sartorius, "Studies of Children's Interests in Reading," *Elementary School Journal,* 31: 656–670, 1931; L. B. Johnson, "Children's Reading Interests as Related to Sex and Grade in School," *School Review,* 40: 257–272, 1932; M. Lazar, "Reading Interests, Activities, and Opportunities of Bright, Average, and Dull Children," *Teachers College Contributions to Education,* No. 707, 1937, 127 pp.; *Twelfth Yearbook of the California Association of Elementary School Principals,* 1940, 154 pp.

[4] Thorndike, *op. cit.*

Yes　No　?　53.　*Murder in the Green House*
　　　　　　　　　Who killed Jeb Wilson? Whose were the giant foot-
　　　　　　　　　prints in the hall? Dr. Van Tine puts his wits to
　　　　　　　　　work.

Yes　No　?　78.　*Cabin Boy for Columbus*
　　　　　　　　　The adventures of Angelo, who sailed with Colum-
　　　　　　　　　bus on his great voyage of discovery.

All the titles were fictitious. The children were therefore telling what
attracted them in the way of titles and content, not what had interested
them in books they had actually read.

At all ages the boys liked the same books. This uniformity rests
in large measure upon their rejection of any title that sounded feminine
or fanciful. Bright boys of one age selected many of the same titles as
dull boys two or three years older. The girls showed less agreement
among themselves, but this lack of agreement may be due chiefly to
their tendency to mark a large proportion of the titles. They refused
to settle down on a few, as the boys did. The correlations between the
interests of boys and girls are practically zero. This statement does not
mean that they never read the same books, but that knowledge of what
a boy of the ages from 9 to 15 likes is no guide whatever to a girl's
preferences. On a book that is highly popular with boys, the girls may
show the entire range of interest, from high to low.

The 88 titles were classified into a number of types in order to
study changes in interest toward them. Interest in realistic or talking
animal stories and mythology was only moderate for either sex at any of
the ages studied, presumably because the period of maximum interest is
below 9 years. Of moderate or high interest to boys and of rather low
interest to girls were stories of boy outdoor activities, sport stories, and
travel stories. Of moderate to high interest to girls and rather low interest to boys were stories of mild child adventure, of child life in other
lands, of magic and phantasy, of love and romance, and of school. Of
moderately high or high interest to both sexes were mystery or detective
stories, tales of adult adventure, and "success" stories. These results suggest that the difference in experiences between the sexes is more important than age or intelligence in influencing the reaction of children
to book titles.

When one wants to make a sound reading list for children in the various grades one uses such results as those presented above, plus data from other studies as to the difficulty of the reading matter, information concerning the popularity of each book among children in each grade as shown by their voluntary withdrawal of it from libraries, and the opinion of adults concerning selection of books and stories. These four criteria do not necessarily agree with each other.[5] Indeed, there is often a flat contradiction between the interest of children and the approval of adults.

B. BOOK LISTS

The reading lists that have emerged from study and research are too long to present in detail. Some of them rest almost exclusively upon children's expressed interests, while others are the result of more or less systematically collected adult opinion as to what children of different ages like. A few lists take account of difficulty. Especially recommended in its method of selecting books is the Winnetka list.[6]

Samples from this list may help to indicate the usefulness of these materials.[7] After the title of the book comes first a typical statement made by some child who read it. The items about each book are given separately for boys and girls because the sex differences in reaction are so great.

Heidi

I liked the part where she was in Frankfurt and the doctor was just finding out about her homesickness. I like the part where Clara got well again.

	Number Who Read Book	Per Cent Liking It	Interest Value	Average Age	Average Reading Grade	Index of Popularity for Book
Boys	53	87	79	11.5	6.9	1,848
Girls	537	96	85	11.1	6.7	

[5] See F. K. Shuttleworth, "A Critical Study of Two Lists of 'Best' Books for Children," *Genetic Psychology Monographs,* No. 4, 11: 247–320, 1932.

[6] C. Washburne and M. Vogel, *The Winnetka Graded Book List,* American Library Association, Chicago, 1926, 286 pp.

[7] Used by permission of the publisher. Items have been taken from the 1926 volume rather than from the 1933 enlargement of the original publication because the former gives statistical data and excerpts of children's opinions in their own words, whereas the latter classifies and characterizes books on the basis of data but does not give the actual figures. See reference on p. 117. (The 1926 issue is out of print.)

This book was read by ten times as many girls as boys (537 and 53). Most of the boys who read it liked it (87%), but more of the girls enjoyed it (96%). The interest values are lower for boys than girls. The average age of those who read this book was 11½ for the boys and a little over 11 for the girls. The average reading grade in which their reading abilities would place those who read the book was high sixth grade for both sexes. The high index number (1,848) is based upon a combination of all reactions to the book.

King Arthur and His Knights

I liked the part where they had a great combat. They fought until their breath failed.

	Number Who Read Book	Per Cent Liking It	Interest Value	Average Age	Average Reading Grade	Index of Popularity for Book
Boys	79	100	89	10.8	5.6	204
Girls	42	90	72	10.2	5.3	

Adventures of Tom Sawyer

I liked the part where Becky and Tom were in the cave and Tom gave Becky his share of the food because he knew he could stand going without food longer than she could.

	Number Who Read Book	Per Cent Liking It	Interest Value	Average Age	Average Reading Grade	Index of Popularity for Book
Boys	449	99	86	12.5	7.7	2,272
Girls	269	98	84	12.6	8.1	

The Princess on the Glass Hill

I liked the part where the man rode up the last time and got the golden apple out of her hand.

	Number Who Read Book	Per Cent Liking It	Interest Value	Average Age	Average Reading Grade	Index of Popularity for Book
Boys	17	94	75	9.5	4.4	42
Girls	51	92	67	10.3	5.0	

Two of these four stories were read oftener by boys than by girls—an unusual circumstance. Girls read practically everything and like almost every book they read. In most cases the average age and reading efficiency of the boys and girls who read the same book are similar, but in the third case above, the girls were nearly a year older than the boys and a half grade above them in reading age. From the Winnetka lists, the teacher gets information about interest and difficulty, but not about adult opinion. In the *Graded Book Lists for Children,*[8] issued by a joint committee from the National Education Association and the National Council of English Teachers, there is a notation after each book as to the type of child who might like it at each of three levels—Grades 1–3, 4–6, and 7–9. Another publication, called *Pleasure Reading for Boys and Girls,*[9] lists a large array of books, classified as to topic and difficulty. The most recent form of the Winnetka list has appeared under the title of *The Right Book for the Right Child.*[10] In this revision an analysis of reading difficulty and an estimate of interest made by librarians have been included. Numerous other book lists, some commercial and some not, based upon a mixture of subjective and objective factors are of help to teachers.[11]

Remedial teachers or teachers who have fifth or sixth grade classes of slow-learning children will find good use for lists of books designed especially for pupils who have the normal interests of their age but a vocabulary too small to read the books that they would otherwise like.[12] These lists contain a large number of books with low ratings for difficulty but of fifth or sixth grade level in content. From them a teacher can recommend books for children whose reading ability is well below the level of their general maturity.

Children should learn to choose their own books just as soon as they begin to read independently, even though some guidance may be given at all stages by teachers, parents, or librarians. The main contribution of adults, aside from general encouragement, should be con-

[8] American Library Association, 1936, 161 pp.

[9] *Bulletin* No. 17 of the *California State Department of Education,* 1935, 99 pp.

[10] M. S. Wilkinson, V. Weedon, and C. Washburne, John Day Company, 1933, 357 pp.

[11] Other reading lists: S. Andrews (Ed.), *Children's Catalog,* The H. W. Wilson Company, 1936, 979 pp. (Grades 1–8); B. E. Mahoney and E. Whitney (Compilers), *Realms of Gold in Children's Books* and *Five Years of Children's Books,* Doubleday, Doran & Company, 1929 and 1936, 796 pp. and 599 pp.; E. Ramsey (Editor), *Reading for Fun for Boys and Girls in Elementary School,* National Committee of Teachers of English, Chicago, 1937, 104 pp.; "Textbooks and Instructional Materials Evaluated by Means of the Lewerenz Vocabulary Grade Placement Formula" (Mimeographed), Los Angeles County Superintendent of Schools, Division of Administrative Research, 1938, 51 pp.

[12] D. Belser and B. A. Belser, "Easy Books for the Intermediate Grades," *Elementary English Review,* 17: 235–239, 285–289, 1940. See also G. Spache and R. C. Pollock, "Remedial Reading Materials," *Elementary English Review,* 19: 131–133, 1942.

centrated upon getting the right book to the right child at the right point of his physical, social, and mental growth.[13] For the purpose of exposing children to all desirable types of reading, there should be a library in every school, and children should be sent there for free reading at least once a week so that they may get the habit of going to a library and choosing their own books. Most children soon find out what types of books they enjoy and need help only in locating what they want. The school librarian can play a vital role in educating children to choose wisely, but her efforts do not reach all the children unless all of them are sent to her. If she has to depend upon voluntary visits she can reach only those who are already spontaneous readers.

Of course, some teachers cannot get full value out of the lists because there is no good library nearby. Even in the poorest school, however, a teacher can provide some degree of variety in reading matter if she assembles a "library" for her room, by having the children lend their own books when they have finished reading them. The children take turns at being "librarian," and no one is allowed to take a book from the room without having it checked by the librarian. The children are urged to take books home and read them, and to read in school whenever they complete their lessons early. Of course, the selection of books is sometimes extraordinary, but the library has the positive merit of being composed of books actually read by at least one child in the room. Moreover, there is sure to be something that is simple enough for even the dullest, or hard enough for even the most mature. Such a library actually does develop in children the habit of reading. Once the habit is established, the task of guiding the child into better types of books is easy as compared with the task of inducing him to read spontaneously at all.[14]

The types of materials that a teacher needs for making reading or pre-reading activities of interest to pupils vary somewhat from grade to grade as the children become more mature. Table 27 contains a list of the types especially useful in each grade. Beginning with looking at pictures and an occasional word in the kindergarten, the materials become more numerous until, in Grade 6, the children are maintaining a wide program of reading activities. The more closely teachers can follow these suggestions, the better the reading in a school is likely to be.

[13] See, for example, W. C. Olson and S. I. Davis, "The Adaptation of Instruction in Reading to the Growth of Children," *Educational Method,* 20: 71–79, 1940.

[14] See also D. P. Hartman, "Wide Reading without a School Library," *Twentieth Yearbook of the Department of Elementary School Principals,* 1941, pp. 415–420.

TABLE 27

The Materials of Reading at Different Levels [15]

Kindergarten	Grade 1	Grade 2	Grade 3	Grade 4	Grade 5	Grade 6
1. Book table	1. Book table	1. Class library	1. Class library	1. Class library	1. Class library	1. Large circulating classroom library
2. Picture books	2. Picture books	2. Bulletin board	2. Incidental reading materials	2. Incidental reading materials	2. Incidental reading materials	2. Collections of poems
3. Illustrated story books	3. Illustrated story books	3. Illustrated collections of stories	3. Bulletin board	3. Bulletin board	3. Collections of poems	3. Story books
4. Illustrated nursery rhymes	4. Illustrated rhymes	4. Books of rhymes	4. Collections of poems	4. Collections of poems	4. Books from public library	4. Class subscriptions to magazines
5. Labels	5. Borrowed library books	5. Books from the public library	5. Books from public library	5. Books from public library	5. Current magazines	5. Other current magazines
	6. Blackboard reading material	6. Blackboard reading material	6. Collections of stories	6. Collections of stories	6. Reference books	6. Reference books
	7. Charts	7. Phrase and sentence cards	7. Informative books	7. History books	7. Geography text	7. Books borrowed on individual cards from public library
	8. Phrase cards	8. Class newspaper	8. Blackboard work	8. Informational books in history or geography	8. History text	8. Geography text
	9. Class records of experience		9. Access to school library	9. Geography text	9. Informational books in geography or history	9. History text
			10. Sentence and phrase cards	10. Arithmetic text	10. Hygiene books	10. Arithmetic text
			11. Riddles	11. Access to school library for reference books or for home reading	11. Arithmetic text	11. Hygiene text
			12. Arithmetic text		12. Use of public library for home reading	12. Informational books in the social sciences
			13. Class newspaper			13. Science books

[15] E. A. Choate, "Interpreting the Program Through the Home and School Association," *Seventeenth Yearbook of the Department of Elementary School Principals*, 1938, pp. 623–628 (p. 626). Used by permission of the National Education Association.

C. INTEREST IN THE COMICS

Within the last twenty-five years the reading of comics has become
a favorite leisure activity among children of all ages, social classes, and
levels of intelligence. On Sunday morning the children of the million-
aire, the college professor, the merchant, the butcher, the bricklayer, the
teamster, the miner, and the day laborer sprawl on the floor, reading
the comics in the morning paper. Disapproval of parents and teachers
has practically no effect. Every time one goes to the corner drugstore
one finds at least one small urchin sitting on the floor in front of the
magazine rack completely absorbed in *Superman* or *Joe Palooka* or
Little Orphan Annie. Books of comics are among the favorite reading
matter of children, even of those who also read good literature. Since
the comics are here to stay and since almost all children read them,
investigators have begun to study them, in an effort to evaluate their
nature as objectively as possible.[16] Their vocabulary is of approximately
fifth or sixth grade difficulty, although the "funnies" are read and enjoyed by children in the lower grades. Each book of comics contains
about 10,000 words, of which about 1,000 are beyond the first thousand
of the Thorndike Word Book. There is some slang, but such words do
not exceed 5 per cent of the reading matter. A study of 16 books of
comics revealed a total of 28,808 words, of which 78 per cent were in
the Gates Primary Test. It is to be regretted that the conversation, such
as it is, is printed in capital letters, since their use encourages pupils to
read letter by letter. If ordinary type were used, children could recognize words by their shapes much more easily than they can when all
letters are capitalized and words have only length and no shape. The
chief appeal of the comics, as revealed in individual interviews, rests
upon the child's love of excitement, adventure, mystery, sport, and
humor. Moreover, books of comics are easily available and cheap. Children can collect them and swap them in a way quite unlikely with real
books.

16 See G. E. Hill, "The Vocabulary of Comic Strips," *Journal of Educational Psychology,* 34: 77–87, 1943, and "The Relation of Children's Interest in Comic Strips to the
Vocabulary of These Strips," *Journal of Educational Psychology,* 34: 48–54, 1943; R.
Strang, "Why Children Read the Comics," *Elementary School Journal,* 43: 336–342, 1943;
R. L. Thorndike, "Words and the Comics," *Journal of Experimental Education,* 10: 110–
113, 1941; M. A. Tinker, "Readability of Comic Books," *American Journal of Optometry,*
20: 89–93, 1943; P. Witty, "Children's Interests in the Comics," *Journal of Experimental
Education,* 10: 100–104, 1941; also "Reading the Comics: A Comparative Study," *ibid.,*
pp. 105–109, 1941.

It seems probable that children learn many new words through reading the comics, and certainly they get much enjoyment. They should, of course, be encouraged to emerge from this rather low level of taste as soon as possible, but probably they will not suffer a great deal even while their devotion to the comics is at its height. This type of reading, like most types popular with children, gratifies certain of the child's drives and expresses his interests, his desire to acquire knowledge, his love of phantasy, adventure, and mystery. Reading often is, and should be, a form of release and fulfillment of emotional drives and interests.[17]

D. READING PATTERNS

A child is showing a reading pattern if he keeps selecting books dealing with the same topics and serving the same interests. Some children read one book about animals after another, while others are insatiable readers of travel stories. Actually, most people are guided in their reading by already established patterns that stem originally from their interests. Thus if an individual has liked one historical novel he is likely to enjoy another; if he is interested in foreign scenes and has liked a story of life in a provincial French town, he will probably enjoy a tale of life in an Indian pueblo. Children begin to show patterns in their reading at an early age. Teachers should make all the use they can of these expressions of interest when they suggest books for further reading. Especially should they guide a child from less to more worthwhile books and from those that are immature to some that are more advanced. A child who loves *Peter Rabbit* can be led by slow stages to the *Jungle Book* and *Black Beauty*. The pattern is the central core that persists through numbers of books which deal with the same kind of interest.

In order to help children follow their interest, "ladders" of books in a given pattern have been devised. A ladder starts with either an easy or a widely read book and suggests other books of similar nature. The sample given below is a ladder of sea stories.[18]

If you liked:

Nordhoff: *Mutiny on the Bounty*

17 K. Friedlander, "Children's Books and Their Function in Latency and Prepuberty," *American Image,* 3: 129–150, 1942.
18 From *A Program of Similarities* by the Minneapolis Public Library. Used by permission of the Library.

Then read:

> Nordhoff: *Men against the Sea*
> Hawes: *The Mutineers*
> Hawes: *Dark Frigate*
> Kingsley: *Westward Ho!*
> Sperry: *All Sails Set*
> Dana: *Two Years before the Mast*

Such ladders are of great value to both children and teachers. They could be constructed for war stories, home stories, tales of foreign countries, animal stories, phantasies, mystery tales, and so on. It may be noted that they should aid in developing taste if they lead the pupil to read well-known books of yesterday or especially well-written modern books. By such means a child starts reading the classics without ever knowing he is doing so.

Another device that has been described is the "Reading Menu." [19] Each child first writes out a complete menu, from soup to nuts, of the best meal he can ever remember eating. Then he substitutes books for food, putting the most solid piece of reading as the entree, somewhat lighter titles for the vegetables, and so on. One such menu appears below: [20]

John's Menu

Lad, a Dog—Terhune

Smoky—James   *Men of Iron*—Pyle

Dance of Kenana—French

Tom Sawyer—Mark Twain

Sea Fever—Masefield

In order to make out the menu, a pupil must at least look over a good many books. When it is completed, he proceeds to enjoy his meal by reading everything on the menu.

E. SUMMARY

Because of the enormous numbers and types of books now available for children, it should be possible to find several in any given field

[19] M. W. Scott and G. A. Granger, "Activities for Increasing Children's Appreciation of Good Literature," *Seventeenth Yearbook of the Department of Elementary School Principals*, pp. 353–358, 1938; see also J. Betzner and R. L. Lyman, "The Development of Reading Interests and Tastes," *Thirty-sixth Yearbook of the National Society for the Study of Education*, Part I, pp. 185–205, 1937; R. A. Putnam, "Cultivating Taste for Nonfiction," *Elementary English Review*, 18: 228–229, 1941.

[20] From Scott and Granger, *op. cit.*, p. 357. Used by permission of the publisher.

in which a child may be interested. Naturally, his work in class cannot always be adapted to him, because he is then a member of a group whose needs must be considered and because the materials in the class readers are so selected as to give drill on fundamental vocabulary, but additional reading can and should be an individual matter. No subject in school can be so easily linked to childhood interests as reading. One further caution should, however, be kept in mind. The books to be read at home should always be easier than those a child is reading in school; they should be so easy that their reading gives him pleasure. A teacher will avoid many difficulties by selecting interesting books that appeal so strongly to childhood interests that the children read them spontaneously.

V · The Difficulty of Reading Matter

The assignment of certain books as basic or auxiliary reading matter for given grades is often made on the basis of the best collective judgment obtainable, without recourse to such objective measurements as already exist. It is, however, better to supplement judgment with evidence whenever possible. Even under the best of circumstances, difficulty is hard to measure or to estimate, because of the many factors that enter into the situation.

Reading matter may be difficult because the words are unusual or highly technical, because the sentences are long and involved, because the thought is obscure or the style clumsy or ornate.[1] Some of these elements are much more easily measured than others. The difficulty of the vocabulary is relatively easy to determine, provided one takes a sufficiently large and random sampling. Length of sentence is easy

[1] See, for instance, C. Burke, "A Study of the Influence of Some Factors of Style on the Reading of Fourth Grade Pupils," *Journal of Experimental Education*, 4: 303–352, 1936; E. A. Davis, "The Location of the Subordinate Clause in Oral and Written Language," *Child Development*, 12: 333–338, 1941; E. W. Dolch, "Fact Burden and Reading Difficulty," *Elementary English Review*, 16: 135–138, 1939; C. F. Elliott, "A Critical Analysis of the Objective Methods of Measuring Reading Difficulty," *University of Pittsburgh Bulletin*, 37: 97–104, 1941; R. F. Flesch, "Estimating the Comparative Difficulty of Magazine Articles," *Journal of General Psychology*, 28: 63–80, 1943; B. F. Holland, "The Effect of the Length and Structure of Sentences on the Silent Reading Process," *Psychological Bulletin*, 30: 668–669, 1933; M. A. Jackman, "The Relation between Maturity of Content and Simplicity of Style in Selecting Books of Fiction," *Library Quarterly*, 11: 302–327, 1941; A. S. Lewerenz, "Measurement of the Difficulty of Reading Materials," *Educational Research Bulletin*, 8: 11–16, 1929; I. Lorge, "Predicting Reading Difficulty of Selections for Children," *Elementary English Review*, 16: 229–233, 1939; H. McClusky, "Quantitative Analysis of the Difficulty of Reading Materials," *Journal of Educational Research*, 28: 276–282, 1934; P. McKee, "Word Lists and Vocabulary Difficulty of Reading Matter," *Elementary English Review*, 14: 241–245, 1937; R. O. Sims, "Concept Analysis of Primers and Preprimers," *Elementary English Review*, 15: 302–305, 1938; M. L. Stewart, "Sentence Length in Reading," *Elementary School Journal*, 41: 130–133, 1940; M. Vogel and C. Washburne, "An Objective Method of Determining Grade Placement of Children's Reading Material," *Elementary School Journal*, 28: 373–381, 1928, and "Grade Placement of Children's Books" 38: 355–364, 1938; C. Walther, "The Reading Difficulty of Magazines," *School Review*, 51: 100–105, 1943.

enough to compute, and the number of subordinate clauses per sentence is not much harder. It might be possible to work out some technique for counting the number of ideas per page, but one doubts that it would be helpful. Indeed, two of the three reports to date [2] are not very illuminating. One investigator found 4 to 8 facts per 100 words in fifth and sixth grade geography books, 3 to 4 facts per 100 words in history books for Grades 5 to 8, 1 to 3 for second to sixth grade science books, and 1 for hygiene books in Grades 1 and 2. If another person were to repeat this count, the number might come out differently, since the analysis rests upon subjective judgment. The second investigator found no difference in the number of ideas per 100 words in fiction and textbooks. The third report [3] concerns the number of concepts in several primers and pre-primers. The former range from 61 to 111 concepts per book and the other from 270 to 408.

The complexity of the thought, the background of information for which it calls, the extent to which reading between the lines is necessary, the potency of the ideas to call forth reactions in the reader are characteristics that can only be estimated, not measured. And presumably such estimates would vary greatly from one reader to another. The available·measures of difficulty as shown by vocabulary and sentence structure or length are all right as far as they go, but they fail to measure what is presumably most important. Consider, for instance, the following poem:

> Under the wide and starry sky,
> There dig a grave and let me lie.
> Glad did I live, and glad will I die,
> And I lay me down with a will.
> And this be the lines you grave for me:
> Here he lies, where he longs to be;
> Home is the sailor, home from the sea,
> And the hunter home from the hill. [4]

This poem contains 38 different words, 35 of which appear in the commonest thousand in the Thorndike Word List. Aside from the word *starry* there is no word that a high first or low second grade child would not be able to recognize. The poem contains no subordinate clauses. It is, so far as vocabulary and sentence form go, eminently suitable for first or second grade children—who would certainly not understand it. In

[2] Dolch, *op. cit.* and McClusky, *op. cit.*
[3] Sims, *op. cit.*
[4] By Robert Louis Stevenson.

considering the methods presented in this section, one should remember that they can measure only certain elements of difficulty. These elements are worth measuring, but they do not include all that needs to be known about reading difficulty.[5]

A. SENTENCE LENGTH AND STRUCTURE

Sentences tend to increase in both length and complexity as reading matter becomes more advanced. If a teacher analyzes a series of readers, she will find that sentence length increases from year to year. If she analyzes enough series she will discover also that no two of them have the same idea as to how long the sentences should be in this or that grade.[6] That is, there is no standard, although each series of readers is reasonably consistent within itself.

The number of subordinate elements and their location in the sentence may both contribute to reading difficulty. Most children do not spontaneously begin sentences with a subordinate clause in either their conversation or their writing, unless they are very bright indeed.[7] Inferentially, then, sentences that begin with a subordinate clause will be harder to read than those with the clause at the end, where the children usually put it, in case they use one at all. Sentence complexity does seem to have some effect upon the difficulty of reading matter especially in the lower grades. In one experiment[8] the same passage was read, once in simple sentences and once in compound and complex sentences. An equal number read each version first, in order to neutralize the advantage that a second reading always has over a first. There were 10 selections, each in two forms, and all of them were read before an eye-movement camera. The mechanical habits were better for the simpler form, and the comprehension was slightly higher. The younger the children, the greater the difference between the two renditions. Below the seventh grade conditional clauses, especially at the beginning of sentences, were hard to read. Two other experimenters[9] found a preference among children for short, simple sentences.

Presumably, norms per grade for length of sentence, number and

[5] See also, Flesch, *op. cit.*, Jackman, *op. cit.*, and McKee, *op. cit.* All three authors object to the usual measures of difficulty because they do not have reference to the difficulty of the thought.

[6] See Stewart, *op. cit.*

[7] See Davis, *op. cit.*

[8] See Holland, *op. cit.*

[9] Burke, *op. cit.* and McClusky, *op. cit.*

types of subordinate elements, and position of these elements could be worked out and might help in standardizing the difficulty of reading matter. Everything that can be measured ought to be, because there are so many elements that must, in any case, rest upon personal opinion.

B. MEASUREMENT OF DIFFICULTY

Vocabulary, like sentence form and length, can be measured with fair accuracy and indicates the level of difficulty, provided the reading matter thus measured expresses ideas within the average child's comprehension. Thus, *Black Beauty* has a more difficult vocabulary than *Treasure Island*, and this fact would lead one to give children the latter book in an earlier grade than that in which the former is appropriate, since most of the ideas in both books are intelligible to children. However, aside from the Russian proper names, Tolstoi's *War and Peace* uses a vocabulary that is no harder than that of *Black Beauty*, but the ideas are beyond the comprehension of most children. If books are first selected as having an appropriate content, they can be measured for difficulty of vocabulary and assigned to whatever grade they belong in, but measurement of vocabulary rarely reflects difficulty of concept and is insufficient by itself for the selection of books.[10]

The methods for measuring vocabulary are not difficult, although a bit monotonous if one has to investigate a large number of books. The three commonest methods are (1) to determine the difficulty of a fair sampling of words in a book by submitting the words to school children and finding to what degree each is known,[11] (2) to determine the frequency in general use of a fair sampling by comparing it with the Thorndike Word Book, on the assumption that frequency and difficulty are correlated,[12] or (3) to work out a formula that is based upon an assortment of measurable elements. The second and third methods are the ones in wide use.

If one uses the second method, one begins by making what is called a "thousand word count." To do this, one examines the first line on every other page of a book and lists the *different* words occur-

[10] A few authors—Thackeray, for instance—use a vocabulary so difficult and varied and a sentence structure so complex that measures of these two elements would show the books to be difficult reading, without reference to the ideas expressed.

[11] H. C. Tilley, "A Method for Measuring the Relative Difficulty of Words among Elementary School Children," *Journal of Experimental Education*, 5: 61–64, 1936.

[12] See B. A. Lively, "A Method for Measuring the Vocabulary Burden of Textbooks," Master's Thesis, Ohio State University, 1927.

ring on these lines. For instance, on the first line of the first page there may be the words *Once upon a time there was a king who;* upon the first line of the third page, the words *many times during each year when the king saw;* and on the first line of the fifth page, the words *each time the king saw him, he was very.* The sum total of words is 27. The 18 *different* words are listed below.

a	he	many	the	upon	when
during	him	once	there	very	who
each	king	saw	time	was	year

Until she has reached a total of a thousand the teacher should list the separate words and keep count of how many words have been examined. In that number she is not likely to find more than 500 that are different, and usually not over 350. There is no need to count the frequencies; the duplicates are included in the total, but each different word is listed only once. If the book is so short that the first line on every other page does not yield a total of a thousand words, the teacher should go back to the beginning and take the first line on the pages she omitted on her first count. If she still does not have the necessary total, she should take the bottom line on every other page. On the other hand, if a teacher has been examining the first line on every other page and finds her total of words more than 500 by the time she reaches the middle of the book, she should take the first line on every third page throughout the remaining half in order to obtain samples from alternate pages all the way through the book. The selection is made in this way to get a random and systematic sample from the entire book. It is not desirable to take the thousand words out of the first few pages, because these may be more or less difficult than the remaining portions.

When a teacher has looked at a thousand words, taken at random, and has listed the different ones, she is ready to estimate the reading

TABLE 28
Norms for the Number of Different Words per 1,000

Primer	208	Fifth–sixth grades	425
First grade	246	Seventh–eighth grades	455
Second grade	294	Ninth–twelfth grades	470
Third grade	340	College	502
Fourth grade	397		

difficulty of the book as a whole. The first method of measuring is to compare the number of different words with the averages for each grade. These averages are given in Table 28. Thus if a book intended for the fourth grade contains 201 different words in a sample thousand, it is too easy. If it contains 462 different words in a sample thousand, it is too hard. The oftener the same words recur in reading matter, the more drill each word receives and the more quickly the reader masters the necessary vocabulary. Consequently the fewer different terms there are, the easier is the reading matter. Even in the most difficult books there

TABLE 29

Tabulation of Thorndike Frequencies for Eight Books [13]

Thorndike Frequencies by Thousands	Primer	Second Grade Reader	Fourth Grade Reader	Kidnapped	Junior High School Science	High School History	College Text in Psychology	Medical School Physiology
Not in List	2	3	11	12	2	7	10	35
19,000–20,000	—	—	1	0	0	0	3	3
18,001–19,000	—	—	1	0	3	2	4	1
17,001–18,000	—	1	0	1	1	0	5	2
16,001–17,000	1	—	1	1	0	3	3	3
15,001–16,000	—	1	2	0	0	2	6	5
14,001–15,000	2	—	1	1	4	1	8	1
13,001–14,000	—	1	2	2	1	6	14	6
12,001–13,000	—	3	2	1	4	3	6	6
11,001–12,000	1	—	1	1	2	3	7	3
10,001–11,000	1	—	2	4	2	3	8	6
9,001–10,000	—	1	2	2	2	5	10	11
8,001–9,000	3	—	6	2	3	8	15	11
7,001–8,000	1	—	1	3	15	10	17	24
6,001–7,000	1	4	2	4	13	15	26	21
5,001–6,000	4	10	8	9	17	13	8	5
4,001–5,000	1	7	3	8	19	28	22	17
3,001–4,000	9	8	20	16	24	33	24	18
2,001–3,000	8	20	27	19	42	48	31	37
1,001–2,000	6	52	71	50	61	81	54	33
501–1,000	16	63	71	55	68	64	38	47
1–500	148	195	213	208	196	184	144	119
Total	204	368	448	399	479	519	463	414
% above lowest 2,000	17	16	20	22	32	37	49	52
% above 10,000	3	2	5	6	4	5	16	17
% above 20,000	1	1	2	3	.5	1	2	8

[13] These figures are based on thousand-word counts found in the master's thesis of Bertha Lively, Ohio State University.

are rarely more than 500 different words per thousand because of the numerous repetitions of such words as *the, and, if, to,* and so on.

The second measure is the determination of the "commonness" in general usage of the different words already listed. One must first look up each of these words in the *Teachers' Word Book* [14] and note down in which thousand or half thousand the word occurs. These Thorndike frequencies are then tabulated as in Table 29. This sample tabulation contains results for a primer, a second grade reader, a fourth grade reader, *Kidnapped,* a junior high school science book, a senior high school history, a college text in psychology, and a medical school physiology. It can be seen that these books are arranged in order of difficulty, insofar as difficulty may be measured by the commonness of the words, although the primer has too high a per cent of unusual words and both the science and history texts are also too loaded with words that are infrequent. The commonness of the words in these various samplings may be estimated by determining what per cent is beyond a given point in the Thorndike list—the first 1,000, the first 1,500, the first 2,000, or any other point. Tentative norms for the per cent of words beyond the first 2,000 have already been established and range from 4 per cent for primers to 36 per cent for college texts.

TABLE 30

Norms for the Per Cent of Words beyond Thorndike's Lowest 2,000

Primer	4	Fifth–sixth grades	24
First grade	8	Seventh–eighth grades	28
Second grade	12	Ninth–twelfth grades	32
Third grade	16	College	36
Fourth grade	20		

None of the books in Table 30 is easy enough as compared to these norms. The primer is notably difficult.

These measures of difficulty, plus others if desired, may be combined into a formula. One of the simplest formulae contains only three variables: the number of different words in a thousand, the number that are not among the commonest fifteen hundred of the Thorndike list, and the number of simple sentences in seventy-five selected at random from the book being studied.[15] Each of these elements has been

[14] See page 42.
[15] Vogel and Washburne, *op. cit.* (1938).

evaluated statistically and each is to be multiplied by a number that weights it so as to give the best possible estimate of difficulty. The formula reads:

$$\text{Number of different words} \times .00255$$
$$+$$
$$\text{Number of unusual words} \times .0458$$
$$+$$
$$\text{A numerical constant equal to } 1.294$$
$$-$$
$$\text{The number of simple sentence} \times .0307$$

This formula is worked out in the sample below with the figures from *Tom Sawyer*. There were 373 different words in the thousand, 117 of these words were uncommon, and 18 of the 75 sentences were simple sentences. Substituting these values in the formula, one gets:

$$
\begin{array}{ll}
373 \times .00255 & = 0.951 \\
117 \times .0458 & = 5.359 \\
\text{Constant} & = 1.294 \\
\hline
 & 7.604 \\
18 \times .0307 & = -.553 \\
\hline
\text{Answer} & = 7.051
\end{array}
$$

The answer gives the proper grade placement, in this case 7.0, or right at the beginning of the seventh grade.[16]

Another formula [17]—and still a relatively simple one—reads as follows:

$$x_1 = .01029x_2 + .009012x_3 - .02094x_4 - .03313x_5 - .01485x_6 + 3.774.$$

The decimals are numerical weightings that have to be used because some factors are more important than others. The expression x_1 is the

[16] Sometimes this formula is given with variations and in reverse: The proportion of words that are repeated, the proportion of words among the commonest 1500, and the proportion of complex and compound sentences. Anyone interested in rating difficulty by such means is advised to send for the *Winnetka Chart for Determining Grade Placement of Children's Books,* Research Department of the Winnetka Public Schools, and the *Grade Placement Formula: Word Tabulation Sheet* by A. S. Lewerenz from the Educational Research and Guidance Section, Los Angeles City School District. Both charts give full directions for tabulation of the raw data and computation of the results by formula.

[17] From W. S. Gray and B. E. Leary, *What Makes a Book Readable?* University of Chicago Press, 1935, 358 pp. (From page 138.)

readability of the book; x_2 is the number of different hard words in a sample 100; x_3 is the number of first, second, or third person pronouns in the sample; x_4, the average number of words per sentence; x_5, the per cent of different words per 100; x_6, the number of prepositional phrases. When the formula is worked out it results in a figure that tells, in terms of the elements measured, how difficult the book will be to read. This method is similar to the one just described, but it includes more elements and smaller samples of each.

Use of the Winnetka Chart with a number of current magazines gives the grade placement so far as difficulties of vocabulary and sentence structure are concerned. Three issues of each magazine were analyzed and the results averaged. The grade placement thus obtained shows that most magazines are suitable for high school and the early years of college.

TABLE 31
Grade Placement of Magazines [18]

Magazine	Grade Placement
True Stories	7.9
Liberty	10.1
Good Housekeeping	10.2
Saturday Evening Post	10.2
Woman's Home Companion	10.3
Harper's	11.0
Readers' Digest	11.7
Scientific American	12.6
National Geographic	13.
Time	14.2
Newsweek	14.4

An occasional excerpt from these magazines might be usable in elementary school, but for the most part, children had better stick to children's magazines.

C. SELECTION OF BOOKS

The ratings of difficulty for a book should be, and sometimes are, combined with expressions of interest on the part of children who have read the book. The grade placement as derived by formula tells how

[18] Walther, *op. cit.* Used by permission of the publisher.

hard a book is to read, but it does not tell how hard, easy, interesting, uninteresting, exciting, or dull the ideas may be, and only children who have read the book can give the necessary information. They are the consumers, and they know what they can and cannot consume, even if they are extremely foggy as to the reasons. It is rarely worth while to ask children why they liked or disliked a book, but their ratings of how well they liked it or how completely they disliked it are reasonably accurate and of great value. By combining measures of difficulty and interest, one can place books in the grade where they will be most useful.[19]

If such measures are not used, books have to be selected and assigned to grades on the basis of opinion. The opinions may be gathered in a systematic way,[20] but they remain more or less subjective. Moreover, they are adult opinions based upon adult reactions to books that will be used by children. Naturally, some items, such as the clearness and size of the type, the spacing of the lines, and the adequacy of illustrations, indices, or headings can be estimated by adults better than by children, but difficulty can be measured better objectively than subjectively and the interest of children be determined more accurately by asking them for their reactions than by asking adults for theirs. Experienced librarians and teachers can often make a good guess about a book's appeal and its difficulty, but actual analysis plus actual trial in a few typical classes will yield more accurate, more detailed, and more reliable results.

D. SUMMARY

Some elements of difficulty, notably sentence complexity and vocabulary, can be rather easily measured, but the measurable items do not give a complete picture of reading difficulty and may even give a false impression if an author has chosen to express adult philosophies in simple English. Those who have the task of selecting books should certainly use all the information they can get concerning measurable elements of difficulty, but they should not trust to these alone. Refusal to use what objective evidence exists and complete dependence upon it are about equally ill judged.

---

[19] See Chapter IV.

[20] See, for instance, J. A. Clement, *Manual for Analyzing and Selecting Textbooks,* Garrard Press, Champaign, Ill., 1942, 119 pp.; and G. Whipple, "Procedures Used in Selecting Textbooks," *Elementary School Journal,* 36: 665–673, 760–775, 1936, and 37: 47–57, 1937.

VI · Reading Readiness

Readiness to read is usually thought of as a problem met only in the first grade. On the contrary, it reappears whenever a pupil starts a new level of work. One should certainly investigate each child for his readiness to read at the first grade level, the fourth, the seventh, the ninth, and at his entrance to college. In each of these grades the pupil meets new types of reading matter, and his work will inevitably begin below the necessary level of achievement if he is not ready before he starts.

The main purpose of the reading readiness program in Grade 1 is the prevention of failure through the recognition of immaturity and the postponement of formal reading instruction.[1] It appears from research already done that from 10 to 50 per cent of the pupils in each entering class are not yet ready to read. The higher per cents are in schools that serve underprivileged children, whose background is meagre and narrow. All evidence goes to show that failures can be prevented if teachers adjust instruction to individual ability and have a sufficiently wide range of teaching techniques and reading materials.

It is desirable to know what skills are necessary for beginning work at each of the successive levels, especially at the lowest. Such a schedule will be presented in the following sections.

A. READINESS TO READ IN THE FIRST GRADE

It has long been an educational assumption that children are ready to read when they are six years old. To be ready, however, a child must have sufficient intellectual development, maturity of speech and sense organs, plus social, emotional, and experiential maturity. Some children

---

[1] For texts that cover the various phases of reading readiness, see, for instance, E. A. Betts, *Prevention and Correction of Reading Difficulties,* Row, Peterson and Company, Evanston, 1936, 402 pp.; M. L. Harrison, *Reading Readiness,* Houghton Mifflin Company, 1939, 2d ed., 262 pp.; M. Stanger and E. Donahue, *The Prediction and Prevention of Reading Difficulties,* Oxford University Press, 1937, 191 pp.

show adequate development along all lines, but many are retarded in one or more fields. It is about equally important that the former should begin reading at once and that the latter should not.

There are various series of tests [2] that measure readiness to read at the entrance to school. Some of these involve a good deal of equipment and technical experience and are relatively hard for a teacher to use. The really essential measurements, however, can be made well enough by means of the simple techniques to be described shortly.

1. **Mental Maturity:** First comes a measure of intelligence. Although the Binet examination is doubtless the best, it demands a considerable amount of experience before one can use it. The average teacher will get more accurate results if she uses such tests as the Detroit Primary Intelligence, the Pressey Primary Classification, or the Pintner-Cunningham Test.[3] These are all group tests. During the first week or two of school, only a few children can be tested at once; the teacher should repeat the examination as often as necessary until she has scores for everyone. From any of these tests a mental age can be obtained.

It appears from research that a child needs a mental age of at least six and a half if he is to learn how to read by the methods of instruction currently in use.[4] Since children enter school at chronological ages from five years eight months until six years four months, it is clear that only those with an IQ of more than 100 have this degree of mental

---

[2] E. A. Betts, *Betts Ready-to-Read Tests and Manual,* Keystone View Company, Meadville, Penn., 1934; A. I. Gates, *Gates Reading Readiness Tests,* Bureau of Publications, Teachers College, Columbia University, 1939; G. Hildreth and N. L. Griffiths, *Metropolitan Readiness Tests,* World Book Company, 1933; *Lee-Clark Reading Readiness Tests,* Southern California Book Depository, Los Angeles; M. Monroe, *Reading Aptitude Tests for Predication and Analysis of Reading Ability and Disability,* Houghton Mifflin Company, 1935; C. R. Stone and C. C. Grover, *Classification Tests for Beginners in Reading,* Webster Publishing Company, St. Louis; *Van Wagenen Reading Tests,* Educational Test Bureau, Minneapolis, 1932.

See also A. I. Gates, G. Bond, and D. H. Russell, *Methods of Determining Reading Readiness,* Bureau of Publications, Teachers College, Columbia University, 1939; A. I. Gates, "Readiness to Begin Reading," in G. Hildreth, *Readiness for Learning,* Association for Childhood Education, Washington, pp. 13–15, 1941; J. M. Lee and D. M. Lee, "Measuring Reading Readiness," *Elementary School Journal,* 34: 656–666, 1934; H. B. Morrison, "Reading Readiness in the First Grade," *Educational Research Bulletin,* No. 5, 1942, 44 pp.; W. E. Pratt, "The Construction of Group Tests of Reading Readiness," *University of Pittsburgh Bulletin,* No. 3, 37: 265–273, 1941; K. A. Ranson, "A Study of Reading Readiness," *Peabody Journal of Education,* 16: 276–285, 1939; F. P. Robinson and W. E. Hall, "Concerning Reading Readiness Tests," *Bulletin of the Ohio Conference on Reading,* Ohio State University Press, No. 3, 1942, 16 pp.

[3] The first and third of these are published by the World Book Company, Yonkers, N. Y.; the second is published by the Public School Publishing Company, Bloomington, Ill.

[4] M. V. Morphett and C. Washburne, "When Should Children Begin to Read?" *Elementary School Journal,* 31: 496–503, 1931.

maturity at entrance. It is, however, possible that a lower mental age would suffice if the teaching were modified.[5]

The mental level shown at entrance by all the children in a large city makes clear the need for having some method for dealing with those who are not yet sufficiently mature mentally to begin reading. The mental ages of 6,943 children were as follows:

TABLE 32
Mental Ages at Entrance to School [6]

	Number	Per Cent
5 years 10 months, or below	2,231	32
5 years 11 months to 6 years 3 months	1,030	15
6 years 4 months to 6 years 8 months	1,134	16
6 years 9 months, or above	2,017	30
Not tested	531	7
TOTAL	6,943	100

According to these figures 32 per cent were not yet ready to leave kindergarten and at least another 20 per cent needed further growth before beginning to read.

2. **Visual Maturity:** If a pupil's eyes are developing at a perfectly normal rate, at the age of six they are still too farsightd to see clearly so small an object as a word. It is not until a normal child is about eight years old that one can be certain his eyes are mature. Four tests of vision are recommended, the last two of which require a stereoscope.[7] The methods of procedure will be described briefly below.

(a) The first test in the series requires that the child be able to distinguish between pairs of letters that look similar. It is not in the least necessary to read the letters. Samples from such a test appear below:

y–g	l–l	i–i	v–w
b–d	o–c	u–v	r–r
d–d	h–k	e–r	t–t
m–n	j–i	p–q	z–y
a–a	y–y	r–s	f–t

[5] A. I. Gates, "The Necessary Mental Age for Beginning Reading," *Elementary School Journal*, 37: 497–508, 1937.

[6] E. L. Woods, "A Study of the Entering 1B Children in the Los Angeles City Schools," *Journal of Educational Research*, 31: 9–19, 1937. Quoted by permission of the publisher.

[7] These tests are based upon Betts tests, but they have been simplified.

All the child is asked to do is to tell, for each pair, if the two letters are the same or different. Immature pupils are unable to distinguish between letters that are similar in appearance. The tendency to reversals, which distresses elementary school teachers, is mainly a sign of immaturity. In a group of five-year-old children not more than 10 per cent will be able to pass such a test because they cannot see any difference between *d* and *b* or *p* and *q*.[8] By the time children are six years old, about half of them have sufficiently mature eyes to see these reversals. It is not, however, until children are seven to eight years old that the eyes are mature enough to avoid such confusions altogether. A pupil's score on twenty such items as those above should be almost without error before he is allowed to begin reading. If further checking is needed in doubtful cases the child may be asked to copy letters, since his tendency to reversals is almost certain to stand out clearly when he copies.

(b) The second test is of the same type as the first, except that it contains words instead of letters. The pupil is asked to tell if two words presented as a pair are the same or different. He does not need, however, to have the vaguest idea of what either word of a pair may mean. A few sample pairs for such a test appear below:

me–my	rat–rate	men–man	eye–eye
out–owe	save–save	zoo–zoom	did–hit
sent–sent	hope–shop	when–then	play–plow
we–woe	bead–bread	king–king	let–let
weigh–right	tall–tall	all–ill	put–pout

If a child cannot see differences in the appearance of words, he will obviously not learn to read. A pupil should give the correct answer to at least three fourths of the pairs.

The next two tests require the use of a stereoscope. In all, there are four cards to be prepared. Each of these cards is $7\frac{1}{8}$ inches long and $3\frac{1}{2}$ inches wide. They may be made out of any stiff white cardboard. Directions for making them will be given shortly.

(c) The first card of this series shows an upright line on one side and a circle on the other. The teacher puts the card in the stereoscope and lets the pupil look at it. The child sees a line with his left eye and a circle with his right. She first asks him if he sees a line (or stick) and a circle (or ball). Then she asks if the line is beside the circle. The

---

[8] See L. Teegarten, "Tests for the Tendency to Reversal in Reading," *Journal of Educational Research*, 27: 81–97, 1933; F. T. Wilson and C. W. Fleming, "Reversals in Reading and Writing Made by Pupils in the Kindergarten and Primary Grades," *Journal of Genetic Psychology*, 53: 3–31, 1938.

pupil should answer that the circle is on top of the line—or that the
line is under the circle. If his eyes fuse correctly, he will see the circle
balanced on top of the line.

The second card has a horizontal line 3 inches long and ⅛ of an

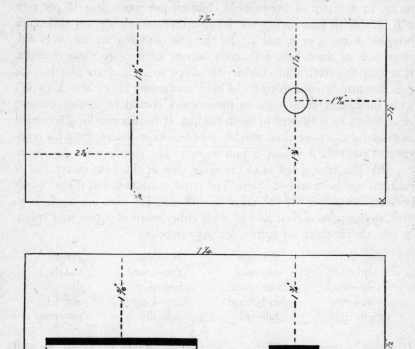

FIGURE 19: Cards for Testing Fusion

inch thick on one side and, on the other, a horizontal line 1 inch long
and ¹⁄₁₆ of an inch thick. When a child looks at this card he sees one
line with each eye. If his eyes fuse correctly he will see a single line
because the one on the right will be seen on top of the longer line and
will become invisible. One merely asks the pupil how many lines he
sees. If he sees two, his eyes are not focusing; if he sees at first two and

then one, his images fuse eventually but the process is not sufficiently automatic for reading purposes. If a child's eyes are mature enough for the strain of reading, he will make no error on either of these two tests for measuring fusion. If the objects in either test constantly shift about,

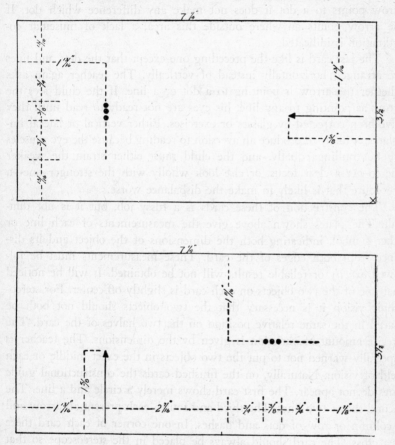

FIGURE 20: Cards for Testing Balance

sometimes fusing properly and sometimes not, the child does not have sufficient visual control to read comfortably.

(d) The last test of vision also requires the stereoscope. It measures the muscular balance of the eyes. There are two cards; on the first, there appears a vertical arrow in the middle of the right field of vision and in the left field a column made up of dots and short lines. If the child's vertical balance is correct, the arrow will point to one of the dots, or between two of them. The plate is so arranged that only dots appear in the area of normal variability. The teacher therefore asks him whether the arrow is pointing to a dot or line. If he reports that the arrow points to a dot it does not make any difference which dot. If the arrow points anywhere outside this area, a lack of muscular coordination is indicated.

The last card is like the preceding one except that the dots and lines are arranged horizontally instead of vertically. The teacher again asks whether the arrow is pointing to a dot or a line. If the child sees the arrow as pointing to any line, his eyes are not ready to read until they have been corrected by glasses or exercises. Either vertical or lateral imbalance is likely to produce an aversion to reading because the eye muscles are not pulling equally, and the child must either strain the weaker one to get a clear focus, or else look wholly with the stronger one—a procedure that is likely to make the disbalance worse.

The construction of these cards is a fussy job, but it is not difficult. The plates shown above give the measurements of each line or other symbol, indicating both the dimensions of the object and its distance from both edges of the card. These measurements must be followed *exactly* or reliable results will not be obtained. It will be noticed that one of the two objects on each card is slightly off-center. For stereoscopic vision it is necessary that the two objects should not both be placed in the same relative position on the two halves of the card. The precise amount of variation is given by the dimensions. The teacher is especially warned not to put the two objects in the exact middle of each field of vision. Naturally, on the finished cards the constructional guide lines do not appear. The first card shows merely a circle and a line. The second shows two lines. The third and fourth each present an arrow and a column or row of dots and dashes. In one corner of each card there is a cross. The card should always be placed in the stereoscope so that this cross is in the lower right-hand corner.

These materials are not, of course, scientifically accurate. Better cards can be purchased by the teacher who can afford them. Nevertheless, these cards, if accurately constructed, are good enough to point out the child whose eyes need attention. A scientific determination of the extent and nature of the defect is not the teacher's business; her job is done when she has found out which children have eyes that do not focus properly and has sent these children to an oculist.

3. Auditory Maturity: There are two simple tests of hearing that a teacher can use to find out if a child's hearing and his perception of what he hears are good enough for reading purposes. These tests are described briefly below:

(a) For the first, the teacher says aloud to the child ten sentences, each six words long, such as "The dog ran after the cat." The pupil is to repeat the sentence aloud after her. If he makes any error whatever, the sentence is counted as wrong. If he does not repeat at least five of the sentences correctly, his hearing—or his retention of what he hears—is defective.

(b) A second test requires the child to differentiate between two sounds. The teacher should use pairs of sounds, such as those that appear presently. The pupil stands beside her, but with his back turned toward her, so that he cannot get any clues from her lip movement. She tells him she is going to make two sounds or noises and that sometimes the two sounds will be just alike, while at other times they will be different. He is to tell her if the two sounds are like or unlike. She then sounds such pairs as are shown below:

b–d	th–sh	a–e	n–n	s–z	n–ng
s–s	k–g	f–f	oo–oo	k–k	a–ai
m–n	o–o	l–l	p–b	f–s	k–kl
r–gr	j–j	t–d	th–th	r–r	v–f

She should, of course, sound—not spell—these letters. The pupil should be able to distinguish correctly at least fourteen out of the twenty-four pairs, or his hearing is not good enough for him to learn to read.

If a pupil makes markedly low scores on these two tests, he should certainly be sent to an expert for ear examination. Although these tests do not measure the extent or cause of the deficiency in hearing, they are good enough to pick out the child whose hearing or perception is inadequate. It is then a job for experts to decide what should be done.

4. Maturity of Speech: A child's speech may be measured by asking him to imitate the sound of each consonant in the alphabet (minus the letters *c* and *q*), plus the common combinations of *th, sh, ch, ng, cl,* and *gr.* This total comes to twenty-five different sounds. The pupil should face the teacher so that he may see her lip movement. He is allowed three attempts, if he needs them, for each sound. If the pronunciation is still incorrect, his effort is counted as a failure. He is not ready to read until he can imitate correctly at least fifteen out of the twenty-five sounds.[9] Any defects of speech should be noted and the pupil given such corrective measures as seem appropriate.

Throughout his first year of school a pupil reads almost no words that are not within his speaking vocabulary. If, however, because of immature speech he does not use the expected number of words, he does not have the necessary background. If his pronunciation is defective, he will not recognize words after he has spoken them.

Children do not master all the consonant sounds and blends at the same rate. The easiest ones—*b, p, m, w, h*—are usually correct by the time the child is three and a half, but the hardest ones—*ch, sh, l, th* as in *these, th* as in *thin, z, s,r,* and *wh*—are usually not mastered until after he enters school.[10] Children who are a little slow in their development will probably not be wholly sure of *f, v,* and *z,* also. Naturally, entering first grade pupils show a larger or smaller assortment of mispronunciations because of their immature speech. Until they can speak with fair correctness they are better off without reading instruction.

5. Emotional Maturity: There are no good measures of social and emotional maturity. A teacher must therefore rely upon her own observation of each pupil. The babyish child who constantly depends upon adults will not make much progress in reading, because he cannot work by himself. The pupil who persistently avoids looking at books, never asks—when he sees a picture—what the words under it are, and wanders off if left to himself during the reading lesson, is not yet ready to read. Until he *wants* to learn, there is not much use in trying to force him. If he were a high school freshman, one would be justified in exerting pressure upon him to learn something worth while and practical. The baby in the first grade, however, cannot be forced because he cannot, even under pressure, direct himself. He is so immature that pressure merely disorganizes him.

A child who is emotionally unstable may also have difficulty in learning to read.[11] Any situation that leads to tension, anxiety, or fear may prevent a pupil from concentrating upon reading or from remembering what he learns.

[9] See also E. W. Dolch and M. Bloomster, "Phonic Readiness," *Elementary School Journal,* 38: 201–205, 1937. Also the *Basic Reading Tests: Word-Attack Series, Tests 1 and 2,* Scott, Foresman and Company.

[10] I. P. Davis, "The Speech Aspects of Reading Readiness," *Seventeenth Yearbook of the Department of Elementary School Principals,* pp. 282–288, 1938. See also S. S. Hawk, "Conditions Affecting Language Maturity," in G. Hildreth, *Readiness for Learning,* Association for Childhood Education, Washington, 1941, 35 pp. (Pages 20–23.)

[11] A. I. Gates, "The Role of Personality Maladjustment in Beginning Reading," *Journal of Genetic Psychology,* 59: 77–83, 1941.

6. **Maturity of Experience:** A child's experiences have to be sufficiently varied to be used as background for his reading. Children from good homes have usually had a fairly wide range of experience, unless they have been overprotected. The matter of necessary experiences is especially important in a school that serves a slum district, because the simple stories children read in the first grade often describe experiences a slum child has never had. He therefore not only fails to recognize particular words, but he does not understand the ideas even after he has learned the words. His first grade reader will undoubtedly contain a story about a family getting into an automobile and driving into the country. The chances are that the slum child has never ridden in an automobile, and he may never have seen a tree, a flower, or any growing thing. He has therefore not much idea what such a simple incident is about. Because of his environment he has seen few pictures, has had few stories read to him, and has made few if any visits to the motion-picture theater. He has not even had these indirect means of compensating for his lack of experience. There is no use in trying to teach such a child to read a story about a farm when he literally does not know what farm animals look like and has no conception of the physical environment under consideration.[12]

An excellent summary of factors influencing readiness to read and of objectives for the readiness program is presented in Table 33. In a given child the factors of environment and maturation fuse, so that it is sometimes difficult to tell which is which. Always they react back and forth, sometimes reinforcing and sometimes inhibiting each other. For instance, a bright child who hears a foreign language at home may still learn to read easily because his maturity compensates for his handicap, whereas a dull child under similar circumstances may have great difficulty because his immaturity and lack of experience in English reinforce each other. Tables like this one give impersonal data, but a teacher should never forget that behind the table there are children. The impersonal abstraction is useful as a summary, but unless it illuminates the individual cases of Johnny and Mary its value is purely academic.

[12] See, for example, G. H. Hildreth, "Information Tests for First Grade Children," *Childhood Education,* 9: 416–420, 1933; G. H. Hilliard and E. Troxell, "Informational Background as a Factor in Reading Readiness and Reading Progress," *Elementary School Journal,* 38: 255–263, 1937; L. Peck and L. E. McGlothlin, "Children's Information and Success in First-Grade Reading," *Journal of Educational Psychology,* 31: 653–664, 1940; P. V. Sangren, "Information Tests for Young Children," *Childhood Education,* 6: 70–77, 1929; F. T. Wilson, "Correlation of Information with Other Abilities and Traits in Grade One," *Elementary School Journal,* 37: 295–301, 1936.

TABLE 33

Factors that Influence Readiness to Read [13]

FACTORS THAT INFLUENCE READING READINESS AT THE PRE-READING LEVEL

ENVIRONMENT

1. Language spoken in the home
2. Reading situation in the home
3. Stability of the home
4. Range of experiences and training provided by
   Home
   Community agencies
5. Home-school cooperation

MATURATION

1. Chronological age
2. Mental maturity
3. Emotional maturity
4. Social maturity
5. Physical status: health, vision, hearing, eye-hand dominance
6. Speech

OBJECTIVES FOR READINESS TO READ

1. Breadth of experiences
2. Language development
   Adequate use of English: speaking vocabulary, accurate enunciation and pronunciation, use of English sentences.
   Comprehension of English: meaningful concepts, understanding and interpretation of stories heard, of conversation, of pictures, of oral directions, and the application of ideas to problems.
3. Audio-visual-motor skills: visual and auditory discrimination, sound blending, ocular-motor control, directional orientation, visual-auditory recall.
4. Study skills: simple library skills and desirable work habits.
5. Personal-social adaptability: care of self, satisfactory participation with a group, desire to read, wider and deeper interests, desirable attitudes, stability, and self-confidence.

[13] J. W. Wrightstone, "Appraisal of Growth in Reading," *Educational Research Bulletin*, No. 2, 1941, 42 pp. (From page 8.) This material is used by permission of the Bureau of Reference, Research and Statistics, Board of Education of the City of New York.

B. INCREASING CHILDREN'S READINESS TO READ

Those children who are not yet ready to begin reading can be helped to become mature in less time than nature alone would produce the same result. They will develop in proportion as they have broadening experiences, since the degree of information that children have is one factor in helping them to learn how to read. Hence, activities that enlarge a child's background of information will be helpful in preparing him for reading. The time intervening between a pupil's entrance to school and the beginning of his formal work in reading should be used as constructively as possible. The projects in which he engages should be such as to help him become emotionally and socially as well as intellectually mature.[14] Some of the activities that are commonly suggested appear in the following list:

TABLE 34

Activities for Developing Reading Maturity

A. Looking

1. Examining and talking about objects
2. Describing objects seen for only a few seconds
3. Naming objects in a picture
4. Discriminating between two objects or patterns that are nearly alike
5. Estimating and comparing sizes, distances, or weights
6. Drawing simple designs from memory
7. Counting objects
8. Matching and sorting colors, designs, or objects

[14] See, for example: Berkeley Public School, "The Kindergarten and Reading Readiness," *American Childhood*, 20: 7–9, 1935; A. I. Gates, "The Pre-Reading and Reading Readiness Program," *Twentieth Yearbook of the Department of Elementary School Principals*, pp. 386–392, 1941; W. H. Johnson, "Pre-Reading Program of the Chicago Public Schools," *Elementary School Journal*, 40: 37–44, 1940, and "Development of the Chicago Program to Aid Pupils Lacking Reading Readiness," *ibid.*, 42: 337–346, 1942; C. E. Manwiller, "Differences in Emphasis on Experiences and Concepts in Readers," *Pittsburgh Schools*, 13: 65–98, 1939; M. Monroe, "A Program to Develop Reading Readiness in Grade One," *Seventeenth Yearbook of the Department of Elementary School Principals*, pp. 273–281, 1938; M. Semmelmeyer, "Promoting Readiness for Reading and for Growth in the Interpretation of Meaning," *Supplementary Education Monographs*, No. 51, pp. 56–62, 1940; E. R. Shank, "Reading Readiness Activities for Slow Children in Grade One," *Twentieth Yearbook of the Department of Elementary School Principals*, pp. 393–399, 1941; L. Teegarten, "Clinical Identification of the Prospective Nonreader," *Child Development*, 3: 346–358, 1932; C. Tutt, "The Preprimer Period," *Childhood Education*, 9: 464–467, 1933; D. Waters, "Pre-Reading Experience," *Education*, 54: 308–312, 1934; L. S. Wright, *The First Grade at Work: A Non-Reading Curriculum*, Bureau of Publications, Teachers College, Columbia University, 1932, 247 pp.

B. Talking

   9. Retelling a story already heard
  10. Describing a picture
  11. Describing an absent object for other children to guess what it is
  12. Choral speaking
  13. Answering questions about a story
  14. Bringing something to school and talking about it
  15. Going on excursions and discussing what was seen

C. Hearing

  16. Carrying out oral directions
  17. Imitating sounds
  18. Discriminating between sounds or tones
  19. Discriminating between letter sounds or syllables

D. Training the muscles

  20. Imitating tapping or other simple movement
  21. Practicing simple rhythmic games
  22. Coloring pictures
  23. Making scrapbooks
  24. Tracing forms, letters, figures, or words
  25. Cutting out and pasting
  26. Copying one's own name
  27. Sorting cards or other objects into compartments

E. Getting ready to read

  28. Arranging letter blocks so as to copy model words
  29. Differentiating between pairs of letters often confused
  30. Copying words already on blackboard
  31. Looking at alphabet books in which each letter is illustrated by one
      word and a picture (*a* is for *ant*, *b* is for *barn*, *c* is for *cat*, etc.)
  32. Looking at attractive picture books
  33. Naming the letters

F. Thinking

  34. Solving simple puzzles
  35. Arranging form boards
  36. Making designs with peg boards
  37. Memorizing jingles, songs, or poems
  38. Deciding upon a story to tell the class

Such activities give children a host of new experiences, practice in working together, and plenty of chances to think. The exercises automatically

point out failures to see or hear well enough for purposes of reading or intellectual handicaps that would interfere with comprehension. Not every child will be interested in every activity, but the total program should be sufficiently stimulating to make the children want to begin reading as soon as possible.

Below appears the case study of an immature child, showing what happens when reading is presented to a pupil who is not yet ready for it.

George was nearly eight years old and in the high-second grade. The teacher reported him as being in constant, but not very serious, disciplinary difficulties. He was also extremely self-conscious, especially about reading, and occasionally became sullen and rebellious when asked to read. When George was tested he showed an I.Q. of 87 and reading ability below the first-grade average. A study of George's school history revealed that he had entered school four months before he was six years old. If, as is probable, he had approximately the same I.Q. as at the time he was tested, his mental age at his entrance to school would have been approximately five years. Throughout the first grade he showed an inability to remember words. This is not surprising in view of his mental development at the time. Moreover, he had a slight speech defect, although it is not clear whether this defect preceded or followed his first efforts at reading. In any case, his failure to pronounce words correctly would be a contributing cause of his inability to learn them. During the first grade George had liked his teacher, but he disliked the teacher of the second grade. His history and behavior suggested that he had been originally too immature to learn reading, that he had been further handicapped by babyish speech, with a resulting failure in his first efforts at reading. This situation had made him self-conscious and unhappy. His dislike for the second-grade teacher, combined with his handicaps, seems to have precipitated his mischievous behavior and his rebelliousness toward reading. George was given forty minutes of training daily for five and one-half months. At the time the training began, he had a mental age of six years and seven months, or approximately the lower limit of mental development necessary for learning to read. At the end of the training his mental age was over seven. He was, then, during the high-second grade just ready to begin reading. His progress during this time was rapid. By the end of the training period, George was reading well enough to go back into his regular class, and his misconduct had disappeared. There appears to have been nothing whatever the matter with this child except that he had immature mentality, immature speech, and immature emotional reactions at the time when he was first given instruction in reading.[15]

---

[15] C. R. Stone, "A Non-Reader Learns to Read," *Elementary School Journal*, 30: 142–146, 1929. Used by permission of the publisher.

C. PREDICTION IN THE FIRST GRADE

The prediction of success or failure in first grade reading is already good and will presumably become better as tests of readiness and methods of teaching improve. Tests of readiness have proven their usefulness [16] as bases for grouping children at entrance to school into those who should learn rapidly and read a great deal, those whose progress will be average, and those who are not yet ready to begin. The first group is often penalized by too slow a start and too deliberate a rate of progress. Children who are ready for reading and have already begun to peep into books at home should not be held back, because their fine enthusiasm may evaporate. As one bright child told his parents, "We don't learn to read yet. We just play being butterflies. And I *don't want* to be a butterfly. I want to read." On the other hand, the immature children are likely to develop most undesirable emotional attitudes toward reading if they are confronted with formal instruction too soon. In general, readiness tests predict success reasonably well. Thus after four months of instruction, the correlations between readiness test scores and reading achievement scores were for seven groups of children, .89, .81, .78, .69, .61, .59, and .51, with an average of .71.

Results from one experiment [17] show clearly the relationship between readiness and success. On the basis of the tests, the children were placed into four groups. The table gives the average score and range of scores per group, the average IQ, mental age, and chronological age, and the average score on reading tests at the end of the year. The children in the first two groups and a few of those in the third reached or exceeded the standard score of 76 points on the reading test. Most of those in Group III and all in Group IV failed to reach it. From this evidence the investigator concluded that an IQ of 105 or more, a mental age of at least 6 years 8 months, and a chronological age of 6 years

---

[16] R. H. Beall, "Identifying Mature and Immature First-Grade Entrants," *Seventeenth Yearbook of the Department of Elementary School Principals*, pp. 255–263, 1938; E. C. Deputy, "Predicting First Grade Reading Achievement," *Teachers College Contributions to Education*, No. 426, 1930, 62 pp.; A. I. Gates, "Prediction of Ability and Disability in Reading," *Psychological Bulletin*, 35: 669–670, 1938, Gates "An Experimental Evaluation of Reading Readiness Tests," *Elementary School Journal*, 39: 497–508, 1939, and "A Further Evaluation of Reading Readiness Tests," *Elementary School Journal*, 40: 577–591, 1940; O. E. Ring, "Effectiveness of a Reading Readiness Program as Shown by Results with Standard Tests," *California Journal of Elementary Education*, 9: 91–96, 1940; S. Roslow, "Reading Readiness and Reading Achievement in the First Grade," *Journal of Experimental Education*, 9: 154–159, 1941.

[17] Beall, *op. cit.* Used by permission of the publisher.

TABLE 35

Readiness Scores and Achievement in Reading

Group	Number of Pupils	Range and Average on Readiness Tests	IQ	MA	CA	Average Reading Achievement Score at End of Year
I	370	90–119 Av. = 98	110	7 yrs. 4 mos.	6 yrs. 6 mos.	87
II	376	75–89 Ave. = 82	108	6 yrs. 10 mos.	6 yrs. 5 mos.	79
III	318	60–74 Av. = 67	103	6 yrs. 5 mos.	6 yrs. 4 mos.	68
IV	261	0–59	92	5 yrs. 9 mos.	6 yrs. 4 mos.	44

5 months were necessary if a child were to be successful in learning to read by the usual group instruction.

In some school districts almost the entire entering class is too immature and too inexperienced to begin reading. A postponement of reading for a semester for all but a few has been found valuable [18] in terms of the subsequent gains made after instruction was begun. Presumably, the postponement prevented the hopeless discouragement that small children develop when they begin their efforts too soon. Several weeks of trying very hard, day after day, and meeting only failure result in a crushing of the spirit and the development of a firm conviction that reading can never, never be learned. Since the postponement would allow the children to become more mature, it would prevent discouragement and therefore produce better reading in the end.

D. FIRST GRADE INSTRUCTION

The teaching of reading in the first grade for those who are ready to learn has changed a good deal from the traditional method of reading sentence by sentence orally until the children had almost memorized their primers. In general, children are taught short phrases first, then words, and letters or syllables only after they have learned to recognize the larger units. Children learn phrases or words by remembering their outlines, not by studying the letters. Since a short phrase gives an even

[18] See, for example, J. L. Thomson, "Big Gains from Postponed Reading," *Journal of Education*, 117: 445–446, 1934; A. I. Gates and D. H. Russell, "The Effect of Delaying Beginning Reading a Half-Year in the Case of Under-privileged Children," *Journal of Educational Research*, 32: 321–328, 1939.

more characteristic outline than a single word, it is remembered better. At entrance to school, 78 per cent of children can retain phrases shown them, but only 25 per cent of them remember individual words shown them and still smaller per cents—11 and 7, respectively—retain syllables and letters.[19] Such a phrase as *happy children* has an outline so distinctive that it is easy to remember. A single long word, such as *gingerbread* or *butterfly* may also be distinctive, but words like *these, those, this, them, three, thin, than,* and *then* are constantly being confused because they look alike.

Often the teaching of reading is integrated with numerous activities in which the children show an interest. For instance, in one first grade room the children kept a diary of each day's events.[20] The teacher wrote the sentences, but at the children's dictation and after much discussion of the proper content and study of words and phrases on the blackboard. The children spontaneously read through the diary often and with great enjoyment. This record contained a total of 3,407 words —of which there were 603 different words and 280 numerals. Such indirect approaches to reading are sometimes found more productive than more direct, formal teaching.[21] Another first grade teacher encouraged the children to dictate to her short "poems" about their experiences and activities. The pupils then learned to read the poems, which they knew almost by heart anyway, by the time they were dictated in their final form. A sample production is shown below:

> This is our room
> We shall work and play
> All, all the day.[22]

Not everyone, however, agrees with the advantages of the indirect approach, and certainly its superiority, if real, is far from being proved.[23]

A comparison of a "direct" versus a "preparatory" approach to

[19] J. E. Ségers, *La psychologie de la lecture et l'imitation à la lecture par la méthode globale, Anvers,* 1939, 394 pp.
[20] Sister Richardine and F. T. Wilson, "A Reading Activity in Grade One," *Elementary English Review,* 15: 129–132, 160, 1938.
[21] M. M. Hobson, "Introducing Reading through First-Grade Activities," *Seventeenth Yearbook of the Department of Elementary School Principals,* pp. 298–304, 1938; J. E. Dickson and N. E. McLean, "An Integrated Activity Program Try-out in the First Grade of the Public School," *Education Method,* 9: 31–42, 1929.
[22] M. Kallen, "Beginning Reading Experiences in the New School," *Elementary English Review,* 16: 27–30, 1939.
[23] See, for instance, C. R. Stone, "The Current Experience Method of Beginning Reading," *Elementary School Journal,* 36: 105–109, 1935; and J. M. Lee, "Reading Achievement in First Grade Activity Programs," *ibid.,* 33: 447–451, 1933.

beginning reading favors the former by a considerable margin,[24] especially in the development of comprehension. The nature of the two programs is outlined in Table 36.

TABLE 36

Descriptions of Two Methods for Teaching Reading

Direct Method	*Preparatory Method*
1. The initial period of general reading readiness activities is replaced by immediate meaningful experiences and reading from books.	1. A period of general reading readiness activities at the beginning of the school year, designed to stimulate a desire for reading, to provide experiences which will aid in the preparation for reading, and to introduce a basic reading vocabulary through informal reading procedures.
2. Each selection read is treated as a literary whole, with the acquisition of reading skills subordinated to the getting and retaining of meanings.	2. A subsequent program of daily instruction in reading from books and supplementary materials.
3. Skill and expertness in getting the author's directions is provided for by means of skill-development-activities supplementary to the reading process, and including (a) the development of a meaningful sight vocabulary; (b) the independent recognition of words; (c) testing for comprehension of form, content, meaning; and (d) oral reading practice in portraying meanings to others.	3. Skill-development-activities are a part of the basic reading program and are provided for through seat work, involving vocabulary drills for recognition, methods of independent recognition of words, and testing for comprehension.
4. The year's instruction in reading is characterized by a series of wholes composed of (a) meaningful preparatory activities *specific* to the selection to be read and involving those experiences and vocabulary necessary for full appreciation of the selection; (b) reading of the selection as a whole, followed by the reading and understanding of its parts; (c) supplementary skill-development-activities; (d) re-reading of the selection as a whole, for the retention and clarification of the acquired meanings of vocabulary and information, and for practice in portraying meanings to others.	4. The year's instruction in reading is characterized by (a) the period of general reading readiness or pre-book program; and (b) a period of more or less formal reading instruction from books for the remainder of the school year.

The preparatory method is the traditional one. For dull children it seems definitely inferior, and somewhat inferior for those of average ability. Bright children learn as well one way as another—they generally do!

A distinctly modern idea is the teaching of beginning reading by

[24] L. K. Dice, "An Experimental Study of Two Methods of Teaching Beginning Reading," *Johns Hopkins University Studies in Education*, No. 32, 1942, 92 pp. See also J. W. Carr, "The Approach to Reading as a Meaningful Process," *Elementary English Review*, 13: 145–146, 1936.

means of moving pictures.[25] The film consists of single words, sometimes with pictures of the objects they represent, accompanied by the
pronunciation of the word and some explanation of its meaning. The·
screen thus becomes an animated blackboard. Films of this kind should
be helpful, because children enjoy them so much and attend to them
better than to what the teacher tells them in class. Silent films for
improving the width of the reading span are also available for children
in the upper grades who already know the words but do not yet read
by phrases.

There is some difference of opinion as to the extent to which oral
reading is to be used in the first grade. Of course, word study is oral;
the matter at issue concerns the advisability of letting children read
connected material aloud. Some teachers feel that all actual reading
should be silent, and a few more or less complete systems for non-oral
instruction have been devised.[26] The pupils learn by what one author
calls the "look-and-see" rather than "look-and-say" method. For example,
the teacher, after teaching the necessary words or phrases at the blackboard, gives a pupil a card on which is printed such a sentence as:
Please stand up beside your desk. The pupil does not read the card
aloud, but if he understands, he gets up. Children taught by such non-
oral techniques are sometimes reported as making more progress than
is usual under the traditional methods of mixed oral and silent reading.

E. READINESS TO READ AT HIGHER LEVELS IN SCHOOL

As stated earlier in the chapter, readiness to read can and should be
measured at the beginning of each new level of work. In the following
brief description it will be assumed that the achievement necessary for
all lower levels is included in each of the upper levels.

1. **Readiness for the Second Grade:** At the beginning of the second
year of elementary school a pupil needs an intelligence of not less
than seven years and a vocabulary of not less than six hundred words.

[25] I. H. Anderson and W. F. Dearborn, "A Sound-Motion Picture Technique for
Teaching Beginning Reading," *School and Society,* 52: 367–369, 1940.
[26] For instance, E. E. Keener, "Teaching Primary Reading by a Non-oral Procedure,"
Elementary English Review, 15: 291–292, 308, 1938; J. E. McDade, "Beginning Reading
by a Non-oral Method," *Seventeenth Yearbook of the Department of Elementary School
Principals,* pp. 305–312, 1938; N. B. Smith, *American Reading Instruction,* Silver Burdett
and Company, 1934, 287 pp. See also, by the same author, *The Unit Activities Reading
Series, Teachers Guide for the First Year,* Silver Burdett and Company, 1937, 21 pp.

His vocalizing should not be loud, although a faint whisper with lip movement is permissible. Four brief informal tests for measuring skills that should have been acquired in the first grade are described below.

(a) The first test is extremely simple. The child should know the name—not the sound—of every letter in the alphabet. He does not need to know them in their alphabetical order. If he does not know the names, he will not understand what his teacher means when she tells him he has left out an *r*, or a *b*, or some other letter in pronunciation.

(b) The second test requires merely the sounding of each consonant in the alphabet. The teacher shows the pupil each letter and asks him to sound it. She also presents him with the common initial combinations of letters: *sh, th, wh, ch, pr, br, cr, wr, tw, cl, pl*, and *bl*. He should make no errors on the single letters and not more than three on the blends.

(c) The third test measures his ability to fuse sounds into words. For this test the teacher uses such a list of words as presented below.

and	when	fast	stop	tame
think	baby	man	left	not
did	good	paid	him	red

She pronounces to the child the successive sounds within each word, sounding each separately and clearly *without the slightest fusion*. For the word *and*, for instance, she first pronounces a short *a* and pauses; then she pronounces the *n* and pauses again; finally she sounds the *d*. The child should be able to fuse the sounds of any word as familiar as those listed above, provided the component sounds are given to him. He should not, of course, see the words.

(d) The last measure is a test of sentence comprehension. A teacher may best use the relevant section of the Gates Primary Reading Tests, but she can test children with sentences selected from first grade readers. A pupil should be able to get meaning from typical sentences of this early level before he attempts more difficult material.

It will be noticed that the main emphasis at this stage is upon knowledge of sounds and mastery of a small but fundamental vocabulary.

2. **Readiness to Read in the Fourth Grade:** [27] So little research has been done in regard to readiness in the fourth grade that one can make only a few suggestions as to what some of the standards for entrance

[27] See, for instance, M. L. Harrison, "Reading Readiness at All Educational Levels," *Peabody Journal of Education*, 16: 167–175, 1938; J. L. Hahn, "Reading Readiness in the Third Grade," *Childhood Education*, 40: 179–180, 1935.

might be. A pupil would presumably need a mental age of not less than 9 years and a general reading vocabulary of not less than 2,000 words. He should be able to read second grade material with not more than 130 fixations per 100 words and not more than 30 regressions, with a speed of not less than 125 words a minute. His vocalizing should not be more than a vibration of the vocal cords, without whispering or lip movement. He should be able to get meaning from both sentences and short paragraphs of third grade difficulty. Not much more can be said at the present time, but sooner or later some one will doubtless make a test for readiness to enter the intermediate grades.

F. SUMMARY

Measurement of readiness to read is relatively new and marks an important step forward. Prevention of reading difficulty by postponement of the first efforts until each child is ready should prove to be a great deal more effective than even the best efforts to cure already established habits of either specific reaction or emotional response. Those pupils who are not yet ready to read can be accelerated in their normal course of development by appropriate treatment. Although readiness is a cardinal problem in Grade 1, it continues to be important at all levels whenever a new subject or new section within a subject is to be introduced.

VII · Remedial Work in Reading[1]

One of the relatively new developments in schoolwork is the class in remedial reading, which has made its appearance at all levels from the primary grades to the upper years of college. Among 300 colleges in 1933, 185 already had classes of this type and 73 more had plans for establishing them as soon as possible.[2] A little over 5 per cent of freshmen appear unable to read their texts without assistance.[3] In the school year 1938–1939, a total of 10,000 elementary and high school pupils were sent to 88 school clinics for diagnosis of their inability to read.[4] The remedial work obviously must meet an acute need, or it would hardly have developed so rapidly in so short a time. Presumably it is an attempted solution for a problem that inevitably arises from the modern policy of promoting almost every child every year. The arguments in favor of the policy justify its widespread acceptance, but the wholesale promotions do send children into the upper grades before some of them have sufficiently mastered the elementary skills they will need, of which the most important is reading.

---

[1] For general presentations of the subject, see, L. Cole, *The Improvement of Reading,* Farrar & Rinehart, Inc., 1938, 338 pp.; D. D. Durrell, *Improvement of Basic Reading Abilities,* World Book Company, 1940, 407 pp.; A. I. Gates, *The Improvement of Reading,* The Macmillan Company, 1935, rev. ed., 668 pp.; A. J. Harris, *How to Improve Reading Ability,* Longmans, Green & Co., 1940, 403 pp.; G. Hildreth and J. L. Wright, *Helping Children to Read,* Teachers College, Bureau of Publications, 1940, 90 pp.; S. A. Kirk, *Teaching Reading to Slow-Learning Children,* Houghton Mifflin Company, 1940, 225 pp.; J. M. McCallister, *Remedial and Corrective Instruction in Reading,* D. Appleton-Century Company, 1936, 300 pp.; P. A. Witty and D. Kopel, *Reading and the Education Process,* Ginn and Company, 1939, 374 pp.

Also excellent, although colored to some extent by their points of view, are G. M. Fernald, *Remedial Techniques in the Basic School Subjects,* McGraw-Hill Book Company, 1943, 349 pp., and M. Monroe, *Children Who Cannot Read,* University of Chicago Press, 1932, 205 pp.

[2] F. O. Triggs, "Remedial Reading Programs," *Journal of Educational Psychology,* 33: 678–685, 1942.

[3] R. L. McCaul, "The Cost of Remedial Reading Programs in Eighteen Colleges," *School and Society,* 56: 361–364, 1942.

[4] D. Kopel and H. Geerdes, "Survey of Clinical Service for Poor Readers," *Journal of Education Psychology,* 33: 209–220, 1942.

In elementary school, at least, a special teacher for children who have difficulty in learning to read will probably become a fixture, because the native endowments of children are so varied that any group method of instruction is almost certain to be inappropriate for some of the children. The most popular methods at the present time are largely visual and are not successful with those children who learn best by ear or by muscular training. Even with an excellent method there are sure to be a few children who get started wrong, develop one or more disastrously bad habits, and become convinced they cannot learn to read; without study, analysis, and remedial teaching they usually do not make much progress. The room teachers can do a little remedial work, but not a great deal, because most of their teaching has to be done with groups and remedial work is highly individual.

The even more recent interest in reading readiness will presumably result in a decrease in the number of children who have to be given remedial work, since it should prevent an appreciable number of failures. If children do not begin their work in reading until they are mature enough to have a good chance of success, not as many of them as is the case at present should develop clumsy and inept habits, or should become too discouraged and bewildered to make normal progress. It is, however, not likely that the remedial program can be dispensed with entirely as long as children are promoted by age rather than achievement.

In the school of forty years or more ago, remedial reading classes were not needed above the primary grades, because those pupils who got beyond Grade 3 were a well-selected group who had passed the rigid standards of the day. In one school in which the writer once worked, the average number of children entering the first grade was 75, but the average size of the graduating eighth grade class was 12. There were two first grade rooms, three second and three third grade rooms, two rooms for Grade 4, one each for Grades 5 and 6, and a combined room for Grades 7 and 8. The principal of the school used to boast that no pupil went from her school into high school without being adequately prepared. She was probably right. An eight-year elimination test that picks 12 children out of 75 ought not to make many mistakes. Most of the retarded children who swelled the ranks in the third and fourth grades were able to read, after a fashion at least, the material of the grade they were in, and they never progressed far enough to annoy teachers in the departmentalized subjects by their inability to read on a more advanced level. When, however, the promotion policy became more liberal, these children—perhaps better taught but no brighter—

appeared in large numbers in junior high and high school, and for a while no one knew just what to do with them. Because ability to read is so important, the remedial reading class was one of the first responses to the difference in pupil material.

In the writer's opinion, a more fundamental approach to the situation is now being made. Teachers are gradually realizing that learning to read is a continuous process that goes on from early childhood until well into adult life. As a pupil progresses through school he meets different kinds of reading matter, and he has to learn how to get meaning from each new type. The assumption that reading is a well-polished tool by the end of elementary school and that teachers of subsequent levels can assume ability to read has been thoroughly disproved. Teachers in junior high school, high school, and college now know that each instructor must teach at least the beginning classes in each subject how to get meaning from their assignments.[5] Language teachers have to show students how to read and study grammars, chemistry teachers have to help pupils both in reading the text and in understanding the problems, and history teachers need to teach both reading for essential ideas and notetaking. The teachers of English literature have known for a long time that they must give instruction in a more advanced type of reading than the pupils have been accustomed to. When, and if, all teachers regard training in reading skill as part of their normal work, remedial reading classes above elementary school should not be needed, because each teacher will contribute her own elements of training. In the meantime, these classes can serve as a stopgap until the materials, methods, and added knowledge that are coming from them are incorporated into the routine work of the subject-matter teachers.

A. THE CAUSES OF POOR READING

There are almost as many opinions as to the causes of failure in reading as there are investigators. Some stress physical causes—such as poor eyesight or mixed dominance; others favor emotional causes; some regard non-readers as merely immature; and still others blame the methods by which children have been taught. There are probably not as many reasons as there are poor readers, but the constellation of causes is certainly different for every child. Many of the difficulties are no more serious than those met by children who learn to read, but for some

[5] See G. O. Blough, "They Can't Read," *School Science and Mathematics,* 38: 627–632, 1938.

reason the failing child cannot solve his problems. In some cases, his woes are simple enough, but there are merely too many of them. Failure to read can be caused by a single bad habit, such as trying to read from right to left, but it can also be caused by the jealousy of an older child for a younger one. Sometimes poor reading is a cause of other difficulties, and sometimes it is caused by them. The only safe assumption to make is that each child in the remedial class is a unique organism, whose failure to read is a by-product of some condition within him that has been intensified by some condition outside him.

A list of possible causes is perhaps worth giving, provided the teacher remembers that a list is only an abstraction and that when she meets the difficulties they will be clothed in flesh and blood, and provided also that she regards the list as tentative and subject to change.[6] The causes have been grouped under four general heads as being physical, intellectual, emotional, or methodological.

TABLE 37

Causes of Poor Reading

I. Physical conditions that tend to influence reading adversely

    A. Defects of eyesight that lead to a blurring of visual images

    B. Visual immaturity

    C. Blurred hearing or failure to hear some of the tones

    D. Left-handedness, especially when combined with preference for the right eye

---

[6] The list is based upon a number of references: A. Bennett, "Launching a Reading Project," *Journal of Exceptional Children*, 5: 121–125, 1939; C. C. Bennett, "An Inquiry into the Genesis of Poor Reading," *Teachers College Contributions to Education*, No. 755, 1939, 139 pp.; G. L. Bond, "The Auditory and Speech Characteristics of Poor Readers," *ibid.*, No. 657, 1935, 48 pp.; R. C. Challman, "Personality Adjustment and Remedial Reading," *Journal of Exceptional Children*, 6: 7–12, 1939; W. F. Dearborn, "Remedial Reading: Case Studies and Recent Experimentation," *Supplementary Educational Monographs*, No. 49, pp. 110–118, 1939; P. Fendrick, "Visual Characteristics of Poor Readers," *Teachers College Contributions to Education*, No. 656, 1935, 54 pp.; A. I. Gates, "The Role of Personality Maladjustment in Reading Disabilities," *Journal of Genetic Psychology*, 59: 77–83, 1941; R. E. Hemphill and E. Stengel, "A Study of Pure Word-Deafness," *Journal of Neurology and Psychiatry*, 3: 251–262, 1940; J. Jastak, "Interference in Reading," *Psychology Bulletin*, 31: 244–272, 1934; M. R. Ladd, "The Relation of Social, Economic, and Personal Characteristics to Reading Ability," *Teachers College Contributions to Education*, No. 582, 1933, 100 pp.; M. I. Preston, "Reading Failures and the Child's Security," *American Journal of Orthopsychiatry*, 10: 239–253, 1940; H. M. Robinson, "Types of Deficient Readers and Methods of Treatment," *Supplementary Educational Monographs*, No. 49, pp. 159–169, 1939; M. Sherman, "Emotional Disturbances and Reading Disability," *Supplementary Educational Monographs*, No. 49, pp. 126–134, 1939; S. V. Wilking, "Personality Maladjustment as a Causative Factor in Reading Disability," *Elementary School Journal*, 42: 268–279, 1941; G. A. Yoakum, "The Improvement of Reading in the Middle Grades," *Education*, 56: 1–6, 1935.

    E. True word deafness or blindness*
    F. Speech defects
    G. Glandular disturbances
    H. Nervousness or neuropsychiatric disorders
    I. Slower physical development among boys

II. Intellectual conditions that tend to influence reading adversely
    A. Low intelligence
    B. Poor memory for visual patterns
    C. Bilingualism or other environmental cause for defective growth in language
    D. Short attention span
    E. Meagre vocabulary
    F. Failure to associate symbols and sounds
    G. Inability to select and discriminate between ideas
    H. Poor memory for ideas
    I. Failure to react to what is read

III. Emotional conditions that tend to influence reading adversely
    A. Insecurity in school or home
    B. Tension, anxiety, worry, or fear (often induced by reading failure during the first few weeks of school)
    C. Emotional immaturity
    D. Lack of interest in reading materials used to date
    E. Lack of persistence
    F. Tendency to be inactive, withdrawn, and solitary
    G. Abnormal attitude toward reading (dislike, jealousy of better readers, antagonism, defeatism, embarrassment, etc.)
    H. Fear of attacking new words

IV. Methodological conditions that tend to influence reading adversely
    A. Overemphasis upon visual instruction for a child with poor visual equipment
    B. Overemphasis upon phonics for a child with poor auditory equipment
    C. Pressure for speed at too early an age
    D. Overencouragement of guessing from context
    E. Lack of method for attacking new words
    F. Lack of training in locating data, in using dictionaries, etc.

---

* This cause is rare, if it exists at all, but until it has been proved a chimera, it has to be listed.

Most of the physical causes have already been discussed. The complete non-readers, aside from mental defectives, are almost exclusively boys, and the great majority of poor readers are also boys. In some remedial groups there are seven boys to every girl, and the proportion is almost never less than seven to three. Throughout their school careers boys are inferior to girls in anything pertaining to language—reading, spelling, composition, foreign language, literature—and boys are superior to girls in anything mathematical or scientific. There is abundant proof that boys develop physically, intellectually, and emotionally more slowly than girls. They mature later, they grow more slowly, their bones ossify at a slower rate, their interests are less mature, their mental and emotional development is more gradual. Since they are already nearly a year behind girls in physical growth at entrance to school, more of them are visually, mentally, and emotionally too immature to learn to read. Consequently, more of them become reading failures.

Nervousness is mentioned only rather casually, if at all, by many investigators, and is often confused with or at least lumped with emotionality. Nervous children may or may not be also emotional, but the two conditions are by no means synonymous. Usually these children have so little inhibition that no emotion is ever suppressed long enough to develop into a complex! They do not generally show abnormal behavior; they simply show too much ordinary behavior. A nervous child sometimes becomes a poor reader because he, or more likely she, is inattentive and easily fatigued. Reading is an especially confining task for those who, with the best of intentions, cannot keep still for more than a few moments at a time.

Perfectly healthy people rarely understand the problems of nervousness. A nervous child is so sensitive to all stimuli that he is constantly overstimulated and cannot relax. In fact, his essential difficulty is a constant nervous tension which produces abnormally early fatigue and prevents normal relaxation. He cannot relax enough to sleep at night or to digest his food properly. As a consequence, his vitality is low, and he is more susceptible to infection than are other children; by the end of an ordinary school day he is pale, his hands are unsteady, his eyes are abnormally bright, and he is in general "wound up" so tight that he cannot stop his activity. The nervous child further shows his condition by becoming excited much too easily and by being overeager to participate in whatever is going on. For example, if he knows the answer to a question, he not only waves his hand frantically but jumps up out of his seat and—if not promptly called upon—shouts the answer anyway. He is far too active; the most difficult thing in the world for him is to sit still. From a teacher's point of view his most bothersome symptoms are undoubtedly his inability to stop talking and his constant squirming. When a teacher stimulates her class by telling them how anxious she is to have them do their best, the nervous child overacts to her remarks and starts a terrific flurry of work. Before school is over, he is irritable, jumpy, and quite unable to concentrate.

Poor ability to visualize or to remember visual patterns is not accepted by some investigators as a cause of poor reading, but the author believes it to be valid, at least in extreme cases. Most people can remember the pattern made by such a word as *butterfly,* but there are individuals who cannot remember well enough to call it to mind or even to recognize it. Such a person learns to read by storing up auditory and kinesthetic memories to reinforce his weak visualizing powers.

In some instances a child does not learn to read because he is emotionally distracted and under tension from some situation in either home or school. For instance, one very shy boy was seated facing the rest of the class on the first day of school because all the regular seats were filled and the extra chairs happened to have been set down facing the other pupils. For the first two weeks he was in an agony of embarrassment and learned nothing. If the janitor had not accidentally placed the chair at the back of the room one day, the child might not have learned to read, merely because he was so miserable. More often, however, the emotion comes after a failure to read and is a result rather than a cause. The fundamental difficulty is usually intellectual or physical immaturity, dulled hearing, blurred vision, or inattention—but the failure to learn soon precipitates emotional symptoms that obscure the original source of trouble. A pupil may be apprehensive and fearful, he may be worried and harassed, he may accept defeat and become convinced of his inferiority, he may quietly withdraw from something he does not understand, he may decide that reading is not worth the trouble it takes to learn, or he may become fiercely aggressive and combative. The reactions depend on what kind of person he is, but once they have developed they will block further learning, even though the original handicap may no longer exist. A few children fail to learn because they are emotionally disturbed, but most poor readers are emotionally disturbed because they failed to learn.

Sometimes the method used in a school, while excellent in itself, is not appropriate for some child in the class. In other instances, a teacher unintentionally overemphasizes some one element in her teaching—such as guessing the meaning of words from context—and immature pupils get the idea that guessing is all there is to the business of reading. Thus, an excellent method may become a handicap for a child who has misunderstood its nature and purpose. It is interesting to note the results of two parallel studies [7] of defects that characterized two groups of poor readers. In the schools that used a largely visual method the children with visual defects failed to make progress, whereas in the schools that emphasized phonics, the poor readers were those who did not hear well.

Although inability to read well enough to keep up with assignments is a phenomenon at all levels in school, the particular symptoms by means of which an inadequacy makes itself felt vary more or less from one grade to another. The elementary school levels have been well characterized as follows:

The composite *first year* reading problem, then, is a child essentially immature—physically, intellectually, or emotionally. He has been forced into intellectual activity—learning to read—for which he is not prepared. He is inattentive and, eager as he may have been to go to school, by the end of the first term he dislikes reading very much. He has also begun to develop habits of evasion or "cover up," or else, trying desperately to read, has begun those erratic mechanical habits which are fully evident only later and by then are chronic.

In the *second and third years,* when it is assumed that the child has acquired the mechanics of reading, reading failure is usually interpreted in terms of the mechanical difficulties observed. Reversals, confusions of similar forms, omissions and substitutions of letters, words, or phrases are common at this level. In the *third year,* such deficiencies take on an acute character because so much more is demanded than the poor reader can perform. This is the point at which the "no phonic ability, word-reading, poor visual discrimination" complaints are most numerous. Here, too, lack of interest is evident.

In the *fourth year,* inability to comprehend reading materials becomes marked and, in the *fifth and sixth years,* increases in seriousness as the scope of reading expands. "Reads words instead of thoughts," "limited vocabulary," are typical reports. The difficulty is often attributed to attitude: "Can't concentrate," "lethargic," "nervous," "not interested." The inability to attack words independently and specific mechanical difficulties, such as reversals and confusions, are recognized as very serious if they persist at this level.

Beyond the sixth year, reading failure is most generally identified with weakness in one or another of the many types of comprehension demanded in these grades. The child who has not learned from the beginning to extract

[7] Bond, *op. cit.* and Fendrick, *op. cit.*

the fullest meaning from his reading is often penalized in these upper grades where he is called upon to interpret a wider range of materials.[8]

The variation in symptoms is of course caused by the differences in the demands made upon pupils by the nature of the work in successive grades.

A word should perhaps be said about the complete non-reader—the otherwise normal boy who cannot recognize as many as ten words after one to five years of honest effort. Such a pupil requires expert assistance. He has already shown that he cannot profit by the usual instruction. If possible he should be sent to a reading clinic, or, if that is not possible, the teacher should write to a reading clinic, describing the boy and asking for instructions as to how to deal with him.[9] A thorough physical examination is also essential.

As can be appreciated, there is no one "cause" for poor reading. Moreover, most of the possible causes are neither unique nor bizarre. They are the same defects and handicaps from which the rest of the human race also suffers. Even severe visual defects, for instance, do not necessarily keep children from reading. The writer knows one boy with a nystagmus who does detailed and accurate statistical work, reads easily, and is even a good draftsman. Yet his younger brother, who had only a slight astigmatism, became a non-reader. At the present stage of knowledge one can give only two general explanations as to why one child fails to learn and an equally handicapped pupil gets along all right. First, some children learn early to compensate for a defect, thus avoiding some of its direct effects and almost all of its emotional concomitants. Second, one constellation of difficulties may prevent learning, while another that looks equally severe from the outside does not—and nobody knows why.

[8] From page 9 of M. Lazar, "A Diagnostic Approach to the Reading Program, Part I," *Educational Research Bulletin,* No. 3, 1942, 25 pp. Quoted by permission of the publisher.

[9] For descriptions and discussions of the non-reader, see, T. H. Eames and R. W. Peabody, "A Nonreader Reads," *Journal of Educational Research,* 28: 450–455, 1935; G. M. Fernald and H. Keller, "The Effect of Kinaesthetic Factors in the Development of Word Recognition in the Case of Non-Readers," *ibid.,* 4: 355–377, 1921; C. A. Ford, "Methods and Results of Teaching a Case of Congenital Word-Blindness," *Psychological Clinic,* 17: 226–233, 1929; A. I. Gates, "Diagnosis and Treatment of Extreme Cases of Reading Disability," *Thirty-sixth Yearbook of the National Society for the Study of Education,* Part I, pp. 391–418, 1937; B. Loudon and G. Arthur, "An Application of the Fernald Method to an Extreme Case of Reading Disability," *Elementary School Journal,* 40: 599–606, 1940; H. M. Robinson, "Treatment of Severe Cases of Reading Disabilities," *Journal of Educational Research,* 32: 531–535, 1939; M. A. Tinker, "Remedial Methods for Non-Readers," *School and Society,* 40: 524–526, 1934.

B. DIAGNOSIS OF READING DIFFICULTY

When a child is sent to a remedial reading teacher, her first task is to find out what is the matter with him. In order to do so, she makes a case history, collecting all relevant facts from numerous sources and giving whatever tests she considers desirable. The outline of a typical history appears in Table 38.

TABLE 38

Plan for Diagnosis of Inabilities in Reading

I. Sensory equipment
   A. Defects of eyesight . . . .
      1. Glasses . . . .
   B. Defects of hearing . . . .
   C. Defects of speech . . . .
      1. Letters mispronounced . . . .
      2. Visual memory . . . .

II. Eye movements
   A. Number of fixations per line . . . .
   B. Number of regressions per line . . . .
   C. Percent of lines hit accurately at the beginning . . . .
   D. Length of span . . . .

III. Degree of vocalization

IV. Ability to read by phrases
   A. Length of longest phrase recognized in one fixation . . . .

V. Rate of reading
   A. Words per minute . . . .
   B. Type of material read . . . .

VI. Vocabulary
   A. Estimated size of general vocabulary . . . .
   B. Special vocabularies
      1. Arithmetic . . . .
      2. Geography . . . .
      3. History . . . .

VII. Comprehension
   A. For sentences ....
   B. For paragraphs ....
   C. For geography text ....
   D. For history text ....
   E. For arithmetic text ....
   F. Ability to get outline from expository matter ....
   G. Nature of errors in comprehension ....

VIII. Phonics
   A. Letters whose sounds are not known ....
   B. Ability to blend sounds into words ....
   C. Ability to divide words into syllables ....
   D. Ability to pronounce long and unfamiliar words ....
   E. Knowledge of prefixes ....
   F. Knowledge of suffixes ....
   G. Number and type of errors in oral reading ....

IX. Intelligence
   A. Mental age .... IQ ....
   B. Evidences of special defects ....

X. Interests
   A. Books read ....
   B. Hobbies ....
   C. Comics ....

XI. Attitudes
   A. Anxiety, inferiority, or other emotional attitudes toward read-
      ing ....
   B. Abnormal emotional attitudes toward school or family ....

XII. Physical condition
   A. Medical report ....
   B. Any symptoms noted during analysis ....
   C. Undue fatigue ....
   D. Nervousness ....
   E. Handedness ....
      1. Preferred eye ....
      2. Reversals ....

At a minimum a child should be given medical and optical examinations, plus a series of reading tests to determine any faults he may have in his eye movements, the degree of his vocalizing, the size of his vocabulary, his methods of attack upon new words, his knowledge of phonics, his ability to comprehend material of different types and levels of difficulty, and his emotional and intellectual attitudes toward reading.

The results of tests are often summarized in diagrams so made as to give a picture of a child's development along many lines. Figure 21 shows a few sample graphs. Those for Children A and B are expressed in terms of grade standing, those of C and D in terms of age. Child A was placed in the low third grade, his intelligence was that of an average child in the high third grade, his arithmetic scores placed him in the low third, his handwriting and spelling were high second, and his reading was high first. Child C had a chronological age of 10 years 6 months, a mental age of 10 years 3 months, a reading age of 8 years 8 months, an arithmetic age of 10 years, a spelling age of 10 years 7 months, and a general growth age (derived from measures of height, weight, and dentition) of 10 years 4 months. The other graphs are read in similar manner. Child A was placed in a grade below his native ability but in accordance with his reading, spelling, and handwriting scores. Whatever else was wrong with this child, he did not lack intelligence. Child B was somewhat retarded mentally, but not enough to explain his educational retardation. Child C was developing harmoniously except for reading. Child D was retarded in all lines, and his physical growth was paralleling his mental, not his chronological, age. These general summaries of a child's growth are useful because they give an over-all picture and prevent a remedial reading teacher from becoming so concentrated upon her single subject that she disregards growth in other fields.

Whatever methods are used and however general or detailed they may be, the results should be summarized and interpreted as a basis for beginning remedial work.

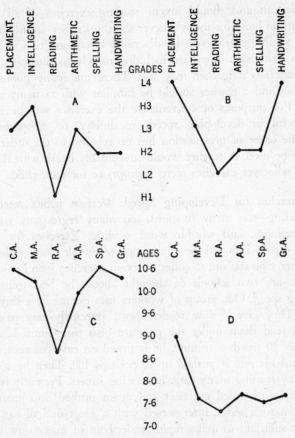

FIGURE 21: Relative Standing in Several Subjects

C. TREATMENT OF READING DISABILITIES

The teacher of the remedial room needs many types of reading matter, exercises, and techniques. She needs also to have good contacts with doctors, oculists, school nurses, social workers, visiting teachers, room teachers, and parents, because she often needs their services both in diagnosis and in treatment. She can, of course, carry out simple recommendations from these specialists, but she can hardly hope to be a specialist herself outside the strictly educational field. For instance, if an oculist sends directions for certain eye exercises for Mary Jane, the teacher can see that the child performs them, but she has no business inventing or assigning eye exercises on her own initiative. On the other hand, she can and should invent reading exercises of all kinds and have them on hand for use whenever she thinks they are needed.

The sample exercises to be described briefly are only a few of the hundreds that exist. They are included merely to illustrate the nature of the materials a teacher may use. There are many published series of exercises and a teacher should be familiar with as many of them as possible. For purposes of convenience the exercises will be grouped as being useful in developing speed, vocabulary, or comprehension, although the order of presentation has no relation to the order in which they may be used. A teacher would presumably begin with the simplest forms of whatever exercises seem appropriate for each child.

1. Exercises for Developing Speed: Certain habits interfere with rapid reading—too many fixations, too many regressions, too small a span, vocalizing, and word-by-word reading. Exercises for increasing speed are directed toward the elimination of one or more of these causes. The teacher who sets out to collect relevant exercises soon becomes aware that there are two schools of thought about the best techniques for developing speed. One group of workers uses essentially a single, simple method. They give a slow reader short, extremely easy passages and have him read them under the pressure of a time limit. If his initial rate is only 80 words a minute, he is timed on easy passages of known length until his rate is pushed up to perhaps 100. Then he consolidates his gains by reading many easy, interesting stories. Presently he is given another series of timed exercises and again pushed into greater speed. Six or eight such series, interspersed with a great deal of easy reading, have been sufficient to make rapid readers out of many slow ones. The main motivation is the interest aroused by the wide reading, and the main training comes from practice, experience, and effort. The treatment is undiagnostic, but it often works.

If a teacher belongs to the school of thought that believes in specific drill for specific defects, she can select any of a number of exercises for slow readers. If she has a Metron-O-Scope she can use it to correct faulty eye movements or to give training in phrase reading.[10] Since the

---

[10] For evaluations of the usefulness of these machines, see, I. H. Anderson, "The Ophthalmograph and Metron-O-Scope Evaluated in the Light of Recent Research on the Psychology of Reading," *Teachers College Journal,* Terre Haute, Indiana, State Teachers College, 12: 60–63, 1941; E. B. Cason, "Mechanical Methods for Increasing Speed of Reading," *Teachers College Contributions to Education,* No. 878, 1943, 80 pp.; F. M. Garver and R. D. Matthews, "An Analysis of Research of the Speed Drills with the Metron-O-Scope to Increase Reading Rate," *Journal of Educational Psychology,* 30: 693–698, 1939; E. A. Taylor, *Controlled Reading,* University of Chicago Press, 1937, 367 pp. (Some of these authors "prove" the machines are valuable and others "prove" they are not!)

length of the exposure is regulated, the machine forces the child to read at a given rate. As he progresses, the machine is speeded up.

Many teachers, however, do not have machines and therefore find it necessary to use other types of exercise, preparing many of them for themselves. Three types are especially recommended for correcting faulty eye movements, vocalizing, and word-for-word reading.

For eye-movement drills, the pupils are grouped into pairs. One pupil in each pair is to read the first exercise while the other watches his eye movements in a mirror; after one pupil has finished an exercise, the two change places. It may seem that children in elementary school are not mature enough to watch each other in this way, but actually they are highly accurate. Moreover, they get great enjoyment out of the procedure and are stricter with each other than an adult would dare to be.

(1) The first drill consists of a sheet upon which single words have been placed in the manner shown just below. The pupil is to read the first word, slide his eyes along the line to the second, then to the third, fourth, and fifth, and then return along the diagonal to the beginning

boy	not	big	run	must
glad	and	child	city	out
look	bread	cut	and	just
play	arm	school	five	men
may	it	but	am	street
bird	half	black	bear	corn
to	any	soon	be	rain
white	still	try	most	of

(on reverse of sheet)

Test:	school	front	bread	sun	rain
	yellow	full	pretty	in	bird
	leg	city	friend	bush	funny
	sand	bread			

FIGURE 22: Eye-Movement Drill, Type (1)

of the next line. The child who is watching is instructed to stop his partner if he detects any extra fixations or regressions. At the end of the reading he shows his partner the words on the back of the page and asks him to pick out the ones he has just read. If the partner can pick out five words that he has seen from a dozen that he has not, he passes the exercise. This test is added to the drill to prevent a purely mechanical movement of the eyes and to put a small emphasis, even in the simplest drill, upon meaning. The children use as many such sheets as they need until each has read two exercises with not more than eight observable regressions per page and with enough word recognition to pass the brief tests.

(2) The second type of exercise consists of pages on which a brief incident is narrated, the story being broken up into groups of one long or two short words each, as shown just below. The reader is to look

The girl	looked	after her	brother	as he
ran into	the old	house.	Then she	followed
after him	as fast	as she	was able	to go.
In the	kitchen .	of the	house	mother
was just	taking	a cake	from the	big oven.
The cake	smelled	so good!	She gave	each one
of them	a thick	piece	and a	glass
of nice	cold milk.	Both the	children	were very
hungry,	and they	ate up	every	crumb
of cake	and all	the milk.	Then the	children
ran out	to the	garden.	Under an	apple tree
they began	to build	a little	play house	from some
boards	that were	left over	after the	new barn
had been	built.	For over	an hour	they kept
on working	but then	it was	too dark	to do
anything	more	until the	next day	so they
returned	to the	house.		

(on reverse of sheet)

1. What did the children eat?
2. What did the children start to build?
3. Why did they stop?

FIGURE 23: Eye-Movement Drill, Type (2)

once at each group of words. The pupil who is watching should stop his partner if he sees extra eye movements. The reader then begins the first line over again. His increased familiarity with the words will allow him to proceed further on each successive rereading. At the end of his reading, he answers three questions. To pass an exercise a pupil must have had not more than twelve regressions on the page and must have answered at least two of the questions correctly. The pupil is not only practicing correct eye movements, but he is also beginning the task of learning to read by phrases, and to get some meaning from what he reads.

(3) The third set of exercises in this series consists merely of paragraphs so typed that the lines are about equal in length to those in a book, and the distance between the lines is a little more than average. They should contain only the simplest possible words. Such an exercise appears in Figure 24. A child is to look first at about the second word in the first line, then move his eyes to the right about halfway to the middle of the line, then look at the middle, then about halfway from the middle to the end, and finally at about the second word from the end; that is, he is to make five fixations at approximately the same places on each line that he has been trained to look at—first with the isolated words and then with the phrases. His partner again checks him. Whenever the reader makes a regression he is to go back to the beginning of the story and start over. As his familiarity with the story increases, his

At our house we have five baby kittens. They are only three days old. One of them is all white. Two of them are white and black. One is all black. The other is black with a little bit of white under his chin; he also has white paws and a bit of white on each ear. All the kittens are still blind, so we do not know what color their eyes will be. Next week their eyes will open. Their mother has one blue eye and one yellow eye. Ever since the kittens were born their mother has been very busy. She has to feed them and keep them clean. Every day she washes each one from his head to the tip of his funny little tail. They are still so weak that they cannot stand up. Every time they try to get up they fall down again. All they do now is eat and sleep. But soon they will begin to play. Then we shall have lots of fun watching them play.

FIGURE 24: Eye-Movement Drill, Type (3)

(on reverse of sheet)

1. How many kittens were there?
2. How old were they?
3. What color were their eyes?
4. Could they stand up?
5. What did their mother do for them?

FIGURE 24: Eye-Movement Drill, Type (3)

eye movements will become approximately correct. At the end of his reading he should comprehend well enough to get at least four of the five questions right.

A teacher needs a file of such exercises, so that pupils may have many duplicate forms. Since the sheets are not marked, they may be used until they wear out. The children should get their own exercises from the file and put them back again.

To decrease vocalization, the teacher may use any variation of an extremely simple technique. The main thing is to render the speech mechanism incapable of pronouncing sounds, even partially. The easiest means of bringing about this result is to have a child put two fingers into his mouth, using them to separate his upper and lower teeth and to hold down his tongue. Nobody can articulate words with his mouth hanging open. If the child, through force of habit, moves his jaws to articulate, he bites his fingers. With the tongue and the jaws both under control, there will be no pronunciation. Instead of his fingers a child may use a ruler or a large-sized eraser. The fingers are better than either wood or rubber, however, partly because the pupil is unwilling to bite them and partly because he always has them with him! Another, if even less elegant procedure, is to let the child chew gum while he is reading. His speech mechanism then ceases to be a problem, not because it is at rest but because it is doing something else. Naturally, a pupil should not persist in these techniques until they become habits. They should be used only until the tendency to pronounce words has been broken.

To give drill in phrase reading a teacher can use a series of flash cards, upon each of which has been typed a phrase of known length. The number in the corner tells how many spaces wide the phrase is.

A few sample cards appear in Figure 25. The children may work in pairs, drilling each other, or each may work by himself. The teacher prepares enough cards so that she will have about five duplicate "decks" with phrases seven or eight spaces wide on each card and perhaps fifteen cards to a deck, which is held together with an elastic. A blank card on top tells the user how wide the spans are in each deck. This card also acts as a shield. The pupil removes the elastic but leaves the cards face up under the shield. Then he moves the shield aside and replaces

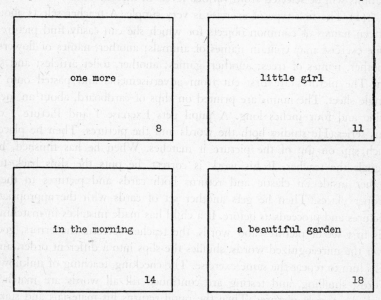

FIGURE 25: Flash Cards for Phrase Reading

it as fast as he can, exposing the phrase below. If he does not grasp it on the first exposure he tries again. He next reaches under the shield and removes the top card. Again he flicks the shield off and back to reveal the new phrase. When he can read phrases seven or eight spaces wide, he progresses to the next series of decks and learns to read those that are nine spaces wide, then ten, then eleven, and so on.

These three types of exercises represent the minimum for the teacher who wishes to use diagnostic drills and has no machine to help her. There are many other types,[11] but she can get along for a while with these

---

[11] C. H. Sievers, and B. D. Brown, *Improvement of Eye Movements: A Graded Series of Reading Exercises,* McGinn Publishing Company, Wichita, Kansas, 1940, 81 pp. (*Manual of Directions,* 43 pp.)

three. Throughout the work she should encourage a great deal of easy, interesting, exciting reading, so that the pupils will have the most favorable opportunities for transferring their new skills to connected·reading matter.

2. **Exercises for Increasing Vocabulary:** As in the case of speed, only a few of the total possible vocabulary exercises will be given. The illustrations will be selected from various levels in the school.[12]

(1) The first type of exercise is very simple. A teacher selects about fifteen names of common objects for which she can easily find pictures. One exercise may contain names of animals; another, names of flowers; another, names of trees; another, games; another, toilet articles; and so on. The pictures are first cut from advertisements and pasted onto a single sheet. The nouns are printed on slips of cardboard, about an inch wide and four inches long. A pupil gets Exercise 1 and Picture 1 of this series. He studies both the words and the pictures. Then he places each slip on top of the picture it matches. When he has finished, he signals the teacher. If his work is correct, he puts the slips back together inside an elastic and returns both cards and pictures to their proper places. Then he gets another set of cards with the appropriate pictures and proceeds as before. If a child has made mistakes in matching his first set of pictures and words, the teacher corrects the errors, goes over the unrecognized words, shuffles the slips into a different order, and tells him to repeat the same exercise. The checking, teaching of unknown words, shuffling, and testing are continued till all words are matched with the correct pictures. Then the pupil returns his materials and starts another exercise.

(2) A variation on this same exercise consists of using a single picture showing several articles. Each slip contains the name of one object in the picture. The slips are then laid upon the appropriate objects.

(3) A third type of self-administering exercise requires from eighteen to thirty small cards—library cards cut in half are excellent. Each pack of these cards should contain words dealing with three topics. For instance, a single pack might include the following words:

[12] For published exercises dealing especially with vocabulary, see, P. W. Birch, *Retrieving the Retarded Reader, with Special Reference to Vocabulary,* Public School Publishing Company, 1940, 24 pp.; T. G. Hegge, S. A. Kirk, and W. D. Kirk, *Remedial Reading Drills,* George Wahr, Ann Arbor, Mich., 1936, 49 pp. (Grades 1–3.); W. J. Osborn, *Remedial and Follow-up Work Bulletins in Silent Reading, No. 1, Vocabulary,* Public School Publishing Company, Bloomington, Ill., 1939, 32 pp.

Farm	*School*	*Automobile*
pig	desk	tires
hay	teacher	horn
carrots	book	motor
horse	eraser	seat
barn	pencil	driver
corn	lesson	gasoline
farmer	class	car

The top card of the pack lists the three main themes. The pupil simply sorts the cards according to topic. If he is successful, he returns them to their proper place and gets a similar pack, dealing with three other subjects. If he makes mistakes, the teacher corrects them, shuffles the cards, and tells him to try again.

(4) A slightly more difficult exercise consists of a sheet of paper on which are typed lines like the following:

1. cat mouse dog chair rabbit
2. yellow blue funny red green
3. jump run hop skip think
4. gun paper kill shoot war
5. game sheet blanket mattress springs
6. clown elephant school circus tent
7. lovely beautiful pretty handsome ugly

The child is to copy off onto a sheet of paper the numbers of the lines and, for each line, the word that is "different" from the other four. He then compares his work with a score sheet, studies his errors, puts the sheets away, gets another, and records the new sheet in the same way. A teacher can use as many of these sheets as she is willing to make. It is best to choose the words for any given sheet from the same half of the same thousand in the *Teachers' Word Book;* in this way, the difficulty of each sheet can be estimated and the series arranged in order from easy to difficult.

(5) In the third and fourth grades, pupils should learn how to divide words into syllables. A series of exercises for this purpose can easily be made. On each of a set of perhaps twenty library cards a teacher writes a polysyllabic word, taken preferably from the regular reading matter of the grade. On the back of the card she divides the same word into syllables. The pupil who works at this exercise takes a package of such cards to his desk, looks at the first word in its undivided form, and copies

it onto a sheet of paper, dividing it into what he thinks are correct syllables. At the end of the exercise, he turns the cards over, checks, and corrects his work. He then puts the package back together again, returns it to its proper place, and gives the teacher his record, which shows how many words he divided correctly. The teacher needs several such packages of cards so that each pupil can receive as much training of this sort as he requires. The ability to divide into syllables is essential in learning how to get acquainted with an unfamiliar word, because it enables one to break it down into pronounceable units.

(6) Another exercise on syllables consists in giving pupils "scrambled" syllables, such as *ti—ful—beau,* or *dent—ci—ac* or *fort—com—ing.* The children are to write on a separate sheet of paper the word they make out of each set of syllables. The syllables for each word may be put on a card, with the corresponding word on the back, or they may be typed on a sheet. Other exercises may be found on pages 60 and 61.

3. **Exercises for Increasing Comprehension:** In a previous chapter [13] a list of specific skills needed for comprehension and another of the specific reading problems met by children were presented. The exercises to develop comprehension are usually constructed so as to meet a common problem, such as the reading of tables and graphs, or else to develop a particular skill, such as finding the main idea of a paragraph. The samples given below are only a few of the total number that have been devised.[14]

a. *Getting the Main Idea from a Paragraph:* An exercise of this type consists of a single typewritten page containing four or five short paragraphs taken from different sources. A sample exercise appears below.

[13] See pp. 87 and 94.
[14] See A. I. Gates and C. C. Peardon, *Practice Exercises in Reading,* Bureau of Publications, Teachers College, Columbia University, 1933; W. J. Osburn, *Remedial and Follow-up Work Bulletins in Silent Reading, op. cit.,* Nos. 2 and 3; D. H. Russell, *et al., Reading Aids through the Grades,* Bureau of Publications, Teachers College, Columbia University, 1939, 90 pp. (225 remedial exercises and activities); *Van Wagenen* and *Dvorak Diagnostic Exercises in Silent Reading Ability,* Bureau of Publications, University of Minnesota (gives training in ten important reading skills); J. A. Wiley, *Practice Exercises in Silent Reading and Study,* Iowa State Teachers College, 1928, 368 pp.
See also E. W. Dolch, *Manual for Remedial Reading,* Garrard Press, Champaign, Ill., 1939; L. G. Elmendorf, A. T. Jameson, and F. C. Perce, *Games and Devices for Remedial Reading,* Institute for Jewish Research, Chicago, 1937; A. I. Gates and M. C. Pritchard, *Teaching Reading to Slow-Learning Pupils,* Bureau of Publications, Teachers College, 1942, 65 pp.; T. F. Hicks, "Diagnostic and Remedial Practices of an Adjustment Teacher," *Supplementary Educational Monographs,* No. 49, pp. 151–159; A. Jameson, "Methods and Devices for Remedial Reading," *ibid.,* pp. 170–178.

Directions: Read each paragraph. Then, on a separate sheet of paper, write *one sentence* for each paragraph, telling what the main idea is. Do not write more than one sentence for a paragraph. Do not copy any sentence out of the stories; make up your own.

a. Devil's Island, the most famous French prison, lies about ten miles off the coast of South America. The island is a solid rock of 34 acres. There is nothing on it except some palms and a dozen small stone cottages. Prisoners are sent there for life, and today it holds only six. They are men who have committed treason or some other crime against France. Captain Dreyfus was on Devil's Island. Each of these six men has a cottage to himself. He is locked in it from six at night until six in the morning. During the day he may do whatever he likes. He has no duties, except that he must care for his own cabin and cook his own food. No one has ever escaped from Devil's Island. The currents around it are so fierce that even a steamer has difficulty in approaching. Then there are thousands of sharks. A French government boat brings food; no other boat ever goes near the place.[15]

b. The worker bees in a hive regard the queen as sacred. The purest honey is reserved for her use alone. Some of the bees watch over her by day and by night. If she has the least accident the news will spread quickly from group to group, and the whole population will rush wildly to and fro. If she is taken away from the hive too early, all work will cease. The young will no longer be cared for, the workers will cease to visit the flowers, the guards at the entrance will leave their posts. Little by little the amount of honey in the hive will become less. The older bees will die and the unborn eggs will never develop because they were not fed. Finally, every bee in the hive will die, even though every flower of summer bursts into bloom before them. But if the queen is restored before the bees have grown too hungry and tired they will receive her with extraordinary, pathetic welcome. They will flock eagerly round her, present her with honey, and escort her back to the royal chamber. Order is at once restored, work resumed, and the hive soon resounds with the gentle buzzing that never is heard unless the queen is alive and well.[16]

b. *Finding the Answer to a Question or Questions:* A single exercise of this type may consist of a series of short paragraphs, about each of which a question is asked, or of two longer paragraphs, about each of which there are two or three questions. It will be noticed that the question *precedes the paragraph,* so that the pupil knows before he starts to read what it is that he is looking for. A sample exercise of this type appears below.

[15] Used by permission of the *Reader's Digest.*
[16] Used by permission of the *Reader's Digest.*

Question: What are the possible uses of a telephone from one part of a building to another?

There are hundreds of possible uses for a telephone from one part of a house to another. One station may be placed at the bedside of a sick person and the other station in the kitchen, so the sick person may call downstairs easily. If you are annoyed by salesmen at the door, you can put one station of your telephone outside the front door and the other in the house. In this way you may talk with each caller without walking through the house. And you can refuse to let anyone in if you do not wish to see him. If you want to, you can put the telephone between your husband's workshop and kitchen. This arrangement makes it easy to call your husband into the house for dinner or for any other purpose, without going outside. You can change this telephone into a sort of loud speaker. The speaking end is put, for instance, in the nursery, where it will pick up any unusual noises made by the baby and will carry them to the kitchen or any other room where the mother is working. Doctors find such telephones very useful between their offices and their reception rooms. A businessman may use such a telephone between his desk and that of his secretary. In a restaurant one can link together the dining room and kitchen. In fact, any two rooms can be joined together in this way.[17]

c. *Drawing Inferences:* This type of exercise is relatively hard to construct. A teacher will find few paragraphs that she can take word for word from books, although she will obtain many suggestions from readers and texts. A type of paragraph demanding inferences appears below.

Directions: Read each paragraph or story and then answer the question about it.

What I noticed particularly during the next few days was the change that had taken place in this quiet town. People that had been friendly now seemed to be bitter enemies. Many of the men in the village had been arrested or were missing. Their property had been taken and their families were wandering homeless, with former friends afraid to offer them food or shelter. The hopes of others had been swept away. Toni had to give up his store because it was ruined. Some of the youngsters who were at the big dance last year were starving. Maria, the postman's daughter, would not get married in the spring because Jaime was a prisoner and would soon be shot. Imprisoned with him were 38 other men from this town, all in danger of their lives.[18]

What do you think was going on that had changed matters in this town?

[17] Adapted, by permission, from material in *Science and Mechanics.*
[18] Adapted, by permission, from the *Reader's Digest.*

d. *Following Directions:* These exercises are really preparatory to the type of reading necessary in any laboratory course. In the elementary grades such a large portion of directions is given orally that pupils obtain relatively little practice in following written instructions. In fact, many adults never learn to do so. When junior high school pupils first start even the most elementary experiments in science, many are unable to read the directions. It seems, therefore, desirable to include such a set of exercises in this series. A sample exercise appears below.

Write down George Washington's name. Cross out the first two letters of the first name. Change the third letter from the end of the last name to an "s." Put a "d" between the "o" and "r' of the first name. Change the second letter of the last name to an "i." Write another "o" in front of the one at the beginning of the first name. Cross out the three letters after the "h" of the last name. Change the last two letters of the first name to "ow." Change the "h" of the last name to an "l." Cross out the first "s" in the last name. Begin the first name with a capital "W." Whose name is it?

e. *Reading Simple Diagrams:* Reading, in the minds of most teachers, is concerned exclusively with literary types of material. A pupil finds it necessary, however, to read maps, graphs, and diagrams in his textbooks in social, biological, or physical science. Such nonverbal materials present real difficulties for the pupil. Very rarely does he obtain help in understanding them from his general training in reading. It seems desirable, therefore, to include a series of exercises that would give training in these special types of reading. A typical sheet from such a series appears in Figure 26. The pupil is to study each diagram and then answer the questions about it. The easiest and simplest diagrams are maps. The pupil occasionally finds bar graphs and curves in his books and as soon as he begins work in any science, he finds schematic pictures of various phenomena. In the textbooks that pupils are required to read in the upper grades of elementary school and in the subsequent years, teachers can find plenty of materials for making up a series of this type.

It will be noted that all these exercises stress meaning, in one way or another. They train children in the different techniques by which they can find ideas. Once a child knows what to look for and how to look for it, he is reasonably certain to find it.

DIAGRAM 1

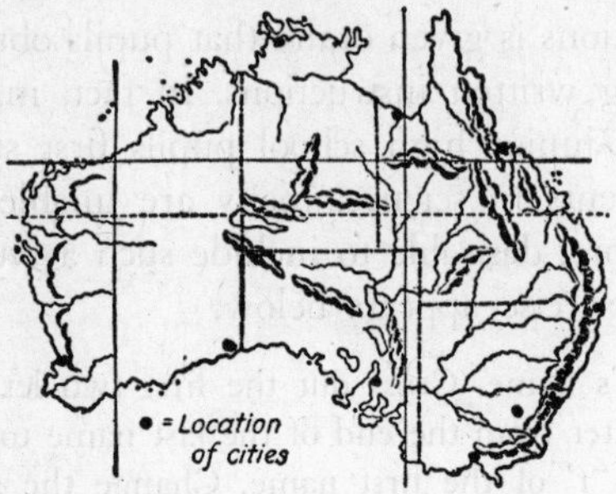

• = Location of cities

DIAGRAM 2

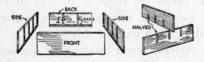

DIRECTIONS: At the left is a map of Australia. Study it and then select the best answer to each question.

1. Where is the biggest harbor? in the northwest   in the southeast   on the west shore   on the east shore

2. Where would you expect to find plains?   in the southeast   in the center of the island   in the western third and the north   along each coastline

3. Where are the cities located? near each other   near the ocean   in the south   at the foot of mountains

4. How many main divisions are shown?   6   3   5   8   16

5. In what direction does the biggest river flow?   north   southwest   west   northeast   south

DIRECTIONS: This diagram shows how many spelling words John had right each day for three weeks. The days are shown down the side and the number right across the top. Study the diagram and then choose the best answer to each question.

1. What was the smallest number of words John spelled correctly on any day?   0   1   2   3   4

2. What score did John make most frequently?   10   7   3   5   0

3. How many times did John get all the words right?   3   5   7   1   2

4. During which week did John do the best work?   first   second   third

5. How many words did John spell correctly during the entire first week?   6   35   5   22   40

DIRECTIONS: This diagram shows the parts out of which a drawer can be made. Study the diagram and then choose the best answer to each question.

1. How many different pieces are needed to make this drawer?   10   7   6   12   9

2. How many partition pieces would you need to go across the drawer from left to right?   1   2   3   4   5

3. How many small compartments would the drawer have when it was finished?   12   7   8   6   20

4. What do you think a "dado" is?   a measurement   the back of a drawer   a partition   a groove   a hinge

FIGURE 26: Exercise in the Reading of Diagrams [19]

[19] The third diagram is used by permission of *Science and Mechanics*.

D. A FEW ILLUSTRATIVE CASES

The teacher of a remedial room soon becomes aware of the fact that the room teachers will probably send her all kinds of children with all kinds of difficulties. Indeed, their only point in common is a failure to read well enough to keep up with the work of their respective grades. The causes are sometimes simple, sometimes complex, sometimes obvious, sometimes subtle. The remedial teacher needs to know as much as possible about causation, but if she keeps an open mind, studies each child carefully, and invents her treatments as she goes along she will do better work than is likely if she has a set routine of procedure or if she comes under the domination of a single theory as regards either causation or treatment.

The following have been selected from a large number as being illustrative of the wide range of problems that confront the remedial teacher. They do not cover all the possibilities by any means, but they may help the reader to see the problems involved more clearly than is possible in a more general discussion.

Ronald from Grade 5 was sent to me because he read so slowly. His comprehension was fair and his vocalizing slight. In disposition he was a slow, plodding, serious child who would probably never do anything very rapidly. When I studied his eye movements I found a curious situation. He had too many fixations per line, but he made almost no regressive movements; the number of pauses usually equaled the number of words, and each pause was abnormally long. In spite of his relative inefficiency, Ronald liked to read. I felt sure there was something I had thus far missed to account for the boy's extreme deliberation and his habit of reading in one-word units. He had some bad habit, but thus far I had not found it and he was presumably unaware of it. Sometimes bad habits pop out only when a child feels himself unobserved and becomes absorbed in what he is reading. The next day I pretended that I was too busy to give Ronald my personal attention and asked him to entertain himself with some books of comics which I kept on hand for children who would read nothing else. Ronald plowed through *Superman* but I discerned nothing abnormal in his behavior. The next day, however, after a few minutes of concentration upon the relaxed enjoyment of *Little Orphan Annie* he began to point. Ronald was a systematic child, and he pointed systematically once at each word. One reason for his long pause was that he was a bit slow of comprehension but another reason was his habit of keeping his eyes and his finger together. Upon investigating the matter further I found that Ronald had arrived in school with the pointing habit and that it was still in evidence in the second grade, where the teacher had "suppressed" it. That is, she had made Ronald feel ridiculous by telling him that pointing was a baby trick, and he had stopped his overt behavior. But his eye movements had remained those of a child who points—one long stare at each word. Like most small boys Ronald was interested in anything mechanical, so I showed him how my simple tachistoscope worked, showed him where I kept several hundred cards containing phrases of different lengths, and turned him loose to re-educate himself for a half-hour each day. He began with such short phrases as "come in" and worked his way up until he could grasp as long a phrase as "with a last glance" at a single fixation. This practice served also to impress upon him the fact that he did not need to look at each word separately. The training in phrase reading plus subsequent work to make sure that his new recognition span transferred to ordinary reading matter required about six weeks. In that time Ronald almost doubled his speed with no loss of comprehension. A bad habit is always bad, but a suppressed bad habit is worse because its invisibility makes it baffling to all concerned.

Mildred was a bright little girl in the upper first grade who was sent to me because she constantly read words that weren't on the page. Her performance was, to say the least, unique. When asked to read aloud she proceeded with great ease, *sang-froid,* and fluency. The only trouble was that the story she read was not the one in the book! It did not even contain many of the same words. I tried another book, this time giving it to her upside down. Mildred launched at once into a simplified version of *Jason and the Golden Fleece,* a story she "read" well, except that it wasn't there. As a final check I gave her a book of stories in French from which she "read" me *Jack and the Beanstalk* with variations. What made Mildred's performance most remarkable was that she went through all the motions of reading and had no idea she was not proceeding normally. I never found out when she began to substitute a bland recital of the many stories her mother had read aloud to her for the story in the book, but presumably some of the commoner tales—*Little Red Riding Hood,* for instance—were in her early readers, and once she had read enough words to identify the story she found recollection much easier than further reading. Since she did not actually read much, she failed to learn new words, and because soon the supposedly learned words were unfamiliar she substituted the recounting of stories for the reading of them. The child was such a poised *raconteuse* that she could keep the class entranced as she "read," and only the teacher seemed to care that the words did not agree with those printed on the page—an attitude that Mildred regarded as typical adult fussiness. Teaching Mildred to read was quite a chore, and even as late as the fourth grade she still occasionally "read" a story to herself and then started to relate it to the class either telling the story inaccurately or substituting another. What finally cured her was the change in the attitude of her audience. First grade children are not critical and will listen to any story that is well told, but as they grow older they begin to get annoyed at inaccuracies. Eventually they start to laugh, and it was the hurt of mockery which finally convinced Mildred that imagination was no substitute for real reading.

William from Grade 8 was of the stuff from which specialists and fanatics are made. He had one interest at once, and it absorbed him to the exclusion of competing stimuli. At the time I knew him his ruling passion was boats. In school he was doing excellent work in arithmetic and good work in geography; his spelling, handwriting, composition, and history were poor, and his reading was very poor. His teachers were sure William could read if he would only exert himself, but they could not seem to stimulate him to the effort. William's own laconic statement of the situation was that most reading was nonsense and not worth bothering with because when you finished a story or assignment you were no better off than when you started it! Since the problem seemed one of motivation, I began to talk with William to discover his interests. In his spare time he built boat models, reading the specifications for them without difficulty from books on woodworking. At the end of the first interview he offered to bring me one of his models. The next day he appeared with a beautifully made sailboat, all his own work. I had come armed with a book on the history of ships, a volume well filled with handsome pictures. William was entranced. For two periods he studied the pictures but on the third day he settled down to read the text and could hardly be separated from it. After two or three other factual books, I gave him *Captains Courageous* and followed it by *Two Years Before the Mast*. He was soon reading stories of the sea willingly, but he continued to balk over the regular reading assignments in English and history. I finally persuaded his English teacher to let him read such books as he would read at all instead of the routine assignments. William was already over 15 when I first knew him. The next year he took out working papers and got a half-time job in a shipyard. In his half day of schoolwork he took mostly mathematics and shopwork. He read *Popular Mechanics* and similar magazines and an occasional book about shipbuilding. He is now a keyman in the business of turning out Liberty ships. William is a living reminder of the fact that no teacher can make a rounded scholar out of a born specialist. The boy's reading difficulties were only expressions of his personality. He is not an educated or cultured man, but within the confines set by his narrow interests he is well informed and capable of informing himself further as necessity arises. When a teacher is confronted by an incipient specialist she might as well abandon any plans of well-rounded development for him and concentrate upon making a *good* specialist.

Frederick, a slow and uncertain reader from the fourth grade, is a star illustration of how to teach reading by not teaching it. Within five minutes of his arrival on the first day in my room Frederick told me that he was unable to read and that he could not learn anything without great effort. His whole manner was shy, diffident, self-conscious, and discouraged. I finally persuaded him to try reading to me from a second-grade book. He hesitated before almost every word and asked me to check his meanings for words several times, by such questions as, "That word is 'horse' isn't it?" When I tried to test his vocabulary with flash cards he became even more hesitant, until he was unwilling to commit himself on any word before he had asked me if it were correct. In one series of 10 words he knew every one, but checked 8 of them to be sure he was right. By the end of the second session with Frederick I had become certain that his poor reading was only one indication of a deep-seated uncertainty. The testimony from his teachers reinforced this assumption. Frederick had such feelings of inferiority that he would not do any schoolwork well until he made a recovery from his attitudes of defeatism. The causes of his discouragement were not hard to find. He had been out of school for a year with infantile paralysis, from which he had made an excellent recovery, and was now grouped with children younger than himself. His illness had left him without much vitality and had broken off his friendships with his age-mates, at the same time throwing him among adults. Intellectually he was unusually mature, but he did not know how to take his place in the rough-and-tumble life of boyhood. He had tried to mix with the boys while he was still too delicate to succeed and had only persuaded himself that he was incompetent. His schoolwork was so much too easy for him that he was sure he must be extraordinarily stupid or he would not be asked to learn things that seemed so simple. He was certain there must be a catch in it somewhere, and he had compensated by becoming preternaturally cautious. With this total picture in mind, I put books aside, because their use would only give him practice in hesitating, and asked him what he would most like to do, of all the things in the world. The answer popped out instantly, "I'd like to know how to turn a cartwheel. All the other kids can except me." I took him to a corner of the playground and spent two or three periods teaching him how. Then I asked him again what he wanted most to do. This time, he wanted to walk on his hands. The next time he wanted to build a model airplane. Then he wanted to write a story about the imaginary hero who flew the airplane just constructed. Presently I noticed that he was mixing with other boys at recess much better than before. I suggested to his room teacher that he be allowed to read his story to the class—a procedure that gave him great pleasure. Next, for nearly two weeks he regressed to a previous level and spent the whole period each day practicing with his marbles! But the practice helped maintain his social prestige. Frederick came to the remedial reading room every day for almost a year, but he rarely read anything. One by one we patched up the deficiencies that galled him, both nonacademic and academic. We worked somewhat on arithmetic and spelling, but he never mentioned reading as being difficult. While this work was going on, the room teacher talked several times with Frederick's mother and gradually persuaded her to let him be a boy instead of an invalid. In the summer between his two semesters with me he went to a boys' camp for almost the entire three months. When he returned it was evident that he was now far superior physically, mentally, and socially to the other pupils in the grade in which he was placed, so he came back to me to be given such extra work as he needed to skip a grade. With this prospect before him, Frederick shed the last vestiges of his inferiority complex. When last I heard of him he was doing excellent work in the ninth grade, was playing on his class basketball and ice-hockey teams, and was on a dance committee. The main thing to note in this story is that Frederick's initial poor reading was only one symptom among many of an underlying maladjustment. It could not be cured until the maladjustment was remedied—and then it cured itself.

Madelaine was a harassed looking small child in the fourth grade. She had in general done well in her first grade work, but in the second she had begun to slip, and in the third she had barely scraped through. Now, in the fourth, she was failing everything. Most of the time she was quiet, inoffensive, and well-behaved, but during the reading period she sobbed steadily and noisily. Her explanation for this behavior was that she "just couldn't read." Since reading threw her into such an emotional outburst, my first move was to tell her that she could amuse herself in any way she liked, instead of reading, providing she was quiet. She spent the first days in the remedial room happily coloring pictures, dressing and undressing a doll, cutting out a family of paper dolls, just sitting in the sun, and playing with a lump of clay. The ease and accuracy with which she colored the pictures suggested that her eyesight was normal. This carefree life went on for some time while I took a look at the home situation. There I found three elements that contributed to Madelaine's emotional state. First, reading had been used as a punishment for misbehavior—and reading in the Bible, at that. Second, reading had been used as a basis of comparison between Madelaine and a younger sister who was making good progress in school. The process of reading had thus been surrounded for years by unpleasant associations. Finally, Madelaine's stepfather of whom she was desperately afraid, had been trying to tutor her in reading at home. I do not believe he intended to frighten the child, although he admitted that he did sometimes become impatient and scold her. He seemed sincere in his efforts to help her and was shocked to be told that she was afraid of him. He was a huge, rough-mannered man and had a loud voice and a heavy hand, and I suspect that from a small child's angle of vision he must have looked like an ogre. The treatment given Madelaine for her supposed inability to read consisted of two parts. I persuaded the mother to stop using reading for either punishment or a basis of comparison between her daughters and dissuaded the father from further tutorial effort.

Then I excused Madelaine from reading for an indefinite period. She came to me each day when her class had its reading period, but she played quiet games or otherwise amused herself. Gradually, her nervous tension decreased, and she became a happy normal youngster, but it was three months before she picked up a book. At first she only looked at pictures, but presently she began to read in short snatches. As soon as she began to use books at all again, I let her curl up on a couch and suck lollypops while she looked at the pictures, thus making association with books agreeable. It was six months before the many unpleasant associations with reading had been sufficiently forgotten and pleasant ones sufficiently well substituted to permit concentrated reading.

David was the small victim of a single bad habit. He was sent to me by his first grade teacher because he seemed to get such confused meanings from what he read. The teacher had tried having David read aloud and reported that the child would read a few words correctly, then make a hash of the next line or two, then skip two or three lines, and again give a perfect performance for several words only to come again to grief. David's reading for me showed the same pattern. Naturally his comprehension was restricted to the occasional line that he had read correctly. When I watched his eye movements as he read, the nature of his trouble was at once apparent. He did not know how to get from the end of one line to the beginning of the next.

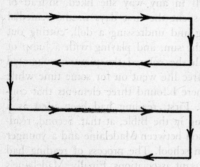

Sometimes he continued across the same line onto the opposite page, sometimes he skipped several lines, and sometimes he wandered by degrees from right to left, picking up a word here and there on the way, but his basic scheme was to read one line from left to right, drop directly down to the end of the next line, and then read from right to left, progressing as shown below: By this arrangement, the child reversed every other line. For some reason David had failed to grasp the idea that lines must always be read in the same direction and the words always taken in the order of appearance. Remedying his difficulty was fairly easy because he had not been practicing his bad habit for very long.

FIGURE 27: Record of Abnormal
Eye Movements

Ellen was a victim of teaching. The method used was one that is in general excellent but it turned out to be inappropriate for this particular child. When I first knew her Ellen was in the fourth grade, where she was doing poor work. Her IQ was 87. Ellen's oral reading performance was somewhat remarkable. She read fluently such words as she recognized at all, laboriously sounded out the first two or three letters of unfamiliar words, guessed a more or less probable meaning—sometimes correcting her guesses several times—and then rushed on without paying attention to the sense of what she read. Her guesses were indicative of her general approach to the problems of reading. Thus, for the word *threaten* she first sounded the *th,* then guessed *this, throw, tree, wood, house,* and *cat.* The first three words were suggested by the initial letters of *threaten,* but the last three were from free association alone. Ellen had been taught to read by the well-known "look-and-say" method. When a child sticks on a word, the teacher is supposed to help her with the initial sound for guidance and then ask, "Now, what do you *think* it must mean?" thus showing the child how to use context to derive meanings for unknown words. The method is sound, but it presupposes more intelligence than Ellen possessed. All she got from it was that when you didn't know a word you just guessed anything that came into your head. I tried to show Ellen how to look through an entire word when it was unfamiliar, but she preferred to go on guessing. She knew most of the sounds and she could, under pressure, sound out and recognize correctly an unfamiliar word that was within her comprehension, but I very much doubt if she is likely to go through this laborious process often of her own volition. The "look-and-guess" technique was well entrenched in her dull mind and it will take a better teacher than I to remove it.

Cecile's reading difficulties were merely one indication of her general immaturity. She was a very pretty little girl in the second grade. Her clothes were always clean and her hair had recently been given a permanent wave, of which she was as vain as a peacock. In disposition she was babyish, willful, self-centered, stubborn, and dependent. She could not put on her own coat, mittens, or rubbers. She was of average intelligence, but she used her ability chiefly to avoid doing what she preferred not to do—reading, for instance. At home her mother read aloud to her, and she saw no reason why she should bestir herself in school. Her mother also fed Cecile, dressed her, bathed her, entertained her, and gave in to her to avoid the scenes that occurred when the child did not instantly get her own way. Cecile had had several temper tantrums in school and often cried. During her first short session with me she was too busy exerting her wiles to get any reading done, but on the second day, when it became clear that I meant business and was not going to succumb to her charm, she stamped her foot and refused so much as to try. Hoping to catch her attention, I got out a picture book, which she promptly threw across the room. Clearly, we were in for a scene. I explained to Cecile that I could not make her read but that if she would not try, she would have to go back to her room. This idea did not please her at all. Evidently, she thought it a great honor to be sent to the remedial reading room! And no doubt she enjoyed the moment when she could show off her clothes and her curls by leaving her regular room in the middle of a period. When I threatened to deprive her of her new prominence, she stated flatly that she would not go back to her room and I could not make her. This time she had gone too far. It was true that I could not make her read, but I certainly could return her to her room. I merely gathered her up under one arm and carried her, letting her yell all she liked. As I sat her down, not too gently, in her seat in her classroom, the crying abruptly stopped and she began to restore clothes and hair to their previous unruffled condition. I took advantage of the pause to tell her that she might come back to my room any morning that she felt like learning to read and that I'd be glad to have her come. Two days later Cecile was back, considerably chastened, and there was never any more trouble. She had not learned to read earlier merely because she was too immature to make the necessary effort. Cecile's room teacher, a visiting teacher, and I all talked with her mother on the subject of letting Cecile grow up. As the year rolled on, the child did mature noticeably and learned to read quickly and with rather less trouble than the average beginner, because she was older. Nothing would have been less appropriate than to put Cecile through an elaborate program of testing and remedial teaching—and how she would have loved the attention!

E. RESULTS OF REMEDIAL TREATMENT

There are literally dozens of reports concerning the results of remedial teaching at all levels of the school system. In most instances the work produced extremely rapid gains. Indeed, when such results first appeared, many people did not believe them because it seemed impossible that a group of poor readers could make such gains in a short time—sometimes three or four years' progress in as many months—especially since they had already been supposedly well taught by the classroom teachers for a number of years without much profit. There is no need to quote a large number of studies because the results are similar, the main differences in the amount of progress from one experiment to another being due largely to variations in the nature and extent of the remedial program and in the length of time that the work continued.[20] In general,

[20] See, for example, E. A. Betts and H. E. Donnelly, "Systematic Instruction and Retarded Readers," *Journal of Exceptional Children,* 3: 118–125, 1937; C. D. Boney and J. E. Lynch, "A Study of Reading Growth in the Primary Grades," *Elementary English Review,* 19: 115–121, 133, 1942; M. E. Broom, "Improvement of Reading Mechanics," *Texas Outlook,* 24: 29, 1940; E. Deans, "Correcting the Reading Disabilities of Nine Selected Pupils," *Seventeenth Yearbook of the Department of Elementary School Principals,* pp. 403–408, 1940; K. B. Hester and F. E. Livingston, "The Remedial Reading Program in the Mt. Lebanon Public Schools," *Elementary School Journal,* 41: 277–282, 1941; G. H. Hilliard and M. Barnes, "The Effect of Specific Drill on Reading Abilities," *ibid.,* 31: 417–426, 1931; J. W. Johnston, J. H. Coleman, and W. S. Guiler, "Improving the

pupils gain an average of about a year in eight to twelve weeks, and some proportion between a fourth and a third gain two or more years in reading ability. Other by-products are sometimes noticed, such as improved adjustment to school life, reduced failures in school subjects involving reading, greater maturity and independence, loss of disagreeable personal characteristics, and greatly lessened tension.

Curiously enough, the exact treatment administered does not seem to make as much difference as one might expect. Almost any reasonable treatment seems to produce results, probably because of the close relationship between all phases of the reading process and because of the highly individualized treatment. The poor reader becomes the center of the teacher's attention. Every item of progress meets with praise and encouragement, which the child laps up the more eagerly because thus far he has had very little where reading was concerned. Soon his galling sense of inferiority leaves him, his emotional resistance evaporates, and he can learn within the limits of his natural capacity. If, in addition to encouragement and attention, one or more specific weaknesses are also remedied, a pupil may make a startling gain.

The specific results from a few outstanding investigations will be presented to show in some detail what changes take place. In the first experiment to be quoted,[21] one group of children received extensive treatment under the close supervision of specially trained teachers. Children in a second group were given help by their regular room teachers, who were supervised to some extent by the specialists. The third group of pupils received the usual teaching of reading but no remedial work. The three groups were equal in reading ability and intelligence at the start of the training. All were poor readers. Table 39 presents the results.

Group C that had no specific training gained a bare 2 months in reading age during slightly more than 8 months. Group B gained 10 months in 7 months' time—a little more than normal progress. Group A gained a year and 2 months in reading age in a little less than 7 months. No one in Group C and only one child in Group B made a gain of over a year and a half, whereas 24 children in Group A gained from a year

Reading Ability of Elementary School Pupils," *Elementary School Journal,* 42: 105–115, 1941; B. Lantz and G. B. Liebes, "A Follow-up Study of Nonreaders," *Journal of Educational Research,* 36: 604–626, 1943; M. Monroe and B. Backus, *Remedial Reading: A Monograph in Character Education,* Houghton Mifflin Company, 1937, 171 pp.; E. F. Mulroy, "Marks Made Following a Program of Remedial Instruction," *School Review,* 44: 753–758, 1936; A. A. Riefling, "Report of Two Reading-English Classes," *School Review,* 50: 587–595, 1942.

[21] Monroe, *op. cit.*

TABLE 39

Number of Years Gained in Reading Age [22]

Years	Group A Closely Supervised	Group B Taught by Teachers	Group C No Remedial Instruction
4.8—5.1	1		
4.0—4.7	2		
3.2—3.9	1		
2.4—3.1	6	1	
1.6—2.3	14		
.8—1.5	46	26	2
.4— .7	17	17	7
0— .3	2	6	41
Number of children	89	51	50
Median gain	1 yr. 2 months	10 months	2 months
Number of months from beginning to end of period	Nearly 7	7	A little over 8

and a half to 5 years of reading age during the 7 months of the experiment. This study shows clearly that close individual attention is essential for rapid progress.

The results from a second experiment are given in terms of individual progress of 25 children who were given training in phrase reading for some number of 20 minute periods between 7 and 22—or a total training time between 2 hours 20 minutes and 7 hours 20 minutes. The number of 20 minute periods used by each child appears in the last column in Table 40. Subject No. 1 decreased his fixations for the same amount of reading matter during the training period from 113 to 92 and his regressions from 17 to 3; he maintained his comprehension at 75 per cent but increased his speed from 285 words a minute to 446. These changes were wrought in only a little over 4 hours of practice. No. 8, an especially inefficient reader, decreased the number of fixations and regressions from 224 to 156 and 46 to 29, respectively, maintained his comprehension at 88 per cent and increased his speed from 144 to 218 words a minute, after 3 hours and 40 minutes of drill. No. 25, in 2 hours and 20 minutes of practice, worked a minor miracle; he decreased his fixations 40 per cent; cut his regression down by 66 per cent, maintained a perfect score in comprehension, and increased his speed by 255 a minute. Nos. 5, 15, and 19 made very little progress, but the others all made an

[22] Monroe, *op. cit.,* p. 146. Used by permission of the publisher.

TABLE 40

Individual Gains in Reading [23]

Subject	Fixations		Regressions		Comprehension		Speed		Number of 20 Min. Practice Periods
	Before	After	Before	After	Before	After	Before	After	
1	113	92	17	3	75	75	285	446	13
2	112	93	14	11	100	100	302	406	15
3	131	92	12	1	63	75	212	374	15
4	184	147	34	21	55	88	136	224	14
5	122	123	28	26	75	88	237	264	15
6	164	125	45	28	63	88	211	308	16
7	216	168	70	44	100	88	175	215	17
8	224	156	46	29	88	88	144	218	11
9	154	113	19	11	63	75	203	309	17
10	126	96	21	15	100	80	247	411	12
11	142	113	12	5	75	75	253	348	11
12	145	121	30	14	100	75	209	294	18
13	124	114	14	19	63	88	197	252	12
14	102	67	12	5	75	88	402	622	10
15	148	144	39	31	63	100	210	232	15
16	144	106	27	11	75	75	237	382	14
17	84	63	15	6	75	88	444	649	10
18	132	108	13	5	63	75	214	364	22
19	106	105	10	10	100	100	310	336	12
20	153	121	35	27	75	75	243	323	8
21	128	84	29	10	75	100	306	481	15
22	131	119	24	14	50	75	259	334	20
23	112	96	5	6	80	75	338	406	10
24	143	134	13	8	50	75	249	331	10
25	108	66	18	6	100	100	342	597	7
Average	139	111	24	15	77	85	256	369	13

	Decrease		Decrease		Increase		Increase	
Per Cent	20		37		16		44	

appreciable gain in one or more respects, No. 17 finishing with the amazing speed of 649 words a minute.

A third investigator concentrated upon the rate of reading in a number of elementary school classes. The progress of two typical groups during 28 and 36 consecutive school days, respectively, is shown in Figure 28. [24] The average speed rose from 101 to 400 words per minute for the 15 pupils in Grade 4 and from 170 to 422 words for the 19 children in Grade 6. The curves rise in a somewhat irregular manner partly because the selections used in the daily tests of speed were of

[23] Taylor, *op. cit.*, p. 270. Used by permission of the publisher.
[24] J. A. O'Brien, *Silent Reading*, The Macmillan Company, 1921, 289 pp. From pages 215 and 221. Used by permission of the publishers.

somewhat unequal difficulty. The main trends are, however, unmistakable.

A teacher who worked with a group of only nine children succeeded in producing in a semester an average gain of .96 of a year in the reading of sentences and of 1.34 years in the understanding of paragraphs, with

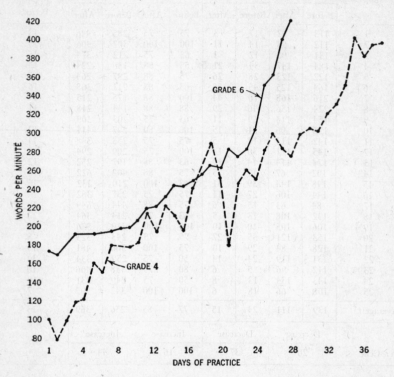

FIGURE 28: Increase in Reading Rate for Two Groups of Pupils

an average decrease of 28 errors in the oral reading of a brief passage.[25] Some children gained as much as a year and a half in comprehension, and three of them eliminated from 37 to 45 errors out of an original 44 to 54.

Such results prove that most poor readers do not need to remain poor readers. Their difficulties can be analyzed and to some extent remedied, even in the case of dull children, although naturally the brighter the child the better his chances for success.

[25] Deans, *op. cit.*

F. SUMMARY

Children may fail to make progress in reading from almost any constellation of existing causes. Sometimes failure to learn can be traced to certain specific, ineffectual methods of work, and sometimes it is merely one evidence of a fundamental and unresolved problem. Because of the many possibilities, careful analysis and diagnosis are necessary before a pupil begins his remedial work. A teacher needs a large assortment of remedial exercises, but perhaps even more she needs the sense to know when and with whom to use what. Remedial teaching, when properly done, is valuable both to the individual child and to the school. To be sure, prevention of error would be a lot better, but remediation is often remarkably effective, although one sometimes wonders if the human interest and sympathy shown toward the child by the remedial teacher and the individual attention showered upon him are not worth more in rescuing Johnny from his difficulties than all the exercises and gadgets.

G. REFERENCES AND PROBLEMS

There are a number of excellent books in which the general nature and problems of reading in elementary school are set forth. One or more of them should be used as additional reading matter with this text.

1. G. L. Bond and E. Bond, *Teaching the Child to Read,* The Macmillan Company, 1943, 356 pp.

2. M. E. Broom, A. A. Duncan, D. Emig, and J. Stueber, *Effective Reading Instruction,* McGraw-Hill Book Company, 1942, 482 pp.

3. A. I. Gates, *The Improvement of Reading,* The Macmillan Company, rev. ed., 1935, 668 pp.

4. G. Hildreth, *Learning the Three R's,* Educational Publishing Company, Minneapolis, 1936, 824 pp. (Chapters 2, 3, 4, 5, 12, 13, 18, 21, 22.)

5. J. M. McCallister, *Remedial and Corrective Instruction in Reading,* D. Appleton-Century Company, 1936, 300 pp.

6. M. E. Pennell and A. M. Cusack, *The Teaching of Reading for Better Living,* Houghton Mifflin Company, 1935, 469 pp.

7. C. R. Stone, *Better Primary Reading,* Webster Publishing Company, St. Louis, 1936, 536 pp.

8. C. R. Stone, *Better Advanced Reading,* Webster Publishing Company, St. Louis, 1937, 292 pp.

9. *Seventeenth Yearbook of the Elementary School Principals Association,* 1938, 704 pp.

10. *Thirty-sixth Yearbook of the National Society for the Study of Education,* Part I, 1937, 442 pp.

11. *Twelfth Yearbook of the California Association of Elementary School Principals,* 1940, 154 pp.

12. *Supplementary Educational Monographs,* Nos. 40, 51, and 52; 1933, 1940, 1941; 226, 355, and 344 pp.[26]

To the Student

The following exercises and projects are included to give you greater insight both into the problems involved in learning the school subjects and into the methods used in research. More are listed than you are likely to use in order that you may have some degree of selection.

1. Five children made the following scores. Work out their IQ, RQ, and AQ. What would you conclude about each?

	Mary	Paul
Intelligence	10 yrs. 6 mos.	8 yrs. 1 mo.
Reading	11 yrs. 2 mos.	6 yrs. 6 mos.
Arithmetic	9 yrs. 1 mo.	7 yrs. 2 mos.
Chronological age	9 yrs. 3 mos.	9 yrs. 4 mos.

Fred	Donald	Betty
9 yrs. 3 mos.	12 yrs. 8 mos.	10 yrs. 1 mo.
9 yrs. 6 mos.	13 yrs. 6 mos.	7 yrs. 6 mos.
9 yrs. 1 mo.	9 yrs. 2 mos.	9 yrs. 9 mos.
13 yrs. 6 mos.	13 yrs. 6 mos.	10 yrs. 11 mos.

2. Make a survey of the class as to the eyesight of its members. How many wear glasses? What defects do the members have? Is there any effect on reading?

3. Each student should bring a mirror to class. (Many of those in the girls' purses are large enough.) The students work in pairs. The mirror is placed on one page of an open book. One student reads, first

[26] The titles of these successive yearbooks are: "The Teaching of Reading," "Newer Practices in Reading in the Elementary School," "Children's Interests," "Improving Reading Instruction," "Reading and Pupil Development," and "Adjusting Reading Programs to the Individual."

See also the references on Reading Readiness on page 134 and on Remedial Reading on page 155.

aloud and then silently while the other stands behind the reader and watches his eye movements in the mirror. (If there are not enough mirrors, the watcher can squat in front of the reader and look at his eyes.) It is desirable that each student should read something very easy, something of average difficulty, something very hard, and something from a foreign language—orally and silently in each. When one has finished, the students change places. Each should try to count the other's fixations and regressions.

4. To investigate vocalization, the students work in pairs. One puts his fingers on the other's larynx. The partner reads aloud, then reads softly, then whispers, then reads as silently as he can. The other is to note the differences in vibration.

5. Using the table on page 26 as a guide to the width of the span (the number of words divided by the number of fixations gives the width of span), divide a given short passage (10–12 lines) into phrases of proper length for training in phrase reading, (a) a second grade child, (b) a sixth grade child, (c) a high school pupil, (d) a college junior. All are assumed to be normal for their grade.

6. Hold a debate on the values of oral reading.

7. Analyze Chapter II of this text for technical vocabulary. List the terms and tabulate the frequency of each. At the end, make a master list for the class. Be careful to distinguish between technical and merely unusual words.

8. List all the words on any two pages. Each student should select a different two. The lists should be combined into a master list for the class. This exercise gives a faint idea of the difficulties involved in vocabulary study.

9. If pre-primers are available, each student or group of students should analyze one for number of words and frequency of use, with results similar to those in Table 9.

10. From the Thorndike Word List, make a list of words similar to that in Table 6. You can select them with the same initial letter if you use *a, c, m, p,* or *s.*

11. Analyze the words in Chapter I of this book for (a) prefixes and (b) suffixes. What and how many of each do you find?

12. Examine this text to determine the reading demands it makes upon the students, using Table 29 as a basis.

13. Make an outline of the chapter on Vocabulary. In what ways does this procedure help you?

14. Look at Table 24 and select any two "lessons." Then make up one lesson of each type. You may make them for any grade or level in school that you prefer, but state which level or grade it is.

15. Write a brief statement about a recent occasion when you have failed to understand what you read. Can you decide why?

16. What books can you remember reading as a child, at what age, and why was each book interesting?

17. What nontechnical books have you read within the last month? With what degree of interest? What characteristics of the books aroused or did not arouse interest?

18. Make a "ladder" on any other topic than the one given on pages 121-122.

19. List what you think would be a "typical" book for (a) a boy and (b) a girl at each of the following ages: 8, 10, 12, 15, 18. Use only well-known titles.

20. What was the favorite book of your childhood? Of your adolescence? Why?

21. Make a thousand-word count of any book and compare its difficulty with the norms on pages 128-130. (You will need a copy of the Thorndike Word Book.)

22. Apply the formula on page 131 to some child's book to determine its proper grade placement.

23. Bring to class a book you know you cannot easily read and try to comprehend a given 2 or 3 pages. What are the elements of difficulty?

24. Find a short selection of either prose or poetry that has an easy vocabulary but expresses complex ideas.

25. Suppose you had a niece whose birthday came in the middle of a semester and you had to decide whether you would send her to school when she was 5 years 9 months old or wait until she was 6 years 3 months. Using only such materials as would be available in the average home, how could you estimate her readiness to read?

26. Write a brief account of something you once tried to learn before you were "ready."

27. Superintendent Jones had read some articles about reading readiness and issued an order to postpone all reading until the second grade. Debate the wisdom of this order.

28. Write a case study of some child or adult who is or has been a poor reader, emphasizing the causes.

29. Select any length of phrase between 10 and 30 spaces and make a set of a dozen flash cards, as shown on page 173. All phrases must be of the same length. Count each space between words as one letter. Note that a phrase or short clause is a coherent unit of thought. The words *white flower* or *very likely* or *twelfth page* are phrases, but *closet and* or *roses that* or *the famous* are not. The clause *let him come* is a satisfactory 12-space phrase, but *became when* cannot be used because it is not a unit of thought or expression.

30. In a book that you have no occasion to look at often, begin on a given page and read for three minutes as fast as you can and still understand what you read. Mark the end of the last line you read and then close the book at once, putting a marker in the page. Later on in the day, begin where you left off and again read for three minutes. Mark the last line and close the book. Read twice each day, trying to increase your speed. At the end of five days, *but not before,* count the lines per three-minute period and make a graph of the results.

Part II · WRITING

HANDWRITING

SPELLING

COMPOSITION

INTEREST AND DYNAMICS IN VARIOUS PHASES
OF WRITTEN WORKS

READINESS TO WRITE, SPELL, AND COMPOSE

REMEDIAL WORK IN WRITING

THIS section includes the results of research in regard to three school subjects which function together although they are often taught separately. In order to write a letter, a paper, a report, or examination, a pupil needs legible handwriting, correct spelling, a knowledge of what to capitalize and when to punctuate, a sense for correct grammatical usage, and an ability to write sentences that hang together. Since these numerous skills function more or less simultaneously, it is necessary that some of them be so automatic that the pupil's mind can be free to concentrate upon the sense of what he is writing.

The first subject chronologically is handwriting. The child often begins to trace the letters almost as soon as he enters school. A little later he begins to study the spelling of words. From that moment on, writing and spelling function together, although not always harmoniously. In the third or fourth grade a child begins to write whole sentences, and at once he needs a number of new skills. As he grows older and the ideas he wants to express become more complex, his sentences lengthen and he has need for more punctuation than formerly and for greater skill in sentence structure. In the end, if he practices long enough, he reaches a stage of development in which the formation of the letters, the spelling of common words, and the use of capitals, periods, commas, and apostrophes become habitual, and he can attend to content, organization, and style. At this point he has a hierarchy of habits, the simpler ones serving as a basis for the more complex.

The elementary school child does not, however, reach this level. He is still fully occupied with the simple habits of writing, spelling, capitalizing, and punctuating. When he concentrates upon forming his letters neatly and carefully he is likely to misspell words, and when he attends to his spelling he forgets to punctuate. A teacher should try to fuse the elementary habits into a smoothly working whole insofar as possible, but only an occasional child will succeed in getting all his habits to function together for more than a few minutes at once.

The three subjects are presented together in this section as a unit of schoolwork partly because of their organic relationship and partly to encourage teachers to obtain as much transfer from one to another as may be possible at each level of schoolwork.

VIII · Handwriting

A given specimen of handwriting may be scored in three different ways. Its general appearance of "quality" is determined by comparing it with a series of specimens and giving it the score of the specimen it most closely resembles. Its "speed" score is found by dividing the number of words a child has written by the number of minutes during which he wrote. Most investigators use only these two measures. It is possible however, if children have written compositions, to obtain a "legibility" score, which is the number of words a person reading the handwriting is able to read per minute. Up to a point speed correlates positively with both quality and legibility, because those who form their letters correctly and have an easy writing movement write at a rapid rate,[1] as is shown by correlations of .40 to .70 between speed and quality. Legibility is also positively related to quality, but may be negatively related to speed if the writer is proceeding at too rapid a rate for his best degree of coordination.

Since the nature of instruction in handwriting depends closely upon the relative emphasis put upon the quality, rate, and legibility of the final product, it is necessary to consider to what extent each element should be stressed. In the past, handwriting has been regarded as an art. At present, however, it is thought of as a tool, which should be so taught as to be as useful as possible. Since handwriting exists for no other purpose than to be read, one must give primary emphasis to legibility. Speed of writing is next to be stressed, because it is of practical value that legible handwriting be produced as rapidly as possible without strain. Quality or appearance is therefore put last, as a desirable but not essential element. If speed is not adversely affected, one may put a moderate amount of emphasis upon quality, but one must consider

---

[1] See, for instance, A. R. Wills, "Investigation of the Relationship between Rate and Quality of Handwriting in Primary School," *British Journal of Educational Psychology,* 8: 299–236, 1938.

whether or not the necessary time could be used to greater advantage, either in the more essential phases of handwriting or in some other subject.

Quality and legibility may at first seem to be the same thing, but examination of a few individual instances will soon reveal the difference. Most conspicuous are the cases of those people whose handwriting has character, an impressive appearance, or a geometrically perfect slant but

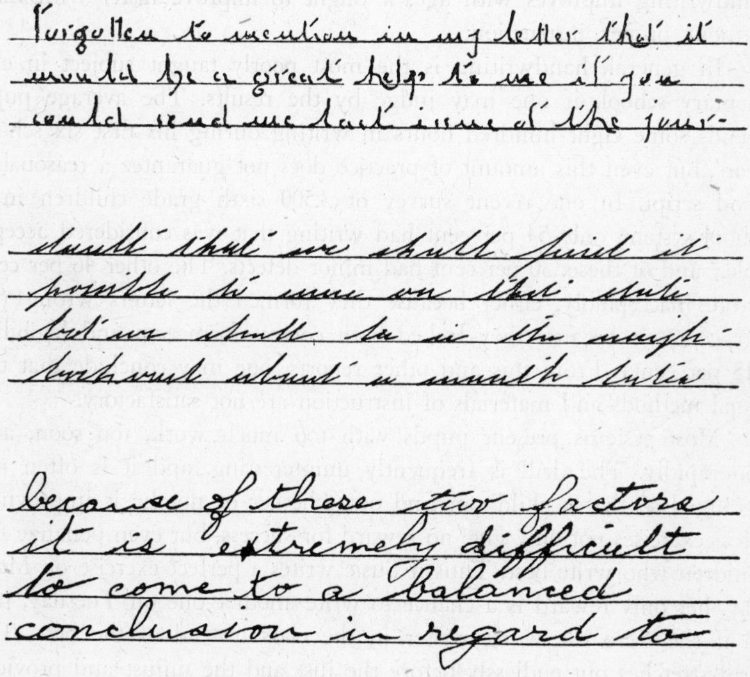

FIGURE 29: Legibility versus Quality

cannot be read. Other people produce a most legible handwriting that is not in the least beautiful. The writing on a single page may show a half-dozen different slants, may be composed about equally of thick, thin, smooth, and rough pen-strokes, and may be abominably spaced; still, the person reading it may be able to proceed without hesitation. Examples of these two extremes are shown in Figure 29.

Various investigators have shown that children improve their hand-writing about as well without instruction as with. One reason for this result is that handwriting will improve almost inevitably as children grow older because their muscular control becomes better. Another reason is the frequent inappropriateness of instruction in penmanship, much of which is so general that it gives children practice in making their errors more and more neatly rather than practice in correcting them. Indeed, a system of instruction can be so poorly adjusted to childish capacities that it actually retards progress. Granted, however, that handwriting improves with age, it ought to improve faster with than without proper instruction.

In general, handwriting is the most poorly taught subject in elementary school, if one may judge by the results. The average pupil spends some eight hundred hours in writing during his first six school years, but even this amount of practice does not guarantee a reasonably good script. In one recent survey of 3,500 sixth grade children in a school system, only 54 per cent had writing that was considered acceptable,[2] and of these, 30 per cent had minor defects. The other 46 per cent wrote inacceptably, either because they formed the letters wrong (28 per cent) or because they lacked both correct formation and legibility (18 per cent). From this and other reports, one may conclude that the usual methods and materials of instruction are not satisfactory.

Most systems present pupils with too much work, too soon, and too rapidly. The drill is frequently uninteresting, and it is often not arranged so that a child can find out whether or not he is improving. Most exercises not only give no reward for success, but even penalize the children who write best. Thus if Susie writes a perfect exercise on Monday, her only reward is a chance to write another one on Tuesday, just as if she were the worst writer in the class instead of the best. The drill stretches out endlessly before the just and the unjust and provides a situation in which learning is slow. A further deficiency in many schools is the failure to teach transfer from practice during the penmanship period to written work in other subjects. Because of these various defects in current methods, children tend to progress in penmanship at a snail's pace. This situation is not necessary, but it is likely to continue until teachers learn to apply the same diagnostic and corrective teaching to handwriting that are already in use in arithmetic, spelling, or reading.

[2] A. Grant and M. M. Marble, "Results of the Cincinnati Handwriting Survey," *School Review*, 48: 693–696, 1940. See also C. Woody, "Teaching Practice and Achievement in Penmanship in the Public Schools of Michigan," *Bulletin of the Bureau of Educational Reference and Research*, No. 151, 1938.

A. MANUSCRIPT WRITING

During the past twenty years there has been agitation over "manuscript" writing. This system calls for the printing of letters instead of the writing of script. Its advocates defend it with the argument that its use permits a child to write the same alphabet that he reads. By using printed letters he can copy directly from his books without translating them into another alphabet. This argument seems sound from an adult point of view, but actually children do not seem to be bothered by the two alphabets, probably because the small letters are much the same in both.[3] In any case, a small child's writing, whether the letters are in print or script, has so little resemblance to anything in a book that one may well wonder how much transfer he is getting.

Any added ease that manuscript writing may give at the beginning is more than offset by various difficulties that arise later. If the print is really copied from books, it is vertical, and vertical writing is known to be more fatiguing than slanted and to depend largely upon finger move ment. Moreover, manuscript writing is almost inevitably slower than practical situations demand,[4] partly because of the features just mentioned and partly because the child takes his pen off the paper between letters.

In about the fourth grade the children are supposedly trained to join the letters, but many of them never learn to do so. Others who do join some of the letters tend to connect the first two or three letters of a word, then leave a space, and then connect two or three more. The result is that a single long word looks like several short ones, and the reader finds the script difficult to read. The sample of writing presented below gives a fair idea of the finished product. It was written by an intelligent, quick-motioned, sixteen-year-old girl who was brought up exclusively on manuscript writing. Her script has character, style, and fairly high quality, but it lacks speed or ease of production. Moreover she leaves spaces in such a way that her writing is hard to read. The word *hours* becomes *h our s, earth* is *ear th, every* is *ever y,* and *four* is *f our.* Incidentally, this girl had the greatest difficulty when she tried to learn Gregg shorthand. Since cursive writing is faster and easier to produce, and since manuscript would—if properly joined—become a

---

[3] Dr. Grace Fernald agrees with me on this point. Neither she nor I have ever found a child who had more difficulty in writing script than in writing manuscript letters. L. C.

[4] Not everyone agrees with the writer about manuscript writing. See, for instance, C. W. Washburne and M. V. Morphett, "Manuscript Writing from Recent Investigations," *Elementary School Journal,* 37: 517–529, 1937.

cursive script anyway, there would seem little justification in teaching children to write the hard way. Incidentally, the assumption that manuscript writing helps children to spell has recently been proven false. Children in various schools were paired as to age and intelligence. One group had been taught manuscript and one cursive writing from their

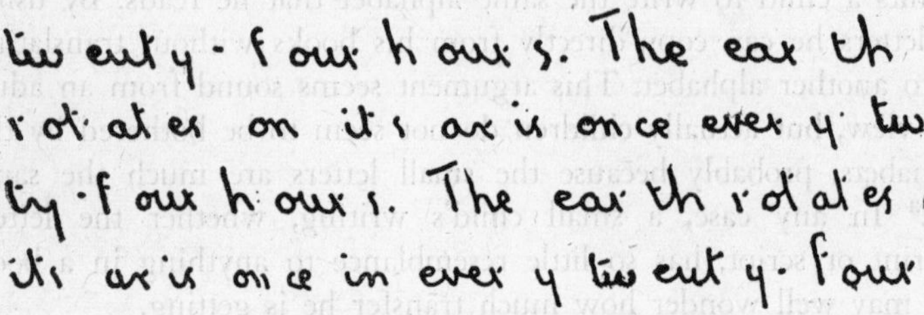

twenty-four hours. The earth rotates on its axis once every twenty-four hours. The earth rotates on its axis once in every twenty-four

FIGURE 30: Manuscript Writing

first day in school. Both groups were alike in ability to spell, and both made the same errors.[5]

B. THE HANDWRITING MOVEMENT FOR CURSIVE SCRIPT

1. Position and Equipment for Writing: A child must be comfortable while he is writing if he is to write well. He should be seated at a desk low enough so that both his feet can rest on the floor and both his arms from the elbows down to the wrists on the writing shelf; it should never be necessary for him to twist in his chair in order to get his writing arm into position. The arm should be flat or nearly flat on the desk. The paper should be placed so that its bottom edge is at right angles to his arm, whether he uses his right hand or his left.

The pen or pencil should be gripped about an inch from the point. The third and fourth fingers rest on the desk; the middle finger is below the pen; the forefinger rests above and to the right of the point, while the thumb opposes it to the left. The fingers and thumb should be relaxed at the joints, but not bent. The direction of the pencil or pen is approximately the same as that of the entire arm; writing with a pencil or pen is simply an extension of writing with one's forefinger.

Individual variations are, however, to be allowed. Children's hands are of different sizes, and the relation between total hand size and

[5] J. W. Varty, "Manuscript Writing and Spelling Achievement," *Teachers College Contributions to Education,* No. 749, 1938, 63 pp.

finger length varies considerably. Most children find writing easier if they rest only the outside of the hand and wrist, rather than the entire width of the wrist, on the desk. The position described in the previous paragraph is in general the best, but there is no harm in minor variations. The main object is the production of script at a high rate and without fatigue. If a child finds a variation in the standard position really better in all ways, the teacher should allow it, provided it does not injure the child physically or lead him into bad habits in subsequent years.

When children are learning to write, their equipment should consist of sheets of paper with ruled lines rather far apart and round pencils with fairly soft leads. They should be encouraged to make their handwriting large. If the lines on the paper are too close together, they can write on every other line. As they grow older they will make their handwriting smaller of their own accord, but they should not be forced to do so until they are ready. At about the beginning of the fourth grade they should start using fountain pens. The defenders of penmanship as a fine art will undoubtedly object to the fountain pen, but since penmanship is a practical tool and not an art, it is more sensible to train children to write well with the implement they will use than with a school pen—an implement they will not use if they can help it. Even if the conservative teacher does not wish to abandon pen and ink altogether, she can postpone their use until after the children can write with a fountain pen, since the latter is an easier implement than the former. Moreover, if a teacher wants to prepare children for daily living she will have difficulty in defending the use of pen and ink against the use of the ubiquitous fountain pen. A relatively fine pen point is probably better than a stub for producing the usual forward slant and is therefore to be preferred. The desirable flexibility of the point depends upon one's style of writing. A school's best procedure is to have on hand fountain pens with different acceptable types of point and to allow each child to experiment till he finds the kind with which he can produce rapid, legible handwriting with a minimum of effort.

2. **Muscular Coordination:** Handwriting proceeds by a combination of finger, wrist, and arm movements. People who have mastered an arm-movement technique and use the fingers only for gripping the pen are usually facile and almost tireless writers, but the amount of practice needed to acquire such facility seems prohibitive for most people. At the other extreme are those who use an exclusively finger movement;

such people are usually slow writers and tire so easily that their script soon becomes illegible. The most practicable arrangement seems to be to use the finger and hand muscles in forming the letters and the wrist and arm muscles to guide the hand across the page. It is not desirable, however, to have the first joint of the index finger bent inward, as this position leads to an alternate lengthening and shortening of all the fingers and the thumb and produces a pronounced finger motion that is almost impossible to integrate with an arm movement. The fingers should move as wholes—that is, the real motion should be in the knuckles, not in either the first or second joints of the fingers or the first joint of the thumb. Since the integration of muscular movements is difficult and calls for a higher degree of control than most small children possess, the teacher must make a choice between beginning with a largely finger movement and adding the arm motions subsequently or beginning with a largely arm movement and then gradually adding the desirable amount of finger movement, until the child becomes old enough to execute both simultaneously. Since there is always the danger that whatever is started will persist without later modification and since an exclusively finger movement is undesirable, it seems best to begin with the arm motion, the fingers being used to grasp the pencil, but not participating to any extent in the formation of the letters. If this is to be the beginning movement, the handwriting will be very large, but that is unimportant. Emphasis on the use of the arm muscles also helps to avoid an overzealous grip on the pencil, a habit that is encouraged by finger movement. In general, children will add what finger motions are desirable as they grow older. If a pupil is already beginning to integrate his movements in the first grade he should not be held back and forced to use an exclusively arm movement; if, on the other hand, his attempts at integration seem premature and ineffective he had better be restricted to the earlier type of movement. One does not expect all children to achieve a given degree of integration at the same age. Rhythm and relaxation are essential to efficient penmanship because they offset fatigue and muscle cramp. Children have difficulty in achieving the easy relaxation and rhythm that are essential to comfortable handwriting.[6]

A discussion of movement must necessarily include a consideration of the slant to be taught. For right-handed people, the easiest slant is usually at an angle of about forty-five degrees to the right from the base line. Slight deviations are of little importance. The slant can be

---

[6] R. Hansen, "The Three R's of Handwriting," *Training School Bulletin,* Vineland, N. J., 39: 2–8, 1942.

controlled most easily by the position of the paper. If a child has developed a comfortable and effective integration but his slant is such as to interfere with either legibility or speed, it is easier to show him how to move the paper a bit one way or the other than to upset his established rhythm. There is nothing sacred about any particular slant or any particular position of the paper; the only criteria are the efficiency of the finished product and the ease with which it is produced.

When a child first begins to write he becomes very tense. He clutches his pencil as if it were a life line, screws up his face, bites his tongue, shuffles his feet, squirms about, and gets into rigid, uncomfortable positions. Because of this effort the handwriting periods should be very short. A fifteen minute period is long enough in the primary grades, twenty minutes is long enough at any level in the elementary school. Handwriting involves eye strain, nerve strain, and muscle strain. The teacher who prolongs the writing drill beyond the children's capacity to stand strain is simply destroying whatever learning has taken place previously.

C. THE LEFT-HANDED PUPIL

Approximately 10 per cent of the population prefers its left hand to its right. Of this number more than half use their left hands for writing. Those who do not, show their native preference by using their left hand to throw a ball, to sew, to whittle, to use an egg beater, to play tennis, or to do anything they have not specifically been taught to do in school. Some children whose "handedness" has been changed by the school for writing purposes seem none the worse for the experience, but others show an awkwardness and general incoordination in all their movements, sometimes including their speech reactions. Hand preference seems to be so innate that one should hesitate a long time before interfering with the natural coordination and balance that come with the use of the preferred hand.

All systems of writing are based upon the assumption that the pupil will use his right hand. The youthful left-hander is therefore forced into a system not adapted to his needs. He is expected to produce writing that slants to the right, and he often imitates his neighbors and tips the page on which he writes in the same direction that they do. His grip on his pen must be somewhat abnormal if he is to avoid pushing the point into the paper. The usual Spencerian slant is a strain for him.

Since his desk usually faces in the same direction as the others, his hand throws a shadow across what he writes. As soon as he begins to use ink he finds that his hand smears each word as soon as he has written it. These difficulties arise, not because he is left-handed but because he has to act as if he were right-handed.

The sinistral inevitably meets certain difficulties because he cannot reverse the direction of his script. If he could write from right to left, he would present no problem. Unfortunately this "natural," completely reversed procedure results in a script like that shown in A of Figure 31.[7] The sinistral must therefore adopt at least the direction of script normal for the right-handed person. In many instances, the grip on the pen, the angle of the paper, the slant of the writing, and the relation of his hand to the base line are also thrust upon him. The result is a maladjustment of position that is often serious.

To understand the difficulties of the left-handed child, one should put oneself into his place, study his problems, and trace his adjustment to them. Suppose that a sinistral in Grade 1 imitates his neighbors in hand position, grip on the pencil, position of the paper, and slant of the script. He then writes as shown in B of Figure 31. There are two objections to this position. In the first place, the pressure of the pencil causes the paper to "walk away" across the desk. If the right hand holds the margin the middle of the paper wrinkles and presently tears. In the second place, the child's hand promptly covers every letter as soon as it is written. Even with pencil this arrangement is inconvenient; with a pen it becomes utterly impossible.

If the sinistral tips his paper so that the lower edge is at right angles to his arm but does not make any other adjustments, he assumes the position shown in C of Figure 31. Only a left-handed child can realize the outstanding difficulty of this position: he cannot see what he has written because his hand is in the way. If he were an adult, he could look over his hand, but a child's trunk is so short that his hand comes between him and his writing. The usual reaction is to lift the wrist and hand a bit and peek under it. This position is shown in Position D— the typical position of the sinistral in the early grades, before use of ink complicates matters.

As soon as ink is introduced the sinistral is again in trouble because his hand smears what he writes. He must abandon Position D and must somehow solve the joint problems of keeping his hand out of the ink, preventing the pen from going through the paper, and of

[7] See p. 12 also.

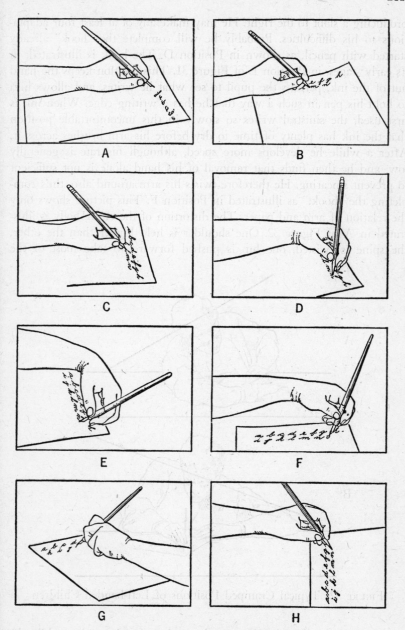

FIGURE 31: Genesis of the "Hook"

producing a slant to the right. He may make any of at least four adaptations to his difficulties. Probably he will complete the "hook" already started with pencil, as shown in Position D. The hook is illustrated, in its early stages, in Position E of Figure 31. This position keeps the hand out of the ink, permits the pupil to see what he writes, and allows him to hold his pen in such a way that he has a writing edge. When ink is first used, the sinistral writes so slowly in this uncomfortable position that the ink has plenty of time to dry before his arm brushes across it. After a while he develops more speed, although his rate is generally low, and he then finds that removal of his hand alone is not sufficient to prevent smearing. He therefore twists his arm around also, thus completing the "hook," as illustrated in Position F. This picture shows only the relation of arm and paper. The distortion of the entire body is illustrated in A of Figure 32. One shoulder is held higher than the other, the spine is twisted, one hip is pushed forward to take most of the

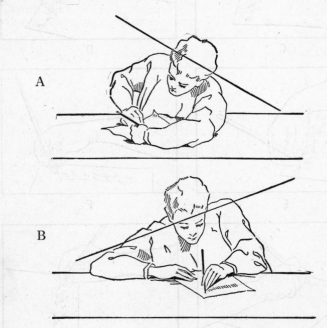

A

B

FIGURE 32: Typical Cramped Positions of Left-handed Children

weight, and in all probability one leg is hanging in midair while the other is hooked around the chair legs. Since children spend many hours each week in writing, this twisted posture can easily do damage to growth.

An occasional left-handed child makes a different adjustment by twisting his hand to the right instead of the left and turning his pen until it occupies the same position that it would occupy if it were being held by his right hand. The terrific strain of this position, which is pictured in G of Figure 31, is obvious. This solution also involves a distortion of the whole body, as illustrated in B of Figure 32. The strain is at least as bad as that for the sinistral who uses a "hook" position.

A few children never alter the position developed when they used pencils, as shown in B or C of Figure 31. Since a pupil's hand immediately smears what is written, he resorts to a laborious, unbelievably slow, but simple method of procedure. He writes three or four letters, lifts his hand off the paper, carefully blots his work with his right hand, writes two or three more letters, and repeats the business of blotting. When he has perfected this method, he moves with the rhythm of a pendulum; his left hand swings in to write, then his other hand swings in to blot. He often produces a clean page, but the hopeless inefficiency of this method is too obvious to need comment.

Finally, there is a small nucleus of intelligent youngsters who discover for themselves the only workable system that produces a "right-handed" slant without serious impairment of effectiveness and comfort. These children merely turn the paper around and write upside down, in the manner illustrated in Position H of Figure 31. With this technique the writing is visible, the movement is comfortable, the pen is held normally, and the hand will not smear the ink if the pen is held far enough from the point to keep the hand two lines below the line of writing. Of the four adjustments of the left-handed child to the use of ink, only this one is comfortable. It is also the only adjustment that practically no teacher will tolerate! Writing upside down is not an ideal solution, but it involves only a mental inversion of the alphabet—a relatively simple trick. There are better methods for the sinistral, but there are also several which are a good deal worse.

In order to avoid the difficulties and maladjustments just described, left-handed children need, first, to turn their desks around and get the light over their right shoulders. They should next tip their papers to the left, so that their left arms will be at right angles to the base of the paper. Figure 33 shows the proper positions of right- and left-handed pupils. It will be noted that the two positions are exactly reversed.

As shown in Position A of Figure 31, the sinistral's "normal" slant is to the left, at an angle of about forty-five degrees from the base line. A slant to the right is, for him, a backhand slant, but the left-hander usually produces it, despite strain and discomfort, because he does not know that any other slant is possible. Either of the two slants in Figure

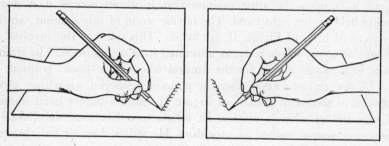

FIGURE 33: Proper Relation of Arm and Paper

34 are easy and natural for sinistrals. If a child is to write at either of these angles, however, he will need a stub pen because the regulation school pen point will go through the paper. He can use either a rather blunt fountain pen or a pen point that turns up, as shown in Figure

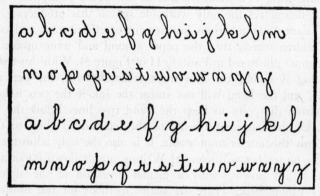

FIGURE 34: Two Alphabets for Sinistrals

35. The resulting script will have slightly thicker lines than may be considered beautiful, but it will be legible and will allow pupils to be relaxed and comfortable.

The right-handed person can keep his hand beside the word that he is writing, or to the right and slightly below the base line, or directly below each word as he produces it. He has a choice because his hand is always resting on the unused part of the page, even if it is held high enough to be actually on the unused portion of the base line. The sinistral has no such choice. His fingers are not so arranged that he can keep his hand to the right of his script, and there is no place at the

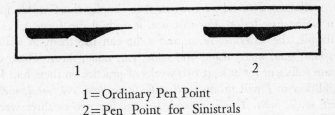

1 = Ordinary Pen Point
2 = Pen Point for Sinistrals

FIGURE 35: Comparison of an Ordinary Pen Point and One that is Easy for Left-handed Children to Use

left that will not smear his writing. He may, of course, hook his arm over the paper and keep his hand far above the base line, but this position is inefficient and uncomfortable. There remains only one place for his hand: below the base line and far enough below to miss the

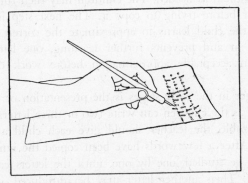

FIGURE 36: Proper Grip on the Pen for the Left Hand

longest loops. Figure 36 shows the proper grip on the pen. This same grip should be taught from the first, even though a child writes with pencil for some years and has no need to keep his hand out of the ink. The shift from pencil to pen involves some unavoidable difficulties; the sinistral's shift from pencil to pen should not be complicated by a change of grip as well.

D. LEARNING TO FORM THE LETTERS

One learns to form letters by forming them—not by executing artificial exercises. Children should begin at once on some of the easy letters, including a vowel or two, so that simple, short words may be written at the first lesson. For instance, if a child can form, so as to be recognizable, the letters *e, m, a,* and *t,* he can use them to write *am, mama, mat, met, meet, team, ate, mate, eat, tame, meat.* These eleven words are sufficient for at least two weeks of practice on these four letters. The addition of *l* will produce *all, tall, lame, late, eel, meal, melt, let, tale, tell, male, malt.* This is enough for another two or three weeks. It is highly desirable that children write letters from the very start and words as soon as possible.

The general procedure in learning a letter is simple. Each child should be supplied with a large, clear copy of the letter to be learned, a large-sized pencil with a rather soft lead, and a sheet of ruled paper. Copying from the board is almost impossible at this stage; every child must have his own copy. The teacher can write the letter on a paper for each child or she can cut the letters out of colored paper or cardboard and use them as needed. The children may then run their fingers over the letter before trying to copy it. The next step is largely trial and error as the child learns to approximate the correct form. Unless boredom sets in and prevents further learning, one letter should be brought to an acceptable approximation before work on another is started.

One danger in the early stages is the presentation of too much too soon. As soon as the children can write two or three letters well enough to be recognizable, the teacher should give each child a model for a whole word. After a few words have been copied the same letters and words should be studied, one by one, until the letters can be written from memory. Then another letter may be introduced, copied several times alone, copied in words containing it in combination with letters already learned, and finally memorized. This same procedure is continued for the remaining letters.

Because the initial steps are so important, the writer makes the following suggestions as to achievement in the first grades: (1) All small letters except *x, z, j, q, k,* and *v* should be taught during the first year, each letter being given approximately two weeks of practice, and no letter being used in the practice material except those already studied.

(2) In the low first grade, each child should be taught the capital or capitals needed to write his first name and, in the high first, the capital or capitals needed for the last name.[8] (3) During the low second grade there should be a review of the twenty small letters already taught and addition of the remaining six. Capitals needed for the name of the school and city may also be given. (4) In the high second grade, all capitals except X, Z, J, Q, K, U, V, W, and Y may be added. (5) Finally, in the low third grade the children learn infrequently used capitals.

Such a spreading out of new letters will permit children really to learn them. Since they have little practical use for writing anything except their names and a few simple words in their spelling lessons, this distribution of letters would seem possible and desirable. Few children can, without strain, acquire even approximate forms for fifty-two letters in as short a time as is commonly required. A child has at least six years in which to learn these fifty-two forms. This is plenty of time to learn each letter thoroughly once, but it is not long enough if the forms are so hurriedly acquired that they must be unlearned and relearned several times. The teachers in the early grades should proceed slowly and emphasize correct letter formation, correct movements, and correct posture. Speed can wait, in fact must wait, if the newly formed habits are not to be disrupted. It is obviously impossible to make letters rapidly and correctly until one can make them correctly—and no end is served by making them rapidly and wrong. The best preparation in the early grades for speed later on is a high degree of legibility produced by relaxed nerves and muscles.

E. ANALYSIS OF ERROR

As children proceed with the task of letter formation, they make numerous errors. At first, they simply do not approximate the shape, but this stage does not last long. As soon as a letter is recognizable its defects can be diagnosed and remedied. In fact, unless defects are diagnosed they are not likely to be remedied.

As an example the writer would like to give an experience of her own in learning how to make the letter q. The first efforts resulted in a page of rather mediocre g's. This she took to the teacher who merely told her to try again because the letter was all wrong. Obediently she covered another page with g's of somewhat better quality—still not noticing that the loop was on

---

[8] For the few pupils needing a small x, z, j, q, k, or v for either name, an additional letter should be given individuality.

the wrong side. This second offering met with neither approval nor the slightest analysis on the part of the teacher. Upon request, she then wrote a third page, this time practically drawing the *g's* and achieving a superlative degree of neatness. However, a suspicion that something more than mere lack of form was the matter had been slowly growing and before presenting this last page to the teacher she showed it to the small boy beside her. Fortunately, he was better at educational diagnosis than the teacher. With his pencil he started to mark over every *g* on the page by bringing the loop up on the proper side. By the time he had corrected two or three, the writer had learned how to make a *q*.

This incident illustrates exactly the difference between trying to eliminate an error by practicing it repeatedly and really eliminating it by diagnosis. Practicing *g's* for years will never produce a *q*. Usually all that a child learns by practicing an incorrectly formed letter is to make it wrong more neatly and more rapidly. Indeed, if the formation is wrong, the better it is written the more illegible it gets, because the more clearly it seems to resemble some other letter.

It is, therefore, necessary to diagnose each child's errors with each letter. In the lower grades, at least, diagnosis should concern itself almost exclusively with letter formation. Slant, alignment, evenness of lines, spacing, and size of script can all be postponed until the child's maturing control makes them possible without strain. If the models from which a child writes all have a uniform slant and spacing, he will develop his handwriting along these lines as rapidly as his nervous system will let him—and no amount of training will produce results any faster, although it may produce them more slowly.

FIGURE 37:
Analysis of a
Letter into Its
Strokes

Study of letters and of the specific strokes by which they are made is useful and profitable.[9] For instance, an *f* may be analyzed into a series of strokes. The pupils can see from such an analysis how the individual strokes are made and can, by comparison with their own writing, see in which movement they have made an error. Handwriting does not demand merely motor learning; part of it is perceptual, and it is by visual perception that a child fixes in his mind just what a letter should look like and just how it is made. Study of letter form, accompanied by analysis of error and a small amount of corrective prac-

[9] D. Leggitt, "Perceptual Learning in Penmanship," *Elementary School Journal*, 40: 764–770, 1940.

tice, results in an appreciable gain in legibility and usually in quality as well.

Extensive analysis of illegibilities in handwriting [10] makes it possible to present an exact list of the most common malformations that make writing illegible. In using such a list the teacher first has the children write a composition or something from dictation. She then

TABLE 41

List of Illegibilities in Handwriting

a like *u*	*f* like *b*	*n* like *u*	*t* like *l*
a like *o*	*f* like *oj*	*n* like *v*	*t*, cross above
a like *ci*		*n* like *s*	*t*, no cross
	g like *y*		*t*, cross right
b like *li*			*t*, cross left
b like *l*	*h* like *li*	*o* like *a*	
b like *k*	*h* like *p*	*o* like *r*	
b like *f*	*h* like *b*	*o* closed	*u* like *oi*
	h like *l*	*o* like *u*	*ur* like *w*
c like *e*		*r* like *i*	
c like *i*	*i* like *e*	*r* like *s*	*v* like *n*
c like *a*	*i*, dot to right	*r* too small	*v* like *r*
	i, dot like -	*r* like half *n*	
d like *cl*	*i*, no dot	*r* like *u*	*w* like *u*
d like *I*		*r* like *e*	*w* like *m*
d like *a*	*k* like *h*		*wr* like *ur*
		s like *r*	
e closed	*l* closed	*s* like *i*	*D* not closed
e like *l*	*l* too short	*s* like *o*	*I* like *cl*
e like *c*	*m* like *w*	*s* blurred	*T* like *L*

reads through the productions and makes a colored circle around every word that she does not instantly recognize. While reading she makes no attempt to diagnose, but merely tries to locate the illegible words. When she has finished reading, she carefully examines the illegible words made by each child and diagnoses what error in what letter or letters caused the trouble. The results of such an analysis usually show that each child is making certain specific errors over and over again, so that his total number of errors is large while the number of different errors is small. To both the child and the teacher this situation is encouraging.

[10] S. L. Pressey and L. C. Pressey, "Analysis of 3,000 Illegibilities in the Handwriting of Children and Adults," *Educational Research Bulletin*, 6: 270–73, 285, 1927; also, *Chart for Analyzing Illegibilities in Handwriting*, Public School Publishing Company, Bloomington, Ill., 1926.

This analytic method of attack provides for individual instruction most of the time. Handwriting is a subject well adapted for individualized teaching. Even small children can direct their own drill while the teacher is explaining particular errors to others. If teachers will use an individual, diagnostic, and remedial method of attack they will find that they can teach children to write acceptably in about half the time now needed. There is no subject in which more time is wasted than handwriting. Much of this time goes into trying to make finished penmen out of children at an age when most of them have not the necessary voluntary control to profit by the drill and in an age when beautiful penmanship is as unnecessary as the whatnot that used to stand in the corner of the parlor.

F. DEVELOPING SPEED AND RHYTHM

By the time children reach the fourth or fifth grades they should be able to produce spontaneously and easily the correct letter forms. The first practical requirement of legibility should be achieved in the lower grades. Actually, most pupils do write well, albeit slowly, as long as they are making their letters large and are using soft pencils. In the third and fourth grades they begin to reduce the size and to write more rapidly. It is at this point that penmanship begins to deteriorate. It is, however, necessary that children should achieve a fair degree of speed, in order to meet the practical requirements of life. If writing is not produced rapidly enough, its legibility and quality will degenerate quickly when the need for an increased rate arises during the later years in school and the subsequent years of adult life. In Figure 38 are two samples of the writing of adults between the ages of forty-five and fifty-five and samples of the writing of these same adults as children in about the eighth grade.[11]

In their childhood these adults "drew" their letters, but the world did not give them sufficient time, so they lost the high quality they had originally achieved. The minimum "safe" rate at the end of elementary school is 90 letters a minute. If a child writes more slowly, he will not be able to meet the demands made upon him by either school or job, and his script will deteriorate markedly as he is forced to increase his rate. Actually, most adults write with a speed of over a hundred letters per

[11] The first sample is from the writer's private file of handwriting specimens. The second is from L. A. Shaw, "Handwriting in 1876," *Detroit Journal of Education*, June, 1922, pp. 23–24. Used by permission of the publishers.

minute but too often their quality has been sacrificed. However, if a
child at the end of the sixth grade can produce ninety legible letters a

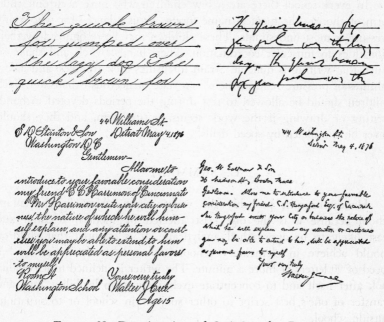

FIGURE 38: Deterioration of Script under Pressure

minute and can keep it up without fatigue for several minutes, he has
the necessary basis for an adult script that will meet the pressure of
business later on.

Speed drills are furnished with most manuals of directions for the
teacher's use in the handwriting class. By the fifth or sixth grade, after
the letters have been thoroughly learned, the children profit by the use
of exercises in which a single letter, groups of related letters, or words
are repeated. Children find such exercises more interesting if they sing
or hum as they write; moreover, they will relax better and will soon
begin to write in rhythm with the music. Some children will write
exactly with the music, some will write in double-time, and a few in
half-time. Even though all pupils are humming the same familiar song,
they do not need to proceed at identical rates. Other speed drills consist of writing a single sentence as many times on successive days as
possible without diminishing the legibility in a short period of time—
perhaps three minutes. The pressure for greater speed must be applied

gradually, and the drills must be short enough to prevent fatigue from offsetting the value of the drill.

In every school there are a few children who have a chronic mild form of chorea—the medical name for St. Vitus's dance—for whom any pressure is most undesirable. These children may be recognized by their difficulties in muscular coordination. Their hands twitch and shake so much that writing is difficult. Strain intensifies their troubles, and a few minutes of pressure reduces them to a state of nervous exhaustion. Such children should be allowed to rest during the periods devoted to handwriting or drawing if the work seems to tire them, and they should never be stimulated by speed drills.

G. SUMMARY

Handwriting is probably the worst-taught subject in elementary school because it is the one least affected by modern research and least likely to be approached analytically. It is essential that children should achieve in elementary school correct letter formation and a speed of 90 letters or more a minute. The writer is inclined to let quality look after itself and to concentrate exclusively upon legibility, rate, and transfer of one's best script to other subjects in school or to situations outside school.

The left-handed pupil presents many problems because he is forced to write the letters of a word in a reverse order from that which is natural for him. Usually he has further and unnecessary troubles because he is taught by methods applicable to 90 per cent of the population but not to him. He may develop a quite abnormal and cramped position unless he receives proper treatment.

IX · Spelling

School pupils of the present day have a great deal of difficulty with spelling, probably more than their ancestors did, because they are taught to read by methods that transfer negatively to spelling. In the "good old days" children were taught to read by first learning the alphabet, then spelling out the words, and then reading orally a great deal. As a result, they actually learned spelling first and reading afterward, and there was a large amount of transfer from one subject to the other. To be sure, their reading was somewhat laborious until they recovered from the method by which they had learned. With the introduction of more efficient ways of teaching reading, children's ability to spell diminished. Children are now taught to glance quickly at words or whole phrases and to recognize them by their outlines rather than by the letters. They see those letters that go above or below the line, but hardly look at the others. The better a child reads, the more fleeting is the glance he gives each separate word. This technique is unexcelled for acquiring skill in rapid, assimilative reading, during which one is interested exclusively in content and not at all in form. As already pointed out, however, this reading by meanings is inadequate even for increasing reading vocabulary and must be supplemented by word study. Even more supplementation is needed for spelling. Whereas the old-fashioned methods of teaching reading automatically taught spelling as well, the modern methods tend to produce excellent readers and abominable spellers. This situation does not call for a return to the teaching of reading by cumbersome and inefficient methods, but rather for a modification in the teaching of spelling to offset reading habits.

If a child is to learn the exact order of letters within a word, he must look at each letter and observe its position. Then he must memorize this order. Spelling is a relatively slow process and requires a concentrated study of every letter—the exact thing a child is emphatically not to do when he reads. If he requires two minutes of study originally to learn the appearance of the word "gingerbread" and if he can subsequently recognize it by a single fixation lasting eight twenty-fifths of a second, he will need a total time of perhaps ten minutes to learn the precise order of letters. The teacher will avoid some of the negative transfer if she will tell the children frankly that spelling is a different procedure from reading and then explain the difference. Such information helps in giving the pupils a different "mental set" for the two types of work. If the teacher uses definite word study in her class, the work in spelling can grow easily out of this, the children being told that they are now to study certain words even more closely than before.

A. THE SELECTION OF WORDS

Because learning to spell is slow and for many children difficult, the problem of a proper selection of words to be learned in detail becomes vital. Children cannot learn to spell all the words they can read nor is there need for such extensive learning. Anyone's writing vocabulary is smaller than his speaking, hearing, or reading vocabularies. The words actually used in writing by both children and adults are already known through many extensive analyses of written material of all kinds. These studies show exactly what words make up the essential core of ordinary writing during childhood, adolescence, and adult life. The words thus found form the basis of spelling instruction in the elementary school.[1] The various studies of word usage in the writing of adults and children show what words are used spontaneously and at what stage of development. They therefore serve as a basis for preliminary assignment of words to different grades. It is also necessary, however, to take account of how difficult each word is to learn. Evidence on this point will be presented later.

[1] W. N. Anderson, "Determination of a Spelling Vocabulary Based upon Written Composition," *University of Iowa Studies in Education,* Vol. 21, No. 1, 1921, 66 pp.; L. P. Ayres, *The Spelling Vocabularies of Personal and Business Letters,* Russell Sage Foundation, 1913, 58 pp.; M. Cox, "The Vocabulary of Third-Grade Children's Letters," Master's Thesis, State College of Education, Greeley, Colo., 1929; J. A. Fitzgerald, "The 1035 Words Most Commonly Misspelled by Minneapolis Pupils in Grades 3–8," Research Department of the Minneapolis Public Schools, 1927; and "The Vocabulary of Children's Letters Written in Life Out of School," *Elementary School Journal,* 34: 358–370, 1934; W. C. French, "A Study of Children's Letters," Unpublished study, Department of Education, University of Chicago, 1925; E. Horn, "A Basic Writing Vocabulary," *University of Iowa Monographs in Education,* First Series, No. 4, 1926, 225 pp.; also, "The Vocabulary of Highly Personal Letters," Unpublished study, University of Iowa, 1922; J. D. Houser, "An Investigation of the Writing Vocabularies of Representatives of an Economics Class," *Elementary School Journal,* 17: 708–718, 1917; G. Spache, "A Minimum Reading-Spelling Vocabulary for Remedial Work," *Journal of Educational Research,* 33: 161–174, 1939; W. F. Tidyman, "A Survey of the Writing Vocabularies of Public School Children in Connecticut," *Teachers' Leaflet,* No. 15, U. S. Bureau of Education, 1921, 18 pp.; W. C. Warning, "An Investigation of the Word Usage of Adults in Written Correspondence," Unpublished thesis, Department of Education, University of Chicago, 1925.

The size of the vocabulary to be taught in any one grade varies considerably from one investigator to another, according to how many and which lists he uses and where he draws the line as to the frequency below which he considers the words to be so uncommonly used that they need not be taught to all children in school. The total number of words assigned to the six elementary grades may vary from 3,000 to 10,000, the load per school day being from 2.5 to 8 words. The variation is not as extreme as at first appears because some lists include several derivative forms as separate words (for instance, *love, loving, loved, lovely,* and *lovable*) while others give only a single basic form.

Between the years 1910 and 1931 there were no less than 27 studies of spelling vocabulary. About 25,000,000 words written by children and adults were read and analyzed for errors. The number of words per study varied from 2,412 to 15,000,000, and the number of different words from 665 to 19,000. Thirteen spelling lists were published on the basis of these analyses, lists varying from 500 to 4,532 words. Studies of errors began to appear in 1914, and by 1931 there had been 10 of them. The

TABLE 42

Source of Words for a Spelling Text [2]

1. Words used by children only and appearing on three or more childhood vocabulary lists	211
2. Words used by adults and having a frequency of 25 or more in the composite adult list	240
3. Words used by both:	
a. Appearing in 3 or more childhood vocabularies regardless of frequency in adult lists	2,297
b. Appearing in only 2 childhood lists and having a frequency of 10 or more in adult lists	456
c. Appearing in only one childhood list and having a frequency of 20 or more in adult lists	277
4. Added from children's letters	23
5. Added from adults' letters	292
6. Added from Commonwealth Study	44
	3,840
Subsequently dropped	−22
Final list	3,818

[2] Items 1, 2, and 3 are from F. S. Breed and W. C. French, *How to Teach Spelling*, F. A. Owens Company, Danville, N. Y., 1930, 177 pp.

number of misspellings studied varied from 1,584 to 5,231.³ As may be realized by now, there has been much work but little agreement among research writers as to how big the spelling vocabulary should be. As good a selection as any from this overwhelming mass of data is given in Table 42 on the preceding page.

In a recent study,⁴ in which the contents of seventeen widely used spellers published since 1929 were analyzed, the investigator selected 8,645 words to be taught in Grades 2 through 8. The number per grade is shown in Table 43.

TABLE 43

Spelling Load per Grade

Grade	Per Year	Per Week	Per School Day
2	392	10	2.0
3	751	19	3.8
4	1,137	28	5.6
5	1,378	34	6.8
6	1,398	35	7.0
7	1,864	47	9.4
8	1,734	42	8.4

In addition, 209 words were listed to be introduced in Grade 1, on the basis of their inclusion in the eight spellers that listed words for this grade. The lists include not only the words, but the frequency with which they appeared in the seventeen spelling books and the range of grades over which they were assigned. The average number of words per day, as shown above, ranges from 2.0 to 8.4. For all grades except the second the numbers seem to the writer to be too high for efficient learning. If teachers taught thoroughly a maximum of two words every day, the end result might be better. There appears to be little agreement among the spellers analyzed as to the proper assignment of a word. For instance, the word *accident* was included in sixteen of the seventeen spellers and assigned from Grade 5 to Grade 8. *Airplane* and *aside,* each listed in thirteen books, had ranges from Grade 3 to Grade 8. All books included *automobile* but placed it anywhere between Grades 3 and 7. Only one word in the 8,645 was used in all seventeen spellers and also placed by all of them in the same grade. Many words, of which *alone*

³ These facts are from W. H. Coleman, *A Critique of Spelling Vocabulary Investigations,* Colorado State Teachers College, 1931, 119 pp.
⁴ E. A. Betts, *The Spelling Vocabulary Study: Grade Placement of Words in 17 Spellers,* World Book Company, 1940, 72 pp.

is typical, varied only one grade in all the books, in this case between Grades 2 and 3. The list includes numerous words that appeared in only one of the seventeen books—for instance, *aristocracy,* assigned to Grade 8 or *axle* to Grade 7. One can only infer from these results that the commercial spellers do not yet use to their full value the results of research in the field. There are plenty of lists, but thus far no one has successfully bridged the gap between research and the schoolroom.

It is not to be assumed that children never use or need any words not included in their spelling lessons. They use many, but such words are either among those assigned to higher grades or else are unusual words that are favored by a single child who happens to know their meaning. Beyond the commonest words, vocabulary becomes a highly individual matter. The most feasible solution is for each child to look up words of which he feels uncertain, keep a record of his errors, and subsequently to learn the correct spelling of each word he has missed. All the teacher or the textbook writer can do is to present the commonest words and to leave the less common to each child's vocabulary study or correction.

1. Use of Spellers: Recently there have been some investigations indicating that spelling books are not especially useful. A good deal of the growth in the subject seems to take place just as well without the spellers as with them. A few items from the results of testing 2,250 pupils in Grades 3B through 6A appear in Figure 39.[5] The children made just as much progress on the words they did not study as on those they did, as illustrated by the two halves of this figure.

It is not altogether clear just how much progress in spelling is due to teaching, how much to wide reading, and how much to mere maturity. Thus the curves in the right half of Figure 39 do not show consistent gain in or immediately after the grade in which a word is studied. In another instance, the children in Grade 4, in an extensive study,[6] could spell 86 per cent of the words assigned to Grade 2, 80 per cent of those from Grade 3, 57 per cent of the Grade 5 words, 40 per cent of the Grade 6 words, and 32 and 28 per cent respectively of those assigned to Grades 7 and 8. These children failed on 14 to 20 per cent of the words they had studied, but they could spell from 57 to 28 per

[5] D. L. Arnold, "Spelling Lessons and Ability to Spell," *Elementary School Journal,* 42: 35–40, 1941. Used by permission of the publisher.

[6] H. A. Curtis and E. W. Dolch, "Do Spelling Books Teach Spelling?" *Elementary School Journal,* 39: 584–592, 1939. See also, L. L. Clifton, "The Textbook and Work Book in Learning to Spell," *Journal of Experimental Education,* 7: 274–276, 1939.

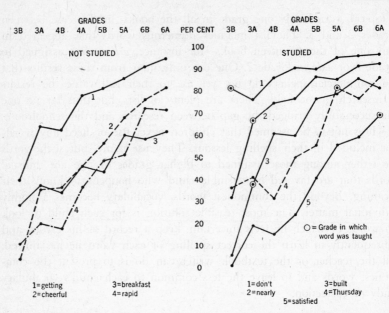

FIGURE 39: Mastery of Studied and Not-Studied Words

cent of words they had not thus far been taught. The words taught in any one grade are certainly not learned there. Thus the Grade 3 words were known by:

23		1
72		2
80		4
84	per cent of the children in Grade	5
95		6
96		7
97		8

Almost three fourths of the words in any given year are known by pupils below the grade in which they are studied, but even with this head start a year's work in Grade 3, for instance, raised the level from 72 to only 80 per cent. In subsequent years, during which the third grade words were assumed as known, growth continued until mastery had reached 97 per cent in Grade 8. Of this final per cent, however, only 8 per cent can be attributed to teaching. The rest probably came from reading and general maturity. If the children in each grade can learn to spell from a half to nearly two thirds of the words for the following year without teaching, it would seem as if teachers might be able to bring about a mastery of the other half to a third; but they do not, although the reasons for the meagre gains are not clear. It is the writer's personal opinion that only by a complete individualization of spelling can progress be made that is commensurate with the effort involved.

If a teacher or a group of teachers wishes to select a textbook, in spite of the evidence that these books are of relatively little value, at least as they are commonly used, there are certain important criteria against which prospective selections should be checked.[7]

1. Are the words selected on the basis of research?
2. Are the words assigned to grades on the basis of research?
3. Are the words grouped according to spelling difficulty, structure, or meaning?
4. Are there provisions for review?
5. Are there lessons that would lead to an appreciation of the value of spelling?
6. Is the work well motivated?
7. Are there practice exercises for the pupil?
8. Are there good suggestions for the teacher?
9. Is the book attractive and the print clear?

It seems as if a spelling book that met these criteria should, if properly used, be of value in helping children learn to spell. Possibly the negative results to date are due to the inclusion of far too many words, with the result that the pupils become confused and discouraged.

B. CHILDREN'S ERRORS IN SPELLING

In general, mistakes in spelling arise from three different and largely unrelated sources. Some are due to defects within the pupil, some to the difficulties inherent in English words, and some to inappropriate methods of teaching. Often all three types of cause fuse together, as in the case of a certain ten-year-old boy with defective vision, who failed such sight words as *neigh* and was taught by a system that put much emphasis upon getting a clear visual picture. The boy had a defect, the word was inherently difficult, and the teaching was inappropriate for this particular child. The many investigators who have analyzed errors have classified them in more or less detail under sundry headings. In one recent article,

---

[7] I. R. Waterman and I. R. Melbo, "Evaluation of Spelling Textbooks," *Elementary School Journal*, 36: 44–52, 1935.

previous studies have been brought together and the many divergent groupings of errors reconciled and combined. Those errors that arise from the nature of the English language are presented first in Table 44.[8]

The above errors arise from the pecularities of the language. If,

TABLE 44
Types of Spelling Error

I. Omissions
   A. Of a single letter
      1. Silent (*throu* for *through*)
      2. Pronounced (*cach* for *catch*)
      3. Of one of a pair of double letters (*suden* for *sudden*)
   B. Of a syllable (*intertion* for *intervention*)

II. Additions or repetitions
   A. Of a single letter
      1. Doubling (*untill* for *until*)
      2. Nondoubling (*untile* for *until*)
   B. Of a syllable (*recoverer* for *recover*)

III. Transpositions and reversals
   A. Phonetic (*cride* for *cried*)
   B. Unphonetic (*baord* for *board*)

IV. Phonetic substitutions
   A. Of a vowel (*injoy* for *enjoy*)
   B. Of a consonant (*prizon* for *prison*)
   C. Of a diphthong (*Ogust* for *August*)
   D. Of a syllable (*purchest* for *purchased*)
   E. Of an entire word (*colonial* for *colonel*)

V. Nonphonetic substitutions
   A. Of a vowel (*stition* for *station*)
   B. Of a consonant (*impossitle* for *impossible*)
   C. Of a diphthong (*fained* for *feigned*)
   D. Of a syllable (*difficould* for *difficult*)
   E. Of an entire word (*comfort* for *concert*)

VI. Confusion of homonyms (*two* for *too*)

[8] G. Spache, "A Critical Analysis of Various Methods of Classifying Spelling Errors, I," *Journal of Educational Psychology,* 31: 111–134, 1940. Used by permission of the publisher.

See also, J. C. Almack and E. H. Staffelbach, "Spelling Diagnosis and Remedial

for instance, the sound *a* could not be spelled as *eigh, ai,* or *ei,* children would not produce such misspellings as *paiy* for *pay,* or *pleigh* for *play,* or *drane* for *drain.* Such sources of error are inevitable and will remain so until simplified spelling gains in favor more than it ever has in the past. To date, spelling reform has had little success, but a change eventually is not impossible. For instance, the Swedes have changed their spelling two or three times during the past century and the Norwegians even oftener. Within the last fifty years the Germans have eliminated all their silent *h's.* Some day the conservative Anglo-Saxon mind may follow suit.

The twenty-six letters of the alphabet do not cause errors in direct proportion to their frequency. Thus, the letter *e* makes up approximately 13 per cent of the total number of letters in ordinary writing, but it produces 23 per cent of all the errors. The letter *t,* on the other hand, contributes 9 per cent to the total usage but only 3 per cent to the errors. The four letters that give rise to the greatest number of errors in proportion to their use are the four vowels, *a, e, i,* and *u.*[9] Many of the errors are presumably due to the failure to pronounce these vowels accurately, especially when they are short.

The errors thus far listed are due in the main to peculiarities of English orthography. Silent letters, double consonants, numerous spell-

Teaching," *Elementary School Journal,* 34: 341–350, 1934; R. G. Anderson, "A Note on a Case of Spelling Difficulty," *Journal of Applied Psychology,* 22: 211–214, 1938; W. F. Book and R. S. Harter, "Mistakes Which Pupils Make in Spelling," *Journal of Educational Research,* 19: 106–118, 1929; F. J. Brittain and J. A. Fitzgerald, "The Vocabulary and Spelling Errors of Second-Grade Children's Themes," *Elementary English Review,* 19: 43–50, 1942; F. R. Dearborn, "A Study of Erroneous Word Concepts," *Elementary English Review,* 6: 3–6, 1929; J. A. Fitzgerald, "Some Reasons Why Children Are Poor Spellers," *Catholic Schools Journal,* 42: 126–127, 1942; A. I. Gates, *A List of Spelling Difficulties in 3,876 Words,* Bureau of Publications, Teachers College, Columbia University, 1937, 166 pp.; I. H. Hill, "Diagnosis of Spelling Difficulties," *Elementary English Review,* 1: 225–230, 1924; H. V. Masters, "A Study of Spelling Errors," *University of Iowa Studies in Education,* Vol. 4, No. 4, 1927, 80 pp.; M. McGovney, "Spelling Deficiencies in Children of Superior General Ability," *Elementary English Review,* 7: 146–148, 1930; J. E. Mendenhall, *An Analysis of Children's Errors,* Bureau of Publications, Teachers College, Columbia University, 1930, 65 pp.; F. A. Ogle, "A Study of Spelling Difficulty," *Field Study No. 1,* State College of Education, Greeley, Colo., 1933; D. H. Russell, "Characteristics of Good and Poor Spellers," *Teachers College Contributions to Education,* No. 727, 1937, 103 pp.; Sister Mary Virgilia, "Some Values of Diagnosis in Spelling," *Elementary English Review,* 3: 39–41, 1926; G. Spache, "Characteristic Errors of Good and Poor Spellers," *Journal of Educational Research,* 34: 182–189, 1940, and "Validity and Reliability of the Proposed Classification of Spelling Errors, II," *Journal of Educational Psychology,* 31: 204–214, 1940; also, "Spelling Disability Correlates: Factors That May Be Related to Spelling Disabilities," *Journal of Educational Research,* 35: 119–137, 1941; D. Speer, "An Analysis of the Sources of Error in 104 Words Misspelled by Primary School Children in the City of Baltimore," *Elementary School Journal,* 28: 362–372, 1928; A. E. Watson, "An Experimental Study in the Psychology and Pedagogy of Spelling," *Teachers College Contributions to Education,* No. 638, 1935, 144 pp.

⁹ Mendenhall, *op. cit.*

ings for the same sound, a large assortment of diphthongs, several pairs of homonyms, and many words for which the spelling and the pronunciation are only distantly related are inevitable sources of error. In addition, there are sundry mistakes that come from the nature of the human organism. The more important of these should be considered.

1. Inattention: The pupil who is not attending to his work can produce errors that baffle the analyst completely. He writes, *The horse was in the prte,* not because he thinks his rendition is a spelling of *pasture* but because he was thinking of something else altogether.

2. Illegible handwriting: Some children write so badly, often because of immature motor control, that neither they nor anyone else can read the words with certainty. A pupil who produced *slyle* may have thought *style* but have made the *t* with a loop and then forgotten to cross it or omitted to do so because it looked so much like an *l*.

3. Anticipation: A child thinks as he writes, and because his mind moves faster than his pencil, he sometimes gets ahead of himself and inserts letters from the words he is about to write into the word he is writing. For instance, such an error as *We are going on tre train* is due to anticipation. It occurs because the pupil is thinking *train* while writing *the.* Usually, these mistakes occur only when successive words have the same initial letter, but not always. Errors of a similar kind come from tacking on an unnecessary letter, as in the sentence, *The young man wore a greens shirt.* The *s* from the last word was written too soon.

4. Mispronunciation: Pupils often pronounce words incorrectly and then spell what they have said. If a child says *gran* for *grand* he is likely to leave off the last letter. Unless a few people in public life begin to say *government* over the radio instead of *govermunt,* children will never learn how to spell the word correctly. Indeed, spelling by ear is almost as often dangerous as it is helpful, because the sounds within a single word may vary in pronunciation even by the same person from day to day. The word *you,* for instance, may contain any vowel from a long *u* to a sound best rendered as *yuh.* Unless pronunciation is exact, it can easily lead one into error.[10]

5. Failure to complete words: When a child writes *understa* for *understanding,* he may have been interrupted, or inattentive, or he may have been unable to proceed any further. Older pupils sometimes make this error because they are in the habit of using abbreviations in their notes—*compre* for *comprehension,* for instance. These shortened forms are not, strictly speaking, errors, but they occur.

6. Reversals, especially among young children: In the first two or three grades some of the pupils are still so immature visually or so predominantly

---

[10] M. E. Kay, "The Effects of Errors in Pronunciation upon Spelling," *Elementary English Review,* 7: 64–66, 1930.

left-handed and left-eyed that they read words or letters backward. They write *saw* for *was, dog* for *good, bone* for *done, qrant* for *grant.*

7. Inadequate hearing: Many pupils fail to hear all the sounds in a word. Sometimes they miss vowels, especially short ones, and sometimes they confuse consonants or fail to hear them. One acquaintance of the writer cannot distinguish *epic* from *ebig,* or *Kentucky* from *Genduggy* because he hears no difference between *p* and *b* or between *k* and *g.* Other people cannot sense a difference between *dawg* and *dog* or between *fish* and *feesh,* or *eighth* and *eight,* or *-ence* and *-ance.* Short vowels are especially difficult, and many children cannot spell correctly such a series as *pat, pet, pit, pot,* and *put* because the short vowels sound so much alike to them.

In some cases errors seem due to the methods used in teaching or to other environmental factors. These causes are in the background and usually fuse with others from the two previous categories. The most common source of trouble in the teaching is the presentation of too many words, too hurriedly. Some teachers emphasize vision almost exclusively, while others try to teach an unphonetic language phonetically. Either extreme is undesirable because it is too narrow, and it may be fatal to those children who do not have the native capacities necessary for profiting by the instruction. The use of a foreign language at home usually has a negative effect upon spelling in English, because a child tends to transfer sounds from one language to another. Thus the child from a German-speaking home spells *shell* as *schell* and the one from a French-speaking home renders *credit* as *credite.*

In the actual writing of words the errors that come from peculiarities of the language, those arising from the human organism, and those that result from inappropriate teaching are intermingled, and it is not always possible to decide which errors come from which source. Of all the types of mistake listed, the most common are the phonetic errors, which make up about 65 per cent of the total.[11] English contains only 44 sounds, but these can be spelled in a variety of ways,[12] and it is not surprising that children constantly interchange them. One discouraging point is the persistence of errors from one level to another. Almost as many college students misspell *necessary* and with the same variations as children in the fifth grade; some of them still invert the vowels in such common words as *friend* or *groan* or *guest,* or even *neither,* and many more are still confused about the doubling of consonants before the *-ing* or *-ed*

[11] Masters, *op. cit.*
[12] Watson, *op. cit.*

endings of verbs.[13] Perhaps the difficulties of the language will prove insurmountable, but better teaching should reduce the number of errors.

A recent study of error has resulted in a small book that should be most helpful to teachers, because the errors on each word are listed separately. A few items appear in Table 45.

TABLE 45
A Few Samples from the Gates List of Spelling Errors [14]

Correct Spelling	Per Cent of Misspellings Due to Errors in Italicized Parts	Common Error or Errors	Per Cent of Total Errors	Average Grade Placements	Grade in Which 90% of Children Know Meaning
be*ne*fit	100	benifit	55	H 7	H 8
b*i*cycle	61, 47	bycicle	33	L 6	H 2
br*ai*d	90, 48	brade	42	L 5	L 5
		brad	23		
b*uy*ing	100	bying	75	L 5	H 1*
cand*i*date	97	canidate	31	H 7	L 7
		canidate	26		
crac*k*er	95	craker	59	H 4	L 3
cre*a*ture	54, 32	creture	50	H 6	H 6
fi*f*th	83	fith	43	L 5	L 4
fir*m*	90, 35	ferm	49	L 6	L 7
		fern	29		
nec*es*sary	90, 73	nessery	14	H 6	L 7
		nessary	13		
nin*e*	85	nin	67	H 3	H 1
p*i*ano	94	paino	30	L 4	L 3
rea*ll*y	91	realy	79	L 6	L 4
se*c*ure	63	sucure	20	L 8	H 8
		sicure	19		

* The grades below L 3 are estimates based upon reading vocabulary lists for Grades 1 and 2.

[13] See, for instance, T. G. Alper, "A Diagnostic Spelling Scale for the College Level: Its Construction and Use," *Journal of Educational Psychology*, 33: 273–290, 1942.

[14] Gates, *List of Spelling Difficulties in 3,876 Words, op. cit.* Quoted by permission of the publisher.

The letter or letters in italics show the place or places in each word where errors most often occur. The second column gives the per cent of mistakes due to the letter or letters indicated. Column 3 contains some common misspellings, with the per cent of errors due to each appearing in Column 4. The average grade placement of each word in a number of spellers and the grade in which 90 per cent of the pupils know the meaning of each word appear in the last two columns. By comparing these two, a teacher can tell whether or not children are likely to know the meaning of a word already or if she needs to teach its meaning along with its spelling.

The items in Table 45 show a number of different kinds of mistakes. All the errors found in *benefit* occurred in one place, and over half of them came from substituting an *i* for an *e*, presumably because an unaccented *e* is pronounced as either a short *i* or a short *u*. *Bicycle*, on the other hand, has a number of misspellings aside from those in the letters marked, and the reversal of *y* and *i* accounts for only a third of them. The misspellings of *necessary* are legion, as is indicated by the low per cents after the two common errors included in the list. The children are prolific in their misspellings of *receive* also, but they concentrate upon the omission of the one *l* in *really*. The average grade placement in a number of spellers is sometimes too low, because the meaning of the word is not yet sufficiently known. For example, the meaning of the word *firm* is not known to 90 per cent of the pupils until a year after it has been taught.

Every teacher should get the Gates list of words so that she may look up the hard places and probable errors in each word before she teaches it, since she can prevent errors more easily than she can correct them. Teachers sometimes underline the most difficult part of a word or else write it in colored chalk. It is doubtful if these procedures help much, although the failure may be due to other factors than the marking. Perhaps the teacher relies too much on the device, or she does not get as much value from it as she might. It may be, however, that the marking merely distracts attention instead of concentrating it.[15]

C. THE GROUPING OF WORDS

There are a number of ways of grouping words for presentation to a class. One relatively popular method is to select for each group words

[15] L. S. Tireman, "Value of Marking Hard Spots in Spelling," *University of Iowa Studies in Education*, Vol. 5, No. 4, 1930, 48 pp.

that deal with a single subject such as: *farm, cow, horse, barn, duck, farmer, grain, pond, field,* and so on. This arrangement may increase interest and it certainly permits of a fairly immediate transfer from spelling to composition—in case the teacher follows study of such a group by a writing assignment concerning life on a farm. The words in a single meaningful group do not, however, assist each other in the actual spelling because they have no phonetic relationship, and they may actually interfere with each other. Grouping upon the basis of phonetic similarity [16] or spelling difficulty is also possible. In the latter case, common words in which the long *i* sound is spelled as *y* might be taught together; *my, fly, by, shy, cry, try, why, dry;* or on a more advanced level: *bicycle, typhoon, dynastic, cyclone, thyroid,* and so on. Probably most common is the grouping on the basis of phonetic similarity. Such groupings should promote positive and retard negative transfer, which is the greatest single source of error. There is, for instance, positive transfer from *clean* to *mean, seam, team, cream, beam, bead, deal, peal, fear, dear,* and so on, but the transfer is negative from *clean* to *seen, receive, beet, seed, equal* or other words in which the long *e* sound is spelled in some other way than *ea.* The transfer is positive also from *all* to *ball* or *call,* but negative to *almost* or *always.* It is therefore most undesirable that a teacher should give pupils a list of words in which the same sound is spelled in different ways or in which the same series of letters is pronounced differently. Such a series as *leave, esteem, receive, been,* and *earnest* is bad because it gives three spellings for long *e* and two pronunciations apiece for *ea* and *ee.* It is, however, possible to group words so as to bring about as much positive transfer as possible and thus to facilitate learning. A few suggested groups are presented below:

hatchet	although	able	all	school	hollow	food
catch	almost	table	call	schedule	fellow	moon
match	always	stable	ball	scheme	follow	pool
	altogether		fall	scholar	yellow	cool
beet	also	knock	hall		pillow	fool
career		knife	tall	voice	shallow	foolish
fleet	cracker	knit	wall	choice		soon
green	pack	know		moisture	sudden	goose
breeze	quack	knew			hidden	hoop
seed	tracked	knob				

A teacher would do well, at the beginning of the year, to go through the entire list of words she is to teach and group them. Words from previous years may also be included, since the children are already familiar with them. There are some words that may be grouped in more

16 See lists on p. 239 ff.

than one way, in which case the point of greatest difficulty within the word should be selected and the grouping based on this. Thus, in the lists above, *school* is put with the other three *sch* words rather than with the *oo* words, since greatest difficulty in it is that the *ch* will be regarded as a *k*. Even with one's best ingenuity, there are certain to be some highly individual words remaining after the clearly related ones have been classified, but even a small amount of grouping is useful.

Teaching of the *-s, -ing,* and *-ed* endings of regular verbs offers an excellent opportunity for grouping words. A week spent in adding these endings to large numbers of regular verbs (those not having a final *-e* being kept separate from those that have) is most effective in reducing the number of errors made in adding these endings. Such an exercise inevitably leads to the derivation of at least one general principle or rule, about which more is to be said shortly.

The question of teaching homonyms,[17] *there—their, new—knew, ate —eight, sight—site,* or *seed—cede,* separately or together is perennial. A review of experiments and opinions favors the following conclusions: If one member of a pair of homonyms is taught in a lower grade than the other, there should be no mention of a possible confusion when the first word is taught. If the two members of a pair are both in the list for the same year the teacher should take up the more widely used member of the pair first. Sooner or later, children have to learn to distinguish between homonyms, but the time to make the distinction is either when the second member is introduced or in a review after both members have been learned separately, and the children are old enough to be interested in rather than confused by two spellings for the same sounds.

D. SPELLING RULES

In days gone by children have memorized many spelling rules, together with lists of numerous exceptions. Within the past two decades, investigators have challenged the value of these rules.[18] One investigator studied the application of the most widely quoted rules to a modern spelling vocabulary of 4,065 words intended for use in Grades 2

[17] K. C. Harder, "The Relative Efficiency of the 'Separate' and 'Together' Methods of Teaching Homonyms," *Journal of Experimental Education,* 6: 7–23, 1937.

[18] For excellent discussions of spelling rules and their possible value in different grades, see L. M. King, "Learning and Applying Spelling Rules in Grades Three to Eight," *Teachers College Contributions to Education,* No. 517, 1932, 80 pp.; and I. C. Sartorius, "Generalization in Spelling," *ibid.,* No. 472, 1931, 65 pp. Also L. B. Wheat, "Four Spelling Rules," *Elementary School Journal,* 32: 697–706, 1932.

through 8, in an effort to determine the value of each rule for such common words as one is likely to write—not for all possible words in the language. A few samples of the results are of interest.

TABLE 46

Spelling Rules [19]

Rule	Words to Which It Applies	Exceptions
1. The plural of most nouns is formed by adding -s or -es to the singular.	250	25
2. Final -e is dropped before a suffix beginning with a vowel.	244	4
4. Nouns ending in -y preceded by a consonant change the y to i and add -es to form the plural.	16	0
6. Monosyllables or words accented on the last syllable ending in a single consonant preceded by a single vowel, or a vowel after qu, double the final consonant when adding suffixes beginning with a vowel. If accent is not on the last syllable, the final consonant is not usually doubled.	97	13
7. i before e except after c or when sounded as a in "neighbor" and "weigh."	101	30
10. In words like calf and half, the -f of the singular is changed to v before adding -es to form the plural.	21	0
11. Final -e is kept before a suffix beginning with a consonant.	1	0
12. When words end in a single consonant preceded by a single vowel the last consonant is called the final consonant. This final consonant is doubled before a suffix beginning with a vowel.	312	28
13. When final -y is preceded by a consonant, the -y is changed to i when adding a suffix beginning with a consonant.	14	0
15. Final -y is changed to i before a suffix that does not begin with i.	32	1
16. All words ending with -full have only one l at the end.	16	0
17. q is always followed by u.	54	0
18. Words of one syllable having a long vowel usually end with a silent -e.	248	339
22. ph often sounds like f.	20	2
25. A final e is dropped before a suffix -er.	19	1
26. A word ending in -y after a vowel usually retains its y before any suffix.	31	0
27. In adding -ing to words ending in -ie, drop the final -e and change the i to y.	7	0

These rules are clearly of unequal value. Rule 18 has more exceptions than it has applications. Ten per cent of the plurals are exceptions, as are 30 per cent of the ie words, and 9 or 13 per cent of the words that do or do not double their final consonants, depending on how the rule is phrased. The other rules taken together have only 8 exceptions, but they apply to a total of only 475 words out of the 4,065 studied, or about 11 per cent. Indeed, one objection to any or all of these rules is that they apply to too few words. For the rules above given the total words affected are 1,383, or 34 per cent of the 4,065, and there are 443 exceptions—well over 10 per cent!

These results might easily discourage a teacher from even trying to present spelling rules, but the author is inclined to salvage whatever can be used, even though the number of words affected is rather small. Perhaps the "rules" might better be called "general principles," since the former word suggests a greater invariability than actually exists. These principles cannot, however, be presented until after the children have already been learning to spell words for three or four years because the technical vocabulary is too difficult, but in the fourth grade one or two simple rules may be introduced, the proper formation of plurals, for example.[20]

1. Plurals are formed by:
   a. Adding *-es* to nouns ending in *-o, -s,* or *-x.*
   b. Changing the *-y* of nouns ending in *-y* to *i* and adding *-es.*
   c. Changing the *-f* of nouns ending in *-f* to *v* and adding *-es.*
   d. Adding *-s* to all other nouns.

To this rule there are as common exceptions the irregular plurals: *men, women, children, teeth, geese, mice.* In teaching this rule, words may be grouped in the fashion shown below, a single group being presented and discussed at any one time.

cow—cows	potato—potatoes	calf—calves	lady—ladies
ball—balls	gas—gases	leaf—leaves	lily—lilies
fur—furs	Negro—Negroes	half—halves	city—cities
eye—eyes	hero—heroes	wolf—wolves	baby—babies
hotel—hotels	box—boxes	shelf—shelves	pony—ponies
laugh—laughs	dress—dresses	elf—elves	party—parties
notice—notices	ax—axes	self—selves	ferry—ferries
root—roots	(Exception:	(Exception:	hobby—hobbies
tomato—tomatoes	autos)	handkerchiefs)	

To help pupils in the addition of the *-ing* ending to verb stems and of the *-able* or *-ate* endings to adjectives, after they begin to write stories and need these derived forms, a second principle may be introduced.

[20] See also King, *op. cit.*

2. If a word ends in *e*, drop the *e* before adding an ending that begins with a vowel.

hide—hiding	devote—devoting
ride—riding	manage—managing
make—making	devise—devising
wake—waking	refuse—refusing
bite—biting	desire—desirable
use—using	fortune—fortunate

Three other relatively minor rules may also be given, since these are either invariable or almost invariable and will, if observed, prevent a small but appreciable number of errors.

3. Although the word *full* has two *l*'s the ending -*ful* has only one.

4. Every *q* is followed by a *u*.

5. The sound of short *i* at the end of a word is usually spelled with a *y*.

wonderful	queen	inquire	daily
beautiful	quiet	require	fully
successful	queer	request	weary
needful	quite	square	fairy
thoughtful	question	squint	pretty

The changing of *y* to *i* to form the plural of nouns has already been mentioned. Two other principles about *y* are also useful.

6. A word ending in *y* after a vowel usually retains the *y* before any ending.

7. A word ending in *y* preceded by a consonant changes the *y* to *i* before any ending that does not begin with *i*.

play—playing,	played,	playable
cry—crying,	cried,	cries
ply—plying,	pliable,	plied
pity—pitying,	pities,	pitiable
ally—allying,	allied,	alliance, allies

The doubling of consonants, especially in inflected verb forms, is the greatest single source of error. The general principle can be expressed clearly enough, but it involves several technical words and it is hard even for sixth grade children to understand:

8. Words of one syllable or words with the accent on the last syllable that end with one consonant preceded by one vowel double the final consonant before an ending beginning with a vowel.

There are some exceptions, but the main objection to the rule is that it involves too many factors for childish intellects. Moreover, before they can grasp the rule pupils need to write for some years many of the commonest words to which it applies. It is possible, however, to explain to children that a double consonant shortens the vowel before it and that a single consonant leaves it long. Therefore *hide* becomes *hiding,* with a single *d,* but *hidden* with a double *d.* This principle does not always work, but it is quite consistent in the case of many common words that children use. If the children understand this phonetic principle they can avoid such errors as:

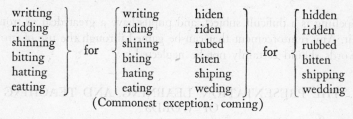

writting		writing	hiden		hidden
ridding		riding	riden		ridden
shinning	for	shining	rubed	for	rubbed
bitting		biting	biten		bitten
hatting		hating	shiping		shipping
eatting		eating	weding		wedding

(Commonest exception: coming)

If a teacher in the sixth grade wants to teach the doubling principle she would do well to proceed by three stages, beginning with vocabulary drill on the special words needed. The rule can then be divided into two parts, one for monosyllables and one for longer words, thus eliminating the factor of accent from the initial section of the rule. Endings beginning with vowels, *-ing* or *-able,* can be contrasted with those beginning with consonants, *-tion* or *-ly.* With the second part of the rule, the emphasis can shift to accent position, with such contrasts as:

> expel—expelling, expellant
> alter—altering, alteration
> occur—occurring, occurrence
> paper—papering
> blunder—blundering

The proper sequence of *e* and *i* when they occur together is a complex matter. There are *ie* rules of which the commonest is the rhyme:

9. "*I* before *e* except after *c* or when sounded as *a,* as in *neighbor* or *weigh.*"

This statement of the matter does not cover all cases, but it has the merit of being easy to learn, and it has no more exceptions than other formulations. A teacher can illustrate the principle by grouping words that are spelled in the same way and can give the rule, a little at a time, as it applies to subsequent groups.

When pronounced as a	*After c when pronounced as one sound*	*After c when pronounced as two sounds*	*All others* ie
freight	receive	society	believe
neighbor	receipt	science	relieve
weight	deceive	conscience	sieve
feign			
rein			

(Exceptions: *either, neither, height, leisure*)

Spelling is a difficult subject, and pupils have a great deal of trouble with it. Any reinforcement that can be gained through the use of grouping words should certainly not be neglected.

E. THE PRESENTATION, LEARNING, AND TEACHING OF WORDS

1. Getting a Clear Impression: The words to be taught in a given half year are listed for the teacher in whatever speller has been adopted for the school system, but she is more or less free to present the words as she likes. The method of presentation, discussion, and study should have as its objective the clearest possible impression of each word upon the minds of the pupils. The suggestions in this section are made with this end in view.

Words should always be presented one at a time, even though they may later be grouped together in order to bring out their similarities. The common habit of writing on the blackboard a list of assorted words is a poor method for making any one word clear. Partly because of eyestrain, partly because vertical reading is an unfamiliar process, partly because isolated words are uninteresting, the pupil usually reads the first two or three carefully, then begins to falter, skips over some, and finally ends with a fairly careful consideration of the last one or two. Words in the middle of a list are barely seen. Since the words of a list are necessarily close to one another and because children's eyes focus none too accurately, whole syllables from one word are likely to be transposed to another. The teacher should make a point of writing each word by itself. She may either write three or four words (the outside number to be taught at one time) at widely separated intervals on the board or may erase each word after it has been studied and put the next in its place.

In studying a word, the pupils must first recognize its meaning and pronounce it. It may next be incorporated in a few sentences to familiarize the children with its use. The teacher should then repronounce it, exaggerating the sounds, especially at the points where errors are likely to occur. For instance, if a word has a double consonant, *both* should be sounded by the teacher. For the word *recommend,* the teacher should say *re-com-mend,* being extremely careful to pronounce only one *c* and both *m's.* In colloquial speech a person sounds a double consonant exactly as if it were single, but in teaching spelling the exaggerated and deliberate sounding of both is a great help. This slow and emphatic pronunciation should then be copied two or three times by the children. If the word has more than two syllables, the teacher should call attention to its length, speaking the word so as to give it a rhythmic pattern that will help the pupils to remember it. They should next look at the word carefully, stare at it, and make a conscious effort to remember its appearance. They should also repeat the letters aloud once or twice. It is a good idea at this point to have the children close their eyes, try to "see" the word, whisper softly to themselves the pronunciation and spelling, and try to write it in the air or with their forefinger on the desk. After they have looked at the board once more to correct any wrong impressions or uncertainties, they should write the word *once* and then score the results against the correct form. Children who have made errors should throw away their copies and start over, time being given them for further study. Everyone should then write the word a second and perhaps a third time, but not more.

All children should be given thorough practice in all ways of getting a clear impression of a word—by looking at it, listening to its sound, pronouncing it, spelling it aloud in a whisper, recalling its appearance, recalling its sound, writing it in the air, and tracing its form if all else fails. In the course of time each child will come to use one or two of these techniques in preference to the others. Some learn excellently merely by looking at words and are disturbed rather than helped by the sounds. Others depend greatly upon the sound and may tend to spell phonetically. For most people, the more senses are used, the better; they need hearing, seeing, and writing to get a clear impression. If a child finds his visual images poor and has to resort to sound he must, in the whispered pronunciation from which he will spell, say every consonant whether it is silent or not, enunciate all double consonants clearly, give all single vowels their exact quality, pronounce all double vowels separately, and separate the diphthongs into their two constituent vowels. All this is cumbersome and should not be resorted to unless necessary, although a small amount of it is often valuable. Thus, the endings *-ence* and *-ance* can always be distinguished by correct "inner" pronunciation, despite the fact that in American speech both become *-unce*. Other such exact pronunciations, to be used regularly by the child with faint visual memories and occasionally by all children for reinforcement of difficult words, are shown below:

> *leave* becomes *le-ave*
> *occasionally* becomes *oc-ca-si-on-al-ly*
> *nineteen* becomes *ni-ne-te-en*
> *tomatoes* becomes *to-ma-to-es*
> *patient* becomes *pa-ti-ent*

The value of such devices may be appreciated if the reader will remember how he pronounces the word *subtle* when he is writing it. Although in speech he says *suttle,* in writing he probably says *sub-tle* to himself to insure correct spelling. Children who have unusually good kinesthetic memory and easily learn rhythms learn best by chanting the letters—after the fashion of pupils learning Latin verb forms, poetry, the bones of the body, or the Lord's Prayer. What such children remember best is neither the appearance nor the pronunciation of the word but the series of more or less rhythmic reactions they themselves make in spelling off the letters. For longer words an accent helps, such as *b-u-s-i'——n-e-s-s'*. Division into syllables is also helpful in long words. All these methods are good but not equally good for all children.[21]

2. Eye Movements in Learning to Spell: The good and the poor speller may be recognized by his eye movements quite as easily as the good and the poor reader. Figure 40 shows the records made by

[21] A relatively old but still helpful article contains a number of good suggestions: J. Sudweeks, "Practical Helps in Teaching Spelling: A Summary of Helpful Principles and Methods," *Journal of Educational Research,* 16: 106–118, 1927.

See also T. G. Foran, "Basic Psychology and Techniques in Spelling," *Education,* 57: 364–366, 1937; E. P. O'Reilly, "Providing for Individual Differences in the Teaching of Spelling," *Twentieth Yearbook of the Department of Elementary School Principals,* 20, No. 6: 503–506, 1941; S. M. Reese, "Spelling as Taught in a Large City System," *ibid.,* pp. 488–495.

two children in studying the word *questionnaire*. The child whose record is at the right spelled well and easily. After an initial regression he took six fixations to get through the word once, then went through it with four, then made one regression, and ended by going through the word again with five fixations. His procedure showed a definite pattern of efficient eye movements. At the end of less than six seconds of study he could spell the word correctly. In contrast, the child whose record is at the left wandered back and forth in the word without much system. He had 24 forward movements and 18 regressions. After studying the word for 18 seconds he had little idea of how it was spelled.[22]

Figure 41 [23] presents another contrast between a good and a poor speller. The first child learned the word *accident*. He started at the beginning, went through it once with seven fixations, then made a return sweep, and went through it again with five pauses. The 13 fixations are numbered in order. His procedure was systematic and his movements were accurate. The second child tried to learn how to spell *biscuit*. His method was rather inefficient. He began in the middle of the word, went backward, and then

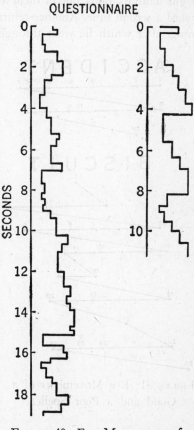

QUESTIONNAIRE

SECONDS

FIGURE 40: Eye Movements of a Good and a Poor Speller

[22] L. C. Gilbert, "A Genetic Study of Growth in Perceptual Ability in Spelling," *Elementary School Journal*, 40: 346-357, 1940. Figure 40 is used by permission of the publishers. See also E. M. Abernathy, "Photographic Records of Eye Movements in Studying Spelling," *Journal of Educational Psychology*, 20: 695-701, 1929; L. C. Gilbert and D. W. Gilbert, "Training for Speed and Accuracy of Visual Perception in Learning to Spell: A Study of Eye Movements," *University of California Publications in Education*, 7: 351-426, 1942; L. C. Gilbert, "An Experimental Investigation of Eye Movements in Learning to Spell Words," *Psychological Monographs*, Vol. 43, No. 3, 1932, 196 pp.

[23] Gilbert, "Experimental Investigation of Eye Movements in Learning to Spell Words," *op. cit.* Used by permission of the publisher. See Figures 3-9 for similar records of eye movements in reading.

forward until he had gone off the end of the word entirely. After this introduction, he started at the beginning and went right through the word with five fixations and again returned to the initial letter and took eight more fixations, one of them a regression, to get almost through the word a second time. Another return sweep took him back to the beginning, after which he went through the word once more in three long jumps. On his next return sweep he made a pause en route, then went through the entire word again, and had gone back to the beginning once more when the record stopped. This pupil was a poor speller, but his technique was not all bad. He made only two regressions, and he was systematic in his attack, although he spread his efforts almost evenly over the entire word, except for the last two letters, which he neglected. It seems a reasonable guess that this child has a visual defect or a poor visual memory because his eye movements, aside from their number, are good. He should have learned the word, but he failed to do so.

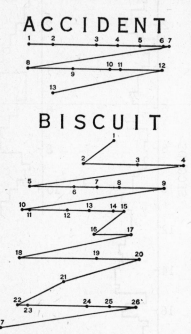

As children progress through the grades, they gradually acquire more efficient habits of word study, presumably through selection of the methods most useful for them. The improvement is reflected in the eye movements used by children as they study words. Pupils who were examined as they passed through the fourth, fifth, and sixth grades show a development from the use of many disorganized fixations to the use of a few that are highly efficient. Figure 42 [24] shows the progress made during three years by the same child in spelling the same word. At first he took 36 fixations and needed over 17 seconds to complete his studying, but he spelled the word incorrectly. A year later he needed only 12 fixations and a little over 6 seconds, but he still misspelled the word, although his second rendition was much nearer to the right form

FIGURE 41: Eye Movements of a Good and a Poor Speller

[24] Gilbert and Gilbert, *op. cit.* Used by permission of the publisher.

than the first. After another year had gone by he took 14 fixations, but they were so short that his time was reduced to 5⅔ seconds, and he spelled the word correctly. The number of regressions was reduced from 20 to 4. In three years this child had changed his method of study from one that was very immature to one that was highly efficient.

3. Organization of the Week's Work: So much for the presentation and learning of individual words. One must next consider the organization, presentation, and study of a unit of work. There have been a few experiments in this field, but the results remain somewhat indecisive, although such evidence as exists points to the general superiority of the type of organization here recommended for those teachers who cannot completely individualize instruction.[25] Its superiority presumably rests upon the fact that the children study only those words they do not know. The schedule below is consequently recommended:

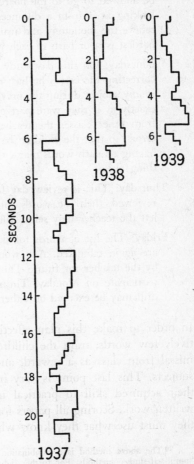

FIGURE 42: Eye Movements of the Same Pupil Studying the Same Word in Three Successive Years

Monday: Dictate twice the words to be studied during the coming week. Not more than ten words should be included. It is best to dictate the series once in the morning and once in the afternoon, using a different order for the words; score papers and tabulate words missed.

Tuesday: Dismiss for the week any children who spelled all words correctly on both tests. Write all the words on the blackboard, but not in a list. Any word missed by a

[25] Breed, *op. cit.*, and C. T. Zyve, "An Experimental Study of Spelling Methods," *Teachers College Contributions to Education*, No. 466, 1931, 89 pp.

majority of the pupils should be taken up first by the whole class. The rest of the period is to be used for individual work. Each child should study only the words he missed on one or both tests. The children may be allowed to go to the board on which a word is written instead of looking at it from a distance, if they want to. Moving around helps relieve the monotony and usually annoys no one but the teacher. The hardest part or parts of each word may be written in colored chalk.

Wednesday: On this day study should be wholly individual, each child correcting the errors he has made in spelling *any* word on *any* paper in *any* subject during the previous week. These words are to be treated exactly as if they were part of the regular lesson. (In reading papers from other classes the teacher should mark and correct all spelling errors, so that the children have the correct form for study.) Children having no such words may either review the week's lesson or do something else.

Thursday: This is review day for all. The words of the week are first reviewed, then the words for the preceding week. In what time is left the teacher may select difficult words from previous weeks.

Friday: The list of words for the week is again dictated and the errors are again tabulated. Any words still missed should be carried along by the teacher for future Thursday reviews. All members of the class participate on Monday, Thursday, and Friday. Those who need no drill may be excused on either or both of the other two days.[26]

In order to make this plan effective, one must concentrate upon relatively few words, train the children to do independent work, use dismissal from class as a reward, and include all words missed in other subjects. This last point is very important. Many children fail to put their acquired skill to practical use and make unnecessary errors in written work. Scoring all papers for spelling gives children the idea that they must use what they know whenever they are writing.

[26] The above method is a combination of the "test-study," the "study-test," and the "pupil-self-study" methods. For further light on these points, see R. S. Thompson, "The Effectiveness of Modern Spelling Instruction," *Teachers College Contributions to Education,* No. 436, 1930, 81 pp., and C. W. Dupee, "A Comparative Experimental Study of the 'Pupil-Self-Study' and the Modern Systematic Methods of Teaching Spelling," *Journal of Experimental Education,* 6: 1–6, 1937, and W. S. Guiler and G. A. Lease, "An Experimental Study of the Methods of Instruction in Spelling," *Elementary School Journal,* 43: 234–238, 1943.

F. SUMMARY

There has been extensive research both into the matter of what words pupils in different grades need to write and into the nature of children's errors. What is still lacking is an adequate application of known facts to the materials of instruction. There are as many different selections as there are spelling books. The data on children's errors is certainly not utilized to its fullest extent in helping teachers to prevent mistakes. In the course of time, the results of research will presumably get into wider use than at the moment.

The main point to remember about the presentation of words is that the child must get the clearest impression possible. Pupils vary from one another as to the means by which this clearest possible impression can be made, and each child should determine at as early an age as he can which methods of procedure are best for him. Children need all the help they can get, except for those fortunate few with crystal clear visual memories, because English is a frightfully hard language so far as spelling is concerned. Sounds and letters do of course have some connection, but it is not invariable as it is in some languages.

X · Composition

Both in school and out, children have constant need for speaking and fairly frequent need for writing. Some of the needs cannot be met by work in elementary school because the children are too immature. Even first grade pupils, however, can make a start on the task of learning to speak clearly and to the point, and each subsequent grade can make its contribution to progress in English. The major uses that children have for spoken or written English at some time during their school career are given in Table 47.

TABLE 47

Life Situations in Which Spoken or Written English Is Used

I. Spoken English

  A. Conversation
    1. At the table, at social gatherings, in discussion groups
    2. During introductions, during calls, at interviews, in greetings and partings, in asking directions, in telephoning

  B. Meetings
    1. Informal proceedings such as class or auditorium exercises
    2. Formal proceedings such as organizations, clubs, committees

  C. Discussions or addresses
    1. Speeches of felicitation, dedication, presentation of gifts, acceptance of gifts; introduction of speakers; inauguration speeches; speeches when retiring from service; impromptu speeches
    2. Reports on meetings, conferences, visits, illustrated lectures, demonstrations, talks
    3. Persuasion talks in membership drives, campaigns of many kinds, applying for work during off hours
    4. Messages, announcements of games, lectures, exhibitions, entertainments, meetings
    5. Explanations and directions as to how to bake a cake; make a radio, a flower box, or other objects; how to reach a park or railway station; how to iron a dress or take care of small children

D. Anecdotes and stories
   1. Telling anecdotes and stories to children in the home, school, or other social group
   2. Telling anecdotes or stories to adults at social functions, on the train, at the dinner table, in informal gatherings of friends, to people who are sick or in trouble, at public meetings

II. Written English

   A. Letters
      1. Business letters to firms for information or supplies
      2. Social letters to school friends, to parents, to children in other communities, to relatives
      3. Informal notes, excuses, invitations
      4. Formal notes

   B. Notices of games, lectures, exhibitions, entertainments, meetings

   C. Reports of committees of school or class, of delegates to class or school council, of president or other official of school council or club, financial reports, savings by class each week, minutes of council or club; reviews of books, articles, speeches, plays; reports of observations, or experiments

   D. Note taking for preparation of papers, stories, discussions, reports; taking class notes

   E. Filling out forms, mailing order blanks, applications for money orders, checks, deposit slips, test forms, telegrams, information blanks or questionnaires, budgets

   F. Making a bibliography

   G. Creative writing for papers, clubs, class newspaper, or magazine; articles in school or local papers, diaries; imaginative writing such as stories, poems, plays [1]

With such an assortment of opportunities it would seem as if a teacher could find plenty of material for giving children practice in such skills as will help them meet the demands made upon them, both in and out of school.

The production of a written composition requires the coordination of several skills and attitudes. One must have something to say and must express these ideas in legible handwriting and correctly spelled words. Nor is this all. During the production the harassed writer must

---

[1] Based on A. L. Threlkeld (Chairman), "Language and Composition," Chapter 9 of the *Fourth Yearbook of the Department of Superintendence of the National Education Association*, pp. 259–260, 1926. Used by permission of the publishers.

drop punctuation marks in the right places, capitalize the right words, write sentences that hang together, and keep a careful eye on grammatical forms. While being mindful of all these specific items he must have enough of his wits left to develop his presentation logically, to paragraph according to meaning, and to select those words that have the most telling effect. If, in addition, he can throw in some graceful personal reflections, a few subtle nuances, and a dash of humor, so much the better. These different activities must go on either in rapid succession or simultaneously. Since a person can think of only one thing at once, some of the simpler reactions must be so automatic that close attention to them is unnecessary.

Until the last two grades of elementary school, children cannot be expected to form letters easily, to spell enough words, to have an adequate vocabulary, or to have mastered simple punctuation well enough to take their attention from these details. Even though they can perform the separate activities well, they do not easily integrate them or keep them subordinated to the expression of their ideas. It is the writer's conviction that the average child would write better English at the end of elementary school if he were never required to produce a formal "composition." Whatever may be won seems to be more than lost through strain and through the practice in making errors incident to the production.

There is, however, plenty of work to be done in English, but it is of a simple nature, properly adapted to the capabilities of the children. In order to adjust work in such a manner, the author would make the following recommendations: that all work in the first grade be oral, that all work except spelling in the second and third be oral, that the work of the fourth grade be concentrated upon the production of simple and compound sentences, that the work of the fifth grade be devoted to the writing of social letters, and that only in the sixth grade should even a homeopathic dose of formal composition work be introduced. The following sections will take up the various types of work above mentioned in, roughly, the order of development in the grades.

A. ORAL ENGLISH

It was mentioned in the chapter on reading that oral composition is an excellent substitute for oral reading. It has all the advantages of reading aloud without the disadvantages. Since speech is obviously acquired mainly "by ear," it is a pre-eminently suitable subject to con-

3

COMPOSITION 253

centrate upon during the years before skills necessary to reading or writing have been developed. An adequate training in coherent speaking is also an excellent preparation for coherent written work later on. Finally, there is no question that anyone's main use of his own language is oral. For all of these reasons concentrated training in oral English would seem logical and wise from the time a child enters school at least until the time he has acquired the tools for written expression.

Work in oral English ought not only to help a child speak correctly but also to help him establish some desirable skills, both social and academic. Table 48 presents two lists of suggestions concerning these by-products.

TABLE 48
Objectives in Oral English

A child should learn:

1. To contribute spontaneously to discussion
2. To contribute courteously
3. To keep to the topic under discussion
4. To tell about one thing at a time
5. To speak clearly so that everyone can understand
6. To think through what he wants to say before he begins
7. To enunciate distinctly
8. To pronounce common words correctly
9. To know when he has finished a simple sentence [2]

A child should:

1. Think before he speaks
2. Know where to find something to talk about
3. Have something to say
4. Be a good listener
5. Talk with enthusiasm
6. Find words that suit his meaning
7. Avoid dominating the discussion
8. Know how to make his remarks fit into the conversation
9. Be sensitive to occasions when he should not talk
10. Speak correctly
11. Have careful enunciation
12. Avoid mannerisms that call attention to himself instead of to what he is saying
13. Be courteous [3]

The direct training in how to speak well should be one of the outstanding phases of public school work. It is hard to see how anything could be much more useful.

[2] M. C. Stevenson, "Oral Language in the Intermediate Grades," *Twentieth Yearbook of the Department of Elementary School Principals,* pp. 269–279, 1941. Used by permission of the publisher.
[3] D. Niles, "Conversation and Discussion," *ibid.,* pp. 287–295. Used by permission of the publisher.

1. Common Errors in Specifics: The training in correct usage should, from the first, stress both the avoidance and the correction of errors in speech. When children talk spontaneously they make a rather large number of errors, but not a large number of types. It appears from research that 76 per cent of all the errors in oral work are of only six types, as listed below:

TABLE 49

Types of Error in Speech [4]

1. Wrong verb used (*lay* for *lie, set* for *sit, can* for *may,* etc.)	19.0%	
2. Confusion of past tense and past participle (*done* for *did, gone* for *went,* etc.)	16.5%	
3. Redundancy (*For what did he go for?*)	13.3%	
4. Failure of subject to agree with verb (*John and Henry is going*)	10.8%	76.0%
5. Double negative (*He hadn't never been there*)	10.5%	
6. Confusion of present and past tenses (*go* for *went, give* for *gave,* etc.)	5.9%	

Naturally, one cannot discuss errors with children in the technical language used in the table to describe the mistakes. One must rather present each usage and correct each error without grammatical explanation. For this purpose the teacher needs a further analysis of the particular words that contribute in the greatest degree to the mistakes of each type. Such a list has been formulated and appears as Table 50 on the facing page. A teacher can make use of this list by centering drill in correct usage on these errors and confusions. She can spend as much time as is needed in having pupils speak sentences using *do, did,* or *done,* presenting sentence after sentence until their ears are trained to the correct expressions. They should say such sentences as *I saw him yesterday, I have seen him before* and so on, until the sound of a sentence tells them which form is correct.

[4] W. W. Charters, "Minimum Essentials in Elementary Language and Grammar," *Sixteenth Yearbook of the National Society for the Study of Education,* Public School Publishing Company, Bloomington, Ill., Part I, pp. 85–110, 1917; H. D. Fillers, "Oral and Written Errors in Grammar," *Educational Review,* 54: 458–470, 1917.

TABLE 50

Specific Errors Made in Speaking [5]

1. Use of *ain't* or *hain't*
2. Confusion of *saw* and *seen*
3. Use of singular verb with plural subject (usually *is* for *are*, *has* for *have*, or *was* for *were*)
4. Double negatives (*couldn't never*)
5. Use of *have got* *
6. Confusion of *come* and *came*
7. Use of *git* for *get*
8. Confusion of *them* and *those*
9. Use of *learn* for *teach*
10. Confusion of *can* and *may* *
11. Confusion of *do, did, done*
12. Use of *and* instead of *to* with infinitive
13. Confusion of *go, went, gone*
14. Use of *I and my brother* instead of *My brother and I*

15. Use of pronouns in objective case as subject (usually in such constructions as *Jim and me went*)
16. Use of *don't* for *doesn't*
17. Use of *this here*
18. Repetition of subject, as in *John, he went too*
19. Use of *that there*
20. Use of *lay* for *lie*
21. Use of *sit* for *set*
22. Confusion of *give* and *gave*
23. Use of *lots* for *many*
24. Use of unnecessary introductory words, such as *well, why, now, so*
25. Use of *leave* for *let*
26. Use of *et* for *ate*
27. Use of *like* for *as if*
28. Use of *run* for *ran*

* Not always wrong. See the next list.

2. **Pseudo Errors:** The experienced teacher may find that some of her old friends are omitted from the above list. Such sentences as *It is me, Can I go?* or *I have got to go now* may seem to her to furnish more errors than some of the categories listed. The acceptance or rejection of a given expression is a matter of the usage of each phrase in the English of cultivated people. A few years ago 222 members of the Modern Language Association, the English Council, the Speech Council, leading scholars of English, leading authors, and outstanding editors were asked to accept or reject a number of sentences as being or not being "informal, cultivated, correct English." The sentences accepted as good usage by 75 per cent or more of these individuals contain elements often classified as errors by teachers. They are not, however, mistakes in the judgment of experts—especially in the minds of the twenty-six leading linguists of the world. The teacher who tries to eradicate them is setting up her personal bias against the reasoned conclusions

5 G. M. Wilson, "Locating the Language Errors of Children," *Elementary School Journal*, 21: 290–296, 1920, and I. Sears and A. Diebel, "A Study of Common Mistakes in Pupils' Written English," *Elementary School Journal*, 18: 172–185, 1917.

of scholars who have devoted their lives to the study of language. The particular sentences that are acceptable but are sometimes regarded as errors are shown below.

TABLE 51

Pseudo Errors [6]

1. I *had rather* go at once.
2. You *had better* stop that foolishness.
3. This is the chapter *whose* contents causes most discussion.
4. He did not *do* as well as we expected.
5. You just had a telephone call. Did *they* leave any message?
6. The women were all *dressed up*.
7. One is not *fit* to vote at the age of eighteen.
8. Our catch was *pretty good*.
9. I can hardly *stand* him.
10. Jane was home *all last week*.
11. I'd *like to* make a correction.
12. I felt I could walk no *further*.
13. I've absolutely *got* to go.
14. That's a dangerous curve; you'd better go *slow*.
15. There are some *nice* people here.
16. Have you *fixed* the fire?
17. I *don't know* if I can.
18. The room is *awfully* cold.
19. *You* had to have property to vote.
20. The kind of apples you mean *are* large and sour.
21. The real reason he failed *was because* he tried too much.
22. They went *way around* by the orchard.
23. We *got home* at three o'clock.
24. There *is* a large *works* near the bridge.
25. None of them *are* here.
26. We will *try and* get it.
27. We *only* had one left.
28. Factories are *mostly* closed on election day.
29. He moves *mighty quick* on a tennis court.
30. It is *me*.
31. *Who* are you looking for?

[6] A. H. Marckwardt and F. G. Walcott, *Facts about Current English Usage*, D. Appleton-Century Company, 1938, 144 pp. (A publication of the National Council of Teachers of English.) Used by permission of the publisher. See also G. R. Johnson, "Will or Shall?" *School and Society*, 49: 779–780, 1939; S. A. Leonard, "Current English Usage," *English Monograph*, No. 1, National Council of Teachers of English, 1932, 232 pp.

32. Drive *slow* down that hill.
33. There *was* a bed, a dresser, and two chairs in the room.
34. They invited my friends and *myself*.
35. *Can* I be excused from this class?
36. Haven't you *got through* yet?
37. *Everyone* was here, but *they* all went home early.
38. He went *right* home and told his father.
39. A treaty was concluded *between* the four powers.
40. I wish I *was* thin.
41. I've no doubt *but what* he will come.
42. My *folks* sent me a check.
43. He came *around* four o'clock.
44. I have *got* my own opinion on that.

The first twenty-two usages were accepted as correct by both linguists and teachers; the second twenty-two were accepted by one group but considered as questionable though not wrong by the other. The above list is given in detail because the acceptance of these expressions as correct is so important in saving time and avoiding confusion. Teachers spend hours trying to eliminate *It is me,* although they are completely unable to do so because the children hear the words repeatedly outside school. This same amount of time can be better devoted to eliminating *I seen him, He done it, He give it to me,* and *He ain't come.* The teacher is strongly advised to accept the sentences in the above list as correct in the speech of children.

3. **Sentence Structure:** In addition to the specific errors in grammar already listed, children have difficulty in their sentence structure because they tend to narrate in terms of long, loose-jointed sentences in which the parts are strung together by "and" or "so." The teacher should try to show children how to divide their sentences into less unwieldy units. To be sure, the looseness of structure is often merely the expression of loosely integrated ideas, but it is partly habit. In any case a first step toward integrated thinking can be made in the lower grades by gradually training children to complete each single thought and then pause before starting another. If a primary teacher can get from children a series of simple declarative sentences free from glaring crudities of expression she may regard herself as successful.

4. **Activities:** In order to talk at all one must have something to say. The quality of what one says is so influenced by the nature of the topic

under discussion that the type of subject matter to be used with small children merits attention. In the first place, generalizations of experience should be avoided. That is, a child should not be asked to tell, for instance, how valentines are made, but rather how he made the particular valentine he has recently completed. Most children enjoy describing what they have done or made or seen. Each child may read a different brief story in an accessory reader and then tell the main events of his story to the class. A variation may be introduced by dividing a longer story into units of about a page and assigning one unit to each child; when all have read their selections, the children tell in order the events of the story, each contributing only one or two sentences. After a holiday or a week end, children may be asked to tell what they did on the previous day. This specific topic is much better than a request to tell about an exciting ride, a happy experience, or a party. Getting from the generalized topic to the specific incident involves the kind of thinking that children do not do well. Occasional use may be made of such assignments as "Why we should wash our hands before eating," or "Why we should watch the traffic lights." Perhaps the most useful kind of exercise is the answering of a relatively simple question such as "Why were you late for school this morning?" "What did you do on the playground during recess today?" "How many people do you have in your family and who are they?" Once in a while each child may be asked to bring into school a flower, a postage stamp, a stone, or other small object and then describe it to the others and answer questions about it. Another interesting device is to have a pair of children stand before the class, one asking the other such a question as "How should I go to get from here to the corner of Oak Street and Parsons Avenue?" The other child then gives the directions needed. (The pairs of children should be assigned by the teacher during the period so that answers to the questions cannot be prepared.) Giving directions is a common type of speech activity—and most people give them badly. Training in introducing people can be made into an interesting and profitable game, with each child labeling himself as to what character he portrays (an old man, a little girl, a mother, the neighborhood grocer, the President, and so on). The children then make the proper introduction to each other, using the correct form and speaking the names clearly. Another interesting variation may be introduced by placing two children with their backs to each other on opposite sides of the room and letting them have a telephone conversation with each other.

The main thing about the assignments to be used is that they should cover a small unit of subject matter, that they should concern some specific happening, that they should concern something recent, that they should be about matters already quite familiar to the children, and that they should require little or no organization beyond a mere chronological sequence.[7]

Of late years an activity described as "choric speaking" has come into vogue. It seems to be a refinement of and improvement on the traditional class singsong produced when the teacher said, "Now, all together." Great emphasis is put upon clearness and accuracy, because every child has to enunciate every word carefully, or the choral result will be unintelligible. In addition to the usual speaking in unison, there may be sundry combinations of individual and group work. The arrangement is much the same as in singing or chanting. Most of the children form the chorus, and from a half to two thirds of the lines are spoken in concert, but here and there children with especially good voices speak individual lines. When the work is well done, the effect is aesthetically pleasing and, what is more important, it seems to be most satisfying to the children. Emphasis is to be put upon the "togetherness" of the situation and the beauty of the lines rather than upon the introduction of too much artistry, or the end result is more likely to be "arty" than artistic.[8]

For the primary grades, then, the main work in English concerns speech, the only written part being the writing of words during the spelling lesson. The teacher has during these years a golden opportunity to teach correct speech. Such training is worth while in itself, and it gives an excellent introduction to written English in the later grades.

B. DEVELOPMENT OF CORRECT SENTENCE STRUCTURE

The smallest unit of coherent thought is a sentence. Skill in the construction of sentences is the beginning of work in composition—and to some extent the end as well. Until individual sentences of fair merit can be produced, work on larger units of expression is of ques-

[7] For good suggestions see L. Abney, "Speech, Voice, and Pronunciation," *Forty-third Yearbook of the National Society for the Study of Education,* Part II, pp. 181–186, 1944.

[8] For suggestions, see, A. M. Othmer, "Values and Proceedings in Choric Speech," *Twentieth Yearbook of the Department of Elementary School Principals,* pp. 302–306, 1941, and E. E. Keppie, C. F. Wedberg and M. Keslar, *Speech Improvement through Choral Speaking,* Expression Publishing Company, Boston, 1942, 279 pp.

tionable value. The work of the fourth grade, therefore, might well be centered around the study and writing of acceptable sentences of those types required by pupils for the spontaneous expression of their ideas.

1. **Types of Sentence:** The first point to be settled is in regard to the types of sentence used, since the number of mechanical skills needed is directly proportional to the complexity of the sentence. The proportion of sentences of each type written by children in different grades appears in Table 52.

TABLE 52

Types of Sentence [9]

	Grades			
	3	*4*	*5*	*6*
Simple sentences	54	51	49	46
Complex sentences	29	31	33	34
Compound sentences	11	10	10	9
Complex-compound sentences	7	9	9	10

The simple sentence is the predominant type in all grades, with the complex sentence—often without need for special punctuation—coming next, and the compound sentence a poor third. Complex-compound sentences require more skill in punctuation than most children have and should perhaps just be ignored when pupils produce them spontaneously.

2. **Skills Needed:** If fourth grade children are to be taught only simple and compound sentences they will need only relatively few technical skills. For convenience, the mechanical skills and technical information will be considered under the heads of sentence structure, grammar, capitalization, punctuation, and vocabulary. There have been many analyses of children's writing, and the common errors in each of these fields are known. The skills listed in this section and the following ones are those that are essential for writing done in the elementary school. The results are based upon detailed analyses of both needs and errors in the writings of well over 3,000 pupils.

[9] W. C. Hoppes, "Some Aspects of Growth in English Expression," *Elementary English Review*, 10: 67–70, 121–133, 1933. See also J. C. Seegars, "Forms of Discourse and Sentence Structure," *ibid.*, 10: 51–54, 1933. Used by permission of the publisher.

a. *Sentence Structure:*[10]

Skills

1. The production of a complete sentence, not a fragment
2. The avoidance of stringy sentences
3. The correction, by rereading, of such omissions or repetitions as are due to inattention while writing

These three rather general skills are fundamentally necessary. The two most frequent errors are the inclusion of too little in a sentence (the use of a fragment) or of too much (a stringy sentence). Errors arising from omitting a word or from writing it twice are neither as frequent nor as fundamental; moreover, they are not errors of sense but of carelessness and can therefore be avoided by a critical rereading of what has been written. The real problem of any sentence is to include exactly the right amount in it. Training along this line can be begun as soon as sentences are written at all.

b. *Grammar:*[11]

Skills

1. Agreement of verb with subject
2. Correct use of past tense and past participle
3. Use of nominative case of pronouns as subjects and of objective case as objects of either verb or preposition
4. Use of right tense for meaning
5. Use of adjectives to modify nouns and of adverbs to modify verbs
6. Use of the correct verb of a pair that sound alike and of the correct member of a pair of homonyms

These errors are much the same as those listed in the section on oral English. Errors in grammar do not, of course, interfere greatly with meaning; they merely give an impression of inelegance and crudity. For this reason they are not as important as errors in sentence structure or punctuation, although they may seem worse because of their offensiveness.

[10] S. L. Pressey, "A Statistical Study of Children's Errors in Sentence Structure," *English Journal,* 22: 197–201, 1933; J. A. Fitzgerald, "The Letter Writing Difficulties of Intermediate Grade Children," *Twentieth Yearbook of the Department of Elementary School Principals,* pp. 332–338, 1941; Sears and Diebel, *op. cit.*

[11] W. S. Guiler, "Survey of English Usage of Elementary School Pupils in Ohio," *Elementary English Review,* 9: 169–171, 182, 1932; Sears and Diebel, *op. cit.;* J. Seaton, "Errors in the Mechanics of English Composition," *Research Adventures in Higher Education,* Public School Publishing Company, Bloomington, Ill., pp. 96–99, 1927; A. W. Wheeler, "A Study to Determine the Errors That Appear in Written Work of Rural and Urban Pupils of Certain School Systems of Kentucky," *Journal of Experimental Education,* 8: 385–398, 1940.

c. *Punctuation:*[12]

Skills

1. Period at the end of sentence
2. Question mark at end of interrogatory sentence
3. Commas to separate members of a series
4. Comma before *and* or *but* in a compound sentence
5. Apostrophe for possessives
6. Apostrophe for contractions

Most simple sentences require only a period or a question mark at the end. The two uses of the comma and of the apostrophe are frequent enough to justify the teaching of these usages as soon as children write at all. They are simple and have the great advantage of being almost invariable. If teachers concentrate on these requirements sufficiently to get periods or question marks at the end of sentences and apostrophes where they are needed, they will have eliminated at least a goodly proportion of all the errors made in writing. It should be noted that errors in punctuation lead to difficulties of comprehension and are therefore of more than formal importance.

d. *Capitalization:*[13]

Skills

1. Use of capital at the beginning of sentence
2. Use of capitals for names of persons
3. Use of capitals for names of cities, states, or countries
4. Use of capital for *I.*
5. Use of capital for names of schools or streets
6. Use of capital for *God.*
7. Use of small letters for all words not included in preceding categories

Most errors in the use of capitals come either from a failure to capitalize the first word of a sentence or from the use of unnecessary capitals for

[12] M. A. Dawson, "Correct Usage," *Forty-third Yearbook of the National Society for the Study of Education,* Part II, pp. 164–170, 1944; W. S. Guiler, "Analysis of Children's Writing as a Basis for Instruction in English," *Journal of Educational Method,* 5: 259–264, 1926; P. L. Harriman, "Sources of Confusion in Punctuation and Capitalization," *Peabody Journal of Education,* 12: 31–35, 1934; C. J. Lee, "Improving the Technical Aspects of Written Language," *Twentieth Yearbook of the Department of Elementary School Principals,* pp. 376–382, 1941; S. L. Pressey and H. Ruhlen, "A Statistical Study of Current Usage in Punctuation," *English Journal,* 13: 325–331, 1924; Sears and Diebel, *op. cit.;* Seaton, *op. cit.;* Wheeler, *op. cit.*

[13] S. L. Pressey, "A Statistical Error of Usage and of Children's Errors in Capitalization," *English Journal,* 13: 727–732, 1934; Guiler, *op. cit.,* Lee, *op. cit.,* Sears and Diebel, *op. cit.,* Wheeler, *op. cit.*

common nouns. Since the names of people and places begin with a capital, children sometimes get the idea that any important word should do so, and they sprinkle capitals for emphasis throughout their sentences.

Of all the errors children make in their written work in elementary school, six, aside from spelling, are outstanding—the use of stringy sentences, the failure to use a capital at the beginning of a sentence, the failure to put a period at the end, the use of unnecessary capitals, the failure to use apostrophes, and the confusion of present and past tenses.[14] These mistakes occur in all grades, although the frequency is a little lower at the end of school than in Grade 3. Since the capital at the beginning and period or other mark at the end of every sentence are invariable usages, and since failures in these two respects are the most frequent of any, it would seem as if the fourth grade teacher might make a valuable contribution to later work in English if she would concentrate a year's work upon these and other relevant skills needed for the production of correctly written sentences.

e. *Vocabulary:*[15]

Fourth grade children cannot be expected to have concepts for many of the terms used in language work, but they do need to know what is meant by those words used by the teacher in showing them how to write sentences or in correcting their mistakes. Words for this purpose appear in the following list:

sentence	period	noun
simple sentence	comma	verb
compound sentence	apostrophe	pronoun
interrogative sentence	capital letter	
subject	present tense	
object	past tense	

The vocabulary that would be needed for explaining errors in grammar does not appear in the above list because such errors are best corrected without explanation. A child learns to say *I did it* instead of *I done it* by ear, not by an explanation of grammatical principles.

14 Wheeler, *op. cit.*
15 R. V. Johnson, "Determination of the Essential Technical Vocabulary for Work in Written English," Doctor's Thesis, Ohio State University, 1927; L. Cole, *The Teacher's Word Book of Technical Vocabulary,* Public School Publishing Company, Bloomington, Ill., 1940, 128 pp.

3. **Content of Written Work:** In the fourth grade, where the task of writing connected material may be begun, the teacher should use a type of assignment that will call for the spontaneous and natural production of simple sentences. Probably the easiest method is to have children write answers to questions, one sentence being written for each answer. As initial practice material a group of easily answered queries may be read by the teacher, such as: "What is your name?" "Where do you live?" "How old are you?" "What game do you like best?" and so on. The children should be required to write whole sentences as answers, not fragments. As soon as the children get the idea, the questions may be based on a story the children have read. In fact, this kind of training offers excellent possibilities for checking on the adequacy of silent reading. A little later it is well to work in questions based on geography and history lessons. An examination or other series of questions can well be used for practice in English. By means of such exercises the children soon come to write perhaps half a dozen short sentences a day, thus obtaining regular practice in sentence structure. At the same time they grasp the idea that one uses skills in written English for the purpose of saying something on paper at other times than during the English class. This early conviction that English is a tool is highly desirable.

Naturally, the teacher must phrase her questions so that the replies may be expressed in easily written sentences. She needs also to keep a wary eye on the probable words in the answers so as to avoid calling for words that cannot be spelled. The content of the questions can be so varied from day to day that the writing does not become monotonous, especially if work in sentence study and sentence analysis is interspersed. One profitable exercise consists in writing on the blackboard a single short sentence, such as "The man played the piano." Each child copies the sentence, and then the teacher asks him to put in a word telling what kind of man it was. Each pupil puts in his own adjective. Then another adjective is added to describe the piano, then an adverb to tell how the man played, a descriptive phrase about him, and so on, each child building up his own sentence until he has such a production as: "The handsome man with the powerful hands played beautifully upon the grand piano that was nearly 100 years old." Every child's sentence is different from every other's except for the words used at the beginning.

If a teacher will use a little ingenuity, she can devise many practical situations that call for a natural and spontaneous writing of sentences. Gradually answers or other exercises that demand two or even three sentences may be introduced. Practice on small but correct units until the sentence becomes a readily used form of expression is the fundamental need.

The work of the fourth grade should, then, center around the production of correctly written, simple or compound, declarative sentences. For this purpose the children require training in the use of six skills in punctuating and seven in capitalizing, further training in correct usage, intensive drill in distinguishing between pairs of words often confused, practice in sentence structure, and meanings for a small number of technical words. All these items are specific and practically invariable. Indeed, they are essential facts, and their mastery demands memory and adequate practice rather than understanding and careful judgment. If attention is centered on them, other types of problem or error being largely ignored, a teacher has time for the establishment of two generalized habits that do involve an elementary degree of judgment and critical understanding. The first—and central problem—is the development of "sentence sense" insofar as the types of sentences practiced are concerned. The second is the habit of invariable, critical rereading of everything that is written. Some children will not, even with the best of teaching, develop these two general habits, because they are not mature enough. However, many children in the fourth grade can make a beginning on these two general habits while they are achieving a fair mastery of simple or compound sentences as units for the expression of ideas in practical school situations.

C. THE WRITING OF LETTERS

Writing letters is the one almost universal use of composition among both adults and children. There are, however, certain additional reasons for choosing letter writing as the first form of composition. A personal letter is largely narrative in type and requires relatively little organization. The thinking involved is therefore simpler than that which underlies a more formal composition. Most children's letters are composed mainly of simple or compound sentences. Perhaps letters require, therefore, few additional technical skills beyond those enumerated, except for the heading, salutation, and ending. These skills are, however, so simple and so invariable that mastering them is well within the capabilities of children. Since letters to friends are informal in style and depend for their content upon what the writer happens to be doing or thinking, children can use their daily experiences as natural material about which to write. For all these reasons a concentration on letter writing during the fifth grade would seem desirable.

1. Sentence Structure: The first question concerns the additional skills and concepts needed for composing a letter. The simple or compound sentence is to be assumed as well enough mastered for use. Study of the writing done by fifth grade children reveals the fact that they use three types of complex sentence with some frequency. They write subordinate clauses beginning with *when,* substantive clauses beginning with *that,* and relative clauses beginning with *that, who,* or *which.* Sentences containing an *if* or a *because* clause are far less numerous, while clauses introduced by *while, since, although,* or other connectives are practically nonexistent.[16] Examples of the three most common types are given below:

1. I was away from home when he came.
2. He saw that I was sick.
3. I like the cake that my mother makes.

The substantive clause (No. 2) is almost invariably used as an object of a verb, not the subject, in the writing of children, and therefore requires no punctuation. The relative clause (No. 3) also needs no commas.

That children use relatively little subordination is shown by the analysis of the compositions written by 482 children in Grades 4 through 9. The total number of clauses was 9,156, of which 6,649—72 per cent—were independent and 2,507 were dependent.[17] That is, there was on the average one subordinate clause to every three main clauses. The children in the elementary grades, however, used even less subordination.

Subordinate clauses beginning with *when, if,* or *because* (No. 1) present more of a problem than either of the other types given because such a clause may be introduced at the beginning, in the middle, or at the end of a sentence and its position affects its punctuation. When the clause comes after the completion of the main clause, a comma is usu-

---

[16] W. J. Osburn, *What and When in Grammar in Terms of Usage,* State Department of Public Instruction, Madison, Wisc., 1924, 17 pp.

[17] L. L. La Brant, "The Occurrence of Dependent Clauses in the Writing of School Children in Grades 4 through 9," *Educational Trends,* 1: 16–29, 1932.

ally not needed. If the clause is inserted into the middle of the main thought, commas are almost invariably required. If it is placed before the main clause, the use of the comma becomes a matter of judgment, except in the occasional sentence in which its omission makes the meaning obscure. The examples below may make this matter clearer.

1. We shall have a picnic if it doesn't rain.
2. We shall, if it doesn't rain, have a picnic.
3. If it doesn't rain we shall have a picnic.

The second type is ruled out at this juncture because children so rarely produce it. The first arrangement is by all odds the most frequent, with the third being used by a few of the more advanced pupils.[18] It takes more forethought than most children possess to place the subordinate clause first. For such complex sentences as children of the age under consideration usually write, then, no more punctuation is needed than for a simple sentence. The occasional sentence requiring a comma can be ignored for the time being, except for the rare child who has already begun to feel a need for commas to make his meaning clearer— but such a one inevitably presents a problem demanding individual instruction.

A sparing use of commas is desirable at any stage but especially at the beginning of composition work. Teachers of the upper grades can persuade children to insert additional commas far more easily than they can bring about the removal of those that are unnecessary and irrational. The correct use of commas to set off clauses can be taught only through the development of a sensitivity to meaning that children do not have. If such usage is presented in terms of objective rules instead of subjective sense, the obedient pupil develops chiefly the incorrect and annoying practice of inserting a comma every six or eight words. The addition of the commonest types of complex sentence does not, then, involve the youthful writer in many situations demanding the use of commas for introducing or setting off clauses.

2. **Specific Skills:** There are only three grammatical usages to be added to the list already given for the lower grades. These are listed below in a form similar to that used in the earlier section.

[18] E. A. Davis, "The Location of the Subordinate Clause in Oral and Written Language," *Child Development,* 12: 333–338, 1941.

a. *Grammar:*[19]
Usages
1. Use of *as if* and *were* instead of *like* and *was* (*He looks as if he were tired*).
2. Use of possessive with gerund (*I did not know about his going*).
3. Use of predicate nominatives after a comparison (*He can swim as well as I*).

Children write enough sentences necessitating correct forms of the above constructions to make teaching of them desirable at this point. Matters presented in the earlier section on grammar are sure to need continuing emphasis throughout elementary school, the drill being given preferably through the use of models rather than by grammatical explanation.

In capitalization the children need to master primarily those usages concerned with letter writing. The list is given below:

b. *Capitalization:*[20]
Skills
1. Capitals for the months of the year and days of the week
2. Capitals in heading
3. Capitals in salutation
4. Capitals in complimentary close
5. Capitalization of titles of people
6. Capitalization of titles of stories
7. Capitals for holidays

These usages are practically invariable, the chief demand upon judgment being the capitalization of words within the title of a story.

A few new skills in punctuation must be added, many of them being those needed for letter writing.

c. *Punctuation:*[21]
Skills
1. Commas in heading of letter or in any address
2. Comma in date
3. Comma after close of letter
4. Colon (or comma) after salutation of letter
5. Quotation marks around the title of a book or story

[19] Seaton, *op. cit.;* Sears and Diebel, *op. cit.;* Wheeler, *op. cit.*
[20] Guiler, *op. cit.;* Lee, *op. cit.;* Pressey, "A Statistical Study of Usage and Children's Errors in Capitalization," *op. cit.;* Sears and Diebel, *op. cit.;* Seaton, *op. cit.*
[21] Guiler, *op. cit.;* Lee, *op. cit.;* Pressey and Ruhlen, *op. cit.;* Sears and Diebel, *op. cit.;* Seaton, *op. cit.;* Wheeler, *op cit.*

All these usages are invariable. The experienced teacher may be surprised by the omission of all references to direct quotations from the above list. Aside from writing done at the request of a teacher, neither children nor adults use direct quotations—except those who are writers by profession—and not even all of them. Nor do children spontaneously quote the actual words of the speaker. Unless required by a teacher to write direct quotations, they will write in indirect discourse, just as anyone else does. Of course, a few highly verbal children will want to use direct quotations, and there is no reason why they should not, provided they are able and willing to master the form, but again that is matter for individual instruction.

Children become confused as soon as they know that there are two kinds of quotations. They do not possess the judgment needed to distinguish clearly between the two, and they consequently use in one situation the punctuation designed for the other. Teaching of direct quotations to children before they are old enough to understand the principles involved may lead directly to errors. All analyses of adult writing show errors that are caused by the insertion of commas before indirect quotations, of quotation marks around such quotations, and of commas before titles. These mistakes are largely the *results of teaching* rather than the results of poor thinking. Since all the world writes indirect discourse and only a few people use the direct form, it seems wise to get the indirect quotation firmly grasped before adding the complications of the direct. A child will write indirect discourse as soon as he writes anything—such sentences as, *She said she would come,* or *My mother asked me to go*—but he can get along happily for some years by restricting his direct discourse to its oral manifestations and omitting its written complexities.

Children do, however, have use for quotation marks around titles. If they are to write letters about their everyday lives, some reference to the books they read or motion pictures they see is almost inevitable.

d. *Vocabulary:*[22] For the adequate understanding of the matters presented in the foregoing paragraphs a child needs a few additions to his technical vocabulary. These terms are listed below:

[22] Johnson, *op. cit.* and Cole, *op. cit.*

heading   title of person   future tense
salutation   title of story
complimentary close   exclamatory sentence
address
                           adjective
                           adverb
colon
quotation marks
exclamation point

The general addition of technical words is necessary if children are to understand the correction of their own errors. A teacher should regard the explanation of new word meanings as an important element in her task of developing correct written English.

3. **Content of Letters:** Children write many letters to many people about many things, although some correspondents and topics are pre-

TABLE

Contents and Recipients

Contents	All Letters	Father Mother	Uncle Aunt	Sister Brother	Whole Family
1. Experiences, activities, events	2,752	15	57	72	3
2. Objects	1,165	10	30	40	2
3. Thanks	282	1	16	7	
4. Greetings	17	1	3	2	
5. Congratulations	2				
6. Sympathy, condolence	48	1		1	
7. Apology, explanation	108	2		2	
8. Animals	557	2	9	14	1
9. Requests	213	6	8	3	
10. School	1,756	3	30	38	2
11. Invitations, acceptances	226	2	4	4	
12. Weather	828	6	22	17	2
13. Inspiration, encouragement	21		1		
TOTALS	7,975	47	180	200	10

ferred to others. In one excellent investigation a total of 7,976 letters written by school children were analyzed for content, a record being kept also of the people to whom the letters were written.[23] The chil-

[23] J. A. Fitzgerald, "Letters Written Outside of School by Children of the Fourth, Fifth, and Sixth Grades: A Study of Vocabulary, Spelling Errors and Situations," *University of Iowa Studies in Education,* Vol. 9, No. 1, 1934, 44 pp. See also R. Selig, "Letter Writing in the Sixth Grade," *Elementary English Review,* 18: 89–95, 1941.

dren were in Grades 4, 5, and 6. Table 53 shows to whom the letters were written and what they were about. The three main topics are daily experiences, school, and objects, with the weather and animals next. The first three constitute 71 per cent of the topics mentioned. Evidently, more letters were written to friends than to anyone else; the favorite relative for epistolary purposes seems to have been a cousin.

When children first begin to write letters they should be content to write short ones—perhaps a half page in length. They might, for instance, practice letter form by writing to the teacher, telling her which of several books they prefer to read, and stating their main reasons for the choice. Any similar type of information may be made the subject of the first practice letters. The next step might be letters to the parents. These may be about a particular happening in school, a story that has been read, a game that has recently been played. These letters are also,

53

of Children's Letters

Grand-parents	Cousins	Other Relatives	Teachers or Former Teachers	School Mates or Former School Mates	Friends	Others
14	548	11	97	45	1,884	6
7	227	3	34	19	790	3
8	58		30	4	158	
	4		1	1	5	
	1				1	
	5		4		37	
	23		9	2	70	
1	135	4	25	7	358	1
	25	2	8	4	156	1
4	365	7	70	33	1,201	3
	50	1	2	3	161	1
4	200	1	24	14	537	1
	8				12	
38	1,649	29	304	132	5,370	16

to some extent, practice ones, but they will serve to provide variety during the period while the children are mastering the form. As soon as possible, real letters should be written. When one of the pupils is at home in bed, the other children may like to write letters to him. Each pupil should compose his own communication, the first drafts being turned in to the teacher. After correction and discussion a final copy on real

letter paper and in ink should be made and—most important of all—
actually sent. There is no inspiration in writing a letter destined for
the teacher's wastebasket. Nor is there much joy in using school paper
for the final copy. Writing a letter on ruled, composition paper is merely
an assignment but writing it on pink stationery is an experience.

There are other letters that children like to write, if the idea is
suggested to them. Letters to authors or to librarians asking about books,
letters to various city officials asking for permission to visit the plants
and thank-you notes after the excursions have been made, letters to
radio stations, and even "fan" letters to motion-picture stars are all interesting and provide excellent practice in composing. Sometimes a
considerable correspondence can be developed between groups of children in different cities whose teachers are acquaintances. The thrill of
really sending a letter is vivid, but it pales into a shadow beside the
excitement of receiving an answer. Composition work is so hard for
children that emotional compensations are badly needed.

Some readers may object to the reading of personal letters by anyone except the producer and consumer. One must remember, however,
that children's letters are granted little if any privacy, anywhere. The
parents will read and edit them whether or not the teacher does. Children do not expect the privacy demanded by adults, and they usually
bring their letters to some adult because they are aware of their own
shortcomings in the matter of composition.

By a judicious insistence upon letter writing as a normal and everyday means of communication between people, a teacher can bring about
a fairly spontaneous writing of twenty-five to fifty letters in the course
of a school year—a total not reached by many children in the course of
their entire public school careers. Since the letter is the most widely
used form of composition, it should be the type of writing first asked of
children.

D. THE BEGINNING OF FORMAL COMPOSITION

If such a course of study as has been outlined above is followed,
the children are reasonably well equipped with the basic skills by the
time they enter the sixth grade. They still need, however, to learn more
about complex sentences, and they should begin to make a written plan
of what they will write before they start. Both these problems demand
certain technical skills which will be discussed in order.

1. The Complex Sentence: In the spontaneous writing of sixth grade children about 35 per cent of the sentences are complex.[24] Many of these, though not all, require one or more commas. Children in this grade use also a certain number of introductory phrases that need to be set off by a comma from the rest of the sentence. A few appositives appear. These various complexities in sentence structure are so confusing that they lead to a marked increase in the number of errors per 10,000 words of written work.[25] The introduction to the complex sentence had probably best be made by careful study and analysis of a large number of sample sentences. Its successful use depends essentially upon this understanding, for the punctuation presents relatively little difficulty if the children grasp the sentence structure.

2. Skills Needed: The new skills needed are not numerous, but they are essential if pupils are to handle complex sentences with reasonable correctness.

a. *Sentence Structure and Grammar:*[26]

Skills

1. Ability to finish the main clause of a sentence in which a subordinate clause has been introduced before the main clause is completed
2. Ability to put a subordinate clause in front of the main clause, setting it off with a comma if necessary for clearness
3. Ability to keep pronouns in agreement with their antecedents

To be sure, these same errors are not unknown in the lower grades, but they do not become frequent until children have ideas of some complexity to express.

The new punctuation skills involved are listed below. As matters now stand, one can expect, in the writing of school children, out of every 1,000 chances, 650 errors in setting off subordinate clauses and 458 errors in setting off introductory words or phrases. The expected number of errors in setting off inserted ideas is not given separately but would be large.[27] In fact, these are the three outstanding new errors in punctuation that appear as soon as sentences become longer and more involved than they were in the earlier grades.

[24] Hoppes, *op. cit.*
[25] Seaton, *op. cit.* and Wheeler, *op. cit.*
[26] Pressey, "A Statistical Study of Children's Errors in Sentence Structure," *op. cit.;* Sears and Diebel, *op. cit.;* Wheeler, *op. cit.*
[27] Seaton, *op. cit.*

b. *Punctuation:*[28]

Skills

1. Use of a comma to set off a subordinate clause
2. Use of commas before and after an inserted element [29]
3. Use of a comma after an introductory word or phrase

These errors, the writer feels, are not due to mere carelessness—as is the omission of a period at the end of a sentence—but rather to a lack of understanding of the function served by commas in the sentence. Children who cannot analyze sentences are almost certain to make these errors in their own writing.

There remain only three more skills in capitalizing that are needed often. The first and third in the list below are of only moderate usefulness to children but the second is needed frequently as soon as children begin to write examination questions in history, because such terms as *French, English, Asiatic, European, Italian,* and so on are sure to be written. For some reason people generally have a tendency to begin such adjectives with small letters.

c. *Capitalization:*[30]

Skills

1. Capitalizing trade names
2. Capitalizing adjectives derived from proper names
3. Capitalizing names of organizations

For an understanding of the complex sentence certain further terms must be added to the technical vocabulary. These terms include those needed to express the fundamental relationships among the parts of the sentence. The vocabulary load is not heavy, but a pupil cannot think clearly without it.

d. *Vocabulary:*[31]

complex sentence	phrase	agreement
clause	introductory phrase	modify
main clause	appositive	preposition
subordinate clause	insertion	conjunction

---

[28] Guiler, *op. cit.;* Pressey and Ruhlen, *op. cit.;* Sears and Diebel, *op. cit.;* Seaton, *op. cit.;* Wheeler, *op. cit.*

[29] At this stage of development the nonrestrictive clause had best be treated merely as one form of inserted element, without which the sentence would still be a sentence.

[30] Pressey, "A Statistical Study of Usage and Children's Errors in Capitalization," *op. cit.;* Guiler, *op. cit.*

[31] Johnson, *op. cit.* and Cole, *op. cit.*

Since the presentation of all mechanical skills in English composition is now at an end, this is as good a time as any to comment upon the various omissions. In capitalization and grammar no common usages or sources of error have been neglected. In sentence structure the main omissions have been with regard to parallel constructions. The need for these so rarely arises in grade school that consideration of them seems unnecessary. In punctuation there has been no presentation of quotation marks for direct quotations, semicolons, colons—except after a salutation —dashes, or parentheses. The matter of the direct quotation has already been discussed. Children rarely write a sentence demanding either a semicolon or a colon, but if either is presented to them, they seem to feel a compulsion to make some use of the marks and proceed to sprinkle them here and there in sentences that do not require them. Most children go on into the upper grades where they receive instruction in these matters, although many of them never will discover what a semicolon is for. The few who do not continue in school are not likely to produce in a lifetime many sentences demanding either a semicolon or colon, or to use either correctly if their sentences do require them. The dash and the parentheses have been omitted because children rarely need them but easily become wedded to their use as a convenient technique for preserving a sloppy sentence instead of rewriting it.

3. **Organizing:** The second main problem for this last grade in elementary school is the organization of material. It was mentioned in the chapter on reading that, as low as the fourth grade, children can begin to use an outline or other type of summary with good effect as a means of getting at an author's main ideas. Recognizing an organization in another person's work is, however, considerably easier than thinking out an organization for one's own productions. Nevertheless, a beginning must be made as soon as children start to write about given topics, for nothing is more productive of a fine crop of errors than aimless writing. Children do not, of course, need rigid outlines, but they should learn to make a plan of some kind *before writing*. On the next page are presented three copies of sixth grade children's plans on the very general topic of "Why Everyone Should Contribute to the Community Chest." Each child has his own method of planning his work, but the important fact is that each had given the matter some thought before actually starting upon his composition.

TABLE 54
Plans for Writing

Plan 1

We should have a Community Chest because:
1. There are lots of poor people.
2. Some of them need help more than others do.
3. The Chest gives the money out more evenly.
4. There isn't ever enough money.
5. When there is a regular drive people give more.
6. The money is used better.

Plan 2.

The Community Chest—I know some poor people (Grants) and they got money last year (over $200) from the Chest and they didn't have any work. The CC helps people fairer because the money is all in one place (tell how many places it was in before). Amount this year ($65,000). Show how it was given. No. of people who gave. One rich man gave $5,000. Tell how money was spent last year, for hospitals, food, clothes, and other things.

Plan 3.

With a Chest

Money given more evenly.
Not much chance for graft.
Drive for money made only once.
Amount of money on hand known for year.
Begun during war.
People give more if they give only once.
You can plan the use of the money better.

Without a Chest

Some poor people get too much and some get too little.
Always some graft.
People always being asked to give.
Money comes in little by little and you never know how much there is.
Before that work not so well done.
People won't bother to give very often.
Money given out without much plan.

Teachers in all subjects can help students develop the habit of planning what is to be written. After some years of teaching, the author became exasperated at the rambling and pointless answers sometimes written on examination papers and introduced a variation in procedure. She passed out the questions and a half sheet of paper at the beginning of a fifty-minute period. Then for twelve minutes she withheld any further supply of paper and instructed the students to read the questions and plan their answers, using the half sheet for notes if they desired. The results showed astonishing improvement in both the form and the content of the answers. An insistence on planning during a period set aside for that purpose before writing is begun will do much to make the pupils' technical skills function as they are supposed to function.

E. SUMMARY

In the primary grades instruction in English is necessarily oral because the pupils are not yet able to write well enough to use language as a means of written expression. The time may, however, be well spent in the elimination of barbarisms from spoken English, in training in speaking whole sentences, in experience of speaking to and with a group of one's peers, and in learning to organize in a simple manner what one has to say. In the writer's opinion the work of the fourth grade is best devoted entirely to the writing of sentences and the mastery of the simple skills that are needed for the purpose. Since letter writing is both the most universal and the easiest form of composition, it seems best to begin with it the process of writing more extensive material than single sentences. With such a plan of work, the children would start formal composition in the sixth grade, except for such contributions as they may make spontaneously as outgrowths of their activities.

Perhaps the main things for a teacher to remember are, first, that the work of the elementary grades should be really elementary, not an attenuated copy of more advanced forms of writing; and, second, that the matters about which children write should be important and interesting to them. Insofar as may be possible, teaching should be individualized, both as to practice in developing skills and as to topics for expression, since children grow in language power more rapidly under individual than group methods of instruction.

XI · Interest and Dynamics in Various Phases of Written Work

Expressing oneself in writing is a relatively difficult and complex performance which requires the simultaneous functioning of many skills and habits. There are, indeed, so many that some of them have to be almost automatic before an individual can write down on paper what he can easily say aloud. During the elementary school years children are still acquiring the basic skills and have not yet reduced most of them to the level of automatic functioning. The task of learning to write is therefore broken up into the subjects of penmanship, spelling, and composition, the last one making its appearance not earlier than the fifth grade after some of the contributing skills have become habits. Children learn to tell stories well orally and to read stories to themselves long before they are able to write them. A teacher cannot therefore use childish enthusiasm for storytelling as a motivation in the beginning stages of handwriting and spelling. These subjects often seem to children rather divorced from reality, as indeed they are, because the uses to which the skills will later be put are not yet apparent. Other motives, then, besides usefulness have to be employed. Some of the auxiliary urges will be presented in the three sections of this chapter. Of course, a teacher should demonstrate the usefulness of the work insofar as she can and she should provide as many situations as possible for practical use, but in the primary grades most motivation is indirect.

A. DYNAMICS IN HANDWRITING

Children have relatively little use for handwriting outside school, but they would probably use their skill oftener if they wrote more easily.

One cannot, therefore, get motivation from an immediately practical value to the children themselves, except as good writing helps them in other school subjects. Nor is the ideal of beautiful penmanship capable of stimulating such activity. Children feel about a model script a good deal as the average adult feels about the life of a saint—something beautiful but not to be achieved by one who is all too full of human frailty. The teacher must therefore find other incentives to stimulate the mastery of a skill that is purely a tool and is not intrinsically exciting.

There are a few things that most children want to write—their names, the names of their parents, their addresses, and so on. They want to put the necessary words on valentines or Christmas cards. They like to copy nursery rhymes to give to their younger brothers or sisters. They like to write notes to each other or brief letters to their friends. They enjoy writing out invitations or acceptances to a party. They are quite willing to write samples for a school exhibit or to exchange samples with children of the same grade in another school. All of these interests can be used whenever they are appropriate. It lends importance to handwriting if papers from other subjects are rated as to handwriting and if marks in handwriting are based to some extent on what the children produce in other classes. The more a legible script can be made to be of practical use in school, the more reason the children will see for working during the handwriting period.

The writer once came across an excellent example of teaching with an almost complete disregard of this principle. She was about to give a test of intelligence to a class of the first grade children toward the end of the school year, when it was found that they could not write their names. The teacher apparently felt some implied criticism and explained the situation. It seems that she had first drilled the innocent children on the small letters taken in the alphabetic order; after polishing off the small "z" she had started through the alphabet again with the capitals and had reached "U." In a couple of weeks more she thought the children would be ready to write their names. These youngsters had labored daily on forms, of the usefulness of which they had not the slightest notion. As far as they knew from anything the teacher had told them, they would be required to go on and on and on for the rest of their school lives drilling on single letters.

The other main motive on which the teacher may rely is a child's interest in getting his work done. This incentive cannot, obviously, be used in the usual handwriting situation because one is never "done."

The situation must be so arranged that children know what they have to do and know when they have done it. To most pupils handwriting drill stretches on forever in monotonous repetition. The teacher's best chances for success lie in setting up a definite and reachable goal and in giving a real reward to those children who reach it. There is no greater incentive than the presence in the classroom of children who have reached the goal and are therefore allowed to spend the drill periods in pursuing other interests. Admission to this leisure group does not signify to children so much an escape from the monotony of drill as an entrance into a socially enviable situation. These children are conspicuously labeled as successes. Nor is their success based on anything more than concentration and work; what they have done, other children in the class can also do, provided they will try hard enough. In handwriting such a reward as inclusion in a privileged group is especially valuable because it gives the overage children in the class what is perhaps their only chance to know success. Because they are older, they have better muscular control than the brighter but younger children. These dullards cannot shine in arithmetic or reading, but they can produce well-nigh perfect handwriting. In using this type of motivation the teacher must be very careful that she does not use the time thus gained to give children some other type of work. The youngsters have earned this time for themselves; as long as they disturb no one else, they should be allowed to do what they will with it.

One child may put his head down on his desk and go to sleep, another may prepare his arithmetic problems, another may read a story, a fourth may read his history assignment, another may draw a cartoon, a sixth may clean out his desk, while another goes out and sits in the sunshine on the school steps. There is nothing reprehensible in any of these activities. Escape from drill because of good work gives children freedom to direct their own activities for a few minutes. At home they are dominated by their parents, at school by their teachers; but the short period of freedom they have earned is theirs. It is no wonder that this type of reward has proved so powerful.

If a teacher uses a diagnostic rather than a general approach to handwriting,[1] the children are more interested because they can see their progress from week to week, sometimes even from day to day. Under the interminable daily drill so often used, improvement can be shown only from the beginning to the end of a semester, a period too long for good motivation.

[1] See Chapter XIII.

B. DYNAMICS IN SPELLING

There is little in a child's social life outside school that can be utilized naturally and easily to motivate the learning of spelling. Few small children write much of anything, and those who do produce an occasional letter are not seriously disturbed by their mistakes. Spelling is not an incidental part of children's games, and it is not useful in doing the chores or in pursuing hobbies. A child does most of his spelling in school. Even here, during the elementary years, he does not use his acquired skills a great deal because his work is largely oral. Some of the experimental schools have been quite successful in bringing about a more spontaneous use of spelling, even in the lower grades, than is usually possible in schools of a more conventional type. Spelling is, then, an almost universal adolescent and adult need that is served by skills so simple they can be acquired in childhood. The motives that help a child through his work in spelling must, therefore, be of a general type that can be attached to the spelling task, even though they are not an integral part of it.

Everyone likes to feel that he is making progress. This general sort of motivation can be introduced into the spelling situation if progress is expressed in terms sufficiently objective to be recognized. Suppose that

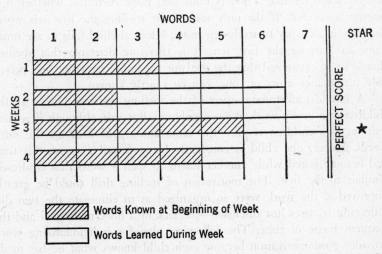

FIGURE 43: A Suggested Record and Report Card for a Month's Work in Spelling

the number of words to be learned per week in a certain grade is seven, plus any additional words missed on each pupil's written work in any subject. If one test is given at the beginning of the week and another at the end, a graph similar to that given above may be constructed. This graph shows, for each of four weeks, the number of words known at the beginning and the added number acquired during the week. If everything is learned by the end of the week, a star is placed after the record. The graph gives the child a definite and attainable objective—the total words for the week; it also tells him how far toward the objective he has already progressed—the words known at the start—and it gives him a reward that he can display if he is successful—the star. Such a graph can be sent home to the parents with the report card at the end of the month. To an adult such a reward as a star may seem inadequate to give the needed stimulation. To the child mind, however, the star is a visible badge of success. The "gold star reward" is old-fashioned, but so are children, and they still love gold or red or blue stars just as much as their great-grandparents did.

One of the unfortunate aspects of the spelling situation is its apparent endlessness. Children are not unduly discouraged by difficulty if they can feel that by hard work they can reach a given goal, but a lack of goal undermines their morale. There is a fundamenal satisfaction in knowing that a job is done and done correctly, whether it is interesting or not. If the only reward for spelling the first ten words correctly is a chance to study ten more, a logical child fails to see much value in learning the first ten. It is therefore desirable that spelling should be so organized that the goal for the entire semester, and preferably for smaller units of time, can be exactly known.

A second unfortunate aspect of the spelling situation is that all the children in a group work about evenly on all words, although it is clear that no two children require the same amount of drill on the same words. Hence, one child is constantly being forced to waste his time and become bored while another learns to spell a word that is already familiar to the first. The motivation of spelling drill could be greatly improved if the work were so organized as to eliminate the two discouraging features just discussed—the lack of a discernible goal and the frequent waste of time. The following plan for individualizing work provides good motivation because each child knows what he has to do and when he has done it.

At the beginning of a semester the teacher groups the pupils in pairs and gives each child a mimeographed sheet of paper containing about thirty words arranged in a number of small groups down the left margin of the page, in the manner shown in Table 55.

TABLE 55

Individualized Work Sheet in Spelling

Words	First Practice Test	Second Practice Test	Third Practice Test	Teacher's Tests			
began							
beyond							
before							
between							
beside							
begin							
bewail							

The teacher dictates the words of the first group or two, scores the papers, and returns them to the pupils. Each child marks on his partner's sheet those words that his partner missed. Each member of each pair starts work by studying the first few checked words on his list. When he thinks he knows them, he and his partner exchange sheets, and each child dictates the indicated words to his partner from his partner's record. The results of this performance are recorded in the first practice column. The two children then proceed to study more words, each from his own list, then exchange papers once more and check each other. The same words are not tested twice on the same day, but are eventually tested three times on different days by the partner. When the children have completed a number of words in this way—about ten or fifteen—they present themselves with their sheets to the teacher. Since the children are handling their own drill, she is free to give tests to children who are ready for them. She seats the children (there may be several of them), lays the sheets out on the desk, dictates the first word checked on the first page to the first child and then while he is writing it, dictates the first word in the second sheet to the second child, and so on until each child has been given a word. By then the first youngster is ready for his second word. She dictates only words that have been checked by the child's partner as being correct on three practice tests. The results of the teacher-dictated tests are entered by her in the first column headed "Teacher's Tests." Children who get through with a unit of work early have a chance to do anything that interests them, provided they are not noisy. Some of them like to help with the teaching of those who are not yet done. When all pupils have finished with the first group or groups of words originally dictated, the teacher presents the next unit of work, and the children go through the same procedure again. Any words correctly spelled at the teacher's dictation are temporarily dropped. Words misspelled are written in at the end of the child's practice list, and he must include them in three more practice tests administered by his partner. In the course of time a child appears again to be tested by the teacher on his second group of words.

Before a word can be finally crossed off as known it must be dictated by the teacher a second time. These review dictations are given without warning, whenever the teacher has time for them. Words known a second time are checked in the second column headed "Teacher's Test" and are then crossed off the list. This review test which may occur at any moment without warning keeps the children reviewing their words and thus giving themselves additional practice. The rule for the elimination of words is, then, that they must be correctly spelled on two successive teacher-dictated tests.[2] When the children finish with one sheet of words they may start on the next, or they may wait until others are done, so that all members of the class may begin new work together.

The above plan gives each child the definite goal of learning—the particular words he should know and does not; it allows each child to concentrate exclusively upon words he has not yet learned; it gives him work in small doses; it gives a definite reward for reaching the goal; and it permits a small amount of sociability along the way. The entire situation is therefore presented so that the mastery of relatively uninteresting, and for the time being perhaps useless, subject matter will require as little time as possible and will lead to pleasant results.

The writer is sometimes asked to discuss the value of spelling games.[3] Most such games seem to be of little use because they give too little drill and give that little too indiscriminately. As an occasional diversion, a short game may be of value, with the realization that it is purely for purposes of motivation. However, care must be exercised in

---

[2] This plan is a modification of the Winnetka Plan for Individualization in Spelling.
[3] See pp. 308–309.

the selection of an appropriate game. The old-fashioned spelling match is as poor a game as could be devised, because those who need the drill most receive the least, while those who are superior to their companions receive the lion's share of a practice that they obviously do not need. The good speller receives sufficient reward without being allowed to monopolize the spelling game as well.

The teacher should realize, then, that spelling is a subject not easily motivated by children's natural interests or readily related to their spontaneous social life. An interest in achievement must therefore be attached to the spelling task.

C. DYNAMICS IN COMPOSITION

It almost goes without saying that few children have a deep interest in the mechanics of English composition. Most youngsters will admit a certain practical value in writing correctly, but the effort involved is so great as to more than offset their rather mild interest. Children work on mechanical elements largely because their teachers want them to do so. Nor can they usually become excited over their progress, partly because it takes place slowly and partly because they cannot be sure they have progressed since they have no way of measuring progress in technical elements by themselves. Any interest that can be utilized as a motive must, then, come from the content. Children, like everyone else, enjoy telling of their experiences. The work in English should therefore use the experiences of the pupils as much as possible, in both oral and written work, so as to utilize the inherent interest.

Because children are relatively weak in generalizing, it is probably best to restrict to specific and recent happenings topics for discussion in either writing or speaking. Such a topic as "How to Collect Stamps" is poor because it is too general. "How I Collect Stamps" is better, but "The Stamps I Collected Last Week" is again an improvement. "My Most Interesting Party" may not suggest anything to children; "My Most Recent Party" is better; "The Party at School Yesterday" is still better. The topics presented to children should also be as objective as possible; that is, they should not demand subtleties of feeling or appreciation of character and motives. For instance, a composition on "The Character of Abraham Lincoln" will generally become either a statement of events or a series of platitudes that would apply equally well to any respectable citizen. Narrating what people did is within the capacity of children; telling how people felt, what they were like, or why they acted as they did is difficult if not impossible because children have not enough experience with people to make the necessary judgments. Especially to be avoided are topics involving abstractions.

It is sometimes desirable to use topics recruited from geography, history, science, or reading. After work becomes departmentalized in the upper grades the use of topics from other fields presents certain practical difficulties, which are by no means insuperable, but during the elementary grades, when the same person is teaching all subjects, there is every reason for the establishment of a close relationship among the subjects. Many a child who cannot write more than three poorly constructed, platitudinous sentences about the beauties of a sunset can produce two pages of correct and interesting material if asked to tell how the Pilgrims lived, or what he has learned in hygiene about how to prevent disease, or what the climate of India is like. In addition to furnishing interest and variety, the use of topics drawn from other subjects in school helps to give children a feeling that composition work is of practical value. It is hard enough to achieve transfer of skills developed during the English period to writing done in other classes; the practice of using in the English class subject matter derived from other subjects helps a good deal. Moreover, exclusive use of "too-literary" topics is likely to lead the more prosaic-minded of the pupils into an active dislike of English. After all, only a few people in each generation produce literature, and they serve a long apprenticeship after leaving school. What the average citizen needs is training in writing about practical matters, since they are what he is going to write about all his life.

In general, work in English as it is traditionally taught is not especially popular among children. If pupils are asked to rank in order of preference the various subjects they study, English composition appears two thirds of the way down on the list. Part of the negative attitude shown is doubtless due to the intense effort required by a curriculum that makes too heavy demands upon childish abilities. Dislike may arise also from the inability of a pupil to know if he is or is not making progress. In part, the lack of interest may come from too much emphasis upon literary topics which are beyond the average child's experiences. Most children probably find the "dosage" of new skills too heavy in all the lower grades. The resulting bewilderment leads not only to poor writing but to an active dislike of English. The attitude of children could probably be considerably improved by a lessening of the dosage and by a better selection of topics.

The work of the National Council of Teachers of English during the last two decades has been outstandingly good in the matter of integrating work in English with life and work both in and out of school. thus increasing the degree of interest and furnishing greater motivation. A few sample activities are listed below:

1. A Christmas Unit: Work in language, art, music, and reading. Reading and dramatization of Christmas stories. Christmas carols. Making and lettering Christmas cards. Writing Christmas letters.

2. Unit on life in King Arthur's Court: Language and reading. Dramatization of stories. Writing of imaginative experiences of characters in the stories.

3. The Spirit of the Refugee: Language, history and reading. Talks by adult or child refugees. Reading of modern accounts of people who have left Europe within the last 10 years and of earlier refugees—in 1848, for example. Writing of letters to a newly arrived refugee child.

4. Incidental Writing for Practical Uses in School: Writing notices, announcements, labels, signs, posters, notes, reports, outlines, summaries, reviews, notices for the bulletin boards, contributions to the school or class paper.

5. Finishing a Story: Composition, spelling, handwriting, art, and reading. The children are given the odd-numbered chapters of a story, already printed, each ending in a situation that has to be solved by the next even-numbered chapter. The project for the year is to complete the book.[4]

Much attention is now paid to what is called "creative" English, or spontaneous productions, both prose and poetry, by the children. It might seem that such a task is too difficult for elementary school pupils, but many children find creative work easier and more satisfying than formal composition. The drill in spelling and mechanics is worked in rather casually between the rough draft and the finished copy, while the child is so interested in his production that he is willing to work in order to polish it. A typical poem follows:

[4] W. W. Hatfield (Ed.), *An Experience Curriculum in English,* D. Appleton-Century Company, 1935, 323 pp. (approximately every other chapter concerns the elementary grades); *Junior English Activities,* Books 1 and 2, American Book Company, 1937; J. B. Opdycke, *Projects in Elementary English,* Oxford University Press, 1931, 726 pp.; *Twentieth Yearbook of the Department of Elementary School Principals,* "Activities Involving a Variety of Language Arts, 1941, Chapter 7, pp. 509–562.

The Sea
Many sorrows it has seen,
Many rocks it has washed clean,
And I'm sure if it could speak,
It would tell of men that seek
Other lands in which to dwell,
Men or ships with goods to sell.[5]

Through the integration of oral and written English with activities of intrinsic interest to children and through the frequent use of creative work, there should be better motivation—with resultant greater mastery —than under the traditional methods of teaching.

D. SUMMARY

It is sometimes difficult to interest children directly in penmanship, spelling, or composition, but a teacher can always attach these subjects to the known interests of children. She can also make clear the usefulness of these subjects by seeing to it that they get used often, at least in school. All three subjects are full of minutiae of no great intrinsic interest to the majority of the pupils and not much more stimulating for the teacher, but children can be led to feel a need for these details and to take pride in their mastery of them. It is essential that pupils should know clearly just what they are supposed to do, just which skills they still lack, and just when they have finished a given task. Such educational engineering as will bring this situation about for each main unit of work does much to furnish the necessary driving power.

[5] M. English, "Creative English," *Education,* 53: 133–137, 1932.

XII · Readiness to Write, Spell, and Compose

This chapter will be very short because there is almost no data concerning readiness to begin these subjects. In the course of time more should appear, but the present selection is meagre. Obviously, there must be measurable elements that contribute to success in each field, but thus far few of them have been investigated.

A. READINESS TO WRITE

Children mature at such different rates and the same child may mature so unevenly in different fields that the problem of readiness is extremely important. Readiness to begin work in penmanship involves maturity of vision, perception, intelligence, muscular control, and attitude.

It has already been pointed out that a pupil needs a mental age of at least six and a half before he begins to read and a mental age of seven before he can be expected to avoid reversals altogether. The necessary mental age for success in penmanship has not been determined, but the writer's guess is that it is not less than six and is probably nearer seven. Sufficient visual maturity for obtaining a clear image of letters is also necessary for handwriting. Seeing letters requires better fusion than seeing words, because the object is smaller. The same visual tests that are used for reading readiness show a child's visual maturity for writing.[1]

Motor readiness can be measured rather easily by means of a simple test.[2] The characters shown in Figure 44 printed or mimeographed down the left margin of a sheet of paper—or down the right margin for left-handed children. The teacher gives each child a sheet and a pencil and asks him to make three copies of each character. He may use as much

---

[1] See pp. 136 ff.
[2] O. E. Hertzberg, "A Comparative Study of Different Methods Used in Teaching Beginners to Write," *Teachers College Contributions to Education,* No. 214, 1926, 60 pp.

time as he likes. A pupil is ready to write, so far as motor control is concerned, when he can copy five of the seven figures successfully, with reasonably good proportions and steady lines, and if he makes a definite attempt to copy the remaining two. This degree of accuracy proves that he has both the necessary muscular control and the visual maturity to copy from a model.

Finally, a child must want to learn how to write before formal instruction is begun. By picking up crayons or colored pencils and imitating the motions of other children who have already begun to write, pupils spontaneously show their desire to write when they are ready to do so, provided there are plenty of writing materials about. Until the desire is there, the child is probably better off coloring pictures or doing other handwork that will develop his muscular control until he has sufficient mental and emotional maturity to make voluntary efforts to learn.[3]

FIGURE 44:
Test of Readiness to Write

B. READINESS TO SPELL

In the writer's opinion a child is not ready to study spelling until he has a mental age of at least seven and a half, a reading vocabulary of some 2,000 words, and sufficient skill in handwriting to make the letters quickly and with reasonable accuracy. Such a standard would postpone the beginning of spelling until the lower third grade, aside from what training may be given orally. One type of preparatory work might consist of having children copy familiar words in their handwriting lesson, thus acquiring the rudiments of spelling while still practicing penmanship. Such monosyllabic words as *go, see, do, me, that, for, the, and, by, if,* and so on are especially good as beginning material and are so familiar that children make relatively few errors and therefore develop confidence in their ability to spell before they are ever called upon to spell independently.

Measures of spelling readiness, aside from the measurement of mental age, would perhaps consist of a test for accuracy in copying, a test of ability to concentrate upon and learn an unfamiliar word, a test of

[3] M. F. Hosmer and E. C. Nystrom, "Readiness for Writing," in G. Hildreth, *Readiness to Learn,* Association for Childhood Education, Washington, 1941, pp. 28–31.

eyesight similar to that used for reading readiness, a test for the recognition of phonetic elements—especially short vowels—a measure of speed and accuracy in handwriting, and a test of first and second grade vocabulary—the words with which spelling instruction begins. It seems probable that most children would be in the third grade before they could pass such a series of tests.

Measures of readiness in higher grades could also be constructed and would be most useful to a teacher in grouping children into sections. Tests for this purpose would include measures of handwriting, of recognition for sounds, of ability to spell words taught in previous grades, and probably of other less obvious elements. It is to be hoped that some teacher who is looking for a good topic to use for her master's thesis will construct the spelling readiness tests that are at the moment still nonexistent. In the meantime, teachers can use either reading readiness tests or can devise informal tests of their own to investigate the ability of each child to begin or to continue work in spelling.

C. READINESS TO COMPOSE

The ability to compose well enough to make the effort worth while rests upon the mastery of a number of simpler skills which must function more or less simultaneously, automatically, and smoothly. Although not definitely proved, it seems reasonable that a child would need a mental age between ten and twelve before he is ready to undertake so complex an activity as a formal composition.

A pupil must be able to make letters with accuracy and ease, so that he can merely decide what words he wants to use and they will "write themselves." Such automatically functioning penmanship is practically unknown below the fourth grade and often is not achieved until the sixth. As long as the production of written symbols is a laborious performance a child will not be able to use his handwriting as an element in written expression without devoting too much of his attention and energy to his script.

A child must be able also to spell most of the words that he wants to use. For the expression of even childish ideas one cannot get far with less than several hundred words, and for ease in writing a much larger number is needed. A child cannot express what he wants to say if he has to warp his ideas in order to use words he can spell, to omit ideas because he cannot spell words he needs, to introduce irrelevant ideas because he can spell the necessary words, or to spell only with such concentration of attention that he forgets what he is saying. If a teacher has ever tried to express herself in a foreign language she knows that she cannot say what she wants to say because she lacks words. Moreover, she is reduced to making such remarks as she happens to have words for. If all she knows is "C'est le chien de mon oncle," then she says either that or nothing, regardless of its appropriateness. The child has the same problem when he tries to write English. Sufficient ease with enough words rarely appears below the fifth grade.

A child must be able to use the few basic capitals and punctuation marks that his simple sentence structure demands. The number of skills is small, but an imperfect mastery leads to diversion of attention from the ideas. He must also have a reasonably large vocabulary from which to choose the words he needs. All too often children have to fall back, unwillingly enough, upon such an expression as "The lion looked awful" or "The lion looked terrible" because they do not have sufficient control over words to call up a more adequate adjective.

A child must be able to make some sort of mental or written plan for saying what he has in mind. When children use long, stringy sentences that wander on and on from one irrelevancy to another, the sentence structure is a reflection of thought that is no better organized. By the third grade they can usually learn to narrate orally a single, short incident well enough for it to have a definite beginning and ending and not too many irrelevancies. But a more compact organization of ideas does not come until later. If a pupil is not mature enough to make some sort of plan before he starts composing, he is not ready to compose.

Finally, he must have something he is eager to write about. If he has nothing to say, he is likely to give himself practice chiefly in making errors when he tries to express his mental vacuum. This difficulty of finding a real content is especially common among dull children and, if topics are too literary, among pupils with practical, unimaginative minds. Unless a pupil has something to say, he is better off silent; at least he is not forming bad habits.

If the above analysis of the necessary previous preparation is reasonably accurate, it should be clear that children do not have the basic skills incident to composition until the fifth grade at the earliest. Some children spontaneously begin composing earlier, but to require coherent writing before that time is to set up a situation which involves so much strain that many pupils develop a lasting conviction of the intense difficulty and uninteresting character of all written work.

D. SUMMARY

At present teachers have little guidance in determining readiness to begin these three subjects, but they can use their own observation to locate those children who are most immature or most lacking in the necessary preparatory skills, experience, and attitudes. For those who seem not to be ready a teacher has to devise her own methods of stimulation, so that they may become more mature as quickly as possible. Sooner or later, further work will be done in analyzing the elements of readiness at various levels and in devising tests, but in the meantime a teacher can do much on her own initiative to prevent children from beginning work in which they are foredoomed to discouragement and slow progress because of their immaturity.

XIII · Remedial Work in Writing

There are as yet no remedial classes in penmanship and hardly any in spelling or composition except in high school and college. In some instances, however, there are general remedial clinics to which pupils doing unsatisfactory work in any subject may be sent. Such an integration has its values since remedial work in several subjects may be combined. At the present time, however, most remedial work in these subjects in elementary school is done by the regular room teachers.

A. REMEDIAL WORK IN PENMANSHIP

During the past decade the writer has devised a series of exercises that are diagnostic and remedial. This series will be briefly described,[1] since it is most useful for remedial work.

The first step in preparing these exercises was to find the frequency of use and the frequency of error for each letter. On the basis of use plus difficulty the letters were taken from their alphabetical sequence and placed in a new order, starting with those that were easy and frequent and ending with those that were difficult or infrequent, or both. The series of letters is: *e, l, m, t, i, h, a, o, f, w, y, p, s, w, c, g, v, b, d, n, k, r, q, j, x, z.* These letters are introduced so slowly that it takes a year to complete the alphabet. Only one new letter is added in each series, and no unpracticed letter is needed for writing the exercises in any series except the first.

The first series of exercises deals with the small letters, the thirteen easier ones during the first semester and the remaining thirteen during the second, thus giving about one and a half weeks to each letter. The

[1] L. Cole, "Heresy in Handwriting," *Elementary School Journal,* 38: 606–618, 1938, and "A Successful Experiment in the Teaching of Handwriting by Analytic Methods," *Journal of Psychology,* 1: 209–222, 1936.

second series presents the eight easiest capitals during the first semester and the other eighteen during the second. These two sets of exercises are commonly used in the fourth and fifth grades. The work of the lower sixth grade consists partly of speed drills and partly of transfer exercises.[2] During it, the children begin to write spelling lessons, tests in geography, or compositions in the handwriting period, as exercises in penmanship.

The work of each series begins with a demonstration and discussion of the proper form of the new letter and of the commonest errors. The errors for four letters appear in Figure 45. The teacher demonstrates

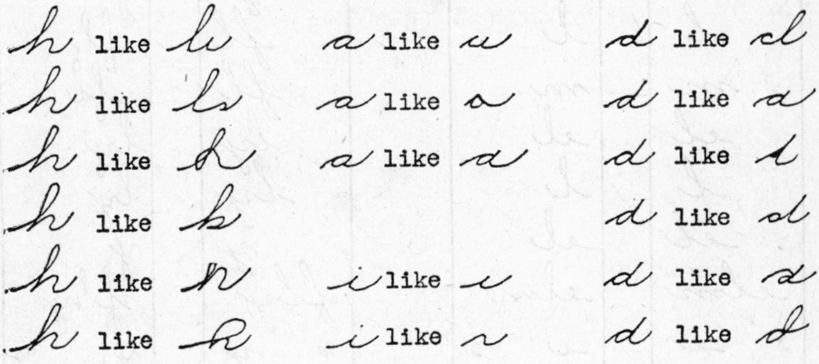

FIGURE 45: Common Errors in the Analysis of Four Letters

the right form, analyzing the strokes,[3] and then she shows the errors. She asks each pupil to look at his last two or three spelling papers, to draw a line around each use of the letter under discussion, then to see what mistakes he made on these already-written papers, and finally to consider how he can avoid them. If children find new malformations, these are added to the list on the board. This first period of study and thought is essential because the pupils need to get a clear picture of the correct formation and a careful analysis of their own errors. Without this perceptional learning they are likely merely to practice their own mistakes.

The exercises are written on cardboard strips, two of which appear in Figure 46. The first strip in each pair is for right-handed pupils and the second for left-handed. The child first practices each new letter several times in isolation with his model beside every practice line so that he does not have to use his own scrawl for a model as he proceeds

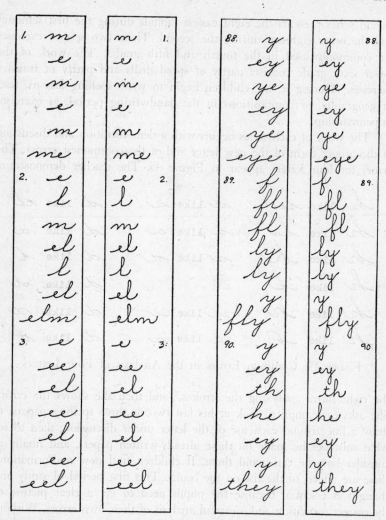

FIGURE 46: Sample Exercises for Right- and Left-handed Pupils

down the page. He has also a brief review of earlier letters. He then at once uses his new letter in a familiar word, which appears on the last line of the exercise. He writes this word three times. Then he puts down his pencil or pen, sits back, studies what he has done, and decides whether or not it is good enough to pass. If he thinks it is, he writes "Yes" in the margin of his paper; if not, he writes "No." Then he goes on to the next exercise. Here he is given more practice on the same letter and writes another familiar word that contains no new problems. Again he tests himself. As the children work, the teacher goes up and down the aisles, helping individual pupils, and adding her "Yes" or "No" to the children's. There are plenty of exercises for the slow learners. Each child takes as many as he needs to pass any three by the teacher's standard and is then excused from the drill until work is begun on the next new letter. The exercises thus reward the good writer by excusing him from drill, at the same time helping the poor writer by concentrating the teacher's efforts upon him. Two or three pupils usually write three good exercises the first day, and several more on the second day; at the end of the first week from a half to two thirds of the children are excused, and the teacher can put all her time upon those who need help most.

At the end of each series except the first there are two exercises of a different character. The children write, in the fashion shown below, one or more of the words that they have already practiced. While they

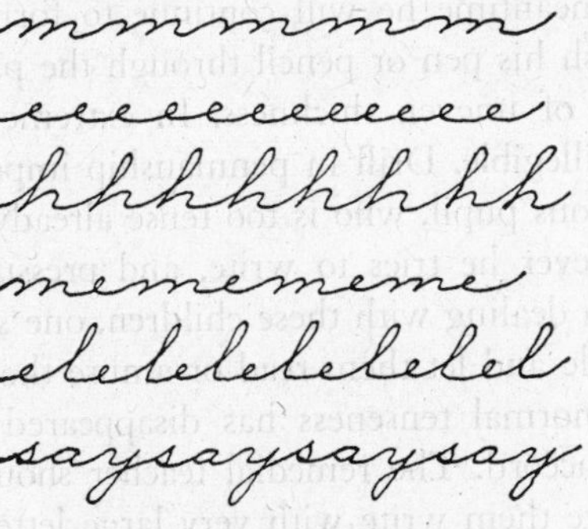

FIGURE 47: Speed Drills

write they sing or hum some familiar song and write in rhythm with the music. The children enjoy this type of lesson and soon begin to relax and write with an easy swing. The last lesson of each series is a "transfer" lesson. The children go over papers from other subjects and copy every word in which they have written incorrectly one of the letters they have already practiced. They are not responsible for letters not yet studied. This exercise brings home to them the need for using their skill all the time.

In about the middle of the first series, the children begin to write an occasional whole sentence composed of words they have already practiced, such as:

I ate all the ham.
I met him at the hotel.
I will meet them at home.

In the second half of the first semester there are a number of such sentences, and they are even more numerous throughout the second semester.

Pupils in the fourth grade use either pencil or fountain pen. The fifth graders use fountain pens exclusively. In the sixth grade those who write well enough are allowed pen and ink as a reward for excellence. The sinistrals, however, continue with their fountain pens.

1. Special Problems in Remedial Work: Nervous, immature, left-handed, and accelerated children present special difficulties to a teacher and appear in the remedial room out of proportion to their numbers. The nervous child has poor muscular control because he has or has had a nervous disease. His control will improve as he recovers from his illness, but in the meantime he will continue to form his letters badly, to splash ink, to push his pen or pencil through the paper, to make lines that are shaky and of uneven thickness. In extreme cases, his writing may be completely illegible. Drill in penmanship imposes an extra-heavy burden upon a nervous pupil, who is too tense already. He puts pressure upon himself whenever he tries to write, and pressure is exactly what he cannot endure. In dealing with these children, one should excuse them from drill for a while and let them read or amuse themselves with quiet games until the abnormal tenseness has disappeared and they start to write of their own accord. The remedial teacher should then give them ruled paper and have them write with very large letters on every fourth line. If the paper has $5/8$ spaces, the small letters will be $5/8$ of an inch high, t and d will be $1\frac{1}{4}$ inches tall, the upper loop $1\frac{7}{8}$ inches, and the loops that go below the line $1\frac{1}{2}$ spaces in length. The large movements needed for writing of this size, or even larger if the child prefers, do not impose the strain that small writing does. The irregularity and shakiness of the lines should be ignored, since they are merely a symptom of illness and will disappear when the pupil gets well. The main thing is to get the letter formation right and then to let the youngster make his script smaller when and if he wants to. The drill periods should, of course, be short, and the pupil should not do any more writing in his other subjects than is absolutely necessary. The remedial teacher's main objective should be to teach relaxation. If some work in correct letter formation can be added without interfering with relaxation, so much the better. If not, it can wait. The immature pupil also has poor control, but he is not sick, merely undeveloped. He also would do well to write a fairly large script. Both he and the nervous pupil should use either a soft pencil or a fountain pen, regardless of what grade they are in.

Children who are bright enough to be accelerated sometimes show a muscular immaturity that is due to their youth. They generally write as well as other children of their chronological age, but more than that is asked of them. The normal eight-year-old child in the low third grade is given less work and more time in which to do it than the bright eight-year-old in the high fourth, who is supposed to keep up with children older than himself. Intellectually, he may have no trouble at all, but his body—though developed beyond the average for his age—may be unequal to the strain. Children grow so fast that there is a considerable gulf between a better-than-average child of eight and an average child of ten. Accelerated children sometimes write illegibly because their minds are so quick that their ideas get ahead of their writing speed, and they scribble as fast as they can in an effort to keep up with their own overstimulating brilliance.

2. Experiments in Remedial Teaching: One experiment is reported of a corrective class in penmanship in high school.[4] The pupils in the class came from two grades, for which the results are given separately. One group contained 40 pupils and the other 29. The corrective work continued for three months. Tests for speed and quality were given at the beginning and end of the period, and also four months after the end of the experiment to see how much of the change was permanent. The results are compared with test results from two control groups. The pupils in the first experimental group lost a little speed during the three months of corrective work, some of which was analytic, but they gained enough during the subsequent four months to give them a net gain of a letter a minute. They had still not gained quite enough to overtake their control group. The second experimental class also showed an initial loss and then a gain after the drill had stopped. In quality, the experimental classes gained 10 and 11 points respectively—the equivalent of two and a half years of normal growth—and they still held over

---

[4] A. E. Traxler and H. A. Anderson, "Group Corrective Handwriting in Junior High School," *School Review*, 41: 675–684. 1933.

TABLE 56

Results of an Experiment in Handwriting

Group	Speed		Quality	
	Gain or loss from Pretest to End Test	Gain or loss from Pretest to Second Test	Gain or loss from Pretest to End Test	Gain or loss from Pretest to Delayed Test
Experimental Group 1	— 3 letters	1 letter	+ 10 points	9 points
Control Group 1	0	2 letters	+ 5 points	2 points
Experimental Group 2	— 1 letter	4 letters	+ 11 points	9 points
Control Group 2	+ 4 letters	6 letters	+ 2 points	3 points

two years of it four months after the end of the experiment. One control group made an unusually large gain for the first three months but evidently lost most of it, since their final standing was only 2 points ahead of their initial score. The second control group showed the usual slow gain. When one subtracts the normal gain from that held at the end of seven months by the experimental pupils, there remains 6 or 7 points, or one and a half years, of gain that seems a permanent possession.

Use of the writer's diagnostic and remedial materials, above described, in eight fourth grade rooms gave interesting results.[5] The 286 children in these rooms were measured at the beginning of the experiment and again four months later when they had completed their drill on half the letters of the alphabet. The measures included speed, quality, decrease in errors of letter formation on the 13 practiced letters, and decrease in errors on the 13 that were not yet practiced. The median speed of the experimental group was 36.5 letters per minute at both beginning and end, showing that the diagnostic work had not caused the children to draw the letters instead of writing them. Nothing was said about quality, yet the children in this group gained 14.5 points, which is more than the normal gain from the beginning of Grade 2 till the end of Grade 5. The letters a, e, f, h, i, l, m, o, p, s, t, w, and y, the easier half of the alphabet, had been studied. On the pretest the median child of the experimental group made 41 per cent of these letters incorrectly; at the end, the corresponding per cent was 21. That is, the pupils had eliminated half their errors. The median for errors on the 13 harder

[5] From unpublished material. The writer is indebted to the teachers and principals concerned in the experiment, in Berkeley, Richmond, Alameda, and Sacramento, California.

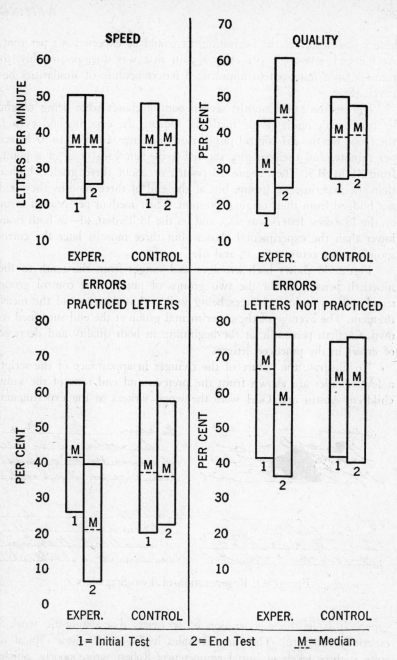

FIGURE 48: Results of Diagnostic Teaching

letters was higher at the beginning, as would be expected—65 per cent. At the end, it was 56 per cent, a gain that was due, presumably, to transfer from practiced to unpracticed letters because of similarities between them.

During the same months several control classes were being taught by traditional, undiagnostic methods. During the experimental period, the speed for the 257 control pupils rose one letter, from 36 to 37 letters per minute, and their quality showed a median gain of .5 of a point, from 41 to 41.5. They began 10 points, or about three grades, higher than the experimental group, but at the end of three months they had not budged from their original position. Their median per cent of error on the 13 easiest letters was 39.5, and on the 13 hardest, 61—in both cases lower than the experimental classes—but three months later the corresponding per cents were 38 and 61.

Figure 48 shows both averages and ranges from the tenth to the ninetieth percentiles for the two groups of pupils. The control group stood still, any minor changes being well within the error of the measurement. The average of the experimental group at the end surpassed its own ninetieth percentile at the beginning in both quality and decrease of errors in the practiced letters.

To illustrate the nature of the changes in appearance of the script, a few samples are shown from the pretests and end tests of the same children. Austin and Gael were the worst writers in the experimental

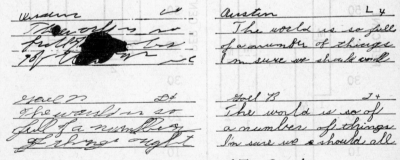

FIGURE 49: Regeneration of Two Scrawlers

group. It is in the regeneration of scrawlers that diagnostic work is especially successful. The three samples in Figure 50 show typical results at three levels of initial competence. Robert wrote poorly, Shirley was exactly at the average for all the classes put together, while Matilda was a superior penman with an oddly cramped style for a right-handed child and the lowest speed in the group. Robert became a low-average writer for his grade, Shirley corrected her tendency toward too-small writing, and Matilda doubled her speed, lost none of her high quality, and achieved an easy relaxed motion.

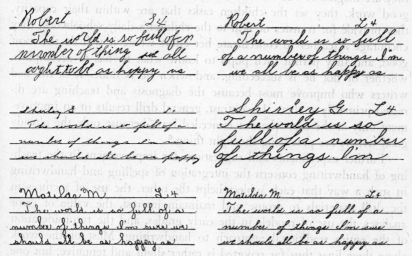

FIGURE 50: Results of Remedial Teaching upon the Script of a Poor, an Average, and a Good Writer

The changes in the script for two left-handed children are shown in Figure 51. David wrote with his arm hooked over the desk top, while Marilyn twisted her hand to the right and got so tired that she needed to rest often and had never finished a written assignment in the time allowed since she had been in school. The relearning of position and

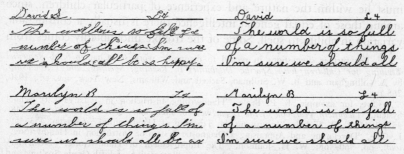

FIGURE 51: Changes in the Script of Two Left-handed Children

slant occupied most of the first month for both these children, but in the remaining three months of practice, they regained and far surpassed their initial rate.

The success of these materials probably rests on seven features: they are diagnostic and remedial, they interest the children, they reward good work, they set the children tasks that are within their capacity, they provide for transfer of skill to the children's daily schoolwork, they encourage a teacher to concentrate her effort where it will do the most good, and they permit each pupil to know what he has to accomplish, whether or not he is succeeding, and when he is done. It is the bad writers who improve most because the diagnosis and teaching are directed primarily at them. In contrast, general drill results in an improvement only at the top, where it is needed least, because only the already good writers are practicing the right thing.[6]

Further experiments and suggestions for improvement in the teaching of handwriting concern the integration of spelling and handwriting in such a way that each subject helps the other, the use of pictures in the drill materials to arouse and maintain interest, the value of error analyses, the use of models in the early grades, and the reconsideration of the entire traditional approach to handwriting. Most of the work along these lines thus far reported is rather slight and tentative, but one hopes the few articles may presage an intensive study of handwriting in the future.[7]

B. REMEDIAL WORK IN SPELLING

Children may fail to learn how to spell for any of a number of reasons. The task before them is admittedly a hard one, because of the unphonetic character of the English language. However, some causes must lie within the nature and experience of particular children, since among those of equal general intelligence there is usually a considerable variation in ability to spell. Some of the trouble undoubtedly comes from

[6] For further suggestions in regard to diagnostic work see Chapter 6 of *Remedial Training for Children with Specific Disabilities in Reading, Spelling, and Penmanship,* by A. Gillingham and B. W. Stillman, Sackett and Williams, New York, rev. ed., 1940, 268 pp.

[7] See, for example, B. P. Beale, "Handwriting Instruction in a Large City School System," *Twentieth Yearbook of the Department of Elementary School Principals,* pp. 448–452, 1941; C. P. Nichols, "Improving the Teaching of Handwriting," *ibid.,* pp. 453–459; L. Cole, "Developing and Appraising a Diagnostic System of Instruction in Handwriting," *ibid.,* pp. 460–468; W. H. Johnson, "The Improvement of Handwriting," *Elementary School Journal,* 43: 90–96, 1942; S. I. Thompson, "Integration of Fifth-Grade Spelling and Handwriting," *ibid.,* 42: 347–357, 1942.

mere immaturity in verbal skills. Once a child gets started wrong he is likely to develop an emotional blocking that will prevent him from learning to spell, even after he has outgrown his original immaturity. Defects of hearing, speech, or vision are especially important as causes of poor spelling, since pupils tend to write down the sounds they hear or make and such letters as they see. Inattention, instability, inefficient habits of work, and general immaturity may operate as causes because they prevent a child from ever getting clear pictures of words.

1. **Diagnosis and Treatment:** Before beginning remedial work one must make sure that a pupil can see, hear, write, speak, and concentrate well enough to spell. A teacher should therefore begin with the same visual and auditory tests used in measuring readiness to read. She can listen to a pupil's pronunciation by having him read aloud and can test his familiarity with the alphabet by dictating the sounds in a random sequence, including both the long and the short sounds of the vowels. A considerable number of poor spellers do not hear some groups of similar-sounding letters, such as *f*, *z*, and *s*, and many can hear no difference between them. Others do not distinguish between *g* and *k*, or *b* and *p*, or *t* and *d*, or *ĭ* and *ĕ*. A record is to be kept of such sounds as are either not heard at all or are heard incorrectly. Remedial work based on those sounds that are missed should then be undertaken to discover whether the failure to hear is due to actual deafness or, as is more frequently the case, to mere ignorance of sound. If a child cannot learn to recognize the letter sounds, he has to be presumed deaf for those sounds; he should, of course, be sent to a specialist for diagnosis and, if necessary, for training in lip reading to supplement his defective hearing. If he does learn the elementary sounds, he obviously hears them, and his previous failure was due to ignorance or carelessness. A child who has been exposed to a given method of teaching for many years and has not learned to spell a reasonable number of words is obviously in need of a new method. His teacher should therefore try out the various techniques already described for normal children and determine which combination is the most efficient for him. If he can hear the sounds and see the letters and if he is not seriously defective in intelligence, there *must* be some combination of techniques by which he can learn.

After a teacher has checked a pupil's vision, hearing, and speech, she must find out what kinds of error he makes before she can hope to give him a type of remedial training that will be appropriate. For her analysis she may dictate words from a standard spelling scale or from the pupil's speller, or she may use a series of diagnostic tests [8] which include measures of ability to pronounce sounds correctly, to give sound equivalents of letters, to spell one- or two-syllable nonsense words, to show adequate auditory discrimination, and to use successfully various methods of studying words. Use of these materials will guide a teacher so that she puts remedial emphasis where it will do the most good.

If a pupil spells most of the sounds in a way that is possible but incorrect for the word in question, he obviously hears well enough but does not have a clear visual image. He cannot, therefore, remember whether *release* is spelled as it actually is or as *reliese* or *releese* or *re- lese,* all of which are phonetically possible. It may be that he has an inadequate visual memory, but it is more likely that he has not looked at words with enough care and has tried instead to substitute sound for sight. In some instances a child's eyes are defective and he cannot see clearly. If a pupil has already shown a preference for learning by ear, he should practice spelling words aloud and listening carefully. Further reinforcement by tracing or writing may also be helpful.

If a pupil's approximations are not phonetic, then he may be deaf for certain sounds but is more probably ignorant of what letters they represent. After the child's hearing and vision have been tested, the teacher therefore needs to give drill in phonics, at the same time training the child to look more intently at words than has been his custom.

It is useful to select four groups of five words each from the same column of the Ayres Scale, using words that are far beyond the pupil's present spelling experience, and then let him study each group in a different way.[9] The teacher should have the words already printed on library cards. She can present the first group wholly visually, one card at a time, not pronouncing the words herself and suppressing any whis- pering that the child may do. It is well to go through the series three times. Then the pupil writes whatever he can remember of each word. For the next series, the teacher pronounces and spells each word, but never shows the card to the pupil. After three repetitions, the child again writes the words just studied. In the third series, the visual and auditory presentations are simply combined. The two elements still untested as possible helps in learning are speech and writing. A fourth

---

[8] Use of the *Diagnostic and Remedial Spelling Manual,* by A. I. Gates and D. H. Russell (Teachers College, Columbia University, 1937) is recommended. Further sugges- tions may be obtained from Gillingham and Stillman, *op. cit.*

[9] These methods are described in detail by Gates and Russell, *op. cit.*

series adds pronunciation by both the teacher and the child to the visual presentation, and a fifth series adds the same element to the auditory. For the sixth technique, the pupil looks, pronounces, and writes each word, while for the seventh he listens, pronounces, and writes. The last series combines everything—seeing, hearing, pronouncing, and writing. By comparing the number of errors per method, a teacher can judge which mode of attack is best.

An occasional child is a complete nonspeller. He either cannot get started at all or else he produces a combination like *nof* when asked to spell *perhaps*. Such a child has some serious defect, on top of which he has probably built up an emotional resistance to spelling. The remedial teacher should have the child's ears, eyes, and speech thoroughly investigated and any defects remedied as completely as possible before she starts her work. These examinations may eliminate, and will at least identify, the basic defect, but diagnosis will not cure the emotional attitude. The beginning has, therefore, to be slow. The teacher would do well to cut out whole words in script from very fine sand paper or from colored paper, after the fashion shown in Figure 52. For the first lesson she can select two or three words that together make a sentence. The pupil then moves his finger over the design for a single word, at the same time saying the word, letter by letter, his voice keeping pace

FIGURE 52: Cut-out for Tracing

with his finger. When he feels that he has learned how a word is spelled, he may copy it in pencil two or three times. Some children like to use a different colored pencil for each letter. After the child thinks he knows the first two or three words, he writes from memory a sentence composed of them and no others. When four or five sentences, with a total of perhaps a dozen words, have been learned in this way, the teacher should dictate them. The pupil then copies each word correctly spelled onto a small filing card; any wrong words go back into future lessons. He files his cards alphabetically and then begins on the new words needed for another series of sentences. A teacher needs 200 or more words cut out for tracing, since some children have to trace that many before they can learn by looking and pronouncing. As the child's file of known words grows he begins to recover from his emotional attitude of defeat, and then he learns more rapidly.

2. Spelling, Word, and Letter Games: Spelling is, for many children, a hard and distinctly dull subject. It needs, therefore, to be enlivened and motivated. The chief dangers in using games are that they will take up far more time than they are worth and that the pupils who already spell excellently will be the only ones who really have fun. It is best to keep whatever competition there may be on a group rather than on an individual basis. A few possible class activities are suggested below:

1. The teacher puts on the board such a series as: *l, e, a, m, s, t* and asks the children to copy the letters on to a paper and then to make as many words as they can from these letters.

2. The class is first divided into two teams. A pupil on one team puts any monosyllable on the board—perhaps the word *mat*. A pupil from the other team crosses out one letter (or the letters for one sound, like *ch, sh, ck*) and makes a new word—such as *met*. A second member of Team One then crosses out a letter of the new word and makes a third one—for instance, *let*. Up comes the second child on Team Two to change the word to *lot*— and so on.

3. The pupils are given cards, on each of which there is a series of syllables, with the word correctly arranged on the back. The pupil writes on a separate sheet each word he can rearrange and compares his answers with the backs of the cards. (This same exercise is used for vocabulary drill.)

al-lo-co-ni	(colonial)
pub-re-lic	(republic)
part-de-ment	(department)

4. The teacher draws on the board two ladders or flights of steps, one for each of the two teams into which the class is divided. Then she dictates one word to each child, taking words from lessons of the previous two or three weeks. If a pupil spells his word correctly, she makes a mark on the next step of the ladder for his side. When the answer is wrong, the team does not progress. The team that gets to the top first wins. A teacher has to use whatever number of steps is best fitted for the spelling ability of the class. Unless one side eventually gets to the top the game remains unfinished.

5. The teacher divides the class into four groups and gives each pupil a number in his group. Then she puts four phonograms—perhaps *-all, -ink, -ing,* and *-and*—upon the board, with some distance between each two. She next gives the class three or four minutes to think up words in each group. Each pupil should write down whatever words he can think of but should not whisper them or talk about them. The teacher next assigns one phonogram to each group, in random order so that the children cannot guess in advance which one they will get. As soon as the phonograms are assigned,

Child No. 1 in each group runs to the blackboard and writes a word using the proper phonogram, directly underneath it. If his teammates accept the word, he runs back to his seat, but if they shout "No" at him he has to erase it before returning. As soon as he is in his seat, Child No. 2 of his team runs to the board and writes another word. At the end the teacher gives 4 points to the side that finished first, 3 to the next, 2 to the next, and 1 to the last. Then she scores 2 points for every correct word, 1 for a questionable word, and subtracts 2 for every erased word—providing it was really wrong. The total points combine speed and correctness with a penalty for errors. The teacher had better choose the sides and assign the order within each team, being careful to put the least verbal children first.[10]

Games enliven spelling drill and may be so devised as to give a good deal of practice in handling words.

3. **Teaching Experiments:** Efforts at remedial instruction have been successful in a number of places.[11] In one instance the investigator worked with a group of 21 fifth grade children. She began by dictating in short series a total of 2,498 words from Grades 2 and 3 of the Jones Spelling Lists. After the papers were scored, each pupil made his own spelling book for the year by listing the correct spelling of all the words he missed. The teacher helped the children analyze their difficulties and to locate the hard parts of words for special study. The number of errors for the 21 pupils decreased from 2,498 before the remedial work to 568 after it. Of the latter number of errors, 52 per cent were made by one child. The seven children in the upper third of the distribution decreased their errors from 161 to 4; those in the middle third, from 774 to 64; and the seven in the lowest third, from 1,593 to 500, of which nearly 300 were contributed by one pupil. The individual records are shown in Table 57 on the next page. From the beginning to the end of this remedial work the average number of errors decreased from 119 to 14—as great a change as could be expected. Some of the children made spectacular gains.

[10] Many other games and exercises are given in E. A. Betts and M. L. Arey, *Teachers Manual for Directing Spelling,* American Book Company, 1941; Gillingham and Stillman, *op. cit.;* H. A. Miller, S. A. Courtis, and G. Watters, *Creative Teaching in the Field of Spelling,* Wallace Publishing Company, Des Moines, 1931, 133 pp.

[11] See, for instance, G. Davis, "Remedial Work in Spelling," *Elementary School Journal,* 27: 615–626, 1927. Table 57 is quoted by permission of the publisher. See also W. S. Guiler, "Improving Ability in Spelling," *ibid.,* 30: 594–603, 1930; G. N. Wells, "The Effect of Specific, Diagnostic, Remedial Procedure in Spelling," Master's Thesis in Education, University of Chicago, 1933, 190 pp.

TABLE 57

Results of Remedial Teaching in Spelling

Child	Number of Errors in Pretest	Number of Errors in End Test	Difference
Jessie	6	0	−6
Paul	10	0	−10
Pauline	10	0	−10
Alice	13	0	−13
Robert	30	2	−28
Sally	36	1	−35
Andrew	56	1	−55
Christine	90	0	−90
Marlene	93	31	−62
Donald	96	6	−90
Dorothy	99	6	−93
Alexander	101	3	−98
Foster	110	12	−98
Maybelle	155	6	−149
Stephen	161	11	−150
Ruth	179	56	−123
Justin	187	33	−154
Carey	202	28	−174
Florence	204	43	−161
Gladys	247	31	−216
Frederick	413	298	−115
TOTAL	2,498	568	
AVERAGE	119.0	14.2	−104.8

C. REMEDIAL WORK IN ENGLISH

1. **Diagnosis:** The pupil who fails his work in English composition offers a fertile field for investigation. Like the poor reader, he may fail to progress for any one or more of a large number of reasons. Perhaps the first things to check are a child's handwriting, spelling, and vocabulary, all of which are more likely than not to be poor. If they are,

his inadequate work in written English may have arisen from too early an effort to write, before he was ready. In the resulting confusion, errors may be made quite at random. The only thing to do is to stop work in English for the nonce and develop the contributory skills. By the time the child can write and spell acceptably he will have had time to forget some of his emotional reactions to failure, and he will be enough older to have a better chance of success.

If, however, a child writes and spells passably, then a remedial teacher has to analyze his written work to determine the technical errors. Once in a while the errors are of many kinds and seem quite irrational and unclassifiable, but usually they are concentrated in a few types. The writer recalls one child whose single basic error was that he would not be bothered with periods. He had written what should have been seventeen sentences, containing an assortment of minor errors, but he used only one capital at the beginning and one period at the end. A short conversation with him revealed that he thought the capital and period belonged only at the start and finish of a composition, and he was rather appalled when told that they were used at the start and finish of every sentence. Another small child produced some curious effects by using a semicolon somewhere in every sentence he wrote—a practice to which he clung stubbornly because his teacher had once told his class that really distinguished writers used semicolons frequently. Through a common error of reasoning this child had decided that if he used enough semicolons his writing would be distinguished! Another small child did not begin the first word of a letter with a capital because he considered the salutation as part of the opening sentence and phrased the whole thing, "Dear Aunt Emma, we are going to have a party." These are not chance errors by any means, nor are they unintelligent.[12]

Often a pupil has a single key difficulty, even when there are many types of error in a piece of written work. Thus, if a child writes long, stringy sentences, he will almost inevitably use too many punctuation marks and in the wrong places. One child of the writer's acquaintance had written a three-page letter, composed of four sentences. He himself evidently felt that something was needed to make his meaning clearer than it seemed to be, so he had broadcast a goodly crop of commas, 119 in all. Nothing would have been sillier for a teacher than to have gone through the motions of correcting his misuses of the comma. They

---

[12] See S. L. Pressey and P. Campbell, "The Causes of Children's Errors in Capitalization," *English Journal*, 22: 197–201, 1933.

were merely a superficial symptom of his bad sentences. He was asked to rewrite his letter in short sentences of not more than 10 words, with no punctuation except the period at the end of each sentence, and then to read over his work and decide if he needed any commas. He eventually put in 3, 2 of them incorrectly, but even 2 mistakes in punctuation are better than 119. Errors in mechanics are likely to form a pyramid on top of a single basic misapprehension or bad habit. The remedial teacher has to analyze what children write, watch them as they write, ask them questions about why they do what they do, and make up her mind, on the basis of all available evidence, as to the nature and seriousness of their errors.

In the sixth grade and perhaps in the fifth, the teacher may use analytic tests, but probably not in the lower grades. Most of the available tests and exercises are too hard even for the fifth and sixth grade children, but a teacher might do well to get copies of as many as she can and to adapt at least a few for her own use,[13] covering the relatively few simple skills necessary for work in the elementary school—use of periods and apostrophes, two or three uses of the comma, and the commonest uses of capitals.

2. **Remedial Materials:** A remedial teacher should be able to construct her own drills. A few items for a proofreading type of exercise appear below. It should be noted that the items dealing with capitals are already punctuated, while those dealing with punctuation have their capitals.

1. my aunt caroline has a birthday on the same day as harold.
2. he lives at 26 duncan street, rochester, new york.

1. Prof Kennedy visited the school this afternoon
2. Can you guess the answer
3. Dorothy needs an eraser a pencil and a sheet of paper

The items on a single page may give practice in only one skill or they may cover two or three, but there should not be too large a miscellany. A somewhat harder type of exercise may be used in the sixth grade by constructing such items as:

[13] *Guiler, Diagnostic Tests in Punctuation and Remedial Exercises,* Rand, McNally Company; *Mullen and Lanz Exercises and Tests in English,* Ginn and Company; *Uhl-Holtz Practice Exercises in English,* Ginn and Company; *Pribble-Brezler Exercises in English,* Lyons and Carnahan.

1. Read this sentence:

    Mary lit the lamp because she could not see.

Rewrite it beginning with the word "because" and putting the words "Mary lit the lamp" at the end of the sentence. Make any other changes you think necessary.

2. Read this sentence:

    Mother bought milk and eggs.

Copy the sentence, putting the word "cheese" after "milk" and before "and." Make any other changes you think necessary.

3. Read this sentence:

    I have asked Mary, Paul, and Catharine to my party.

Copy the sentence taking out "Mary" and the comma after it. Make any other changes you think necessary.

In the first item of this exercise the pupil has to see that he needs a comma to prevent the reader of the sentence from starting off, "Because she could not see Mary." In the second, he has to sense that he has a series after he changes the sentence, and in the third that he has lost the series and should remove the second comma. Skills in punctuation and capitalization can be developed by means of exercises, if necessary, but the best "remedial" treatment is prevention of error by the inclusion of only a few skills in the elementary curriculum.[14]

For pupils who have a weak sense for sentence structure it is sometimes helpful to use an exercise [15] composed of disarranged sentences, such as:

1. of oak piece an is furniture chest a
2. mother me watch my a gave lovely

With younger children it is best to put each word on a separate slip of paper, keeping the slips for each sentence clipped together or in an envelope. The child can then actually rearrange the words until he finds the solution. Older children can do their rearranging on paper and in their heads.

14 The teacher will find excellent suggestions for exercises and activities in W. S. Guiler and R. L. Henry, *Remedial English: A Plan for Individual Study,* Ginn and Company, rev. ed., 1938, 80 pp. Much of the work recommended is above elementary school level, but a teacher can derive many good ideas from this reference.

15 H. D. Gibbons, "Reading and Sentence Elements," *Elementary English Review,* 18: 42–46, 1941.

The remedial teacher is almost certain to find several children whose difficulties are with the content rather than the form of what they write. Their written work rambles in an incoherent way, or the content has practically no relationship to the title, or the production is awkward, stilted, dull, and banal. These faults and shortcomings are much harder to correct than errors in mechanics. One can reduce incoherency somewhat by showing a pupil how to plan what he wants to say or by letting him tell the plot of his production orally before he starts to write. However, a change of subject is usually more helpful than anything else for irrelevancy and banality. If a child has nothing to offer on such topics as "An Exciting Experience," "My Best Friend," or "Why I Like School," he might be allowed to read a short story or a section in a textbook and summarize what he has read. Some children do not write readily about themselves, and many have neither the objectivity nor the vocabulary for describing their own attitudes and reactions. As one boy of twelve once explained to the writer, after he had been asked to write about a day in the country, "All we did was run around, but we had lots of fun, only I don't know why." This same boy sat down and wrote two pages of reasonably correct English on the subject of how to make a kite and followed up this production with a really good summary of an encyclopedia article on Sir Walter Raleigh. Almost any child has or can find something to write about, but the teacher does not always succeed in discovering what it is. If a teacher in a remedial room studies a pupil long enough she becomes well acquainted with him and can help him a good deal in finding topics and in thinking clearly about them.

3. **Experiments in Remedial Teaching:** There are not many reports of remedial work in elementary school, although there are plenty for the higher grades and college. Three studies, however, report excellent gains by use of remedial materials in both recognition and avoidance of error.[16] In two cases, the improvement transferred to written work also. Thus, the children in an experimental group reduced their errors on tests in mechanics from a range of 40 to 61 errors to a range of 37 to 45, and at the same time reduced their errors in written work 44 per cent. In

[16] M. S. Schindhelm, "The Improvement of the Quality of Written Composition through a Remedial Program in Grades 5 and 6," University of Iowa, Master's Thesis, 1940, and J. E. Thomas, "The Elimination of Technical Errors in Written Composition through Formal Drill," *University of Iowa Studies in Education,* Vol. 8, No. 2, 1932, 43 pp., and P. C. Warner and W. S. Guiler, "Individual vs. Group Instruction in Grammatical Usage," *Journal of Educational Psychology,* 24: 140–151, 1933.

another case, correction of error and individualization of teaching resulted in a drop of 32 per cent. Errors can be eliminated, but they often are not either because of the mistaken idea that maturity will get rid of them without specific teaching, because the drills used in correction are not individualized, or because children do not know what errors they have made. When work is really individualized so as to give each child drill where he needs it, there are great gains in mechanical correctness. There are gains also in power to use English as a means of expression.[17]

D. SUMMARY

While relatively few experiments in remedial teaching have been carried on in the field of language, enough has been done to show that diagnosis and corrective, individualized teaching are as effective as in other subjects. The diagnosis should be as specific as possible. A teacher needs to know which errors a child makes in forming which letter, which words he fails to spell correctly, and which skills in English he does not have. It is not always possible to find out why a child makes the errors he does, but at least a teacher can discover which ones he makes, and she can often find the reason also by observing him at work or by asking him enough questions. In English especially do the errors tend to pile themselves on top of one or two "key" difficulties. In this situation only a thorough analysis has much chance to move the key logs and break the jam.

Certain types of children are more likely to need remedial work than others. In penmanship the young, accelerated child, the nervous pupil, and the sinistral furnish the greatest proportion of scrawlers and scratchers. In spelling, the children with visual or auditory defects and the immature make up a high proportion of the failures. Defective vision or blurred hearing prevents a child from getting a clear impression of either the appearance or the sound of a word, while immaturity reduces the attention span to so short a duration that a pupil does not get through studying a word before he interrupts himself. In English, the nonverbal child, the pupils from foreign homes, the underprivileged, and a fair number of the boys regardless of intelligence or background are likely to have difficulty. The dullards often have good penmanship and are fairly good spellers but they usually come to grief in composi-

---

[17] B. E. Roberts, "Thinking, Writing, Growing," *Elementary English Review*, 18: 13–16, 28, 30, 1941.

tion work, fundamentally because they cannot think well enough. A teacher may expect different types of children to have difficulty in each of the three subjects.

E. REFERENCES AND PROBLEMS

One or more of the following books should be used for supplementary reading in each field.

I. Handwriting

1. G. M. Fernald, *Remedial Techniques in the Basic School Subjects,* McGraw-Hill Book Company, 1943, 349 pp.

2. A. Gillingham and B. W. Stillman, *Remedial Training for Children with Specific Disabilities in Reading, Spelling and Penmanship,* Sackett and Williams, rev. ed., 1940, 268 pp.

3. G. Hildreth, *Learning the Three R's: A Modern Interpretation,* Educational Publishers, Inc., Minneapolis, 1936, 824 pp. (Chapters 8, 13, 16.)

4. P. V. West, *Changing Practices in Handwriting Instruction,* Public School Publishing Company, Bloomington, Ill., 1927, 142 pp.

II. Spelling

1. F. S. Breed, *How to Teach Spelling,* F. A. Owen Company, Danville, N. Y., 1930.

2. T. G. Foran, *The Psychology and Teaching of Spelling,* Catholic Education Press, 1934, 234 pp.

3. Hildreth (No. 3 above) Chapters 7, 15, 24.

4. H. A. Miller, S. A. Curtis, and G. Watters, *Creative Teaching in the Field of Spelling,* Wallace Publishing Company, Des Moines, 1931, 200 pp.

5. A. E. Watson, *Experimental Studies in the Psychology and Teaching of Spelling,* Teachers College, Columbia University, 1935, 144 pp.

III. English

1. D. L. Brown and M. Butterfield, *The Teaching of Language in the Primary Grades,* The Macmillan Company, 1941, 236 pp.

2. F. Jenkins, *Language Development in the Elementary Grades,* Thomas Nelson and Sons, 1936.

3. P. G. McKee, *Language in the Elementary School,* Houghton Mifflin Company, 1939, 500 pp.

4. P. G. McKee, *Reading and Literature in the Elementary School,* Houghton Mifflin Company, 1934, 591 pp.

5. J. B. Opdycke, *Projects in Elementary English,* Oxford University Press, 1931, 726 pp.

6. C. J. Trommer and T. A. Regan, *Directing Language Power in the Elementary School Child,* The Macmillan Company, 1933, 497 pp.

7. *Forty-third Yearbook of the National Society for the Study of Education,* Part II, 1944, 257 pp.[18]

8. *Twentieth Yearbook of the Elementary School Principals Association,* pp. 229-671, 1940-1941.

To the Student

The following brief projects and exercises are included to give you greater insight both into the problems involved in learning and into the methods used in research. More are listed than are likely to be used in order that you may have some degree of selection.

1. Analyze 6–8 pages of your own handwriting. Exactly what errors do you make in which letters?

2. Analyze the small letters of the alphabet into their individual strokes, as shown in Figure 37. How many different strokes are needed for the 26 letters?

3. If there are both manuscript and script writers in your class, give a test in handwriting and score the papers for both speed and legibility. (See pages 202 ff.) Is there any advantage to either group in either respect?

4. Debate the question of manuscript writing.

5. After analyzing your mistakes (Exercise No. 1), practice 5–10 minutes a day to correct them. Later on, analyze another paper. Have you eliminated any errors?

6. If you are left-handed and use a cramped position, you would do well to reform yourself. At first, the changed position will seem

---

[18] Both these yearbooks contain material on spelling and handwriting as well as on composition.

awkward, but the greater ease will soon become apparent. Keep a "be-fore-and-after" record of your speed and legibility.

7. Make a survey of the position used by all the left-handed people known to all members of the class.

8. If you can get copies of childhood writing, duplicate the presentation in Figure 38.

9. Give a spelling test to pick out the poorest spellers in the class. Then divide the class into groups, each of which should investigate one poor speller, using the methods described on pages 305-306.

10. If possible, study the best and the worst speller among children in a given grade in school.

11. Borrow spelling papers from an elementary school and analyze the errors, using the classification on page 231 and the following pages.

12. Get from the school library several textbooks in spelling. One or two from the nineteenth century are good for comparison with more modern ones. What is the load of words per grade? Can you find out on what basis they were selected? Are they grouped for teaching?

13. From the Gates List of Spelling Errors select 10–12 words for which you can explain *why* the errors listed were made.

14. Analyze a composition or letter written by a child, classifying the errors under Capitalization, Punctuation, Grammar, and Sentence Structure. Combine results for the class. What errors are frequent? What technical words would you need to explain the errors to the children who wrote the compositions?

15. Debate the pseudo errors listed in Table 51. Wherein do they differ from the real errors listed in Table 50?

16. Analyze the last essay examination you wrote as to type of sentence, using the classification in Table 52. What proportion of each did you use?

17. Select from the class two students who are greatly interested in English and two who greatly dislike the subject. Can you find out what elements attract or repel these students? Are the causes in their nature or in the subject matter?

18. Write out a plan for a paper on the following topic: "The Learning of Spelling by School Children Could be Greatly Accelerated by the Application of Modern Methods Based upon Research." Compare several good types produced by various members of the class.

19. Let each student in the class determine the sentence length of 100 sentences taken at random from a single standard author. The number of different authors will equal the number of students. Then compare the results. In the opinion of the class, is sentence length an element in the ease or difficulty of reading the authors' works? (Warning: The results of this investigation will vary, according to what authors are selected for study.)

20. Analyze any 2–3 pages in this text for the number of ideas they contain. All students should work on the same selection and compare their results.

21. Suppose you were the teacher of this course and that you wanted to limit the enrollment to those who were "ready" to take it. What elements would you include in your tests for readiness?

22. Describe a project or activity that would require an integration of handwriting, spelling, reading, and composition as natural and integral elements.

23. John is a thirteen-year-old boy in the high sixth grade. All you know about him is that he dislikes composition work and never writes more than two or three sentences on any topic because he "has nothing more to say." What characteristics and history would you expect him to have?

24. One great problem of handwriting is to bring about transfer from the handwriting period to written work in other subjects. The same problem arises in the case of skills in composition. What methods can you suggest in each subject for increasing the amount of transfer?

25. Make up several groups of words for spelling, as suggested on pages 235-242.

26. Answer the questions on page 229 concerning any textbook in spelling.

Part III · ARITHMETIC

THE FUNDAMENTAL COMBINATIONS

HIGHER OPERATIONS WITH INTEGERS

COMMON FRACTIONS

THE SOLUTION OF VERBAL PROBLEMS

INTEREST AND DYNAMICS

READINESS TO COMPUTE

REMEDIAL WORK IN ARITHMETIC

IN THE past, arithmetic has been both overemphasized and under-learned. The present generation of teachers has inherited the remains of a curriculum based upon a combination of practical requirements that no longer exist and an educational theory that has been proved largely false. In previous generations the schools were forced by circumstances to graduate every year a small army of clerks and book-keepers who were highly proficient in arithmetic. Every man or woman who sold anything had to be able to reckon the cost of the total from the price of a given unit. Thus, the butcher who sold a roast that weighed 5⅝ pounds at 17¢ a pound had either to calculate with fractions or cut off the ⅝ths. The woman who sold 6⅔ yards of cloth and 1⅓ yards of velvet ribbon found not only fractions but a sound knowledge of measuring units necessary. In all concerns someone had to add long columns of figures in order to keep the books, and someone had to calculate profits and losses. Since business concerns were small there could be no specialists for this task; the work was therefore done by thousands of small shopkeepers. Every operation in a bank was worked out on paper. Indeed, every item of the entire business done in the world had to go through someone's head. Under such circumstances the only practical procedure for the schools was to train everyone in such operations as percentage, discount, profit and loss, partial payments, simple and compound interest, measurement of all kinds, and common fractions. It was essential also that children be highly accurate in all these operations because the errors they might make as adults were so costly in time. A bookkeeper who could not add a column of forty three-place numbers without error at least nineteen out of twenty times was not employable because he wasted to much of his firm's time in running down his mistakes. The emphasis on arithmetic by the schools was, then, quite justified.

Modern conditions, however, are different. The butcher weighs his roast on a weighing machine on which is a scale that tells him the correct total without any calculation. The woman measures her cloth and ribbon with a measuring device that not only tells her the cost but even removes the need for knowing how many feet or inches there are in a yard. The clerk in a grocery store, the bookkeeper, the bank clerk all use adding machines; interest is simply read off a table. Most business concerns are large enough to employ some sort of trained accountant who has been through a special school after finishing his general education. The housewife buys most things in packages or else by the dozen or the pound. In other words, while the business of the world still has to be computed, the details never go through anyone's head. If the elementary school is to confine its efforts to the teaching of what is universally needed, the amount of arithmetic is inevitably going to be small, although the number of concepts may be as great as ever, since ideas of size and extent and worth permeate so many of life's activities.[1] It is the amount of actual computation that has been reduced.

In addition to the practical requirements of the society in which our grandfathers lived there were also two theories concerning the value of arithmetic, the basic assumptions of which pervaded the schools and led to the extensive drill in arithmetic.[2] The theory of mental discipline presupposed that certain subjects trained the mind so generally that the person who had the training could think better on any subject whatever than the person who had not. It is, of course, perfectly obvious that those who survive a long training in a difficult subject are in general better thinkers than those who fall by the wayside. In interpreting this fact, however, the protagonists of formal discipline appear to have made the common error of mistaking the cart for the horse. The survivors of any long and difficult course of study are better thinkers at the end than those who are eliminated for the excellent reason that they were better thinkers before they started. Certain individuals survived several years of intensive work in arithmetic, for instance, because they could think unusually well; they did not think unusually well because they lived through the drill in arithmetic. Any difficult subject eliminates the incompetent thinkers, as can easily be shown by the use of modern tests and modern experimental techniques. The drill theory is also losing ground rapidly. It rested upon three assumptions that have gradually come into disrepute: the idea that learning was largely a matter of sense impressions, the conviction that sheer repetition was the best technique for learning, and the supposition that intellectual abilities were built up out of successive hierarchies of simple skills. Psychologists are no longer sure that any of these assumptions are true. There has conse-

---

[1] P. L. Spencer, "Arithmetic: A Basic Social Study," *California Journal of Elementary Education*, 5: 144–152, 1937.

[2] R. DeV. Willey, "Functional Arithmetic, 1893–1940: A Review of Typical Theoretical Discussion and the Theory to Which It Has Led," *Journal of Educational Psychology*, 33: 105–117, 1942. See also Sister W. Marguerite, "Reaction against Formalism in Arithmetic, 1890–1919," *Catholic Educational Review*, 35: 225–236, 1935.

quently been a change in the teaching of arithmetic, by diminishing the amount of sheer repetition and increasing the emphasis upon development of concepts.

Present-day attitudes have led to a greater emphasis upon the social values of arithmetic, with resulting elimination of those skills that have little if any social value. Much emphasis is now placed upon the use of numbers by children in their daily lives, rather than upon the use they may have for arithmetic after they grow up. Educators are also trying to fit the curriculum to the intellectual maturity of the children in each grade, and the harder topics are consequently being pushed on into the later years. Teachers use less drill and make more effort to make arithmetic intelligible. Instead of stressing memory, they stress more and more the development of concepts of number and relationship. Both the content and the methods of teaching have therefore been greatly changed during the last fifty years.

In terms of mastery, the results are rather hard to interpret. There are two reports[3] that compare the results on the same examinations over a period of time—in one case, 1846 to 1906 and in the other 1916 to 1939. The mastery between the two earlier dates increased, presumably because of better teaching methods and in spite of the larger enrollments and decreased degree of retardation. By 1939, however, the mastery per grade was below that of 1916. As the holding power of the schools increased and as the promotion policies became more lenient, the average ability of pupils per grade has decreased because children of low ability were not only not eliminated but were promoted each year to the next grade regardless of mastery. This process, begun soon after 1890, has become increasingly common. For a while, the lowering of "pupil material" per grade could be offset by better teaching, but as more and more dull children were promoted to higher grades there came a time when teaching skill could no longer compensate for the lowered level of ability.

The work of the elementary grades, then, must center around the everyday activities of adults or children, and should be so presented as to be as useful as possible. Considerable study has been given to the matter of desirable content from this point of view.[4] From these investi-

---

[3] See V. W. B. Hedgepeth, "Spelling and Arithmetic in 1846 and To-day," *School Review*, 14: 352–356, 1906, and M. E. Boss, "Arithmetic Then and Now," *School and Society*, 51: 391–392, 1940.

[4] For samples of research because of which the course in arithmetic has been greatly reduced, see A. D. Bowden, "Consumer's Uses of Arithmetic," *Teachers College Contributions to Education*, No. 340, 1939, 64 pp.; E. I. Hansen, "The Arithmetic of Salespersons," Master's Thesis, University of Iowa, 1934; G. M. Wilson, "What Research Reveals on

gations it would seem that children should at some time acquire skill in the following operations:

TABLE 58

Basic Skills in Arithmetic

1. The number series up to 1,000,000
2. Addition as difficult as that of 8 three-place numbers or 6 four-place numbers
3. Subtraction as difficult as that of a three- from a four-place number
4. Multiplication as difficult as that of a four- by a three-place number
5. Division as difficult as that of a four- by a three-place number
6. Addition, subtraction, multiplication and division of the following fractions: $\frac{1}{2}$, $\frac{1}{4}$, $\frac{1}{3}$, $\frac{3}{4}$, $\frac{2}{3}$, $\frac{2}{5}$, $\frac{3}{5}$, $\frac{1}{8}$, $\frac{3}{8}$, $\frac{1}{5}$, $\frac{3}{8}$
7. Addition, subtraction, multiplication and division of two- or three-place decimals
8. Percentage involving 5%, 10%, 20%, 25%, 33⅓%, 40%, 50%, 66⅔%, 75%, 80%, 90%, and the same per cents plus 100
9. Roman numerals up to 100, for 500 and for 1,000
10. Keeping a cash-account (including budgeting)
11. Retail buying
12. Measurements of: inch, foot, yard, rod, mile, square inch, square foot, square yard, acre, square mile, cubic inch, cubic foot, pint, quart, gallon, bushel, ounce, pound, ton, dozen, penny, cent, nickel, dime, quarter dollar, minute, second, hour week, month, year, century, day
13. Addition and subtraction of mixed numbers, the fractions being those listed above
14. Simple interest
15. Arithmetic as applied to business:

    a. discount   f. profit and loss
    b. commissions   g. borrowing money
    c. transportation costs   h. wholesale and retail prices
    d. insurance   i. taxes
    e. investments   j. saving money
16. Reading and constructing simple graphs

This list obviously includes many items that could not be taught in elementary schools because of the immaturity of the children. For instance, the concept of what "per cent" or "interest" means is not grasped

Proper Drill Content of Elementary Arithmetic," *Mathematics Teacher,* 28: 477–481, 1935; C. T. Wise, "A Survey of Arithmetical Problems Arising in Various Occupations," *Elementary School Journal,* 20: 118–136, 1919.

by three out of every four pupils until the ninth grade level, and the term "rate of interest" until the tenth.[5] Any teaching of interest or percentage would therefore have to be postponed beyond elementary school. The writer would strongly urge the restriction of the elementary school curriculum to the first twelve items of the above list. The material thus included, plus the thirteenth item, is usually presented in the first six grades, but much more work is generally included under each heading than the writer has in mind (as will shortly appear). It was stated at the beginning of the chapter that arithmetic was usually underlearned. No other result can be expected of an overdose of arithmetic administered to childish intellects. Certain arithmetical facts, together with everyday problems to which they apply, are entirely appropriate for children. Strictly adult uses of arithmetic are out of the question, as are complicated processes and all uses of such large quantities or such small fractions as do not occur in the ordinary individual's experience. The outstanding need in elementary school is to teach a small amount of highly useful arithmetic and teach it thoroughly. There is no better preparation for either the work of the upper grades or the requirements of adult life.

For more than a decade, investigators have known how advanced a mental age is needed if 90 per cent or more of the children are to master each process in arithmetic.[6] According to these results the various types of problem would be placed as shown in Table 59.

TABLE 59

Mental Age and Grade Placement of Operations in Arithmetic

Grade	Operation	Mental Age at End of Year (*In Years and Months*)
Low 1	Addition combinations with sums of 10 or less	6–11
High 1	Addition combinations with sums over 10 50 easier subtraction combinations	7–5

[5] A. Claret, "Récherche Expérimentale sur la notion de pourcentage," *Achives belges de Science et de l'éducation*, 1939, No. 4, pp. 87–100.

[6] See R. L. West, C. E. Greene, and W. A. Brownell, "The Arithmetic Curriculum," *Twenty-ninth Yearbook of the National Society for the Study of Education*, Part II, pp. 65–144, 1930.

See also C. W. Washburne, "Mental Age and the Arithmetic Curriculum," *Journal of Educational Research*, 23: 210–231, 1929, and "The Grade Placement of Arithmetic Topics," *Twenty-ninth Yearbook of the National Society for the Study of Education*, Part II, pp. 641–670, 1930; also "The Work of the Committee of Seven on Grade Placement," *Thirty-eighth Yearbook of the National Society for the Study of Education*, Part I, pp. 299–324, 1939.

TABLE 59—*Continued*

Grade	Operation			Mental Age at End of Year (*In Years and Months*)
Low 2	50 harder subtraction combinations			7–11
High 2	Multiplication combinations			8–5
Low 4	7 4 2 6 9 + 3	764 − 531		9–11
High 4	741 − 617	231 − 197	822 × 3	10–5
Low 5	6958 + 6445	37812 + 64387	78 16 33 46 + 21 4728 − 3119	10–11
	803 × 5 34 × 32	638 × 6		
Low 6	3212 − 2648	6)312	51)306 42)882	12–0
High 6	236 961 834 + 372 (88%)	704 − 496 (86%)	786 − 98 (86%)	12–6
		80008 − 3799 (86%)	312 × 403 (86%)	
	7894 (86%) × 8	6)3168 30)600	8)2432 (88%) 72)1872 (87%)	
			47)4653 (86%)	

Several operations usually thought of as belonging in elementary school are too hard, even for the high sixth grade. Of the eleven examples in the last section of Table 59, only two were solved by more than 90 per cent of the pupils. Data on a few still harder examples appear in Table 60 on the next page.

If one is willing to follow research to its normal conclusion one has to postpone into junior high school most of the more difficult operations with integers. Not everyone, however, is willing to accept these

TABLE 60

Operations Too Difficult for Elementary School

378	9438	89	$9\overline{)4755}$	(82%)
912	27	x76		
624	121		$79\overline{)3558}$	(69%)
583	480	(78%)		
171	6124			
264	7		$37\overline{)21830}$	(57%)
382	83	493		
194	135	x487	$46\overline{)52276}$	(75%)
(75%)	(72%)	(64%)	$36\overline{)15484}$	(50%)

conclusions as they stand. The basic objection seems to be that the studies just mentioned assume teaching to be as good as it ever will be. The assignment of processes to this or that grade may, however, be necessary at the moment only because teaching is not good enough to permit an earlier presentation. It might be better to concentrate upon improved teaching than to solve the problem by mere postponement.[7]

In the distribution of the work in arithmetic through the grades, the following arrangement is suggested:

TABLE 61

A Suggested Curriculum

Grade One: (*First Semester*) Counting forward to 100 and backward to 0 by ones. (*Second Semester*) Fundamental contributions in addition for numbers up to 5 plus 5.

Grade Two: (*First Semester*) Counting up to 500 by 5's or 10's; to 100 by 2's. Units of measure for handling money. (*Second Semester*) Fundamental combinations in subtractions. Addition of three digits, all less than 5.

Grade Three: (*First Semester*) 100 multiplication combinations. Units of measure for time. Bridging the tens (18 plus 6 or 27 plus 4.) (*Second Semester*) 90 combinations in division. Units for measuring weight. Writing of Roman numerals up to twenty. Measuring of fractions.

---

[7] For further discussion see W. A. Brownell, "Critique of the Committee of Seven's Investigation on the Grade Placement of Arithmetic Topics," *Elementary School Journal*, 38: 495–508, 1938.

Grade Four: (*First Semester*) Units of measure for length, for liquid and dry measure. Addition of any 5 digits. Carrying adding two two-place numbers. (*Second Semester*) Borrowing. Subtraction of a two- from a three-place number, or of one three-place number from another.

Grade Five: (*First Semester*) Short and long multiplication of a two- or three-place number by a digit or two two-place numbers by each other. Addition of five three-place numbers. Subtraction of a three- from a four-place number with only one borrowing. (*Second Semester*) Addition, subtraction, multiplication, division of two common fractions, using only ½, ¼, ¾, ⅓, ⅔, ⅕, and ⅛. Units of measure for area. Cubic measure.

Grade Six: (*First Semester*) Beginning of long division, using problems that require neither carrying nor borrowing. Subtraction of three- and four-place involving several borrowings. (*Second Semester*) Writing of remaining Roman numerals up to 50 and the multiples of 10 up to 100. Short column addition (four three-place numbers). Subtractions involving zeros in minuend. Short divisions with zero in quotient. Long divisions in which trial quotient is correct.

What arithmetic is taught in elementary school should be really "elementary." The majority of pupils continue in school and can be given larger doses of arithmetic later on; the few who do not progress beyond the sixth grade are quite unlikely to enter occupations in which more arithmetic than that outlined above is needed.

In all grades, work in the fundamentals should be accompanied by practical problems. For Grades 2, 3, and 4 these should be only one-step problems. In Grades 5 and 6 some of the problems should require two steps; during the last half of the sixth grade, an occasional three-step problem may be introduced.

The above scheme is based, first, upon what appears to be the assimilative capacity of children and, second, upon common, practical needs. Finally, it is an outgrowth of observation of the totally inadequate mastery achieved by the average child in his first six years of school. In no other subject does the school waste so much time in drilling children on that which they cannot yet learn. It would seem more sensible to begin formal arithmetic in the third grade and then to continue it up through the ninth or tenth grades than to teach the subject too soon, as is done at present.

XIV · The Fundamental Combinations

The first and in many ways most important step in elementary school arithmetic is the learning of the combinations in addition, subtraction, multiplication, and division. They form the basis upon which all other processes rest. Conversely, failure to master these simple combinations causes errors in one problem or advanced process after another.[1] Throughout the grades the one outstanding source of error in every analysis is ignorance of the basic number facts. It is therefore essential that a teacher make every effort to get, not reasonably correct, but absolutely correct responses from every child to every combination.

A. THE FOUR OPERATIONS

1. **Addition:** The total number of addition combinations involving 0, 1, 2, 3, 4, 5, 6, 7, 8, and 9 is one hundred. These are as follows:[2]

$0+0, 1+1, 2+2$, etc. $= 10$		$1+0$ through $9+0$	$= 9$	
$0+1$ through $0+9$	$= 9$	$2+1$ through $9+1$	$= 8$	
$1+2$ through $1+9$	$= 8$	$3+2$ through $9+2$	$= 7$	
$2+3$ through $2+9$	$= 7$	$4+3$ through $9+3$	$= 6$	
$3+4$ through $3+9$	$= 6$	combi-	$5+4$ through $9+4$	$= 5$	combi-
$4+5$ through $4+9$	$= 5$	nations	$6+5$ through $9+5$	$= 4$	nations
$5+6$ through $5+9$	$= 4$	$7+6$ through $9+6$	$= 3$	
$6+7$ through $6+9$	$= 3$	$8+7$ through $9+7$	$= 2$	
$7+8$ through $7+9$	$= 2$	$9+8$	$= 1$	
$8+9$	$= 1$			

100 combinations

[1] C. Washburne, "Primary Grade Origins of Later Remedial Cases," *Childhood Education*, 16: 29–33, 1939.

[2] The horizontal form, $1 + 4 = 5$, is used here to conserve space. Normally children learn the vertical forms, $\begin{array}{r}1\\+4\\\hline 5\end{array}$ and $\begin{array}{r}4\\+1\\\hline 5\end{array}$.

331

It should be noted that this series contains all combinations with the larger of the two numbers above the smaller and again with the larger below the smaller. That is, $\frac{9}{+4}$ and $\frac{4}{+9}$ are both listed. Unless both positions of the figures are taught there are sure to be some children who can recognize a combination in one form but not in the other. To be sure, the second form is learned quickly because the problem is merely one of identification with an earlier presentation already learned, but both need to be specifically taught.

These one hundred combinations must first be checked by counting, in order to give them meaning. The preliminary counting should, however, not be allowed to continue. Its cumbersomeness should be carefully demonstrated so that children can have some real reason for abandoning it. To the immature mind counting often seems more efficient than learning the answers, but even small children are capable of comparing the time required to count out the answer to 9 + 8 with that required to say an answer already learned. Perhaps the most accurate statement of the desired situation is that children should be able logically to prove the correctness of their answers, but that they should know the answers so well that proof is unnecessary. Once the children really understand the number relationships involved in the addition combinations, they are ready to study them. Some degree of drill is necessary. A teacher has to find the golden mean between giving children so much drill that boredom offsets the practice and giving them so little that the combinations are inadequately learned. Short, intensive drills and frequent voluntary self-drills, plus use of the number facts in problems brought in by the children themselves, are best for keeping interest and effort at a high level.

A teacher should have on hand several sets of cards, on each of which a number combination appears on one side and the answer on the other. Children like to drill each other or to go through the cards by themselves. They will do much of their own memorizing if such materials are provided.[3] In any case the number combinations should be mastered to the point of spontaneous, automatic response; otherwise they are of no use. Moreover, unless the children can react quickly and

[3] For an account of a machine for giving drill, see H. L. Smith and M. T. Eaton, "A Diagnostic Study of Effectiveness in Arithmetic," *Bulletin of the School of Education,* Indiana University, 15, No. 2: 3-49, 1939.

accurately, they are laying up trouble for themselves throughout their remaining years in school.

In learning combinations it is desirable that no set order of presentation be used. The combinations do not normally function in a series and therefore should not be learned in a series. A single number fact, such as $5 + 3 = 8$ should be given isolation, proved by the counting of objects, studied, and at once used in a number of verbal problems. It is a good idea, after $5 + 3 = 8$ has been learned, to present on the same day $3 + 5 = 8$, thus enabling the children to identify the two combinations and to learn both with little more energy than they need to remember one. After one or two pairs of combinations with zero have been learned further condensation can be achieved by teaching the general principle that zero added to any number gives the number it was added to as an answer.

There is evidence to show that some amount of generalizing about the relationship of numbers to each other will help in the learning of the combinations. In a recent experiment,[4] children who merely drilled on the combinations did not learn as rapidly as those with whom the teacher used part of the drill period for pointing out relationships. The difference was small but might easily have been appreciably larger if the experiment had lasted longer and if the children had been a little older. Generalizing could certainly be used to good effect when the teacher is showing children how to "bridge the tens." If they can count and if they already know the answer to $9 + 4$, they can work out for themselves, under the teacher's guidance, what $19 + 4$, $29 + 4$, $39 + 4$, and other similar sums must be. Counting of objects may help in proving that the combinations are still true from one series of tens to the next. Combinations in the higher decades may well be postponed till the third grade, when the children are old enough to grasp the principle.

Children's concepts of number grow slowly. The first concept they develop, some time before they have reached school age, is the difference between "one" and "more than one" or "many." Later on, they add such definite concepts as "two," "five," or "ten" and general ideas for such terms as "equal" or "add." These latter concepts do not develop until a child is about seven years old. First and second grade children do not yet have the concepts needed for learning addition and subtraction, but they have the necessary capacity to learn the simplest forms of these processes if the teacher first develops their concepts by means of

---

[4] C. L. Thiele, "The Contribution of Generalization to the Learning of the Addition Facts," *Teachers College Contributions to Education*, No. 763, 1939, 84 pp.

concrete materials and if she teaches at first in terms of objects, not abstractions. As soon as children can count objects correctly, they can begin to add by means of counting, even though they may not yet be ready for generalizing. That is, they can see that two pencils plus three pencils are five pencils, but not necessarily that $2 + 3 = 5$.[5]

Investigation has already shown which combinations are hard and which are easy. A combination of several studies [6] on this point results in the following list of the hardest and the easiest combinations:

Hardest		Easiest	
$9+6=$	$6+7=$	$2+1=$	$1+1=$
$8+6=$	$5+9=$	$1+1=$	$1+7=$
$8+5=$	$5+8=$	$9+1=$	$1+2=$
$7+9=$	$4+7=$	$2+2=$	$5+1=$
$7+5=$	$8+9=$	$6+1=$	$5+5=$
$6+9=$	$9+8=$	$5+5=$	$4+1=$

Comparison of these two columns suggests the conclusion that, for addition, hardness is largely a function of the mere size of the numbers and the necessity for getting out of one decade into another. The easy combinations are either a number plus itself—a total that is reinforced by multiplying—or a number plus 1—a total that is achieved by counting.

2: **Subtraction:** The total number of subtraction combinations is also 100. These are composed of items as follows:

$$
\left.
\begin{array}{l}
18-9,\ 17-9,\ 16-9,\ \text{etc. to}\ 9-9 \quad =10 \\
17-8,\ 16-8,\ \text{etc. to}\ 8-8 \quad\quad\ =10 \\
16-7,\ 15-7,\ \text{etc. to}\ 7-7 \quad\quad\ =10 \\
15-6\ \text{to}\ 6-6 \quad\quad\quad\quad\quad\quad\ =10 \\
14-5\ \text{to}\ 5-5 \quad\quad\quad\quad\quad\quad\ =10 \\
13-4\ \text{to}\ 4-4 \quad\quad\quad\quad\quad\quad\ =10 \\
12-3\ \text{to}\ 3-3 \quad\quad\quad\quad\quad\quad\ =10 \\
11-2\ \text{to}\ 2-2 \quad\quad\quad\quad\quad\quad\ =10 \\
10-1\ \text{to}\ 1-1 \quad\quad\quad\quad\quad\quad\ =10 \\
9-0\ \text{to}\ 0-0 \quad\quad\quad\quad\quad\quad\ =10
\end{array}
\right\} \text{combinations}
$$

100 combinations

[5] For further discussion of concepts see W. A. Brownell, "The Development of Children's Number Concepts in the Primary Grades," *Supplementary Educational Monographs*, No. 35, 1928, 241 pp.; N. R. Russell, "Arithmetical Concepts of Children," *Journal of Educational Research*, 29: 647–663, 1936.

[6] F. L. Clapp, "The Number Combinations, Their Relative Difficulty and the Frequency of Their Appearance in Textbooks," *Bureau of Educational Research Bulletin* Nos. 1 and 2, University of Wisconsin, 1924, 20 and 126 pp.; H. V. Holloway, "Ar

In teaching these subtraction facts it is desirable to show, by use of objects and counting, that each is the exact reverse of some addition fact. Thus, when the teacher is presenting $16 - 7 = 9$, she should compare it with $9 + 7 = 16$. Having the children discover for themselves which is the corresponding combination in addition can be made into an interesting exercise. The fundamental facts should be understood by such procedures as these, but they must also be learned. As soon as each fact has been memorized it should be used in practical problems.

A consideration of the hardest and easiest combinations in subtraction reveals some interesting facts. The hardest combinations are usually the reversals of those hardest in addition: [7]

Hardest		*Easiest*	
$16-9=$	$15-7=$	$2-1=$	$4-1=$
$15-9=$	$11-3=$	$3-2=$	$8-7=$
$14-9=$	$13-9=$	$1-1=$	$8-1=$
$14-5=$	$16-7=$	$3-1=$	$4-2=$
$13-5=$	$13-8=$	$9-1=$	$3-3=$
$13-4=$	$14-6=$	$9-9=$	$0-0=$

Their difficulty is then a function of the same two conditions previously given, plus the insufficient learning of the hardest addition facts. The effect of a failure to master these sums in addition begins, at this point, to roll up like a snowball. At the other end of the list, easiness is evidently due to one of four situations: the subtrahend is one less than the minuend, the subtrahend itself is 1, the subtrahend is the same number as the minuend, or it is half the minuend. The first two types are easy because they rest directly on counting. The third type can be reduced to a general principle that a number minus itself gives zero, while the fourth type is reinforced by multiplication. It should be noted

Experimental Study to Determine the Relative Difficulty of the Elementary Number Combinations in Addition and Multiplication," Doctor's Thesis, University of Pennsylvania, 1914, 102 pp.; G. M. Norem and H. B. Knight, "The Learning of the 100 Multiplication Combinations," *Twenty-ninth Yearbook of the National Society for the Study of Education,* 1930, pp. 551–568; H. Rebarker, "A Study of the Simple Integral Processes of Arithmetic," *Peabody College Contributions to Education,* No. 26, 1926, 90 pp.; R. T. Rock anad T. G. Foran, "A Comparison of Studies on the Relative Difficulty of the Number Combinations," *Educational Research Bulletin of the Catholic University of America,* Vol. 5, No. 8, 1930; S. M. Washburn, "The Relative Difficulty of Number Combinations in 1937 as Determined by Repeating Clapp's Investigation," *Pittsburgh Schools,* 13: 133–140, 1939; C. Washburne and N. Vogel, "Are Any Number Combinations Inherently Difficult?" *Journal of Educational Research.* 17: 235–255, 1928; L. R. Wheeler, "A Comparative Study of the Difficulty of the 100 Addition Combinations," *Journal of Genetic Psychology,* 54: 295–312, 1939.

[7] Clapp, *op. cit.* and Washburn, *op. cit.*

that for adding or subtracting, the zeros give only a moderate amount of difficulty.

3. **Multiplication:** The hundred multiplication facts involve the same pairs of figures as those in addition, with the $\times$ instead of the $+$ sign between the members of each pair. Because the figures are similar and because the addition combinations are learned first, there is always grave danger that the children will react to such exercises as 2×3 with a 5 instead of a 6. It is imperative, in introducing the process of multiplying, to concentrate attention upon the sign, so as to diminish this source of confusion as much as possible. Since multiplying is a totally new performance it should be introduced by concrete demonstration. An exercise such as 3×4 should be illustrated by using three groups of objects, four in a group, and then having the children count the total. This same demonstration may be used to show that multiplying is a short-cut technique for adding a number to itself several times. The first few combinations should be thoroughly discussed and illustrated until the children grasp what this new process means. Then, when a dozen or so combinations have been memorized, deduction of new facts from those known may be begun without recourse to objects except when the pupils are in doubt. For instance, if they have learned through demonstration that $3 \times 4 = 12$, they may be asked to work out what 4×4 would be by counting up four more units from 12. Care must be taken, however, that children use counting only for deduction or for proof and that they do not substitute it for learning.

The easiest combinations [8] are those involving zeros, those in the series from 1×1 to 1×9 and from 9×1 to 1×1, and those of a number less than 5 multiplied by itself.

The most difficult combinations are mostly old friends, as shown below: [9]

Hardest		Easiest (except for zeros)	
$7 \times 9 =$	$6 \times 7 =$	$1 \times 1 =$	$1 \times 5 =$
$9 \times 6 =$	$8 \times 7 =$	$5 \times 1 =$	$1 \times 4 =$
$6 \times 9 =$	$6 \times 8 =$	$7 \times 1 =$	$1 \times 2 =$
$7 \times 6 =$	$8 \times 6 =$	$1 \times 8 =$	$2 \times 1 =$
$9 \times 7 =$	$7 \times 7 =$	$1 \times 6 =$	$2 \times 2 =$
$7 \times 8 =$	$8 \times 9 =$	$1 \times 3 =$	$2 \times 4 =$

[8] W. A. Brownell and D. Carper, "Learning the Multiplication Combinations," *Duke University Studies in Education,* No. 7, 1943, 117 pp.; Clapp, *op. cit.;* Holloway, *op. cit.;* Washburn, *op. cit.;* L. R. Wheeler, "A Comparative Study of the Difficulty of Learning the Multiplication Combinations," *Journal of Genetic Psychology,* 59: 189–206, 1941.

[9] Wheeler, *op. cit.*

These hardest combinations show, in general, the same pairs of figures that were poorly learned for both addition and subtraction. The snowball is gathering more momentum with each new process. Combinations of 9's, 8's, 7's, and 6's are almost always underlearned and combinations of 1's and 2's—except for 1×1, which children are inclined to add rather than multiply—overlearned.

4. **Division:** For division it seems best to limit the number of facts to ninety, omitting the series running from $0\overline{)0}$ to $0\overline{)9}$. Handling zeros is bad enough even at best, but $0\overline{)9} = \infty$ reduces the average pupil to confusion. In practical problems one never has zero as a divisor. The facts to be learned are, then, as follows:

$$
\left.
\begin{array}{l}
81 \div 9,\ 72 \div 9,\ \text{etc., to } 9 \div 9\ \ = 9 \\
72 \div 8,\ 64 \div 8,\ \text{etc., to } 8 \div 8\ \ = 9 \\
63 \div 7 \text{ to } 7 \div 7\ \ = 9 \\
54 \div 6 \text{ to } 6 \div 6\ \ = 9 \\
45 \div 5 \text{ to } 5 \div 5\ \ = 9 \\
36 \div 4 \text{ to } 4 \div 4\ \ = 9 \\
27 \div 3 \text{ to } 3 \div 3\ \ = 9 \\
18 \div 2 \text{ to } 2 \div 2\ \ = 9 \\
9 \div 1 \text{ to } 1 \div 1\ \ = 9 \\
0 \div 9 \text{ to } 0 \div 0\ \ = 9
\end{array}
\right\} \text{combinations}
$$

90 combinations

In presenting these combinations it is preferable to use the form $9\overline{)81}$ rather than $81 \div 9$ because the former symbol will persist into long division whereas the latter has to be abandoned. Moreover, the sign $\div$ is sometimes mistaken by pupils for a minus. Dividing should be demonstrated as the reverse of multiplying. It is also desirable to demonstrate that dividing is a short-cut method of subtracting. This can be done by assembling, say, twenty-four objects in groups of threes and then subtracting out a group at a time, noting that eight subtractions are needed. Time spent in illustrating these relationships is more than saved in the shortened time needed to learn the combinations. Again, however, pupils should be cautioned against the waste involved in reasoning out an answer instead of knowing it. Memorizing without understanding is disastrous, but understanding without memorizing is not much better.

Study of the hardest and easiest combinations [10] reveals that the old, familiar combinations of 9, 8, 7, and 6 are still weak. A second contribution to difficulty is the odd fact that a number divided by 1 is still

Hardest		*Easiest*	
9)54	1)3	5)20	3)21
6)54	5)5	2)8	3)9
4)28	8)56	2)12	7)21
7)56	8)24	2)14	2)4
4)36	4)24	5)10	5)25
1)1	9)63	2)10	2)6

the same number—a fact that children find hard to believe—especially $1 \div 1 = 1$. Any number divided by itself, such as $6 \div 6$, seems to many children to be the same as the number minus itself, or $6 - 6$; they therefore get 0 instead of 1 as an answer. Finally, there is a type of difficulty well illustrated by the relative positions of 4)24 and 6)24 as compared with 7)21 and 3)21. All combinations with 24 as the dividend are hard because this figure can be factored in so many ways: 6×4, 8×3, 12×2, 4×6, 3×8, 2×12. The two divisions with 21 are easy because 21 can be factored only as 7×3 or 3×7. The easy combinations are those that are factorable in only one way, those in which the divisor is 2, and those involving 5 and its multiples.

There are, then, 390 combinations, of which 175 are reversed forms of another 175, while the remaining 40 consist of the numbers from 0 through 9 added to, subtracted from, multiplied by, or divided into themselves. The mastery of these 390 facts is the main business of three years of school. This load is sufficient to keep the average child well occupied. If time is wasted by overteaching some of the combinations, others are sure to be neglected. If answers are learned erroneously, these mistakes will persist through all succeeding operations. This is one time when a 95 per cent accuracy is not even "good"; for work in later grades or in adult life nothing less than 100 per cent is efficient.

B. DRILL, ERRORS, AND SPEED

1. Drill: In reviewing the points discussed in this section one is impressed with the similarities of the difficulties from one process to an-

---

[10] Washburn, *op. cit.* and Clapp, *op. cit.*

other. One may hazard the guess that adequate concepts for the digits above 5 are not built up and that adequate drill is not given to any handling of them. Indeed, various studies have shown that the exercises used in textbooks usually tend to give more practice with the smaller than with the larger numbers. The following facts from one excellent study may be used as samples: [11]

$$\left.\begin{array}{l} 2+2= \\ 2-2= \\ 2\times2= \\ 2\div2= \end{array}\right\} \text{received} \left\{\begin{array}{l} \text{four} \\ \text{eleven} \\ \text{eight} \\ \text{over } 40 \end{array}\right\} \text{times as much practice as} \left\{\begin{array}{l} 8+8= \\ 17-8= \\ 9\times8= \\ 72\div9= \end{array}\right.$$

In multiplication alone there were, in a single, widely used text, 7,355 uses of 2 as either multiplier or multiplicand, as compared with 2,171 uses of 9, and 1,906 uses of 0; that is, over three times as much practice was provided with 2's as with 9's and nearly four times as much as with 0's.

Another investigator studied the uses of each digit in all four operations. A small section of results for the position of the digits in addition combinations in one textbook appears in Table 62.

TABLE 62

Frequency of Drill with Each Integer in One Text [12]

Integer	Times Used as Lower Number in Combination	Times Used as Upper Number in Combination	Total
0	617	205	822
1	628	237	865
2	1,124	1,018	2,142
3	934	947	1,881
4	732	640	1,372
5	715	598	1,313
6	721	850	1,571
7	580	854	1,434
8	673	924	1,597
9	706	1,157	1,863

[11] E. L. Thorndike, "The Psychology of Drill in Arithmetic: The Amount of Practice," *Journal of Educational Psychology*, 12: 183–194, 1921.

[12] O. S. Lutes and A. Samuelson, "A Method for Rating the Drill Provisions in Arithmetic Textbooksk," *University of Iowa Monographs in Education First Series*, No. 3, 1926, 148 pp. Used by permission of the publisher.

These figures are to be read as follows: a 0 was used 617 times as the lower figure in a combination, such as $\dfrac{7}{+0}$ or $\dfrac{38}{+20}$ or $\dfrac{379}{+104}$, but only 205 times as the upper figure, $\dfrac{0}{+7}$ or $\dfrac{20}{+38}$ or $\dfrac{104}{+379}$. The children therefore, got three times as much practice with zeros in one place as with them in the other. The figure 2 occurred about evenly in the two positions, but 6, 7, 8, and 9 were more often the upper number than the lower. The writer of this arithmetic text seems also to have liked 2's better than any other number, since he used them oftener. In order of frequency the digits are 2, 3, 9, 8, 6, 7, 4, 5, 1, 0, an order that does not coincide with the facts about their difficulty. Since all combinations with 7, 8, and 9 are hard, they should certainly have more practice than those with 2 and 5, which are easy, but in this text they got an almost equal amount. A teacher would do well to analyze the frequency with which she gives drill on each combination and try to arrange the work so that practice on numbers above 5 will far exceed practice on those below.

Not only does the amount but also the distribution of the practice need consideration. A hard combination should be reviewed oftener than an easy one. A teacher can help to distribute the practice where it is most needed if she analyzes all the materials to be used for a semester— textbook, problems, and practice exercises—and plans for the proper amount of drill for each combination. Such an arrangement as that presented in Table 63 is recommended. These samples show the distribution of drill for half a semester for a pair of hard combinations, four of medium difficulty, and two that are easy. It should be noted that the amounts of drill differ in three respects: the total number of opportunities, the initial amount of practice, and the length of time intervening between successive reviews. Thus, for $7+1$ the total number of repetitions is 30, the initial dosage is 8, and the average number of school days between practices is 3.3. For $5+4$ the three corresponding figures are 45, 12, and 2.0; for $9+6$, they are 88, 20, and 1.1. Such planning ahead will do much toward bringing about a real mastery of the fundamental facts.

It remains to say a word about the nature of the drill period. It should be short but intensive. It is better to have three periods of five to ten minutes each than one long period. Ten minutes of intensive drill at once is enough.

TABLE 63

Planning of Drill in Arithmetic

		Easy Combinations		Average Combinations				Hard Combinations	
		7 + 1	1 + 7	5 + 4	4 + 5	3 + 6	6 + 3	9 + 6	6 + 9
First Week	M.	8	5						
	T.	3	3	12	10				
	W.	2	2	5	5	12	10		
	Th.			3	3	7	7	20	15
	F.	1	1	2	2	4	4	10	10
Second Week	M.			2	2	2	2	10	10
	T.	2	2				1	8	8
	W.			1	1	1		3	3
	Th.					2	2	2	2
	F.	2	2	2	2			1	1
Third Week	M.	1	1	1	1			3	3
	T.							1	1
	W.	1	1	1	1			3	3
	Th.					2	2	3	3
	F.			2	2				
Fourth Week	M.			2	2			3	3
	T.					2	2		
	W.	2	2						
	Th.							2	2
	F.					1	1	1	1
Fifth Week	M.	1	1	1	1	1	1	1	1
	T.			1					
	W.							2	2
	Th.					2	2	2	2
	F.					1	1	2	2
Sixth Week	M.							1	1
	T.			2	2			1	1
	W.							1	1
	Th.					1	1	1	1
	F.								
Seventh Week	M.	2	2					1	1
	T.								
	W.					2	2	2	2
	Th.								
	F.							2	2
Eighth Week	M.			2	2	1	1		
	T.							1	1
	W.							1	1
	Th.							1	1
	F.			1	1				
Ninth Week	M.					2	2		
	T.								
	W.	1	1						
	Th.							2	2
	F.						1	1	1
Tenth Week	M.							1	1
	T.								
	W.			1	1				
	Th.					1	1		
	F.	2	2						

2. **Errors:** A most frequent source of error is the mere guessing of answers on the part of a child who does not know the correct response. The chances that a guess will be correct are infinitely less than that it will be wrong; most guesses thus result in errors. Children should be trained to omit answers of which they are not sure, because allowing them to guess answers merely gives them practice in making incorrect responses. Children will not stop guessing answers, however, as long as the slightest odium is attached to the response, "I don't know." Many teachers convey by their attitude the feeling that an omission is worse than an error. Quite the contrary! Omissions do no harm; it is errors that do the real damage.

Moreover, errors are remarkably persistent and can be eliminated only by geat effort on everyone's part. One investigator has checked the occurrence of particular errors on the papers or in the recitations of certain children and has found interesting, though most distressing, results.[13] Thus, one child on twenty-three successive days gave the following oral responses to $4+6$: 8, 8, 10, 8, 10, 10, 8, 10, 10, 10, 10, 8, 10, 10, 10, 10, 10, 10, 10, 8, 10, 10, 10. In all cases errors were corrected on the spot and the child made to repeat the combination correctly. Even at the end of the twenty-three opportunities this child was still not sure of the response. An error is not a negative thing; it is not a mere failure to get the right answer. It is a positive response that is just as persistent as the right answer. Teachers often forget that a child's neurons are quite as willing to learn $6+8=13$ as $6+8=14$. The right answer has no superiority over the wrong, until it has been associated with a pleasant condition of affairs—namely, the approval of the teacher and the emotional satisfaction of the learner. It is therefore desirable to prevent errors rather than to rely upon a hope of correcting them.

For the prevention of errors there are at least three constructive suggestions. The first is to penalize errors far more heavily than omissions. For instance, if an omission counts nothing against a child's score, but a mistake counts two points, children will not be stimulated to guess. If one child has 14 correct answers, and 6 errors on 20 exercises, while another has 14 correct responses and 6 omissions, both would, by usual methods of scoring, receive a score of 14. That is, omissions and errors count exactly alike and, since there is always a chance that a guess will be right, children are actually encouraged to guess. However, if the method of scoring recommended above is used, the latter child

[13] G. Myers, *Prevention and Correction of Errors in Arithmetic,* The Plymouth Press, 1925, 75 pp.

would receive a total sccre of 14, while the former would get only 2:14 right answers minus 6 wrong ones, each counting 2 points, would equal 14−12, or 2. Such a scoring device would soon stop guesswork and would put a high premium upon accuracy. A second suggestion for the prevention of errors consists in the avoidance of fatigue or emotional strain. As soon as a child is tired the number of errors increases. Children make most of their mistakes in the last third of the arithmetic period. The drill periods should, therefore, be short, intensive, and carefully planned. Finally, errors may be avoided by eliminating the pressure for speed. This point is so important that a section will be devoted to it shortly.

If a child is already making errors there is only one course to pursue —analyze his work, find the precise errors, explain them to him, and let him drop other assignments in arithmetic until the errors are corrected. The correction of mistakes, even after their cause is located, is a dreary task, but it has to be done and at once, or progress becomes slower and slower until the child develops a settled conviction that he cannot learn arithmetic—and then the damage *is* serious.

3. **Speed:** Children need to make the combinations with reasonable speed, partly as a practical matter and partly to prevent them from persisting in counting after they no longer need it. The point that seems often forgotten, however, is that children will answer quickly enough when they *know* the answers. Each child will then answer at a rate of response that is natural to his particular nervous system. If the pressure for speed requires him to write or speak quickly answers of which he is not sure he will become upset and either "stall" completely or guess. In any case too early or too great a pressure for speed causes strain and results in mistakes. Until all combinations are learned to an errorless perfection—and this state is not a Utopia if teachers will concentrate on what children do not know—speed is destructive. After combinations are perfectly known, special emphasis on speed is generally unnecessary because complete accuracy produces its own speed. The child who is abnormally slow in his answers to such problems as 7+6 is probably counting; but even for him speed is inadvisable because it will merely make him count faster and will ruin the only method he knows.

There seems to be some confusion between the concepts of "speed" and "hurrying." Speed is the natural concomitant of a well-learned, fully coordinated, effortless response. It comes of its own accord when the learner is ready for it. Hurrying is the result of a pressure for speed

beyond one's normal reaction time. To hurry is primarily to disor-
ganize. Children should proceed at whatever rate they elect, so long
as they are actually applying themselves and not dawdling, until accuracy has been achieved. Sufficient speed will usually follow; if it
does not, there is no harm in a small amount of pressure, but care
must be taken not to use so much that there is a lowering of accuracy.
Arithmetic without accuracy is useless, but arithmetic without high
speed is merely a bit inefficient. Throughout the elementary school years
teaching and learning effort should be put on the task of getting the
right answer, with confidence that continued practice and a maturing
nervous system will produce adequate speed as the years roll on.

C. SUMMARY

The 390 fundamental facts in arithmetic are the basis for all calculation and must therefore be learned thoroughly. Extra time spent at
this initial stage saves hours of remedial work later on and prevents
many errors from ever being made. Conversely, any uncertainty about
these facts will dog a child's footsteps throughout his school days at
least and will influence adversely every subsequent arithmetical process.
The only practical criterion is a perfect score, because an incorrect response is of no conceivable use. A teacher should, of course, introduce
plenty of variety into the necessary drill and should be careful to build
up the children's concepts of number so that the facts may have real
meaning for them, but the only practical objective remains the mastery
of all the 390 basic facts.

XV · Higher Operations with Integers

After the fundamental combinations have been learned there remain certain more complicated tasks, of which the most important are column addition, subtraction involving borrowing, short and long multiplication, and short and long division. Two central difficulties pervade all of these operations to a greater or lesser degree. A child must first learn to manipulate numbers that are not written on the paper before him—often at the same time disregarding some of those that are. He must, second, develop an understanding of the difference between the "places" in a number of more than one place. Drill on these relatively difficult operations produces only confusion until after children have the mental maturity to juggle figures in their heads and to understand the meaning of the "places." Moreover, children need to go slowly at first and to learn thoroughly what they learn at all. It has, therefore, been suggested that this work be postponed until the fourth grade and then be spread out over the remaining years of elementary school.

A. COLUMN ADDITION

The first step from the addition combinations to column addition should involve only one new requirement—the handling of partial sums that are carried in the head but not written down. Such problems as those below, requiring no carrying, are to be used. The height of the column may well be increased to eight digits until the children have developed an attention span long enough to last for a single, fairly tall column and have had adequate practice in carrying partial sums in their heads. Such columns require them to add a number that is seen to one that is not. Thus, in the first example, the child adds $4+7$ and gets a mental 11, to which he adds the visible 6.

```
        9
        3
  6     5
  7     7
 +4    +2
```

The next step in column addition involves the process of carrying and should be begun with only two small numbers so that other source of difficulty may be ruled out temporarily. Here the child has to find out what number to carry and then add it to those he sees. When the fundamental process of carrying has been grasped, further variations should be introduced. For such a problem as appears below the child must handle partial sums as well as carry. As the height of the column increases there is a demand for a longer and longer attention span. It is therefore desirable to distribute the work in column addition through two or three grades, adding to the height and number of the columns as the children develop better powers of attention until a practical objective has been reached. Many children who perfectly understand partial sums and carrying still make errors in column addition because they are required to add columns that are too long for their attention span. Practice will lengthen the span somewhat, but maturity will lengthen it more.

$$\begin{array}{r} 49 \\ +36 \\ \hline \end{array}$$

$$\begin{array}{r} 38 \\ 42 \\ 29 \\ +26 \\ \hline \end{array}$$

There are three outstanding errors in the carrying process itself. The first is a failure to carry at all, plus the writing down of the answers to each column separately. The second error is the failure to carry, plus the complete dropping of the carried number. The third type of error consists in carrying the wrong number. The actual operations in these three types of error are shown below:

$$\begin{array}{r} 49 \\ +36 \\ \hline 715 \end{array}$$ The child adds: *9+6 are 15, 3+4 are 7*, and puts down both complete numbers.

$$\begin{array}{r} 49 \\ +36 \\ \hline 75 \end{array}$$ The child adds: *9+6 are 15, write down 5 and carry 1; 3+4 are 7.* In this there is no actual carrying of the 1.

$$\begin{array}{r} 49 \\ +36 \\ \hline 121 \end{array}$$ The child adds: *9+6 are 15, write down 1 and carry 5; 5+3 are 8, +4 are 12.* He has carried the 5 and written the 1.

In actual practice these errors are often combined with mistakes in the combinations and are not easily recognizable, but they can be located if the teacher will use a series of simple problems such as that given first in this section.

Studies have been made [1] of the eye movements used by children who add well and by children who add poorly. These photographic records reflect clearly the differences in technique. Figure 53 shows five such records.

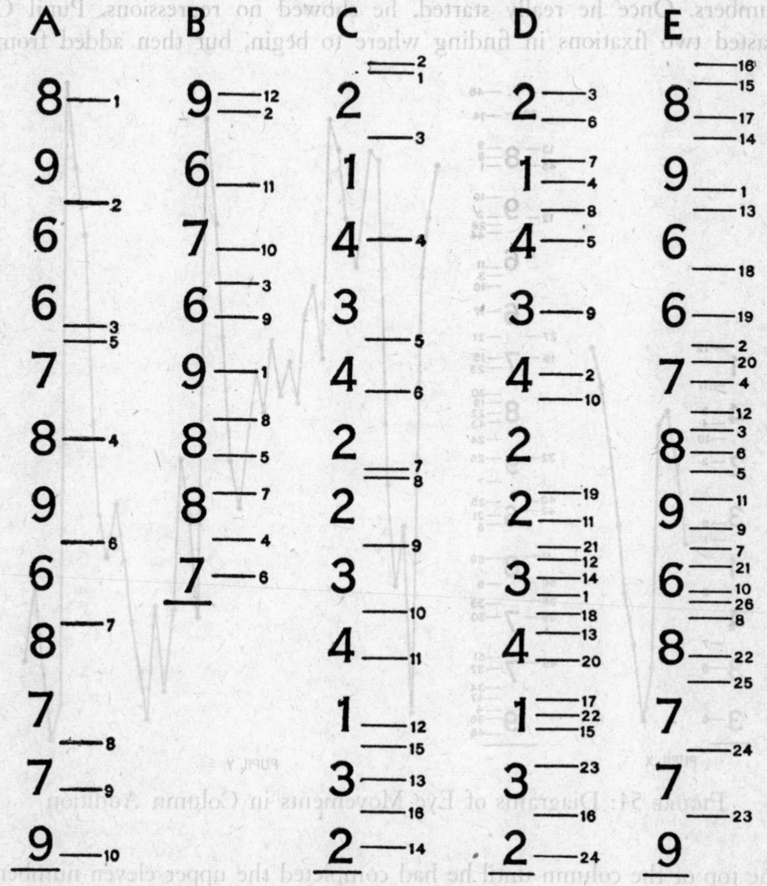

FIGURE 53: Record of Eye Movements during Column Addition

Pupil A added well. He started at the top of the column of figures (shown at the left) and made ten fixations (shown by the small figures at the right). There were twelve figures in the column he added, so that he must sometimes have seen more than one digit at a glance. His fifth

[1] G. T. Buswell and L. John, "Diagnostic Studies in Arithmetic," *Supplementary Educational Monographs*, No. 30, 1926, 212 pp. Figures 53 and 54 are from this reference and are used by permission of the publishers.

fixation was a regression, but otherwise the pauses are in order. Pupil B first made five fixations in a totally random order, apparently examining the column before getting down to work. Then he proceeded from the bottom of the column to the top, using seven fixations to add eight numbers. Once he really started, he showed no regressions. Pupil C wasted two fixations in finding where to begin, but then added from

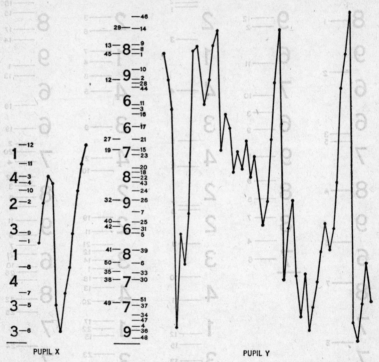

PUPIL X   PUPIL Y

FIGURE 54: Diagrams of Eye Movements in Column Addition

the top of the column until he had completed the upper eleven numbers with eleven orderly fixations. At this point he "ran out of breath" and required five more pauses—one of them a regression—to add on the last number. Pupil D shows even more clearly both the inability to get started and the shortness of attention span. He rambled about for five fixations before he decided to begin at the top, then he added the first nine figures in eight pauses. Here he went completely to pieces and used eleven fixations—five of them regressions—to add the last three figures. Pupil E was hopelessly lost. It is impossible to tell in which direction he thought he was adding. He rambled about, used twenty-six fixations—half of them regressions—and finally stopped in the middle of the column without ever getting an answer.

The records of Pupils X and Y, shown in Figure 54, present a contrast in the procedures of two children. Pupil X began in the middle, glanced toward the top, then toward the bottom, where he settled down to work and added the column in seven fixations and without regressions. His performance is recorded first in the same manner as the results in Figure 53, and then a diagram of the eye movements is made, to the right of the column, for the purpose of bringing out the up-and-down movements of the eyes as clearly as possible. Pupil Y used 51 fixations in trying to add a column of twelve digits. His record suggests that he could not even make up his mind whether he wanted to add up or down. He simply rambled about— sometimes up, sometimes down—and he did not succeed in getting an answer. Upon his own admission, he was hunting around to find combinations of numbers he could add.

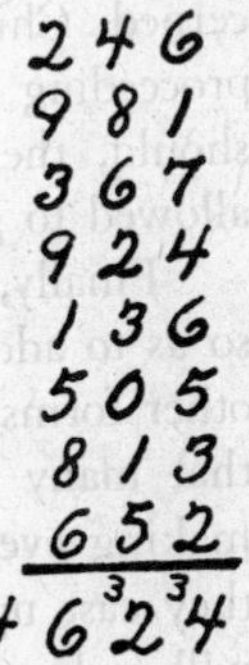

The good "adder," like the good reader, proceeds accurately and rhythmically. He shows few fixations, almost no regressions, and a wide enough visual span of comprehension sometimes to see two numbers; moreover, his attention span lasts until he has finished his task.

$$
\begin{array}{r}
246 \\
981 \\
367 \\
924 \\
136 \\
505 \\
813 \\
\underline{652} \\
4\,6\overset{3}{2}\overset{3}{4}
\end{array}
$$

FIGURE 55: An Aid to Accuracy in Addition

There are three further points to be discussed in regard to column addition. One is the oft-disputed matter of whether or not children should be allowed to write down the figure to be carried, in some such fashion as is shown below. In the writer's opinion, they certainly should be not only allowed but encouraged to do so. To begin with, children need to *see* the number in order to be sure of adding it. Secondly, their attention span is so short that they cannot be sure of getting up the second column before they run out of breath; if they pause anywhere they must go back to the very beginning and start over unless the carried number has been written down. In the third place, an adult working under normal business or social conditions usually writes down these numbers because he may be disturbed before he can complete the addition, and he does not want to waste time. Far from being a crutch, therefore, the writing down of these numbers is only common sense.

Provided they are written so small that they cannot be mistaken as part of the answer they do no harm and a great deal of good. Arithmetic is not a disciplinary subject. The additional mental strain of carrying all numbers in one's head will not produce greater thinking capacity; it will produce only more errors. Arithmetic is complicated enough for the child mind without an insistence upon unnecessary and impractical sources of confusion. The main thing is accuracy and efficiency, not mental gymnastics.

The second matter is the old question of whether it is more efficient to add a column upward or downward. The answer is that it does not make a penny's worth of difference so far as the initial addition is concerned. Children should be trained always to check their addition by proceeding in the opposite direction from that first taken. Each child should, therefore, add in both directions eventually, but he may be allowed to go initially in either direction he likes.

Finally, there is the matter of combining numbers within a column so as to add more rapidly. This is an excellent plan for adults but, like other forms of sophistication, decidedly not for children. The main idea that many children obtain from suggestions for combining is that by making even tens one can avoid the trouble of adding. Consequently, they cast up and down the column looking for pairs of numbers that will make ten, add some figures twice and some not at all, spend more time than they would have needed to add the numbers in order, and finally emerge with an incorrect answer. A graphic illustration of this procedure is shown in Figure 54. For the average child the attempt to combine figures simply breaks down previous habits and leads to mistakes. Later on, when children are old enough to exercise reasonable judgment in the matter, this short cut may be introduced for the benefit of those who are able to use it, but during elementary school the less said about it the better. An educational psychologist sees many children whose progress in arithmetic has been almost stopped because they substituted for orderly addition a frantic search for numbers that will make ten. Combining numbers is an excellent procedure if one is able to do it correctly, but it is not adapted to childish mentalities.

B. SUBTRACTION

There are three different methods of subtraction. Although they are of varying merit, a teacher in the upper grades should allow each child to continue with whichever method he has started, since the difference between the methods is not great enough to warrant the breaking down of a habit of subtraction that is already functioning. Naturally, if one is teaching a child who has had no previous teaching, one would select the most efficient method. The three techniques are illustrated below by quoting what the pupil would say to himself in learning to subtract 39 from 82.

(a) Decomposition Method

$$\begin{array}{r} 82 \\ -39 \\ \hline 43 \end{array}$$

"Take 1 from 8 and make 12, then 9 from 12 is 3; since 1 has been taken from the 8, it is now a 7, and 3 from 7 is 4."

(b) Austrian Method

$$\begin{array}{r} 82 \\ -39 \\ \hline 43 \end{array}$$

"$9+3$ is 12; write down the 3 and carry 1; $1+3$ is 4, plus 4 is 8."

(c) Equal-Additions Method

$$\begin{array}{r} 82 \\ -39 \\ \hline 43 \end{array}$$

"Take 1 from 8 and make 12, then 9 from 12 is 3; $1+3$ makes 4, and 4 from 8 is 4."

Of these three methods, the first is the most common, but it is the hardest.[2] The Austrian is clearly the best, with the third method a good second. Although the decomposition method trails along as a bad third, a child who has learned it should be allowed to use it. Since it is the commonest technique, the discussion of borrowing will be phrased in its terms, but the general principles would be the same for the other methods, although the phrasing would be somewhat different.

1. Borrowing: The first problem in borrowing is to show how the numbers are decomposed. Thus, for the above problem, the 82 is decomposed into 12 and 70. The 9 is taken from the 12 and the 30 from the 70. This may be demonstrated as follows:

$$\begin{array}{r} 82 = 70 + 12 \\ -39 = 30 + \ 9 \\ \hline 40 + \ 3 \\ \underbrace{\hphantom{40 + 3}} \\ 43 \end{array} \qquad \begin{array}{r} 43 = 30 + 13 \\ -27 = 20 + \ 7 \\ \hline 10 + \ 6 \\ \hline 16 \end{array}$$

---

[2] J. T. Johnson, "The Relative Merits of Three Months of Subtraction," *Teachers College Contributions to Education*, No. 738, 1938, 76 pp.

Naturally, not enough examples should be worked out in this way to set up a habit. When it comes to solving actual problems, children should be shown that they can get the same result with less effort by borrowing.

Problems like the above are relatively simple. Such an example as that below makes a further demand. The child subtracts 7 from a 12, of which he sees the 2; then he must subtract 8 from a 13 that is not only not in sight but is represented by a 4; next, he must subtract 9 from a 12 that is not there, at the same time ignoring the 3 that is; finally, he must remember that the remaining 2 has become a 1. This business of continued borrowing calls for the highest order of concentration. For this reason the process of borrowing should be mastered with the use of two-place numbers, and the solving of more complex forms left till later.

$$\begin{array}{r} 2342 \\ -987 \\ \hline 1355 \end{array}$$

The outstanding error in subtraction is the failure to take account of the borrowing. Thus, for 82 minus 39, a child gets an answer of 53 instead of 43. He has taken 9 from 12, written down 3, and then taken 3 from 8. For the continued borrowing, as shown by the problem below, the errors are due either to shortness of attention or to the intrusion into his attention of the numbers a child is actually looking at. Once the subtraction procedure is understood, mistakes occur when there is either a breakdown in concentration or an error in computation.

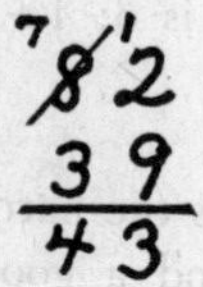

The writing of figures to help in the decomposition of the minuend is of definite value[3] Thus the problem of subtracting 39 from 82 may be made simpler and the degree of accuracy improved by crossing out the numbers that have to be reduced. This procedure has in the past been regarded as a "crutch" and therefore frowned upon. Research has shown, however, that pupils do better work in less time with it than without it. If one still believes that mental arithmetic trains the mind, then presumably one would disapprove of anything that made the discipline less severe. If, however, a teacher is interested in helping children learn to subtract quickly, easily, and accurately, she would do well to teach them how to aid themselves by writing in

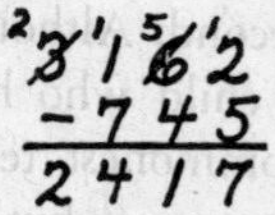

FIGURE 56: An Aid to Accuracy in Subtraction

FIGURE 57: An Aid to Accuracy in Long Subtraction Problems

[3] W. A. Brownell, "Borrowing in Subtraction," *Journal of Educational Research*, 33: 415–424, 1940. Similar material by the same author appears in "Learning as Reorganization," *Duke University Studies in Education*, No. 3, 1939, 87 pp., also as "A Study of Learning in One Phase of Arithmetic," *Journal of Genetic Psychology*, 24: 457–465, 1941.

numbers, according to whichever method they use. These interpolations are especially valuable in working out a long problem, because the child's attention span often does not last long enough for three or four successive borrowings. Most children drop their "crutch" voluntarily after a while, but even if they do not they still get the right answer oftener and more quickly with than without it.

C. MULTIPLICATION

When one multiplies 36 by 8, one has to add as well as multiply. That is, 8×6 is 48, the 4 is carried, 8×3 is 24, and the carried 4 is then added to the 24 to give an answer of 288. As an introduction to multiplication it is advisable to provide drill on the addition facts that will be needed, such as: $56+1=$, $56+2=$, $56+3=$, $56+4=$, $56+5=$, $56+6=$, so that children will have a chance to review these combinations necessary to multiplication. There are 175 such combinations.[4] This number may seem forbidding, but most of them are either easy or already known. The drill on these combinations is chiefly a review in bridging the tens. The number added is always a digit from 1 to 8 —since the highest possible multiplication is $9 \times 9 = 81$ and carry 8. The number to which the digit is added is always a product of two other numbers. That is, there is no need to review $17 + 6$ because a child will never get 17 as a partial product, but he needs $27 +$ any number from 1–8 because $9 \times 3 = 27$. These combinations are constantly used and must be known if frequent and unnecessary errors are to be avoided.

With these combinations as background, children are ready to learn "short" multiplication with an example such as the following:

$$
\begin{array}{ccccc}
23 & = & 20 & & 3 \\
\times 4 & = & \times 4 & + & \times 4 \\
\hline
92 & & 80 & & 12 \\
& & & 92 &
\end{array}
$$

Demonstration of the process after the fashion shown is suggested so that the children can see that the answer obtained is true. The main stumbling block here is again a matter of carrying. In this instance the 1 of the 12 is carried and added on to the second product. The pupil says, "4×3 is 12, write down the 2 and carry 1; 4×2 is 8, + the 1

[4] W. J. Osburn, *Corrective Arithmetic,* Houghton Mifflin Company, 2 vols., 1924, 1926, 182 and 274 pp.

that was carried is 9." This process is a little more difficult than carrying in addition because the carried number cannot be added until after the next multiplication has been made; the learner must put the carried number on some sort of mental shelf while he applies himself to multiplying, after which he must take it down again and add it to his product. It should be noted that neither the carried number nor the partial product to which it is added is seen.

"Long" multiplication involves repetitions of the performance shown above, plus the proper addition of the partial results. The process of multiplying 234 by 28 can be demonstrated as being equal to multiplying 234 by 8 and then by 20. The pupil has to see that he does not

$$
\begin{array}{r} 234 \\ \times 28 \\ \hline 1872 \\ 468 \\ \hline 6552 \end{array}
=
\begin{array}{r} 234 \\ \times 8 \\ \hline 1872 \end{array}
+
\begin{array}{r} 234 \\ \times 20 \\ \hline 4680 \end{array}
\left[=
\begin{array}{r} 1872 \\ +4680 \\ \hline 6552 \end{array}
\right]
$$

multiply by 8 and then by 2. The "place" of the second number must be made clear to him. It can be demonstrated, if a teacher thinks it worth while, that 234 multiplied by any numbers whose sum is 28 is always the same. For instance:

$$
\begin{array}{r} 12 \times 234 = 2808 \\ +16 \times 234 = 3744 \\ \hline 28 \qquad 6552 \end{array}
\quad \text{or} \quad
\begin{array}{r} 6 \times 234 = 1404 \\ 9 \times 234 = 2106 \\ 5 \times 234 = 1170 \\ +8 \times 234 = 1872 \\ \hline 28 \qquad 6552 \end{array}
$$

Children should also be shown that the moving of each successive partial sum to the left is not arbitrary, but is caused by the presence of zeros that are not actually there but are understood. Thus, 1234 multiplied by 637 can be analyzed as follows:

$$
\begin{array}{r} 1234 \\ \times 7 \\ \hline 8638 \end{array}
\quad
\begin{array}{r} 1234 \\ \times 30 \\ \hline 37020 \end{array}
\quad
\begin{array}{r} 1234 \\ \times 600 \\ \hline 740400 \end{array}
\quad
\begin{array}{r} 8638 \\ 37020 \\ 740400 \\ \hline 786058 \end{array}
$$

In actual multiplication, the zeros are omitted and the numbers merely moved over. This writing down of partial products is new and should

$$
\begin{array}{r}
1234 \\
637 \\
\hline
8638 \\
3702 \\
7404 \\
\hline
786058
\end{array}
$$

be carefully demonstrated so that the children may understand what they are doing.

The chief source of error in short multiplication is the simple failure to add the number carried. Occasionally, however, a child is so dominated by the idea of adding that he adds the second part of his problem instead of multiplying. Thus, he solves 4×23 by saying: "4×3 is 12, write down 2 and carry 1; 1 plus $4+2$ makes 7, so the answer is 72." In the long form most of the mistakes are due fundamentally to inattention; there are so many things to be remembered that the child reaches the end of his attention span before he reaches the end of the problem. Some of the errors may be avoided by having pupils rest for a moment after each partial product and again just before they begin the final addition. A ten-second pause at these points will diminish fatigue and hence promote accuracy. Errors in the process itself are not as common as errors in the fundamental combinations. Practice with the combinations and an introduction of "breathing spells" will help prevent mistakes, but the avoidance of too-long problems until greater maturity is reached will help even more. For the introductory work in long multiplication the numbers should have only two places and should be below 5—32×21, for instance, not 79×86—thus reducing the computation to its simplest form until the process itself is mastered. The addition of more places to either the multiplicand or the multiplier involves nothing new, only a prolonging of the same type of calculation.

D. DIVISION

It has been suggested in the plan of work on page 329 that all work in division beyond the learning of the ninety basic facts be postponed until the sixth grade. Long division has been taught in most schools in the fourth grade, but the results certainly speak for themselves all too loudly. At the end of the fourth grade not more than half the pupils can solve long division problems; in fact, 10 per cent of the more able pupils who have continued in school long enough to enter college still cannot solve them. There is so much bewilderment about long division that a postponement at least into the sixth grade would seem highly desirable.

As an introduction to division, children need drill on the uneven division, such as $9\overline{)58}$, $2\overline{)3}$, $5\overline{)24}$, $7\overline{)25}$ and in the subtraction of numbers in the higher decades, such as $22-21=$, $23-21=$, $24-21=$, $25-21=$, $26-21=$, and so on. These operations are needed for both short and long division. For instance, in the example $7\overline{)2583}$ the child must first know the answer to $7\overline{)25}$, then the answer to $25-21$, then to $7\overline{)48}$, then to $48-42$, and only at the end does he have an even division, $7\overline{)63}$. To divide correctly, a child needs to know 174 subtraction combinations in the higher decades and 360 uneven divisions.[5] Most of these facts are either already known or easily deduced by the children, provided they are old enough to be learning long division. However, a review of them is desirable, for all of these facts will be used continually and some of them at least will be unknown or unrecognized. Moreover, some children who know that $7\overline{)49}$ gives 7 for an answer are baffled by $7\overline{)53}$ because "it won't go," and they are unable to get started. A teacher should remember that the drill on the fundamental division combinations gives practice only on those particular divisions in which there is no remainder. In short or long division problems, and in most practical life situations, there are remainders. A pupil needs to know how to put any digit into any one- or two-place number, whether there is a remainder or not. Thus, he should be as familiar with $4\overline{)14}=3$ and 2 over as he is with the special case of an even division in which $4\overline{)12}=3$ and nothing over. The remainders are new and need more practice than the subtractions.

With this preparation children are ready to learn short division, which is relatively easy. A child should certainly be allowed to work out his answers as shown in the example.[6] This form prepares him for

    [5] Osburn, *op. cit.*

    [6] See H. T. Olander and E. P. Sharp, "Long Division versus Short Division," *Journal of Educational Research*, 26: 6–11, 1932. See also F. E. Grossnickle, "Experimenting with a One-Figure Divisor in Short and Long Division," *Elementary School Journal*, 34: 496–506, 590–599, 1934; L. John, "The Efficiency of Using the Long Division Form for Teaching Division by One-Digit Numbers," *ibid.*, 30: 675–692, 1930; L. T. Johnson, "Short Division or Long Division First?" *Chicago Schools Journal*, 12: 55–56, 1929.

$$65.66 = 65\tfrac{2}{3}$$
$$6\overline{)394.00}$$
$$\underline{36}$$
$$34$$
$$30$$
$$\underline{}$$
$$40$$
$$\underline{36}$$
$$40$$
$$\underline{36}$$
$$4$$

long division and produces more accurate results in short division. There is plenty that a child has to carry in his head without forcing him to multiply 6×6, to subtract the unseen 36 from 39, to prefix an unseen 3 in front of the 4, to think how many times 6 will go into 34, to multiply 6×5, to write down the 5, to subtract the unseen 30 from the 34 of which only the 4 is visible —and so on. All of this is unnecessary torture which produces errors without being of practical use. A child can save so much time and avoid so many mistakes by writing out the entire process that he more than compensates for the time needed to write the extra figures.

To be sure, children should be shown that the whole thing *can* be done mentally, and some of the better students may be encouraged to try the more adult form of solution. Most of them, however, will find the mental exercise too severe. Even if children grow up without learning to perform short division mentally, there is no great harm done. The average individual will use short division perhaps 50 times a year; if he requires an extra 15 seconds because of writing out the process he will waste only $12\frac{1}{2}$ minutes. The one real requirement is that he should get an accurate answer every one of the 50 times. At least through elementary school there should be no effort to force the child into an adult form of "short cut," the usefulness of which is problematical even in the case of average adults.

Long division is a complex process that includes estimating the first figure of the quotient, short multiplication, subtraction, bringing down the next number of the dividend, and then performing the entire series of operations over again as many times as needed. The process may best be introduced by choosing those divisors and dividends that will require no carrying during the multiplication and no borrowing during the subtraction, as in examples (1) and (2) in Table 64 on the next page. There are thirty-eight such examples if one restricts the introductory work to the division of a two-place into a three- or four-place number. The next step is to introduce carrying by itself, as is shown by two examples, (3) and (4), for which borrowing is not needed. There are thirty-six exercises of this type. The third group of exercises, illustrated by (5) and (6), introduces borrowing, but there is no need to carry. There are thirty-three exercises of this kind. This gradual adding of difficulties not only makes the learning easier but permits the teacher to diagnose sources of error. A combination of carrying and borrowing skills is

TABLE 64

Arrangement of Examples in Long Division [7]

11	24	34
(1) 13)143	(2) 32)768	(3) 47)1598
13	64	141
13	128	188
13	128	188

57	44	67
(4) 52)2964	(5) 42)1848	(6) 81)5427
260	168	486
364	168	567
364	168	567

91	38	96
(7) 43)3913	(8) 82)3116	(9) 68)6528
387	246	612
43	656	408
43	656	408

92	204	201
(10) 87)8004	(11) 24)4872	(12) 25)5025
783	48	50
174	72	25
174	72	25

now indicated. The next pair of examples, (7) and (8), require both operations, but the trial divisor is still the right divisor. There are thirty-four such problems in the list. Until this point the troubles with trial divisors that will not work have been purposely avoided. The solving of such situations as shown by the next two exercises, (9) and (10), constitutes one more step in the learning of long division. For introducing this difficulty there is a list of thirty-four relatively easy exercises, thirty that are harder, and finally thirty-three that are very tricky indeed. There remains one more source of trouble, the handling of a zero in the quotient, as shown in examples (11) and (12). For this purpose a series of twenty-eight examples is given. The analysis just presented includes all possible divisions of any two-place into any three- or four-place number and favors a diagnostic and gradual approach that

[7] From Osburn, *op. cit.* Used by permission of the publisher.

seems most desirable for presenting long division. The procedure is hard enough even at best without the introduction of exercises in a random order and a consequent mixture of difficulties.

It is now known what mental age is needed before a child can be expected to master the various types of division example just demonstrated.[8] For a problem with a one-, two-, or three-figure quotient, in which the trial quotient is the correct one, a mental age of 10 years 11 months is needed. For a one-figure quotient in which the trial quotient has to be corrected, the mental age is 13 to 14 years; and for a two- or three-figure quotient, involving one or more corrections of trial divisors, the minimum mental age for success is between 14 and 15. If there are zeros in the quotient but no other difficulties, the mental age should be at last 13. Even at these ages, children may still get as many as 25 per cent of the answers wrong. The harder types of long division should, therefore, be postponed until junior high school.

Pupils have to be taught how to estimate the quotient so as to get a trial divisor and how to correct this trial divisor if it is too large. Thus in solving $47\overline{)611}$ the child sees that 47 goes into 61 only once, but in solving $47\overline{)846}$, he may think that since 4 goes into 8 twice, 47 will go twice into 84. He has to learn also that when a remainder is bigger than the divisor, his quotient is too small.[9]

Thus far nothing has been said about remainders to problems. In life situations, problems in either long or short division have remainders more frequently than not. It is, therefore, a mistake to give children only those exercises that come out even. However, divisions that come out with remainders can be left until after the children have become acquainted with the elements of long division. There is nothing to be gained by introducing this final element of confusion into the picture until children have achieved some facility with the process and will not be disorganized by having a piece left over. Later on, after they have been introduced to decimals, they can be taught to go on dividing to two or more decimal places. Or, they may be taught to leave the remainder as a common fraction.

The errors in both short and long division are legion, but they are due chiefly to children's inability to keep the many operations under control and to the early fatigue that comes from their efforts to do so. The

[8] L. J. Brueckner and H. O. Melbye, "Relative Difficulty of Types of Examples in Division with Two-Figure Divisors," *Journal of Educational Research*, 33: 401–414, 1939.

[9] See F. E. Grossnickle, "An Experiment with Two Methods of Estimating the Quotient," *Elementary School Journal*, 37: 668–677, 1937.

introduction of systematic pauses after each new member is brought down will do much to offset the fatigue. Errors are made in the multiplication or subtraction combinations, in carrying, in borrowing, in bringing down the same number twice or in omitting one number, in handling zeros, in copying numbers. Except for zero difficulties these errors are usually due not to a failure to understand or even to an ignorance of the necessary facts, but rather to an exhaustion of attention. The same child rarely makes systematically the same type of error from problem to problem, thus showing that his difficulties are not due to any one deficiency or bad habit. He scatters his errors among many types because he gets tired and inattentive at different places in different problems.

A comparison of children who are successful in long division and those who are unsuccessful shows that the former are superior—even when matched in intelligence—in their ability to estimate and place correctly the first quotient figure, in their accuracy with the fundamental combinations, in their ability to find any errors they make, and in their knowledge of technical words, such as "dividend," "divisor," and so on.[10] The successful pupils are characterized also by having a history of success in previous work in arithmetic. The failing pupils are not usually failures in general and may be quite superior in reading and other subjects. Often they show their incapacity in arithmetic almost from their first day in school. Presumably, they are the pupils who either began arithmetic before they were mature enough intellectually to understand it or else were frightened by older children or adults into a conviction that they could not learn.

E. CHECKING THE ANSWER

Nothing has been said to date about checking answers. This is one habit children should be specifically taught. They presumably already know that the subtraction combinations are the opposite of the addition ones and that division is the opposite of multiplication. They need, therefore, only to apply what they know.

Every column of figures should be added both up and down. The remainder and subtrahend in a subtraction exercise should be added to

[10] R. H. Koenker, "Certain Characteristic Differences between Excellent and Poor Achievers in Two-Figure Division," *Journal of Educational Research,* 35: 578–580, 1942. See also F. E. Grossnickle, "Comparison of Achievement of Pupils who Are Good and Poor in Learning Division with Two-Figure Divisors," *Journal of Educational Research,* 34: 346–351, 1941.

see if they will produce the minuend. Multiplication can best be checked by inverting multiplicand and multiplier. Checking by division can be used after the children have studied it, provided they are accurate enough in long division; otherwise, they are more likely to make errors in the checking than in the original process. To check division, the divisor and quotient should be multiplied. Because accuracy is paramount in the practical demands of life, it is better to have children solve two problems and check them for errors than to have them work four without finding out if their answers are correct. The constant checking also serves to keep all processes polished and ready for use.

F. SUMMARY

In teaching the higher operations a teacher is more likely to be successful if she follows a plan of presentation by which she introduces one difficulty at once, instead of taking examples in the order in which they occur to her. For instance, the three examples $46\overline{)9398}$, $46\overline{)7958}$, and $46\overline{)4216}$ may seem of about equal difficulty, but they are not. The processes of carrying and borrowing are hard enough for children to learn without introducing unnecessary complications by refusing to let them use the simple aids that permit them to stop in the middle of a problem without losing their place. As soon as the pupils know all the processes they should begin to develop the habit of checking all their work for accuracy. The teacher can help to establish this habit if she presents only as many problems as can be checked in the available time and if she gives less credit for an unchecked answer, even though it is right, than for one that has been properly proven.

XVI · Common Fractions

Common fractions have traditionally been assigned to Grade 5. Research indicates, however, a postponement of certain of the more difficult problems, although a beginning with simple materials may be made in the second semester of the fifth grade. The necessary mental age for the introduction of fractions has been reasonably well established.[1] For the addition and subtraction of similar fractions ($\frac{1}{3} + \frac{2}{3} =$) a child needs a mental age of at least 9 years 6 months. For handling dissimilar fractions ($\frac{1}{3} + \frac{1}{4} =$) he needs a minimum mental development of 13 years 2 months. If a child has to subtract a sum such as $1\frac{7}{8}$ from $4\frac{1}{3}$ he needs a mental age of nearly 14 years. The writer feels that the mental age given for adding $\frac{1}{3}$ and $\frac{1}{4}$ is higher than it needs to be because of the complicated methods of work often taught, and that a mental age of 11 or 12 would suffice if a simpler method were used. It is therefore suggested that the first work in fractions be introduced in the fifth grade, but that the harder problems be distributed through the sixth, seventh, and eighth grades.

It has always appeared to the writer that there is more confusion in regard to common fractions among pupils and students at all levels in school than could possibly be necessary. Children seem to master work with fractions poorly, and they seem to use methods that are unnecessarily clumsy. The source of much difficulty is undoubtedly the assumption that children must be taught to add $\frac{1}{2}$ and $\frac{1}{3}$ by a method which can, if necessary, be transferred to the addition of such unlikely sums as 23/175 and 19/75. Actually, the demands of life require the handling of very few fractions and in groups of not more than three and usually not more than two. If schools would confine their efforts to producing faultless results with the half dozen most frequently used fractions, work in this field would be both easy and interesting to children.

In making work with common fractions clear, a teacher is likely to have better success if she gives careful attention to the following

[1] L. E. Raths, "Grade Placement in the Addition and Subtraction of Fractions," *Educational Research Bulletin*, Ohio State University, 11: 29–38, 1932.

suggestions: (1) Only the commonly used fractions should be presented. This restriction means that problems will deal mainly with 1/2, 1/3, 1/4, 1/5, 1/8, 2/3, and 3/4 plus a little work with 2/5, 3/5, 4/5, 3/8, 5/8, and 7/8. Most of the problems should deal exclusively with 1/2, 1/3, 1/4, 2/3, and 3/4, since these fractions constitute 90 per cent of all fractions used in daily life,[2] and half the problems should use 1/2 since this one fraction makes up 60 per cent of all the fractions used outside school. (2) Adequate concepts for fractions should be built up. The fractional parts of a whole are easy enough to demonstrate. Moreover, they can be understood at relatively early ages. Many children know what a half is when they enter school. By means of objects that can be divided and put back together again pupils can develop the necessary concepts long before they begin to compute with fractions.[3] What is often neglected is the concept that the larger the numbers in the denominator become, the smaller is the fraction. Children are inclined to carry over their ideas about integers and to suppose that because 2 is smaller than 8, 1/2 is smaller than 1/8. Similarly they expect the product of two fractions to be larger than either and the quotient to be smaller. Since $6 \times 2 = 12$ and $6 \div 3$, the first answer larger than either component and the second smaller than the dividend, they are quite unprepared to find that the opposite is true when dealing with fractions, and that $1/5 \times 1/6 = 1/30$ while $1/5 \div 1/6 = 1 1/5$—the first answer smaller than either component and the second, larger. This reversal of affairs must be explained or pupils will be suspicious of answers which are correct and satisfied with those which are wrong. More time spent on developing an understanding of what a fraction is and less time spent on complicated ways of getting a simple answer will result in fewer errors. (3) All unnecessary techniques, designed primarily to make easier the handling of very small fractions, should be omitted. They are unnecessary and highly confusing. They waste more time than they save, and they cause more errors than they eliminate. The chief of these are canceling, finding the lowest common denominator, and calculating the highest common multiple. For operations with two fractions there is no need for these operations. Any denominator and any multiple will do as well as any other. If a higher denominator than absolutely necessary is used, the numbers will become larger than they need to be but not too large for accuracy as long as the pupils

---

[2] G. M. Wilson, "What Research Reveals on Proper Drill Content of Elementary Arithmetic, *Mathematics Teacher*, 28: 477–481, 1935.

[3] See Chapter XIX on *Readiness to Compute*, p. 401.

start with fractions that are common. In any case, the children will make fewer errors even with the larger numbers than they do when they try to cancel or to factor.

A. UNNECESSARY PROCESSES COMMONLY USED

Some common denominator is of course necessary in order to add two fractions, but any one is as good as any other. To add 1/6 and 2/3 one can proceed in any of three ways:

$$1/6 + 2/3 = 1/6 + 4/6 = 5/6$$
or
$$1/6 + 2/3 = 2/12 + 8/12 = 10/12 = 5/6$$
or
$$1/6 + 2/3 = 3/18 + 12/18 = 15/18 = 5/6$$

The answer is the same, no matter which denominator is used. There are three objections to figuring out the lowest one. First, the child must learn to factor (6 into $2 \cdot 3$ in the above problem) and factoring is a hard thing to explain to children. High school students, in spite of their intellectual advantage over fifth grade pupils, still have trouble in understanding what factors are. Second, a good deal of mental arithmetic is involved. In adding 1/6 and 2/3 a pupil must think "3 goes into 6 twice and 2 times 2 is 4, so 2/3 becomes 4/6." Every additional mental operation produces its quota of errors. Third, the operation cannot be reduced to a formula because one cannot know in advance how much factoring or multiplying this or that problem will call for. Each addition must therefore be figured out by itself.

The highest common multiple is even less justifiable. Suppose, for instance, that a pupil wants to reduce 24/36. He can proceed in either of two ways. According to the first method, the child has to analyze as follows:

$$24 = 2 \cdot 3 \cdot 2 \cdot 2$$
$$36 = 2 \cdot 3 \cdot 3 \cdot 2.$$

Therefore the highest common multiple is $2 \cdot 3 \cdot 2 = 12$, and $24/36 \div 12 = 2/3$. The second process consists in dividing the fraction by any factor one happens to think of and then dividing again, continuing for as many divisions as necessary. For instance:

$$24/36 = 12/18 = 6/9 = 2/3$$

By the second method, one actually divides by each common multiple—in the above case, 2, 2, and 3—instead of dividing by all three at once.

The technique of canceling is also unnecessary as long as one is using commonly employed fractions. To most children canceling is a source of confusion and error. In the first place, they use it for adding or subtracting and so get into trouble. Second, they become bewildered by the various crossed-out numbers and often manipulate the wrong ones. Third, the canceling itself is often done incorrectly, especially as children show a lamentable tendency to subtract instead of divide. One especially confusing mistake is made when a child cancels the same number in the numerator of one fraction and the denominator of the other and obtains a 0 instead of a 1 in both places. These errors are demonstrated below:

(1) Pupil has crossed out only the 0 of the 10 in the first numerator and has read the 1 and 2 as a 12.

(2) Pupil has canceled by subtracting in the numerators instead of dividing.

(3) Pupil has canceled when adding.

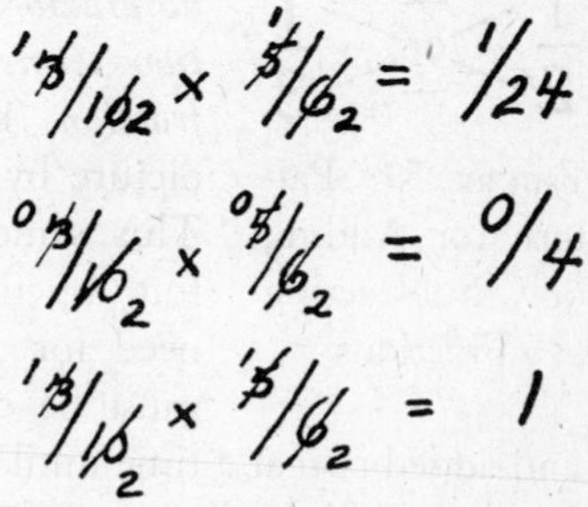

FIGURE 58: Typical Errors in Cancellation

The above problem can be solved easily and quickly without canceling.

$$\frac{3}{10} \times \frac{5}{6} = \frac{15}{60} = \frac{3}{12} = \frac{1}{4}$$

This procedure is not only more accurate but takes less time.

B. A SIMPLIFIED METHOD

In the place of the complicated methods often taught, the writer would suggest a simplification. Addition and subtraction may be taught together as one unit, multiplication and division as another. Both procedures may be reduced to a simple and invariable series of steps. A few examples and a verbal description are given below.

1. Recommended Steps for Adding or Subtracting: The rule for these two operations is: *Multiply the numerator of the first fraction by the denominator of the second. Write down the product and follow it with the sign between the two fractions. Then multiply the numerator of the second fraction by the denominator of the first. Write this product after the sign. These two numbers together form the numerator of the answer, so draw a line under them. Now multiply the*

$$2/3+1/2=\frac{4+3}{6}=7/6=1\ 1/6$$

$$3/4+1/3=\frac{9+4}{12}=13/12=1\ 1/12$$

$$2/3-1/2=\frac{4-3}{6}=1/6$$

$$3/4-1/3=\frac{9-4}{12}=5/12.$$

FIGURE 59: Pattern for Adding or Subtracting Fractions

two denominators and write the product as the denominator of the answer. Then add or subtract the two terms of the numerator and reduce the final fraction. This procedure can be reduced to a visual picture by drawing lines such as appear at the left. This same technique can be extended to three or four fractions if necessary, although one rarely has need for adding more than two. If a longer series must be combined they can be grouped into pairs and added two at a time until the total is achieved. Even such an unlikely problem as the following may easily be solved, in sections:

$$3/4+5/6+2/3-1/5$$

$$3/4+5/6=\frac{18+20}{24}=38/24=19/12$$

$$2/3-1/5=\frac{10-3}{15}=7/15$$

$$19/12+7/15=\frac{285+84}{180}=369/180=123/60=2\ 3/60=2\ 1/20$$

This process may seem clumsy, but it is both quicker and more accurate than trying to add a series of several fractions over a single common denominator, as shown below:

$$3/4+5/6+2/3-1/5=45/60+50/60+40/60-12/60=$$

$$\frac{135}{60}\ -\ \frac{12}{60}\ =\ \frac{123}{60}\ =\ 2\ 3/60\ =\ 2\ 1/20$$

2. Process for Multiplying or Dividing: The rule for these two operations is: *Multiply the two numerators and write the product as the numerator of the answer. Multiply the two denominators and write the product as the denominator of the answer. Then reduce the answer. For division the procedure is exactly the same except that the second fraction is inverted before the solution is started.*

$$2/3 \times 1/2 = 2/6 = 1/3$$
$$2/5 \times 5/6 = 10/30 = 1/3$$
$$2/3 \div 1/2 = 2/3 \times 2/1 = 4/3 = 1 \ 1/3$$
$$2/5 \div 5/6 = 2/5 \times 6/5 = 12/25$$

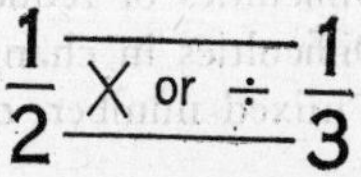

$$\frac{1}{2} \overline{\quad \times \text{ or } \div \quad} \frac{1}{3}$$

This process may again be easily remembered by drawing a pattern. These operations are not

FIGURE 60: Pattern for Multiplying or Dividing Fractions

difficult either to understand or to handle; that is why work with fractions has been placed in the suggested curriculum before long division.

C. ANALYSIS OF CHILDREN'S ERRORS

Although there are many possible errors in the handling of fractions, only relatively small number are frequent. If a "frequent" mistake is defined as one made by 10 per cent or more of the pupils, those based upon a total of 21,065 errors, in Table 65, would be classed as being common.

TABLE 65

Children's Errors in Fractions [4]

Addition:	Per Cent
1. Lack of comprehension of the process	20.2
2. Difficulty in reduction	17.5
3. Difficulty in reducing improper fraction	17.1
4. Errors in computation	13.8
	68.6

Subtraction:	
1. Difficulties in borrowing	24.3
2. Use of wrong process	20.3
3. Difficulties in reduction	14.6
4. Lack of comprehension of process	14.6

[4] L. J. Brueckner, *Diagnostic and Remedial Teaching in Arithmetic,* John C. Winston Company, Philadelphia, 1930, 341 pp. From pp. 215–217 used by permission of the publisher.

TABLE 65—*Continued*

5. Errors in changing fractions to common denominator	8.3
6. Errors in computation	8.2
	90.3

Multiplication:

1. Errors in computation	28.7
2. Lack of comprehension of process	28.6
3. Difficulties of reduction	17.3
4. Difficulties in changing from improper fraction to mixed number, or *vice versa*	11.6
	86.2

Division:

1. Wrong process used	31.1
2. Lack of comprehension of process	12.1
3. Errors in computing	13.8
4. Errors in reducing	8.9
5. Difficulties in changing from mixed number to improper fraction, or *vice versa*	15.8
	81.7

In this study as in others [5] the analysis shows confusion of the four processes with each other, failure to reduce, failure to understand the process, and errors in computation. The division technique is poorly understood and is confused with other processes. It is not especially difficult, but it is usually taught at the end of a year when both teachers and pupils are weary and the time remaining is inadequate. Failure to reduce answers is a singularly persistent error, presumably because this operation comes at the end of a problem when attention is running low. With less confusing and tiring methods of getting the answers, a goodly proportion of these errors should disappear.[6]

D. AN ANALYTIC PLAN OF PRESENTATION

If a teacher wishes to present problems in the addition of fractions in order of intrinsic difficulty she can follow an excellent plan that has been worked out. This plan has the further advantage that it makes

[5] For instance, R. L. Morton, "An Analysis of Pupils' Errors in Fractions," *Journal of Educational Research,* 9: 117–125, 1924.

[6] If a teacher wishes to continue with the traditional manner of teaching fractions, she will be helped by examining "Schemata for the Analysis of Drill in Fractions," by G. M. Ruch, F. B. Knight, E. O. Olander, and G. E. Russell, *University of Iowa Studies in Education,* Vol. 10, No. 2, 1936, 58 pp.

diagnosis of error easy, since each step adds only one new complication.[7]

TABLE 66

An Analytic Approach to the Teaching of Fractions

Description of Operation	Illustration

Addition of:

a. Two similar fractions, the sum of which is not reducible to an integer

    a. $1/3+1/3=2/3$

b. Two similar fractions, the sums of which are reducible to an integer

    b. $1/3+2/3=3/3=1$

c. Two similar fractions, the sum of which is reducible to lower terms

    c. $1/4+1/4=2/4=1/2$

d. Two similar fractions, the sum of which is reducible to a mixed number that needs no further reduction

    d. $3/5+3/5=6/5=1\,1/5$

e. Two similar fractions, the sum of which is a mixed expression that must be reduced

    e. $5/6+5/6=10/6=1\,4/6=1\,2/3$

f. Two dissimilar fractions with an L.C.D. that is the product of the given denominators and a sum that is not reducible

    f. $1/3+1/4=4/12+3/12=7/12$

g. Two dissimilar fractions with an L.C.D. that is the product of the given denominators and a sum that is reduced to a mixed expression not further reducible

    g. $4/5+7/9=36/45+35/45=$ $71/45=1\,26/45$

h. Two dissimilar fractions, the L.C.D. of which is the same as the denominator of one of the fractions and which gives a sum that is not reducible

    h. $1/2+1/4=2/4+1/4=3/4$

[7] A. L. Becker, "Remedial Work in the Addition of Common Fractions," *California Journal of Elementary Education*, 9: 43–47, 1940. See also D. C. Steele, "Teaching and Testing the Understanding of Common Fractions," *University of Pittsburgh Bulletin*, No. 3, 37: 317–328, 1941.

TABLE 66—*Continued*

Description of Operation	*Illustration*

Addition of:

i. Two dissimilar fractions, the L.C.D. of which is the same as the denominator of one of the fractions and which gives a sum that is reducible

i. $1/6+1/2=1/6+3/6=4/6=2/3$

j. Two dissimilar fractions, the L.C.D. of which is the same as the denominator of one of the fractions and which gives a sum that can be reduced to a mixed expression not further reducible

j. $5/6+1/3=5/6+2/6=7/6=1\,1/6$

k. Two dissimilar fractions, the L.C.D. of which is the same as the denominator of one of the fractions and which gives a sum that can be reduced to a mixed expression that is itself further reducible

k. $5/6+1/2=5/6+3/6=8/6=1\,2/6=1\,1/3$

l. Two dissimilar fractions, the L.C.D. of which is neither one of the given denominators and the sum of which is not reducible

l. $1/6+1/4=2/12+3/12=5/12$

m. Two dissimilar fractions, the L.C.D. of which is neither one of the given denominators and the sum of which is reducible

m. $1/10+1/6=3/30+5/30=8/30=4/15$

n. Two dissimilar fractions, the L.C.D. of which is neither one of the given denominators and the sum of which is a mixed expression that is not reducible

n. $9/10+1/4=18/20+5/20=23/20=1\,3/20$

o. Two dissimilar fractions, the L.C.D. of which is neither one of the given denominators and the sum of which is a mixed expression that must be reduced

o. $5/6+3/10=25/30+9/30=34/30=1\,4/30=1\,2/15$

By use of this classification for presenting and analyzing problems, one teacher succeeded in reducing the number of wrong answers in a sixth grade class on a given unit of work from 276 to 82. This same analysis is used for subtraction. A similar analysis could be worked out for multiplication and division.

E. VALUE OF CONCEPTS

A good many teachers and investigators have felt that children fail to develop a proper understanding of fractions, even when they are able to get the right answer to typical examples. High school and college

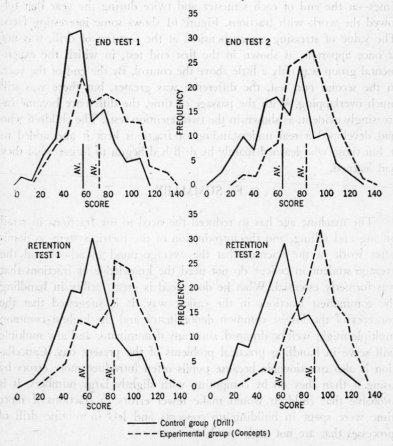

FIGURE 61: Comprehension versus Drill in Fractions

teachers report that their students seem to have forgotten how to handle fractions—another bit of evidence which suggests failure to comprehend fractions when they were originally taught. More emphasis on concepts and less on drill should give children a better grasp and a better retention of processes with fractions. To investigate this hypothesis two carefully equated groups of high fourth grade pupils were taught by different methods, one stressing the usual drill and the other stressing concepts and comprehension with very little drill.[8] The investigator measured the standing of the two groups in accuracy of operations with fractions and in understanding of them. In both respects the experimental pupils were superior. The test for understanding was given four times—at the end of each semester and twice during the year that followed the work with fractions. Figure 61 shows some interesting facts. The value of stressing comprehension, at the sacrifice of drill, was not at once apparent, as shown in the first end test, in which the experimental group was only a little above the control. By the end of the year, in the second end test, the difference was greater, but there was still much overlapping. With the passage of time, the difference became increasingly evident, as shown in the two retention tests. The children who had developed a real understanding of fractions kept it and added to it, but those who learned mainly by drill had begun to forget what they had learned.

F. SUMMARY

The machine age has so reduced the need to use fractions in retail buying and selling, and the introduction of the metric system so dominates work in the sciences that the average pupil in school and the average student in college do not need the knowledge of fractions that was formerly essential. What he does need is great facility in handling the commonest fractions in the easiest way. It is suggested that the concepts of the lowest common denominator and the highest common multiple might well be dropped, since any denominator and any multiple will serve in handling practical problems of the present day. Cancellation is also questionable because pupils often introduce more errors by using it than they do by computing with slightly large numbers. It is probable that children would make fewer errors in fractions if more time were spent in building up concepts and less in routine drill of processes that are not understood.

[8] D. C. Steele, "Teaching and Testing the Understanding of Common Fractions," *University of Pittsburgh Bulletin,* No. 3, 37: 317–328, 1941.

XVII · The Solution of Verbal Problems

Since arithmetic cannot be justified as a form of mental exercise, it is clear that the solution of practical problems such as are often met in daily life is its *raison d'être*. Only in the schoolroom does one meet such abstractions as $73 \div 5 =$ or any other arithmetical process in isolation. In life outside school, the situations are always concrete—seventy-three dollars are to be divided among five people, or seventy-three exercises are to be spread over five days, or seventy-three cents are to be divided among five purchases. For purposes of drill the numbers are removed from their normal setting in problems, just as words are divorced from their context during the spelling lesson. Although the artificial isolation is desirable to make clear the item to be learned, words are normally spelled only in context and number combinations are normally used only in verbal problems. It should never be forgotten that work with combinations is only a means to an end. When children complain that arithmetic has no practical value, their attitude is probably based on a lack of application of what they have learned to the practical affairs of life.

The time to introduce the first verbal problem is on the day that the first addition combination is learned. As more number facts are acquired they should be worked into problems. The facts themselves are relatively uninteresting, but they can lead to highly diverting puzzles —provided the problems used require in their solution only facts already known to the pupils. In the preceding chapter little reference was made to application; it is assumed, however, that every new fact and operation will be used in problems, and that work in problem solving will go hand in hand with drill.

In general, children have a rather hard time with problems. Their troubles seem due to a number of causes. They have not mastered the fundamental processes well enough to use them easily. They do not have an adequate technical vocabulary. They try to read problems by the same methods found to be effective in reading narratives. They become lost in the mazes of unnecessarily complex problems. They do not have an attention span long enough to permit solution of the average problem without moments of inattention, during which they forget what they are doing. They have had little experience with situations involving reasoning and so do not know how to "see through" problems. Their background of facts is meagre. Obviously, nothing can be done about those sources of difficulty that are mere indications of immaturity, but one can do a good deal in making problem solving more efficient by presenting more appropriate problems, by teaching children specifically how to read them, and by improving their mastery of the fundamental facts and processes. This chapter will deal with these points.

A. UNDESIRABLE CHARACTERISTICS OF VERBAL PROBLEMS

1. Types of Problem: A teacher has only to read through the problems presented in almost any textbook to realize that some of them are unnecessarily confusing and difficult. Some involve situations and objects quite unfamiliar to children. Others contain irrelevancies, or they are artificial and uninteresting. They may require so many manipulations that the average child cannot keep them all clear in his mind. They often use larger numbers than would be needed in ordinary circumstances, or they may present outdated situations. Problems can be, and have been, enormously improved in recent years, but there is room for even more improvement.

These points may perhaps be made clearer by examples taken from arithmetic texts.

1. A farmer raised 44 bushels of wheat per acre. His wheatfield contained 92 acres. If he improved his yield by 10½ bushels per acre, how many more bushels would he get from his field than formerly?

2. A woman wants to buy a rug for a parlor which is 14'6" by 12'6" and she wants to leave a 3-foot border all the way around the room. What size must the rug be?

3. A train leaves New York and travels at an average speed of 32 miles per hour to Chicago, which is 950 miles away. A second train leaves an hour later and travels at an average speed of 40 miles an hour. If both trains

maintain an even rate of speed, how many miles from New York will the first train be when the second overtakes it?

4. A merchant buys 500 dresses at $1.14 apiece. He sells them for $1.98 each. What is his profit?

5. A nail is driven through a 2-inch plank so that 1.236 inches stick out on one side and .0927 inches on the other. How long is the nail?

6. In a field 20% of the animals are cows, 60% are sheep, 15% are goats, and 5% are pigs. If there are 200 animals, how many are there of each kind?

7. An elderly gentleman deposited $1,000 for his granddaughter the day she was born. If no more money is added, and if the interest is 2½ per cent, how much will there be when she is 18 years old?

8. If 100 pounds of potatoes cost $7.00, how much would 3 pounds cost?

9. If a woman bought a dress that cost $5.00 and if she spent ⅓ of the money in her purse, how much did she have?

10. A house has 35 windows and 7 rooms. How many windows would there be in each room?

Problems 1, 3, 4, 7, and 8 are concerned with matters about which children know little or nothing. Children do not undertake scientific farming, dispatch trains, buy five hundred dresses at once, deposit $1,000 at a time, or buy potatoes in 100 pound lots. Problem 2 has no actual solution. The indicated size of rug would be 11′ 6″ by 9′ 6″, which is not a standard size; the lady would have to make up her mind whether she preferred to use a rug 8′ by 10′ or 9′ by 12′. Problems 5 and 6 present abnormal ways of arriving at the desired information. If one wants to know how long a nail is, there are simpler methods than the one indicated. The field of animals must have been arranged for the problem, since this assortment of livestock would not normally occupy the same quarters; nor does the farmer calculate the number of animals he owns from the percentage that each kind forms of the total. He counts them. Problems 1, 3, and 5 involve the use of unnecessarily large or complex numbers. Problem 3 contains the totally irrelevant fact of the distance between New York and Chicago; this figure is not used. The trains might as well be going anywhere. Moreover, this problem presents an artificial situation, because trains do not travel at uniform rates, and they pass each other at points where passing seems indicated in view of all the trains using the tracks. Problem 7 is one of those deceptively simple-looking problems that take a half-hour to work out, but

it can be solved in 10 seconds by a bank clerk who reads the answer—
the correct answer—from a table. Problem 9 is plainly silly; if the lady
knew that $5 was ⅓ of her money she must have known already that
she had $15, and does not therefore need to figure it out. Problems 8
and 10 give easily calculated answers—21¢ for three pounds of potatoes
and 5 windows per room—only these answers are in all probability
wrong. If 100 pounds of potatoes cost $7.00, 3 pounds will cost at least
25¢ and more likely 28¢ or 30¢, because of the differences in wholesale
and retail prices. The 35-window house probably has two or three windows in the basement, another two or three in the attic, perhaps one
or two in closets, two to four in hallways, and one to three in toilets—
none of which are mentioned. The remaining 27 to 20 windows are
probably distributed unevenly, from six in the parlor to one in the hall
bedroom. There is no reason why such elements of improbability, irrelevancy, and unnecessary difficulty should be introduced into problems.

2. **Characteristics of Problems:** There have been certain investigations into the extent to which various factors influence the solving of
problems. One excellent study consists essentially of eight minor investigations, each concerned with a single factor. In all instances, extreme
care was taken to keep constant all possible elements except the factor
under consideration. Four of the eight investigated elements were shown to
influence the production or prevention of errors. These are listed in Table
67. The use of an objective, familiar objects, and small numbers, plus the
elimination of nonessentials, would evidently prevent many errors. It
should be noted that the younger children are more distressed by irrelevancies than the older. The use of unfamiliar situations is not as dis-
turbing as might have been expected. This fact is reinforced by finding
in a recent experiment with 257 school children, 134 of whom did better
work on noncomputational problems involving familiar objects, while
123 scored higher on those that centered around unfamiliar things.[1]
Research on the same problem by another investigator results in a quite
different conclusion.[2] The investigation involved 4,000 elementary school
children. The work done on problems involving familiar situations was
superior to that done on problems with unfamiliar situations. The children got 13 per cent more correct answers, made 5 per cent fewer errors
in computation, used the right processes in 24 per cent more of the prob-

[1] J. Sutherland, "An Investigation of Some Aspects of Problem Solving in Arithmetic,"
British Journal of Educational Psychology, 11, 215–222, 1941, and 12: 37–46, 1942.
[2] H. M. White, "Does Experience in the Situation Involved Affect the Solving of
Problems?" Education, 54: 751–755, 1934.

TABLE 67

The Percentage of Errors Made by Children on Problems Involving or Not Involving Given Elements of Difficulty [3]

	Grades 4—5	Grades 6—8
1. Problems in Which the Setting Was:		
(a) Not objective	74.6	56.1
(b) Objective	63.8	41.9
(c) Difference	10.8	14.2
2. Problems in Which the Numbers Were:		
(a) Large	70.5	43.4
(b) Small	58.3	30.0
(c) Difference	12.2	13.4
3. Problems in Which the Objects Used Were:		
(a) Unfamiliar	68.5	44.3
(b) Familiar	63.2	39.0
(c) Difference	5.3	5.3
4. Problems in Which There Were:		
(a) Nonessential elements	64.4	60.3
(b) No nonessentials	35.7	45.3
(c) Difference	28.7	15.0

lems, and omitted 9 per cent fewer of the problems, and left 4 per cent fewer incomplete. It is not, therefore, clear to what extent familiarity with the situation described in a problem is a factor in influencing the thinking of children.

It has sometimes been supposed that imaginative problems would be easier for children than those that are stated in the baldest possible terms. The following versions of the same problem illustrate the difference in the two types.

Conventional: If A has $1.20 and B has $.42 how much money would there be if each contributed ⅓ of what he had to a common undertaking?

Imaginative: Mary and Louise are little girls. Mary is 10 years old, and Louise is 8. They have been asked to Evelyn's birthday party and they want to give her a present. Mary has $1.20 in her bank, but Louise has only $.42. If each one takes a third of her money, how much will the two girls have all together, with which they can buy a gift for Evelyn?

[3] L. L. Hyde and F. L. Clapp, "Elements of Difficulty in the Interpretation of Concrete Problems in Arithmetic," *Bureau of Educational Research Bulletin*, No. 9, University of Wisconsin. 1927, 84 pp. Used by permission of the publisher.

This particular kind of effort to make problems more interesting has not been especially successful. The imaginative problem seem to be just as hard, if not harder.[4] Perhaps the children regard the added details as irrelevancies and are unable to find the problem as easily in the longer as in the shorter form. It is the writer's guess that the imaginative problem introduces as many difficulties as it eliminates. It requires more reading; it favors a narrative type of reading matter, thus encouraging the use of eye movements inappropriate for reading in mathematics; it introduces numerous nonessentials; and it surrounds the actual problem with so much narrative material that the children cannot find it. The formal type of problem may be uninteresting, but it is at least clear and concise. Instead of trying to make problems resemble short stories, it would probably be more efficient to give specific training in how to read problems, so that children would not try to read them as if they were fairy tales.

There is some evidence to show that if children are given problems that deal with their own daily lives, they do better work than they usually do with the traditional, adult type of material. In one case,[5] children in the third grade brought to school problems of their own, which were later formulated by the teacher and class into teaching and learning units. By deriving the materials of arithmetic in this way, a teacher gets better motivation and usually better mastery of subject matter.

3. **Complexity and Sequence:** Several studies have measured the effect of complexity by presenting children in different grades with problems involving different numbers of steps from one to five.[6] The general upshot has been that below the sixth grade only one-step problems are regularly solved with reasonable accuracy, and that at no level are prob-

[4] See, for example, M. G. Wheat, "The Relative Merits of Conventional and Imaginative Types of Problems in Arithmetic," *Teachers College Contributions to Education,* No. 359, 1929, 124 pp.; E. W. Bramhall, "An Experimental Study of Two Types of Arithmetic Problems," *Journal of Experimental Education,* 8: 36–38, 1939; and G. A. Kramer, "The Effect of Certain Factors in the Verbal Arithmetic Problem upon Children's Success in the Solution," *Johns Hopkins University Studies in Education,* 1933, No. 20, 106 pp.

[5] H. L. Harap and U. Barret, "An Experiment with Real Situations in Third Grade Arithmetic," *Journal of Educational Method,* 16: 188–192, 1937; H. L. Harap and E. Mapes, "Learning the Fundamentals in an Activity Curriculum," *Elementary School Journal,* 34: 515–526, 1934; F. Reid, "Incidental Number Situations in the First Grade," *Journal of Educational Research,* 30: 36–43, 1936; E. Salt, "Functional Arithmetic in the Second Grade," *Educational Research Bulletin,* 21: 217–226, 246, 1942; E. Troxell "Opportunity for Number," *Childhood Education,* 27: 64–69, 1927.

[6] See, for example, W. J. Osburn and L. J. Drennan, "Problem Solving in Arithmetic," *Educational Research Bulletin,* 10: 123–128, 1931.

lems requiring more than two steps correctly solved with frequency. In fact, the accuracy in three-, four-, or five-step problems is so low that use of them may lead to serious confusion.

It would not seem to an adult that the order in which one carried out the necessary operations in a problem would affect its difficulty, but evidently it does. If a problem has two steps that require two different processes, some sequences are easier than others, although it is not easy to see why they should be:

1. Subtracting, then adding is harder than adding, then subtracting.
2. Adding, then multiplying is harder than multiplying, then adding.
3. Dividing, then adding is harder than adding, then dividing.
4. Dividing, then subtracting is harder than subtracting, then dividing.
5. Subtracting, then multiplying is harder than multiplying, then subtracting.
6. Dividing, then multiplying is harder than multiplying, then dividing.[7]

In judging which problems are easier or harder than others, these facts may be of use to a teacher.

Verbal problems may be difficult because they are artificial, because they involve matters of no concern to children, because they contain irrelevancies, because the numbers are too large, or because the reasoning requires too many steps. Presumably, the use of problems taken from the children's daily lives would prevent most of these difficulties.

B. ADEQUATE TECHNICAL VOCABULARY

Children encounter their first technical vocabulary while they are studying arithmetic. Naturally, they should not be burdened unnecessarily with strange words, but a certain core is essential to an understanding of the concepts involved. These essential words may, for convenience, be divided into three groups: the names of symbols or operations, the terms used in measurement, and those words used chiefly in problems at the time this list was compiled. The various investigations already made in the field were carefully studied, and only those words were included concerning which there was general agreement among the in-

---

[7] G. Berglund-Gray and R. V. Young, "The Effect of Process Sequence on the Interpretation of Two-Step Problems in Arithmetic," *Journal of Educational Research*, 34: 21–29, 1940. See also J. S. McIsaacs, "The Effect of Process Sequence upon the Interpretation of Three-Step Problems in Arithmetic," *University of Pittsburgh Bulletin*, 37: 220–228, 1941.

vestigators.[8] The vocabulary is not large, but it is essential for understanding work in arithmetic.

1. Terms Dealing with Notation, Numeration, Symbols, or Processes: The words needed for work in fundamentals are listed below and are grouped according to topic. The Thorndike frequency also appears in the column to the right of the terms.

TABLE 68

Technical Vocabulary in Arithmetic (A)

	Thorndike Rating		Thorndike Rating
A. Nomenclature		20. multiplication	10
1. amount	1b	21. plus	8
2. count(ing)	1b	22. product	2b
3. equal	1b	23. quotient	9
4. number	1a	24. remainder	3b
5. Roman numeral		25. row	(1b)
6. square root		26. sign	(1b)
7. whole number		27. subtract	6
8. zero	5a	28. subtraction	12
		29. sum	2a
B. Fundamental Processes with		30. take away	
Integers		31. times	
9. add	1a	32. total	2a
10. addition	2b		
11. answer	1a	C. Fractions	
12. borrow	(3a)*	33. cancel	8
13. carry	(1a)	34. common denominator	
14. column	3a	35. common fraction	
15. difference	1b	36. denominator	20
16. divide	1b	37. factor	7
17. division	3a	38. fraction	5a
18. minus	10	39. improper fraction	
19. multiply	2a	40. invert	6

* The parentheses are to warn the teacher that the high frequency of a word is based upon nonarithmetical uses.

[8] S. S. Brooks, "A Study of the Technical and Semi-technical Vocabulary of Arithmetic," *Educational Research Bulletin*, 5: 219–222, 1926; G. T. Buswell and L. John, "The Vocabulary of Arithmetic," *Supplementary Educational Monographs*, No. 38; University of Chicago Press, 1931, 146 pp.; L. Cole, *The Teachers' Word Book of Technical Vocabulary*, Public School Publishing Company, Bloomington, Ill., 1936, 128 pp.; L. C. Pressey and M. K. Elam, "The Fundamental Vocabulary of Elementary School Arithmetic," *Elementary School Journal*, 33: 46–50, 1932.

TABLE 68—*Continued*

	Thorndike Rating		*Thorndike Rating*
41. mixed number		51. third	1a
42. numerator			
43. reduce	3a	52. decimal fraction	
44. terms	(2a)	53. demical point	
45. fifth	7	H. Signs and Symbols	
46. fourth	1b	183. +	
47. half	1a	184. —	
48. hundredth	8	185. ×	
49. quarter	1b	186. ÷	
50. tenth	3a	189. "	

To assist the teacher in the task of developing vocabulary, tests based on this list have been made.[9] The items of the test are "keyed" to the list. That is, word 6 on the list is measured by item 6 of the list. A few sample items from this test appear below:

TABLE 69

Sample Items from a Vocabulary Test

Directions: After each of these questions, there are five answers. You are to draw a line under the one you think is right.

2. If you said each set of numbers below out loud, which would be counting?

   2—7—3—1   2—0—5—0   8—5—1—0   1—2—3—4   10—15—16—18

4. Which is a number?   7   W   ans.   %   @

5. Which is a Roman numeral?   101   A.B.   pi   .0006   XI

21. Which problem contains a plus?

   $6-2=4$ $6+2=8$ $6 \times 2 = 12$ $6 \div 2 = 3$ $6 \times 1 = 6$

35. Which of the following is a common fraction?

   10   3%   ⅓   .01 $2 \times 5 =$

Directions: Look at the fractions below; then answer the questions about them by writing the answers.

   (A) 1/2   (B) 2/3   (C) 6/5   (D) 3 1/2   (E) 1/5

[9] Cole, *op. cit.*

TABLE 69—*Continued*

33. If you were going to multiply 1/2 by 2/3 what number would you cancel?

34. If you were going to add 1/2, 1/3, and 1/6 what common denominator would you use?

36. In (B) above, which is the denominator?

39. Which is an improper fraction?

41. Which is a mixed number?

42. In (A) above which is the numerator?

43. Which of the following fractions would you reduce?

   1/2   2 2/3   12/16   39/41

44. In (E) above what are the terms?

Directions: Just below there is a list of words with a number in front of each. Below the list, there are some explanations. Each word is explained, or defined. You are to find the definition for each word. For instance, the first word is "apiece." Look through the explanations until you find the one that tells you what apiece means. Then write the number in front of "apiece" (141) in the space just before the explanation you have selected. Then match the other words in the same way. There are more explanations than words.

141. apiece   143. bill   145. cash   147. charge account
142. bargain   144. budget   146. change   148. customer
                                               149. discount

( ) an estimate of what one ex-   ( ) each one
    pects to spend   ( ) a man's total income
( ) a per cent of profit   ( ) actual money as compared with
( ) a person who buys something   a check
( ) an arrangement by which a   ( ) something purchased at an un-
    store allows a person to pay   usually low price
    once a month for things bought   ( ) small amounts of money, such
    during the month before   as dimes and nickels
( ) a reduction in the price of   ( ) a statement of what a person
    something   owes someone else
( ) a market list   ( ) an expense account

By tabulating the test results a teacher can easily see which words the children do not know. If, in tabulating, she puts down the children's names instead of marks, she finds out which child does not know which word. Such a tabulation is presented in Table 70.

TABLE 70

Tabulation by Pupil of Scores in Vocabulary

Words	Children Who Failed to Recognize Each Word	Total Failures per Word
1. add	Mary	1
2. addition	Mary, Ethel, Paul	3
3. carry	Mary, Paul, Enid, Florence, Alice, Fred, Ellen	7
4. sum		0
5. column	Mary, Paul, Alice, Donald, Ellen, Frank	6
6. plus	Mary, Alice, Ellen, Clara, Roscoe, Frank	6

These results tell the teacher that the word *sum* is known by the entire class and the word *add* almost known, although the longer form, *addition,* is a little unfamiliar, since three pupils did not recognize it. Several children failed to recognize the other three words. If the teacher looks over the names, she sees that Mary failed everything but *sum;* that Paul, Ellen, and Alice missed half the words; that Frank missed two; that the other children whose names appear on the list missed one each; and that any children whose names do not appear answered all six items correctly. She knows, therefore, to whom to apply corrective teaching. The teacher should regard the mastery of these few but absolutely essential terms as an important part of her work in problem solving.

2. Terms Needed for Work in Measurement: The distribution of work suggested in Chapter XIV calls for some attention to measurement in each half grade. The work is thus arranged, partly to introduce variety, partly to furnish a basis for practical problems, and partly to provide children with the commonly used facts about measurement. The chapters on fundamentals contained no section on units of measure. The interrelations of the various units are, however, also fundamental facts, although of a different category from the number combinations. It was felt, however, that in measurement, vocabulary was a most important element and that the units of measure belonged more with problem solving than with work in the fundamentals. It is therefore included in the present chapter.

The necessary terms are those given to the units of measure. These names are listed in Table 71.

TABLE 71

Technical Vocabulary in Arithmetic (B)

	Thorndike Rating			Thorndike Rating
D. Units of Measure				
54. ounce	3a		81. penny	2b
55. pound	1b		82. century	2b
56. ton	3a		83. day	1a
57. feet	(1a)		84. hour	1a
58. foot	(1a)		85. minute	1b
59. inch	1b		86. month	1a
60. mile	1a		87. second	1a
61. rod	2a		88. week	1a
62. yard	(1a)		89. year	1a
63. acre	2b		90. annually	12
64. square inch			91. daily	2b
65. square foot			92. quarterly	15
66. square yard			**G. Abbreviations**	
67. square mile			167. bu.	6
68. Cubic foot			168. doz.	7
69. cubic inch			169. ft.	4a
70. bushel	3a		170. gal.	7
71. gallon	5b		171. hr.	7
72. peck	3b		172. in.	6
73. pint	4a		173. lb.	4b
74. quart	3b		174. min.	12
			175. oz.	4b
75. dozen	2a		176. pk.	7
76. pair	1b		177. pt.	6
			178. qt.	5a
77. cent	1b		179. sq.	6
78. dime	4b		180. wk.	12
79. dollar	2a		181. yd.	5a
80. nickel	4b		182. yr.	11

In presenting these terms to pupils, it is desirable to demonstrate each adequately. There are many children who can repeat, parrotlike, the table for units of length without having the foggiest idea of how long any of the units actually are. Because their learning is all too often mere verbalism, children are satisfied with absurd answers to problems. Exercises in guessing weights and lengths—with subsequent checking by actual measurement—are useful in giving the words a substantial meaning.

3. **Terms Used in Presenting Problems:** Naturally, not all the words that may be used in any problem are included here. These few terms are those that appear often. The words divide themselves rather naturally into the groups presented in Table 72.

TABLE 72

Technical Vocabulary in Arithmetic (C)

	Thorndike Rating		Thorndike Rating
E. Practical Measurement		144. budget	8
93. breadth	3b	145. cash	3b
94. broad	1a	146. change	(1a)
95. capacity	4a	147. charge account	
96. contain	1b	148. customer	3b
97. deep	1a	149. discount	10
98. depth	3a	150. exchange	2b
99. dimensions	7	151. expense	2b
100. distance	1b	152. gain	1b
101. height	1b	153. less	1a
102. high	1a	154. loss	1b
103. length	1a	155. net	(2a)
104. long	1a	156. order	(1a)
105. measure	1a	157. per	2b
106. rate	2a	158. price	1b
107. size	1b	159. profit	2b
108. space	1b	160. purchase	2a
109. speed	2a	161. receipt	3b
110. thick	1b	162. retail	6
111. volume	3a	163. sale	2b
112. weigh	2a	164. trade	1b
113. weight	1b	165. wholesale	7
114. wide	1a	166. worth	1b
115. width	3a		

F. Words Used in Problems Concerning Retail Buying	
141. apiece	5a
142. bargain	
143. bill	1b

H. Signs and Symbols
189. "
190. '
191. °
192. $
193. @
194. ¢

It should be noted that one group of terms is used especially in measuring and another in making purchases.

All words dealing with problems of interest, with business generally, and with the measurement of other geometrical figures than a quadrilateral, have been omitted. The suggested course of study postpones these matters until children enter the junior high school, when there is a better chance of such topics being understood. Assuming that arithmetic is begun in Grade 2, the number of words on this list of essentials calls for mastery of an average of seventeen words per semester. Such a burden is not excessive. What is of utmost importance is that the words be really understood and thoroughly mastered. They are essential to both the learning of the fundamental processes and the solving of problems, and they form the basis for the technical mathematical vocabularies subsequently needed in high school or college. The teacher should never feel that she is teaching isolated words; she should, rather, realize that she is teaching elementary ideas in terms of which a child must do his thinking in arithmetic and without which his thinking will not be good enough for reaching the solution to many of the verbal problems that he will be asked to solve. A child's vocabulary will grow more or less as he passes from grade to grade and is exposed to more and more special terms, but his growth can be accelerated by specific training, especially when there are as few words as are needed for elementary arithmetic.

Elementary school pupils do not succeed in mastering even the relatively small number of basic words they need almost daily. Growth

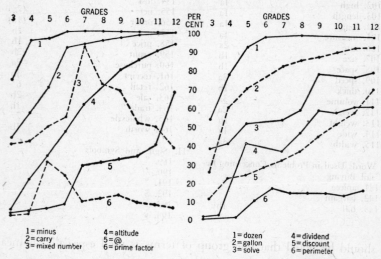

1 = minus   4 = altitude
2 = carry   5 = @
3 = mixed number 6 = prime factor

1 = dozen   4 = dividend
2 = gallon   5 = discount
3 = solve   6 = perimeter

FIGURE 62: Mastery of Vocabulary in Arithmetic

in each of several terms is shown by the curves in Figure 62.[10] The words *minus* and *dozen* are already well known by the third grade; *carry* also shows an early mastery. The symbol @ is learned late. The curves for *mixed number* and *prime factor* show what happens to terms that either are not used or are too difficult. The former was well mastered in one grade, but barely a third of the pupils still knew its meaning at the end of high school. The latter was not known by more than 30 per cent at any time, but this degree of achievement had become

[10] L. C. Pressey and W. S. Moore, "The Growth of Mathematical Vocabulary from the Third Grade through High School," *School Review*, 40: 449–454, 1932.

practically zero by Grade 12. The word *perimeter* was not known by as many as 20 per cent at any time.

Of the 106 terms in arithmetic studied in this research, 34 were learned by 95 per cent or more of the pupils in at least one grade, 45 were known by 80 to 94 per cent, and 20 by 50 to 79 per cent, leaving 7 that were never known by as many as half of the children.

The vocabulary shown in Figure 62 is based upon analysis of problems in textbooks. If, however, elementary school arithmetic were restricted to those problems brought in by pupils, the vocabulary would be somewhat different and probably smaller.[11] The effect of easy or difficult words upon the reading of verbal problems has been amply demonstrated.[12] When definitely familiar terms were used, the pupils got 15 per cent more answers right than when the problems were expressed in definitely unfamiliar words.

Arithmetic texts often do not give drill on technical terms in proportion to either their difficulty or the need to know them. In five books

TABLE 73

Sample Frequencies for Two Words in Five Texts

Term	Total Uses in Text	Number of Different Pages on Which Term Appeared
Minus:		
Text 1	1	1
Text 2	3	3
Text 3	3	1
Text 4	18	12
Text 5	2	1
Subtraction:		
Text 1	48	34
Text 2	64	41
Text 3	30	27
Text 4	46	31
Text 5	93	51

[11] See R. de V. Willey, "Vocabulary for Arithmetic in the Elementary Grades," *Elementary English Review,* 19: 64–66, 1942.
[12] Kramer, *op. cit.*

intended for use in Grade 3, the following amounts of drill were given to the two words *minus and subtraction*.[13] Experience with the word *minus* varied from 18 uses on 12 pages to 1 use on 1 page. The term *subtraction* appeared from 30 to 93 times on 27 to 51 pages. It would seem as if textbook writers ought to make up their minds! An additional burden in these tests was the use of proper names in the problems. These names constituted from 5 to 15 per cent of the total number of words in each book.

In the course of time the essential vocabulary will probably become smaller, as the work in problem solving becomes more and more functional. Eventually, also, there will be agreement, based on research, as to how many repetitions of each term are needed in order to guarantee mastery.

C. THE READING OF PROBLEMS

At the present time children are trained in rapid, silent reading from their first day in school. They are encouraged to read by phrases, to omit nonessential words, and to grasp sentences as units. For discursive types of reading matter this training brings excellent results, but as a technique for reading problems it is almost as bad as it could be.

Children constantly try to read problems as if they were stories. They soon find, however, that this method will not work. Most of them then resort to stumbling around through a problem. Their customary eye movements are disturbed, and they are often taught no other type of movement that might be substituted. The transfer from rapid, assimilative reading to both spelling and arithmetic is negative. The solution is not, however, to make pupils read stories as if they were problems in arithmetic, but rather to supply a special method to be used when a verbal problem is to be understood.

It is instructive to note what eye movements are used by those who read problems well.[14] The numerals are usually read by a fixation on each figure. The pauses are relatively long. The regressions are few and the rhythm fair. There is likely to be considerable vocalizing. These characteristics are very nearly those of good, oral reading, except that there are rather more fixations. If training in good silent reading is

---

[13] E. V. O'Rourke and C. D. Mead, "Vocabulary Difficulties of Five Textbooks in Third-Grade Arithmetic," *Elementary School Journal,* 41: 683–691, 1941.

[14] P. W. Terry, "How Numerals Are Read," *Supplementary Educational Monographs,* No. 18, University of Chicago Press, 1922, 110 pp. Used by permission of the publisher.

destructive to good oral reading, or vice versa, it must be even more destructive to the efficient reading of problems and numbers. The reading of the numbers themselves is especially hard, because only a person who is continually handling numbers can see more than one of two digits at once.

As shown in Figure 63, the person reading the problem apparently read the first of the two numbers as he came to it but left the detailed reading of the second till later, since only one fixation was accorded it.

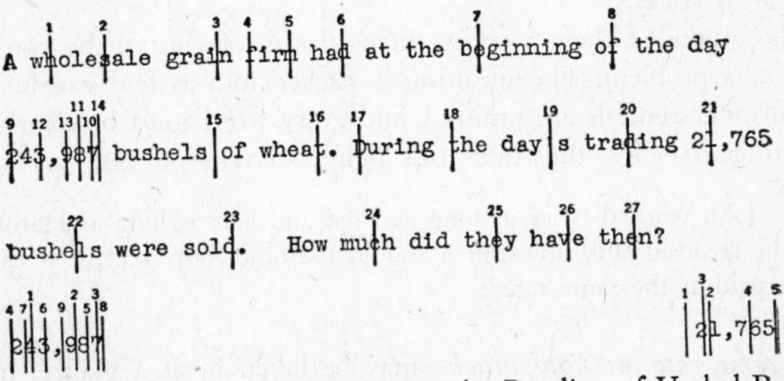

FIGURE 63: Record of Eye Movements in the Reading of Verbal Problems

The two numbers were again read in isolation. The first required a total of nine fixations for six digits and the second a total of five for the five digits. There was not a single regression in reading the words—a fact that shows the reader to have been skilled in the ordinary techniques of silent reading—but he made three regressions in reading the first number in the problem.

In the above sample, twenty fixations were used to cover the twenty-seven words in the problem, not counting either the numerals or the fixations used to read them. This number should be compared with the fifteen needed for the first twenty-seven words of Figure 3.

The strong tendency for the reading of numbers to interfere with the usual rhythm should be especially noted.[15] It is partly for this reason

---

[15] Formulae are even harder to read than numbers. A line of print in which there is a formula requires 62 per cent more time and four to five more fixations than are needed by the same person for reading a line without a formula. Moreover, there are three times as many regressions. (M. A. Tinker, "A Photographic Study of Eye Movements in Reading Formulae," *Genetic Psychology Monographs*, 3: 65–182, 1928.) Even such simple formulae as πr^2 or $2\pi r$ disrupt eye movements badly. Analysis has also shown that high school pupils have much difficulty in reading mathematical symbols, even more than in reading numerals. (J. S. Georges, "The Nature of Difficulties Encountered in Reading Mathematics," *School Review*, 37: 217–226, 1929.) Almost 40 per cent of the failures to understand problems came from failure to grasp the meaning of symbols. The symbols such as $\cong$, @, $\chi°$, $\therefore$, $\div$, or ∞, are especially hard to read.

that two readings—one for sense and one for the insertion of the actual figures—are recommended. The first reading is usually accomplished with almost as many fixations as there are words, especially if the problem is so short that the reader hardly gets started before he is done. The second reading concentrates attention on the numbers, around each of which there is a small group of fixations very close together. From this point on, the individual studies rather than reads; he glances back and forth within the problem, using exactly the type of movements characteristic of study.

The source of these reading difficulties is, of course, the condensed nature of a problem. The meaning is packed into as few words as possible, all nonessentials are omitted, and every word must be clearly read. The problem below illustrates this point. Certain phrases—*as long as,*

> John worked twice as long as Fred and half as long as Harold. If he received 80¢, how much should the other boys receive if they are paid at the same rate?

at the same rate, or *how much*—may be taken in at a glance, but for the most part the reader must proceed word by word. The sentences below are introduced for purposes of contrast; they contain the same number of words as the above problem, but are far easier to read.

> John went with his brother to a pond where they liked to swim. After swimming for about an hour, John suddenly became very cold and was barely able to reach the shore.

A problem is, then, a peculiar type of reading matter. It is too short to allow either speed or rhythm to develop. It is so thoroughly saturated with meaning that everything is essential. It contains special stumbling blocks in the form of numbers. It requires study after it has been read. Since it is such a special type of reading matter, children should be specifically taught how to attack it.

The first thing, perhaps, is to explain to children—not once but many times—that a problem is not merely a highly condensed story. They should be warned against trying to read it as they would a book. It is wise to tell them to read slowly and to look at every single word. Some degree of vocalization should be permitted, since it will help impress the meanings. In the earliest problems, numbers below 10 should be used so that a single fixation will do for the numbers as well as for the words. If a problem is not understood in one such reading, the children should be instructed to go back to the beginning and reread as often as necessary. In the middle of the third grade the idea of two readings, one for meaning and one to insert the numbers, may well be introduced. No effort should be made to hurry children at any stage. Word-for-word reading and back-and-forth studying constitute the essential methods of approach.

D. THE TEACHING OF PROBLEM SOLVING

For many years teachers have been trying to improve the ability of children to solve problems, but without conspicuous success, perhaps because many of the problems presented in texts were beyond the reasoning abilities of children. Until recently, only three methods have been shown to be helpful—intensive drill on fundamentals, drill in vocabulary, and extensive experience with easy problems.[16] The first was helpful because it made the operations a little more certain and thus eliminated a proportion of computational errors and left attention a little freer to consider what processes ought to be used and in what order. The training in vocabulary was useful because an understanding of technical words is a *sine qua non* of correct thinking in a specialized field. The third method gave enough experience with simple problems to allow each child to build up a method of attack and possibly to recover from any fear he may earlier have had.

Children may be taught to analyze problems as a means of attacking them. A common type of problem analysis is illustrated by the following sample:

The Problem

The children in the third grade rooms of two schools were going on a picnic. In one room there were 37 pupils, and in the other there were 32. Counting the two teachers, how many would there be at the picnic if everyone from both rooms were there?

16 For accounts of typical experiments see L. J. Brueckner, "Improving Pupils' Ability to Solve Problems," *Journal of the National Education Association,* 26: 175–176, 1932; R. Dresher, "Drill in Mathematics Vocabulary," *Educational Research Bulletin,* 13: 201–204, 1934; H. A. Greene, "Directed Drill in the Comprehension of Verbal Problems in Arithmetic," *Journal of Educational Research,* 11: 33–40, 1925; R. D. Horsman, "A Comparison of Methods of Teaching Verbal Problems in Arithmetic in Grades 5, 6, 7, and 8," *University of Pittsburgh Bulletin,* 37: 163–168, 1941; W. S. Monroe and M. D. Engelhart, "The Effectiveness of Systematic Instruction in Reading Verbal Problems in Arithmetic," *Elementary School Journal,* 33: 377–381, 1933; C. W. Stone, "An Experimental Study in Improving Ability to Reason in Arithmetic," *Twenty-ninth Yearbook of the National Society for the Study of Education,* 1930, pp. 589–599; C. M. Washburne and R. Osborne, "Solving Arithmetic Problems," *Elementary School Journal,* 27: 219–226, 297–304, 1926.

The Analysis

1. What fact are you asked to find?

   The number of children in   The number of teachers
   both rooms
   The number who did not go   The total number who were going
   to the picnic

2. Which of the following facts is given in the problem?

   The age of the children   The cost of the picnic
   The number of teachers   The number of children who were
                                    sick

3. In which of the following ways would you get the answer to the problem?

   37 plus 32   2 plus 37 plus 32
   37 plus 32 minus 2   37 minus 32

4. About how large would you expect the answer to be?

   100   150
   75   50

Some children seem to profit by drill of this type, but for the slow readers the reading load is too heavy.

One further suggestion has been made—that the introductory problems of each type be dramatized, so as to help the children see the people and experiences behind the wording of the problem.[17] The first retail-buying problems, for instance, may be acted out between two children, one of whom is the clerk and the other the purchaser. This procedure is not the same as the altering of the wording to introduce a number of imaginative details. The problem remains unchanged, but the children learn to read into it a meaning that relates it to life outside a book.

More recently a plan has been proposed for a gradual introduction of several different elements of difficulty in solving problems.[18] The purpose of this presentation was to arrange problems in a series from the easiest to the hardest, so that children might begin with those that involved the smallest number of difficulties. The idea is thus parallel to that behind the arrangement of long division examples shown on

[17] E. Wilson, "Improving the Ability to Read Arithmetic Problems," *Elementary School Journal*, 22: 380–386, 1922.

[18] R. M. Gill, "The Effect of Using Graded Verbal Problems in Arithmetic for One Year in Grades 4 and 5," *University of Pittsburgh Bulletin*, 37: 123–126, 1941.

page 358. In carrying out this experiment the investigator constructed for each grade from 4B through 5A a series of twenty-six lessons in problem solving. The lessons in each series increased in difficulty in six different respects. The first problems required only one step, the numbers were small, no unfamiliar words were used, the problems were about definite objects, there were no unnecessary words, and all symbols were omitted. The hardest problems in each series had two steps and presented sixteen different process sequences. The numbers were of moderate size, and there were more of them. Some abstract or unfamiliar words were introduced, and the problems contained both symbols and a few elements which were pertinent to the problem but not needed for the solution. Each series was thus devised so as to present the pupils with the easiest possible problems first and then gradually to introduce complications. There is some evidence that use of these series results in better progress in problem solving. A fourth or fifth grade teacher would do well to have a copy of the series for her grade for her own guidance and to study the problems in the children's textbook in the light of this research. If problems are presented in a random order, the difficulties from one to the next are likely to vary considerably, and the children are almost certain to become involved in complexities they are not ready to handle.

E. SUMMARY

It is always advisable for a teacher to check the problems in her texts to make sure that they do not have characteristics which make them inappropriate for children. Modern texts are greatly improved in this respect over those of former times, but one still finds some problems of questionable value and usefulness. To be successful in problem solving a child needs to know the meaning of those special terms that constantly appear in the wording of the problems or are constantly used by the teacher in explaining them. He must also develop a technique of reading that is different from that which he has learned for the reading of stories. A successful method of teaching problem solving includes instruction in vocabulary, in special reading skills, and in reasoning. The brightest children in the class will reason well because they are bright, but those of less native capacity can be helped a good deal by proper teaching.

XVIII · Interest and Dynamics

Arithmetic is, on the average, not one of the more interesting subjects in the primary grades. Reading is rated highest, then handwriting, with arithmetic and spelling rather low.[1] In the later grades, however, arithmetic rises in the pupils' estimation until, in Grade 5, it is at the top. Such general statements do not, however, do more than reflect group opinion. They do not tell what the range of attitudes is, nor do they tell why particular children feel the way they do.

When one comes to consider the individual child one usually discovers that arithmetic tends to be either liked very much by pupils or else disliked most heartily. Personal interviews with representatives from both emotional extremes give interesting information. Many children like arithmetic because it is so obviously useful. In this case there has evidently been a successful transfer from the training in school to daily life outside. Other children seem to regard arithmetic as a puzzle which, like any other puzzle, is interesting to solve. These youngsters have no utilitarian end in view. They are those fortunate ones who have not yet been given work so far beyond their capacity that the interesting puzzle has become a hopeless maze. Then, there is a third group of pupils who like arithmetic because they know what they have to do, they know when they are done, they know when they are right, and they know when they are improving. That is, the objectivity of arithmetic appeals to them.

At the other extreme of emotional attitude is a considerable group of children who dislike arithmetic because they do not understand it and can make no progress. These pupils are simply mired in the Slough of Despond. Others, although they do satisfactory work, find arithmetic mechanical and boring. Still other pupils complain that arithmetic is useless. Further inquiry reveals an almost complete failure of arithmetic to function in their lives. Since most of these children are girls,

---

[1] L. B. Baisden and W. J. Burkhard, "Children's Preferences in School Subjects of the Curriculum," *Twelfth Yearbook of the California Association of Elementary Principals,* pp. 41–47, 1940.

it is a fair guess that the types of arithmetical problem used have been suited primarily to adult, masculine activities in which they have little interest.

By considering both the praise and the blame one can derive certain definite suggestions for making arithmetic more interesting for children. The first is, obviously, to keep the learning problems within the capacity of the learner. As soon as work becomes too hard the pleasure derived from getting the answer to a puzzle is lost; soon a chronic feeling of failure is developed, effectually preventing enough further learning for the re-establishment of a pleasurable attitude. The second suggestion is that arithmetic must be so applied that it is useful to the pupils. Children have some need for arithmetic, and there are many situations into which arithmetic can easily be introduced, even though the children do not spontaneously think of using it. Planning what to buy with a given amount of money, dividing possessions evenly among a group, planning refreshments for a party, working and saving to buy a bicycle, measuring ingredients for a cake, making measurements for building a boat, timing children to see who runs fastest, scoring games, doing errands at the store—there are dozens of childish activities into which skill in arithmetic could enter. Practical application should be based on such activities. One way of making transfer to the children's lives certain is to have them bring in instances of their uses of arithmetic outside school. These experiences are then made into problems. Whatever the method for making arithmetic useful may be, it is essential that the practical nature of the subject be demonstrated repeatedly.

A. CHILDREN'S USES OF ARITHMETIC

Many investigations of children's uses of arithmetic have been made, both as to the nature of the problems and as to the computations involved. In one study, elementary school children turned in 1,687 uses of arithmetic outside school, and in another, 2,484.[2] These problems were

[2] E. Wahlstrom, "The Computational Arithmetic in the Social Experience of Third Grade Children," *Journal of Educational Research,* 30: 124–129, 1936, and R. de V. Willey, "A Study of Arithmetic in the Elementary Schools of Santa Clara County, California," *Journal of Educational Research,* 36: 353–365, 1943.
See also L. J. Brueckner, "Social Problems as a Basis for a Vitalized Arithmetic Curriculum," *Journal of Experimental Education,* 1: 320–323, 1932; M. M. Culver, "A Study of Children's Interests in Arithmetic," *Twelfth Yearbook of the California Association of Elementary School Principals,* pp. 60–70, 1940; R. de V. Willey, "Social Situations Which Lead the Elementary School Pupil to Natural Arithmetical Experience," *ibid.,* pp. 70–81; C. N. Robinson, "Children's Arithmetic Needs Arising in the Home Environment," *ibid.,* pp. 54–59.

distributed among a number of activities in the per cents indicated for
the two studies in Table 74.

TABLE 74

Uses of Arithmetic Outside School [3]

	Per Cent		Per Cent
1. Using money	25	1. Using money	35
2. Measuring	20	2. Counting	17
3. School subjects	20	3. Work situations	12
4. Time	12	4. Games & amusements	14
5. Objects	11	5. School activities	10
6. Pets	7	6. Gifts	4
7. Distance	5	7. Saving	3
	100	8. All others	5
			100

In both cases, the handling of money is the most important use made of
arithmetic. As pupils advance through school, however, they use arithmetic for many purposes. A comparison at different levels of development appears in Figure 64.

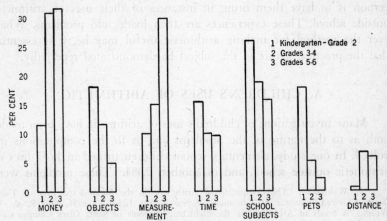

FIGURE 64: Uses of Arithmetic at Different Levels

It is interesting also to know how large the sums are with which
children deal and what operations they perform with the figures. One

[3] Quoted by permission of the publishers.

excellent study of third grade children gives the following information on these points.

TABLE 75

Sums Involved in Extraschool Arithmetic [4]

	Number of Uses	Per Cent
Addition:		
1. Basic facts	235	23
2. Single column	89	19
3. Two or more columns (no carrying)	336	33
4. Two or more columns (with carrying)	213	11
5. Broken column	112	11
6. Addition by ending	20	2
TOTAL	1,005	99
Subtraction:		
1. Basic facts	152	19
2. Harder subtraction	349	44
3. Harder subtraction (with borrowing)	295	37
TOTAL	796	100
Multiplication:		
1. Basic facts	164	74
2. Harder multiplication		
One multiplier	57	25
Two numbers in multiplier	2	1
TOTAL	223	100
Division:		
1. Basic facts	23	58
2. Harder divisions		
One digit in division	9	22
Two digits in division	8	20
TOTAL	40	100

Most of the column additions were of one- or two-place numbers, and usually there were only two of them. In two thirds of the harder sub-

[4] Wahlstrom, *op. cit.* Quoted by permission of the publisher.

tractions, the children used one- or two-place numbers in the subtra-hend. Most of the practical problems (78 per cent) met by the children involved only one step. Practically half of the 1,164 problems involved addition only. Over a third required subtraction. Multiplication was needed for 10 per cent of the operations, but division was scarcely used at all.

It would seem as if arithmetic might be made more interesting and appropriate if the problems were of the same type that the children meet in their daily lives and if the processes involved were such as they were capable of handling. Indeed, some investigators would limit the work of the elementary school to those operations that will actually be used from day to day by children, letting adulthood look after its own arithmetical needs, instead of trying to prepare children for them.[5]

The transfer from arithmetic in school to its use outside school would, however, be better if the school were to teach the same methods that the children will use. The greatest single use of arithmetic is the making of change in retail buying. The big difference between such operations in real life and in school is that the child soon learns to make change by counting from the amount spent to the amount given the clerk, instead of subtracting as he doubtless has to do in school. For this reason, transfer from school problems involving retail buying and change making to similar activities in life situations is less than it might be. What actually transfers is the counting by ones, fives, and tens that is done in the first and second grades. School children have also many occasions in which they want to measure something, but they sometimes proceed in a manner different from that demanded by the school. Thus if a boy is building something, he is less likely to make actual measure-ments in inches to get two pieces of material of the same length than to lay one length against another and use the first as a measure without respect to its length in inches or feet. Children who are quite capable of solving simple problems in school do not always use their skill in meeting situations outside of school.

B. AROUSING INTEREST

One reasonably certain way of arousing interest in problem solving is to create a situation in which children are known to be interested and then to group several problems around it. Thus, if a teacher wants

⁵ See, for instance, C. Washburne, "Functional Arithmetic," *Educational Method* 16: 167–171, 1937.

to show her pupils how to calculate an average she may ask each of them to run a hundred yards and have them time each other with a stop watch; perhaps such a test has already been given during the work in physical education. After each child's time has been found, averages, differences between the fastest and slowest, average increase from one trial to another, and the number and percentage of children surpassing a certain standard can all be calculated from the figures. In this instance, the work in arithmetic is deliberately initiated with an activity that is interesting to children. Arithmetic may often derive motivation from association with other subjects in the curriculum. If Christmas is approaching and the children wish to make greeting cards in their art class, the opportunity to teach square measure may be capitalized by having the children measure the length and width of their cards and calculate the square inches in each. Whenever problems can be grouped about an activity there is certain to be more interest than is otherwise likely.

Children are usually not interested in many typically adult problems, some of which are survivals from a generation of pedagogues who were concerned chiefly with mental training. The resultant lack of interest is primarily the fault of the school and will be overcome in proportion as teachers change the type of problems from those concerning mature occupations to those involving childish interests and activities. Most children really like puzzles and "thinking" games of all kinds. The school has therefore the best of native attitudes out of which to develop an interest in problem solving.

A third suggestion to be derived from the statements of children is the desirability of emphasizing the objectivity of arithmetic, so as to get children interested in progress per se. There is no other subject in which the goals are so definite in these early grades. If a child has one hundred combinations in multiplication to learn and already knows thirty-two of them, he knows exactly how many and what combination he still lacks. If, two weeks later, he knows forty-seven out of the one hundred, he can see that he is progressing. Every use should be made of objective tests and of recording devices. If a child has ten weeks in which to learn the one hundred facts and if he is given a test every two weeks, he can be shown how to make a simple line graph of his progress. By setting up a goal and by diagramming a child's progress toward that goal, a teacher may capitalize on the natural objectivity of arithmetic and can interest children in progress that is so easy to demonstrate.

Finally, arithmetic may be made more interesting by use of games, projects, or activities.[6] Children can help keep attendance records, health records, weather charts, temperature charts, scores in games, or scores on school tests. All of these activities involve more or less arithmetic. Seasonal interests in making kites or playing marbles can be utilized for experience in measuring or counting. Those children who bring a lunch to school can learn to compute the average cost. Pupils can get practice in change making through dramatizations of storekeeping. Some of the exercises used for drill in the fundamentals are arranged in the form of a game or puzzle. When arithmetic is taught incidentally during an interesting activity, the results in terms of mastery are at least as good as under conditions of more formal drill.[7] Perhaps the best thing would be to combine interest and drill by giving the latter only when it is adequately motivated by the former. One should not make the mistake of supposing that interest alone or drill alone is enough.

C. SUMMARY

Probably the surest way to arouse interest in arithmetic is to have children bring problems to school and then to base the drill upon the processes and number facts needed for the solution. To be sure, the teacher has to do some adapting and changing or the children would not get enough practice on some of the combinations, but the connection with childish experiences should be preserved. The second-best way for arousing interest is to group problems around activities in which the pupils are already interested.

[6] See p. 416 ff. for a list of games.
[7] See, for instance, K. Dissinger, "An Experiment in Storekeeping in the First Grade," *Instructor,* 52: 22–23, 1943, and L. Goforth, "A Classroom Experiment in Teaching Reading and Arithmetic through Games," *Educational Method,* 17: 231–235, 1938.

XIX . Readiness to Compute

Readiness to do arithmetic is, like readiness to read, often thought of as being a problem of the first grade. Actually it continues to be a problem at all levels of education. The proportion of entering pupils in Grade 1 who are not yet ready to learn $2 + 2 = 4$ is not much higher than the per cent of high school freshmen who are not yet ready for $(a + b) (a - b)$ or of college freshmen who are unprepared to face $a^2 + ab = 6b^2$. However, the bulk of the work done to date has been with small children.

A. READINESS IN THE FIRST GRADE

Most children bring a variety of simple number skills and number concepts to school with them. They almost always know the numbers up to 5 and many of them can count to 20 or higher. In a typical group of seventy-six entering children, all but twenty-one can count higher than 10, and twenty can count at least to 90.[1] They know the meaning of *first* and *second* and sometimes they know several of the ordinals. Seventy per cent know what half an apple or half a pie is, and 61 per cent can identify half a dozen. About 40 per cent can tell which picture in a series shows a quarter of a pie. Only 18 per cent are unable

[1] W. A. Wittich, "A Number Readiness Test," *School Executive*, 61, No. 7: 11–13, 1942. Figure 65 from this reference is used by permission of the publisher.
See also W. A. Brownell, "The Development of Children's Number Concepts in the Primary Grades," *Supplementary Educational Monographs*, No. 35; L. J. Brueckner, "Readiness Tests in Arithmetic," *Journal of Educational Research*, 34: 15–20, 1940; B. R. Buckingham and J. MacLatchy, "The Number Abilities of Children When They Enter the First Grade," *Twenty-ninth Yearbook of the National Society for the Study of Education*, 1930, pp. 473–524; D. Carper, "A Study of Some Aspects of Children's Number Knowledge Prior to Instruction," Doctor's Thesis, Duke University, 1941; J. W. Dickey, "Readiness for Arithmetic," *Elementary School Journal*, 40: 592–598, 1940; A. Grant, "An Analysis of the Number Knowledge of First Grade Pupils According to the Level of Intelligence," *Journal of Experimental Education*, 7: 63–66, 1938; J. MacLatchy, "Number Abilities of First Grade Children," *Childhood Education*, 11: 344–347, 1935; K. McLaughlin, "Number Abilities of Pre-school Children," *ibid.*, pp. 348–353; A. R. Polkinghorne, "Young Children and Fractions," *ibid.*, pp. 354–358; N. R. Russell, "Arithmetical Concepts of Children," *Journal of Educational Research*, 29: 647–663, 1936; G. Woody, "Arithmetical Background of Young Children," *Journal of Educational Research*, 24: 188–201, 1931.

to write any numbers at all. Half of the others can write some or all of the numbers up to 10. The more intelligent children can read numbers up to about 25 and know the answers to a few of the simplest addition and subtraction combinations. Their vocabulary of arithmetical terms is small, but they do know such general adjectives of size or weight or distance as *long, tall, short, big, small, light, heavy, far,* or *near.* Many of them know *number, add, pound, mile,* or *equal.* Probably about a third of the entering pupils have sufficient knowledge to start work in arithmetic at once, and another third have not long to wait.

There is fair agreement as to what a child needs in order to be ready for beginning work in formal arithmetic. He must first have a general mental development of at least seven years [2] and a long enough memory span to remember the combinations after he learns them. He needs also a real interest in numbers and a sufficient degree of concentration for developing good habits of work. Most of this preparation is intellectual rather than social or emotional.

The children who enter school without proper maturity may simply be allowed to wait for a while. Good results have been obtained by just letting the children grow.[3] It is, however, possible to help children build up the concepts they need by furnishing a wide background of number experiences. A child may be encouraged to handle objects until he learns how many different things are meant by *2, 5, 3, 9,* or any other number up to a 100 at least, and 500 is better. Play with small objects, such as blocks or marbles, usually furnishes many experiences that can be used as a basis for an apprehension of the smaller numbers. For acquiring an idea of how many objects are denoted by such numbers as *48, 74,* or *196* a small child has few experiences unless they are furnished in school.[4] For the really large numbers children have no experiential basis for comprehension. A number such as 8,069 means simply "a lot" or "a big number," because children do not experience 8,069 units of anything together at one time. Probably this lack of apprehension is at the bottom of many errors in copying, since an inversion of the figures from 8,069 to 8,906 results merely in another "big number" which is apparently

[2] B. R. Buckingham, "When to Begin the Teaching of Arithmetic," *Childhood Education,* 11: 339–343, 1935.

[3] See, for example, L. P. Benezet, "The Story of an Experiment," *Journal of the National Education Association,* 24: 241–244, 301–303, 1935, and 25: 7–8, 1936; J. S. Taylor, "Omitting Arithmetic in the First Year," *Educational Administration and Supervision,* 2: 87–93, 1916.

[4] Many suggestions for activities and exercises that make the four fundamental processes meaningful are given in A. Polkinghorne, *Foundations in Arithmetic,* Association for Childhood Education, Washington, 1937, 32 pp.

quite as satisfactory to the child as the original. Appreciation of what is meant by numbers of different magnitudes comes only slowly. At all levels of work in school, care should be taken that operations with numbers do not outstrip apprehension of their meaning. Thus, many a child in the upper grades who makes the mistake of bringing down the same digit twice in a long division problem is not astounded by finding that 83 goes into 39,757 all of 4,789.84 times instead of 479 times, because all large numbers are essentially meaningless to him. For a beginning of work in arithmetic some grasp of numbers up to 500 is probably sufficient, but attention to the building up of number concepts cannot be relaxed at any period in school or the learning will become mere verbalism.

Before a child is ready for formal work he needs to know both the names of the numbers and their serial order. That is, he must be able to count. There is no better basis for arithmetic than a fluent counting forward or backward. By counting a child builds up his number concepts, ascertains the relations between numbers, and senses the repetition over and over again of the series up to ten. But the names alone as a memorized flow of sounds are not sufficient. The names must be accompanied by the counting of actual objects. Many a small child can produce the names of the first four numbers—in much the same singsong used in nursery rhymes—but is unable to count four actual objects. What attention is given to number work in the lower first grade should center around the establishment of facility with the number series up to 100. Actual counting of objects and games involving numbers should be used generously. It is not enough that children be able to plod up the series from 1 to 100. Ability to begin anywhere and go in either direction is needed. A little later, counting by 5's or 10's forward or backward up to 500 should be achieved. There is little use in beginning formal work until children handle the numbers up to 500 with such ease that any number in the series means something to them, both as an actual amount and in its relationship to other numbers. It is more economical to take the time needed for mastery of the series before beginning formal work than to start before the series is fully known.

Study of readiness to begin arithmetic has not progressed as far as study of readiness to begin reading, but a few tests have been prepared and a little experimenting has been done with them.[5] A copy of one such test appears in Figure 65.[6] Children who are not yet able to pass

[5] Brueckner Readiness Tests in Arithmetic, John C. Winston Company, Philadelphia; J. T. Johnson, "Chicago Arithmetic Readiness Test," *Chicago Schools*, 21: 121–123, 1939.

NUMBER READINESS TEST

Name_____ Age_____ Date_____

ABSTRACT COUNTING
1. Say, "How far can you count?" (orally and without concrete objects)
   1___2___3___4___5___6___7___8___9___10___over___

CONCRETE COUNTING
2. Say, "How many blocks are there here?" Show 3 blocks___7 blocks___
                                                5 blocks___9 blocks___

WRITING NUMBERS
3. Say, "How many numbers can you write?" Supply paper. Check correctly written numbers: 1___2___3___4___5___6___7___8___9___10___
                                                          over 10___

ADDITION
4. Abstract counting (without blocks). Say, "Can you tell me how many
   one and one are? Can you tell me how many two and three are?" etc.
   (Use combinations given below. Write "A" in space if combination
   is correctly given).

5. Concrete counting (with blocks). Say, "Here are two blocks and
   here are three more. Can you tell me how many there are in all?" etc.
   Enter a "C" in the blank if the concrete combination is known.

1. 1 + 1 A___C___	6. 2 + 3 A___C___	11. 3 + 6 A___C___
2. 2 + 2 A___C___	7. 1 + 3 A___C___	12. 2 + 6 A___C___
3. 3 + 3 A___C___	8. 2 + 4 A___C___	13. 1 + 6 A___C___
4. 4 + 4 A___C___	9. 3 + 5 A___C___	14. 2 + 7 A___C___
5. 1 + 2 A___C___	10. 1 + 5 A___C___	15. 1 + 7 A___C___

SUBTRACTION
6. Abstract subtraction. Say, "Do you know how many are left when you
   take one away from eight?" etc.

7. Concrete subtraction. Say, "When I take two blocks away from five
   blocks, how many are left?"
   Go through all of the combinations given below and enter the proper
   symbols, "A" or C," in the blanks if the combinations are known.

1. 2 − 1 A___C___	6. 5 − 3 A___C___	11. 7 − 2 A___C___
2. 3 − 2 A___C___	7. 6 − 2 A___C___	12. 8 − 3 A___C___
3. 4 − 1 A___C___	8. 6 − 4 A___C___	13. 8 − 1 A___C___
4. 4 − 2 A___C___	9. 7 − 6 A___C___	14. 8 − 5 A___C___
5. 5 − 1 A___C___	10. 7 − 4 A___C	15. 8 − 7 A___C___

FRACTIONS
8. Say, "How would you cut this pie in half? Draw a line to show how
   you would cut it."
   Say, "Draw a line to show when the glass would be half full of milk."
   Say, "Draw a line through the apple to show where you would cut it
   in half."
   Say, "Draw a line around a half-dozen of the eggs shown here."

   Repeat the instructions for one-fourth and one-third.

A. One-half

B. One-fourth

C. One-third

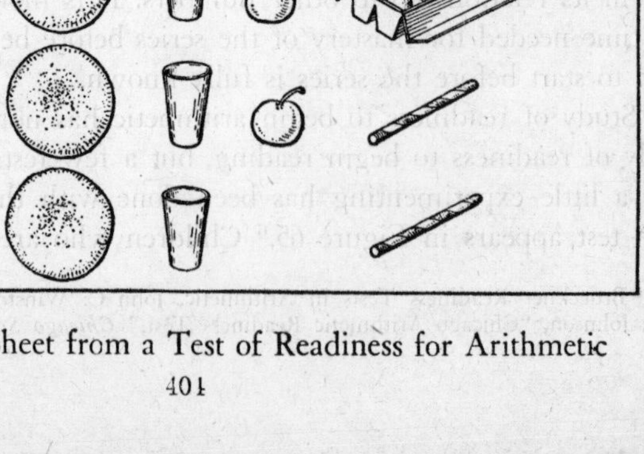

FIGURE 65: One Sheet from a Test of Readiness for Arithmetic

a test of this type have a degree of unpreparedness for which they probably cannot compensate by extra drill.[7] They not only begin work as "slow" in arithmetic, but their failure to develop adequate concepts before entrance to school influences their work in subsequent grades.

The work children do in the beginning phases of formal work in arithmetic is apparently correlated quite highly with their degree of preparedness in the traits measured by tests thus far devised. Those children who are able to pass a readiness test at entrance to school should certainly be allowed to begin work in formal arithmetic at once, but those who cannot pass it will only become confused and apprehensive if the teacher tries to teach them the number combinations. She can simply let them alone, or she can help them to discover arithmetic for themselves by enriching their number experiences.[8]

B. READINESS AT HIGHER LEVELS

Tests of readiness for pupils to begin any phase of arithmetic can be made by analyzing the elements required for making a successful beginning of the work. For instance, readiness to start long division consists of several specific skills:

1. Knowledge of the place value in three-place numbers.
2. Knowledge of the multiplications used in division.
3. Knowledge of the difficult division combinations.
4. Knowledge of the division process with one-figure divisors and 2–4 figure dividends.
5. Ability to judge the correctness of a quotient.
6. Ability to complete the work to determine the correctness of a given quotient.
7. Knowledge of the subtractions used in division.
8. Ability to multiply mentally a two-place by a one-place number.
9. Ability to compare the product of a two- and a one-place number with the proper digits in the dividend.[9]

Tests that measure these capacities predict success in long division with considerable accuracy. In the course of time it is probable that readiness

[6] Wittich, *op. cit.*, p. 11. Used by permission of the publishers.

[7] G. Hildreth, "Number Readiness and Progress in Arithmetic," *Journal of Experimental Education*, 4: 1–6, 1935.

[8] See, for instance, R. Thompson, "Discovering Arithmetic," *Peabody Journal of Education*, 16: 271–276, 1939.

[9] L. J. Brueckner, "The Development of Readiness Tests in Arithmetic," *Journal of Educational Research*, 34: 15–20, 1940. Used by permission of the publisher.

tests at various levels will be prepared. Teachers can then restrict their teaching of each successive process to those who are ready to learn it. Such a situation would be an educational Utopia!

C. SUMMARY

Some small children are ready for arithmetic when they enter school, and most children have developed many elementary mathematical concepts during their preschool years. Those who are ready should certainly not waste time by postponing their contact with material that would interest them, but those who are still immature or inexperienced should play with numbers and ideas about numbers until they acquire the necessary background and attitudes.

XX · Remedial Work in Arithmetic

Most teachers have done more or less individual, remedial teaching in arithmetic because so many pupils have difficulty in learning the material, but relatively few remedial classes or sections have been established in elementary school, although one does find them in both high school and college, often under the supervision of the science departments. Until the war emphasized the great need for mathematics in a mechanized world, people seemed inclined to minimize defects in arithmetical skills and to concentrate attention upon defects in reading and, in high schools, in written English. One would think that diagnostic and remedial work would be easier in arithmetic than in any other subject because the subject matter is so objective. However, no elaborate programs or remedial classes have thus far appeared, although one finds an occasional brief report of successful remedial work on a small scale.

A. DIAGNOSIS OF ERROR

The makers of tests have analyzed the processes involved in such a detailed manner that a teacher can easily study individual children, if she wants to. One such analysis for the operations with integers will be presented in some detail.[1] Many of the errors that children make may be deduced from their written work, but others can be noted only if children solve problems by thinking out loud. The recommended procedure is to test children individually, asking each to talk as he thinks, so that the teacher can follow his mental operations. Some children,

[1] G. T. Buswell and L. John, "Diagnostic Studies in Arithmetic," *Supplementary Educational Monographs,* No. 30, University of Chicago Press, 1926, 212 pp. Used by permission of the publisher. See, for an analysis of multiplication, L. V. Burge, "Types of Error and Questionable Habits of Work in Multiplication," *Elementary School Journal,* 33: 185–194, 1932. Also F. J. Schonell, *Diagnosis of Individual Difficulties in Arithmetic,* Oliver Publishing Company, 1937.

especially those who are abnormally slow, often get the right answer by wrong, involved, or clumsy methods. One such child who was sent to the writer for analysis added 6 by adding 5 and then counting up to 1, subtracted 9 by subtracting 10 and counting backward one number, and multiplied 486 × 7 by the following technique:

$$486 \times 10 = 4,860$$
$$\underline{- 1,458}$$
$$3,402$$

$$10 - 7 = 3$$
$$3 \times 486 = 1,458$$

The child usually got the right answer, but he was extraordinarily slow. When he did his work aloud, it appeared at once that he could do nothing with 6's, 7's, 8's, or 9's.

The errors listed in Table 76 are grouped by operation. The analysis for one pupil appears with the addition and subtraction lists and that of another child with the other two. Pupil E.R. made the combinations correctly, but he was unfamiliar with the processes involved. He made three different kinds of error in carrying and two kinds in subtracting. He also wandered about in the column when he was adding, grouping, or splitting numbers, losing his place, retracing to find it again, omitting numbers, and failing to note which column they were in. What he needed was a good explanation of carrying and borrowing, plus practice in an orderly progression up or down a column of figures. The second child, M.W., knew how to multiply and divide, but made many errors in his calculations and showed confusion when dealing with zeros. He was reduced to counting nine different times because he could not recall combinations. The teacher studied this pupil further to find out exactly which combinations he did not know, since ignorance of the combinations is rarely spread evenly over all of them. The ones that M.W. did not know were:

8+7=	8×7=	17−8=	72÷8=
7+8=	8×6=	16−8=	48÷8=
8+6=	8×5=	15−8=	56÷7=
6+8=	8×9=	14−8=	56÷8=
8+5=		13−8=	42÷7=
5+8=		13−7=	32÷8=
8+9=		15−7=	28÷7=
9+8=		13−7=	48÷6=
8+4=		13−6=	42÷6=
4+8=		14−6=	24÷6=

TABLE 76

Analysis of Error in Fundamentals

A. Column Addition	E. R.	B. Subtraction	E. R.
1. Errors in combinations		1. Errors in combinations	
2. Counting		2. Did not allow for having	2
3. Added carried number last	2	borrowed	
4. Did not add carried number	1	3. Counting	
5. Retraced work after partly		4. Errors due to zero in minuend	
done	4	5. Said example backward	
6. Added carried number irregularly		6. Subtracted minuend from subtrahend	
7. Carried wrong number	1	7. Failed to borrow	8
8. Irregular procedure in column	3	8. Added instead of subtracted	
9. Grouped two numbers	7	9. Error in reading	
10. Split numbers	1	10. Used same digit in two columns	
11. Used wrong fundamental operation			
12. Lost place in column	6		
13. Disregarded column position	2		
14. Omitted one or more digits	1		
15. Read numbers wrong			
16. Dropped back one or more tens			

C. Multiplication	M. W.	D. Division	M. W.
1. Errors in combinations	7	1. Errors in combinations	6
2. Error in adding the carried number	2	2. Errors in subtraction	2
3. Wrote rows of zeros		3. Errors in multiplication	4
4. Other errors in addition		4. Used remainder larger than divider	
5. Carried wrong number		5. Found quotient by trial multiplication	
6. Used multiplicand as multiplier		6. Neglected to use remainder within example	
7. Forgot to carry		7. Used wrong operation	
8. Errors due to zero in multiplier	2	8. Omitted digit in dividend	
9. Used wrong process		9. Counted to get quotient	2
10. Counted	4	10. Repeated part of multiplication table	1
11. Omitted digit in multiplier		11. Used short division form for long division	
12. Wrote carried number		12. Wrote remainders within example	
13. Omitted digit in multiplicand		13. Omitted final remainder	3
14. Errors due to zero in multiplicand	1	14. Omitted zero	2
15. Counted to get multiplication combination	3	15. Counted in subtracting	
16. Error in position of partial products		16. Used too large a product	
		17. Said example backward	
		18. Used remainder without new dividend figure	1

M.W.'s *bête noire* was obviously 8, although he was not very handy with either 7's or 6's. The combinations with digits below 5, the zero combinations, the 9's, and the operations with a number by itself seemed to have been well learned. A variation of this oral technique consists of having a pupil do problems aloud in front of a dictaphone.[2] The record is then studied and analyzed at leisure.

A fairly good analysis of error can be made from study of the scores on a test, provided the test is sufficiently diagnostic and covers the entire field, although a pupil's method of procedure is not always obvious. Each skill has to be measured separately, or one cannot be sure just which of a child's reactions are incorrect. The skills measured by each subtest of one comprehensive, diagnostic series are listed in Table 77.[3]

TABLE 77

Subdivisions of a Diagnostic Test

A. Fundamental processes with whole numbers
. 1. Basic addition facts
2. Basic subtraction facts
3. Basic multiplication facts
4. Basic division facts
5. Basic vocabulary in arithmetic
6. Basic rules of arithmetic
7. Higher decade addition
8. Column addition
9. Carrying in column addition
10. Harder carrying in column addition
11. Checking errors in subtraction
12. Borrowing or carrying in subtraction
13. Additions used in harder multiplication
14. Carrying in addition used in multiplication
15. Complete process of multiplication
16. Short division involving carrying

[2] M. T. Eaton, "The Value of a Dictaphone in Diagnosing Difficulties in Addition," *Bulletin of the School of Education,* Indiana University, No. 4, 14: 5–10, 1938.

[3] G. M. Ruch, F. B. Knight, H. A. Greene, and J. W. Studebaker, *The Compass Diagnostic Tests in Arithmetic,* Scott, Foresman & Company, 1925.

See also the list of skills presented in E. L. Merton, G. O. Banting, L. J. Brueckner, and A. Souba, "Remedial Work in Arithmetic," *Second Yearbook of the Department of Elementary School Principals,* pp. 395–411, 1923, and the *Brueckner-Kellogg-Van Wagenen Analytical Scales of Attainment in Arithmetic,* Grades 3–8, Education Test Bureau, Minneapolis. The *Thirty-fourth Yearbook of the National Society for the Study of Education* (1935) is devoted to papers on diagnosis.

17. Multiplications, additions, and subtractions needed in long division
18. Complete process in long division

B. Fundamental processes with fractions and whole numbers
    1. Changing fractions to equivalent forms
    2. Finding common denominators
    3. Reducing fractions
    4. Addition of fractions and mixed numbers
    5. Expressing mixed numbers as improper fractions
    6. Subtraction of fractions
    7. Reducing mixed numbers
    8. Canceling in the multiplication of fractions
    9. Reducing fractions and mixed numbers to the best form for an answer
   10. Multiplication of fractions
   11. Cancellation in the division of fractions
   12. Changing from the multiplication to the division form
   13. Division of fractions

C. Fundamental processes with decimals
    1. Notation of decimals
    2. Changing fractions and mixed numbers to decimal forms
    3. Changing decimals to fractions or mixed numbers
    4. Addition of decimals
    5. Subtraction of decimals
    6. Place values of decimals
    7. Pointing off in multiplication of decimals
    8. Dividing decimals by pointing off
    9. Location of decimal points in division
   10. Changing remainders to decimal form
   11. Division of decimals

D. Fundamental processes with denominate numbers
    1. Knowledge of the tables of measure
    2. Reducing denominate numbers
    3. Borrowing in denominate numbers
    4. Addition of denominate numbers
    5. Subtraction of denominate numbers
    6. Multiplication of denominate numbers
    7. Division of denominate numbers

E. Mensuration
    1. Vocabulary of mensuration
    2. Mensuration of plane surfaces
    3. Mensuration of solids

4. Finding areas and volumes
5. Formulas used in mensuration

F. Percentage
   1. Relation of fractions and per cents
   2. Relation of decimals and per cents
   3. Expressing areas in per cents
   4. Fundamentals of percentage

G. Interest
   1. Vocabulary of interest
   2. Special forms
   3. Budgets
   4. Computation of interest
   5. Computation of discount
   6. Use of interest tables

H. Problem solving
   1. Mastery of fundamental processes
   2. Comprehension of material read in problem
   3. Knowledge of what is given in problem
   4. Knowledge of what is called for in problem
   5. Probable answer to problem
   6. Knowledge of proper processes to use in solving
   7. Knowledge of proper order of these processes
   8. Recognition of correct solution

One rarely has occasion to use more than one section of this series at once. Unlike the diagnostic test given previously, this one is usually not done aloud, although it may be, if so desired in individual cases.

B. EMOTIONAL ATTITUDES

In almost every room in an elementary school there are at least two or three children who are so afraid of arithmetic that they learn slowly and are uncertain of such facts as they do learn. Some of them have developed the fear because their earliest efforts were unsuccessful, but for most of them some small failure in their initial efforts was merely objective proof of an inability that they believed to be inborn. Their parents or older children told them, perhaps before they ever entered school, that arithmetic was hard and that no success was to be expected. As soon as these children are presented with 1 + 1 they become convinced that they cannot possibly learn it. If such a child's work in arithmetic is poor, his parents refuse to worry about it, on the grounds that their child will be stupid in arithmetic, just as they always were. What they do not know is that they and their ancestors before them were taught a curriculum so hard that failure was inevitable for a fair share of the pupils. Mild forms of anxiety concerning arithmetic are common among children, and a few pupils have a degree of fear that almost paralyzes them. Such children should be sent for remedial work, if there is anyone to send them to, or helped by the room teacher as often as possible. Arithmetic should, of course, be so taught as to prevent anxiety and to allay any fears that the children may bring with them from home. If a child is never asked to learn what is beyond him, if his errors are promptly analyzed and explained to him, and if he is taught by means of problems taken from his daily life, he should like rather than dislike arithmetic.

When a child who fears arithmetic comes to a remedial class, he should receive treatment similar to that described in earlier chapters for those who are emotional over their failure to read. The first thing is a lessening of the strain by a dismissal from work until the pupil voluntarily asks for it. In the meantime he should play with sundry puzzles and games, all of which involve counting or simple forms of the elementary processes. Or a pupil may make something out of cardboard for which he needs to make measurements. This indirect approach takes time, but it neutralizes the fear that is preventing progress. When the anxiety disappears, a teacher can begin an analysis.

C. REMEDIAL METHODS

1. **Development of Concepts:** Since many children lack the basic concepts, it is wise to have on hand many small objects—blocks, pebbles, marbles, toothpicks, or beans, for instance—by means of which a pupil can count out combinations or problems. The old-fashioned frame with colored beads strung along wires is also useful. For demonstrating fractions it is desirable to have spheres or other solids sawed into halves, fourths, eighths, thirds, fifths, or tenths. With them, it is easy to demonstrate what a common denominator is, what size each fraction is of a whole, and so on. The time spent in building up concepts is well spent, since failure in arithmetic is often due to a child's substitution of sheer verbalism for true comprehension. Some pupils fail to grasp the meaning of the numbers themselves, while others have no clear concept of

the processes. The former are uncertain of their answers to such problems as 7 + 6 or 16 − 9 or 4 × 8 or 42 ÷ 7, they tend to guess at answers, and they are satisfied with a solution that is ridiculous — 9 × 7 = 630, for instance. The latter are able to compute fairly well as long as they are given a cue as to what they should do, but they are unable to decide for themselves when faced with a problem. While they may answer $6\sqrt{36}$ correctly, they do not know what to do when asked how much each of 6 children would get if 36¢ were distributed evenly among them, because they have no clear idea of what division is and they are lost if they do not have the cue of the form $\sqrt{\ }$ to guide them.

One author [4] has devised some excellent techniques for developing concepts of size, of process, and of fractions. The pupil acquires ideas of number by counting out beans or other small objects into piles and proves the basic combinations in similar fashion. To get an answer to 6 × 3 he counts out 6 piles with 3 beans in each

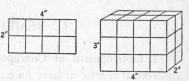

6 × 3 = •• •• •• •• •• •• = 18

4)‾27‾ = •• •• •• •• •• •• •• = 6¾

6 + 7 = •• •• •• • = 13

15 − 8 = ✓ ✓ ✓ ✓ ✓ ✓ ✓ • • • • • • • = 7

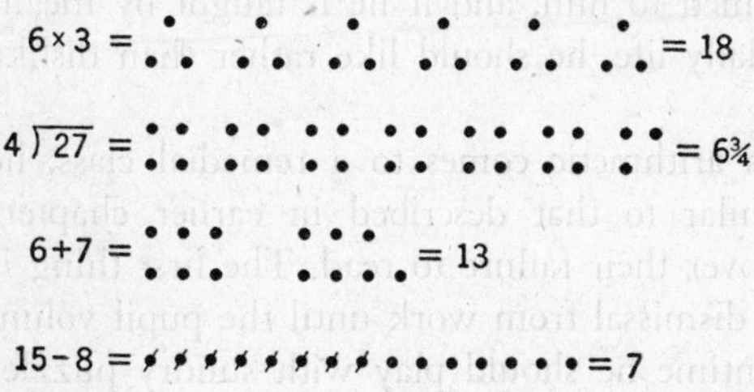

FIGURE 66: Graphic Solutions of Exercises

pile as in Figure 66 and then counts the total. To solve $4\sqrt{27}$ he arranges 27 beans into groups of four, as in Figure 66. He can then see at once that 4 will go into 27 six times with 3 over. To add 6 and 7 he arranges two groups and then counts them together. He can illustrate the subtraction of 8 from 15 by using beans or by making 15 dots, crossing out 8 of them, and then counting those that are left.

FIGURE 67: Graphic Solutions of Square and Cubic Measure

Small square pieces of cardboard and square blocks are used for demonstrating facts about square and cubic measure. Thus a child can put together pieces of cardboard to illustrate the problem: If a table top is 4′ × 2′ how many square feet are there in it? By putting the cardboard squares together the pupil gets a picture of the table top and can count the 8 squares. Similarly, he can

---

[4] G. M. Fernald, *Remedial Techniques in the Basic School Subjects,* McGraw-Hill Book Company, 1943, 349 pp. The excerpts shown in Figures 66–71 are used by permission of the publisher.

use the blocks to illustrate this problem: If a box is 3 inches tall, 4 inches wide, and 2 inches deep, what is its capacity? He builds the required cubic space, studies the figure, and then counts the blocks. Having demonstrated square and cubic measure to himself many times, he is then shown—and proves by further experiment—that he can get the same answer more quickly by multiplying the dimensions. As soon as a child sees what is involved he should, of course, be helped to generalize and to use the short cut of computation, but until the figures and processes have meaning, he is better off arranging his answer so that he can see it.

The same author has a simple but ingenious way of building up concepts for fractions by means of dividing sheets of paper into appropriate sizes. A few representations for the size of fractions appear in

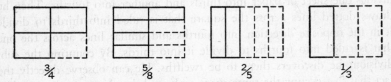

FIGURE 68: Paper Folded and Cut to Illustrate Various Fractions

Figure 68. After a little experience a child can fold and cut a paper to show any commonly used fraction. Operations with fractions may also be demonstrated with paper. Thus, $\frac{1}{2} \times \frac{3}{4}$, $\frac{1}{4} \times \frac{1}{3}$, $\frac{1}{2} \times \frac{1}{3}$, and $\frac{4}{5} \times \frac{2}{3}$ may be visualized as in Figure 69. By such means a pupil builds up concepts as to the size and behavior of fractions.

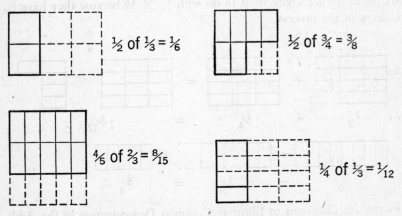

FIGURE 69: Diagram to Illustrate the Multiplication of Fractions

Hardly any children have a clear idea of what happens when one fraction is divided by another. They memorize the rule and hope for the best, but they make many errors and they easily forget the process because the whole procedure means nothing. With the aid of a sheet of paper properly ruled a pupil can begin to see the light. As soon as he sees that ½ ÷ ¼ means *how many times does* ¼ *go into* ½, he can soon discover that it will go in twice. Figure 71 on the next page demonstrates the solutions for ½ ÷ ¼, ½ ÷ ⅓, 1 ÷ ½, ⅓ ÷ ⅕, and ⅙ ÷ ⅓. After a pupil has verified enough problems he can be shown the computational short cut, which will then have meaning for him.

Addition and subtraction of fractions and the concept of a common denominator are easy to demonstrate. To add ⅔ and ¾ a pupil first divides one sheet of paper into thirds and another into fourths. Then he draws dotted lines across the square that is ruled into thirds to divide it in the opposite direction into fourths and similar lines across the one that is ruled into fourths to divide it into thirds. By counting the subdivisions he discovers them to be twelfths. He can observe directly the fact that 9/12 occupy the same space as ¾ and that 8/12 must be equal to ⅔. By cutting out and putting together the two fractional parts he can see why he has to reduce the answer. Figure 70 illustrates also the subtraction of ¼ from ⅞.

This visualizing and manipulation of fractions makes them fun instead of blind drudgery. It is the conventional short cuts, not the fractions themselves, that are puzzling. Many pupils who know that an apple pie that is first halved and then each half cut into thirds will yield six pieces do not know what to do with ½ × ⅓ because they have no concept of the process.

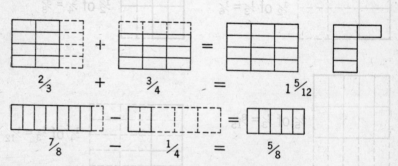

$$\frac{2}{3} \quad + \quad \frac{3}{4} \quad = \quad 1\frac{5}{12}$$

$$\frac{7}{8} \quad - \quad \frac{1}{4} \quad = \quad \frac{5}{8}$$

FIGURE 70: Diagrams to Illustrate Common Denominators in the Addition or Subtraction of Fractions

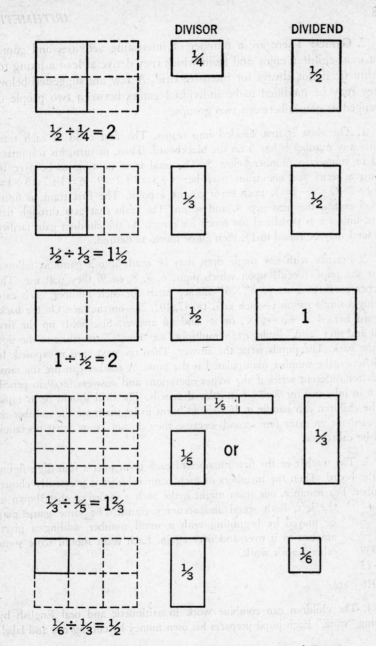

DIVISOR **DIVIDEND**

½ ÷ ¼ = 2

½ ÷ ⅓ = 1½

1 ÷ ½ = 2

⅓ ÷ ⅕ = 1⅔

⅙ ÷ ⅓ = ½

FIGURE 71: Diagrams to Illustrate the Division of Fractions

417

2. **Games:** There are a number of interesting activities and games that most children enjoy and from which they derive at least a liking for arithmetic if not always for intensive drill. A few are suggested below. They may be modified to be individual games between two people or arranged as games between two groups.

1. The class is first divided into teams. The first child of each team writes any number below 5 on the blackboard. Then, in turn, his teammates add or subtract a number below 5. The total is at no time to be over 10. Thus, a series for one team may be: $4+3=7+2=9-6=3+2=5+1=6-4=2+7=9-4=5$. Each error counts 1 point. The first team to finish gets 5 points, the next gets 4, and so on. The team that gets through first wins, unless it is penalized too much for errors. As the children gain facility, the total may be raised to 15, then 20 or more, as desired.

2. Practice with any single digit may be made into a game as follows: First the pupils decide upon which digit, 6, 7, 8, or 9, they will use. The teacher prepares a set of $8'' \times 5''$ library cards for each number, each card having a single number—such as 7, 18, 47, 102, 28—on the face. On the back, toward her, is a $+$, $-$, $\times$, or $\div$ and an answer. She holds up the first card and says "add," "subtract," "multiply," or "divide" according to the sign on the back. The pupils write the answer. Then the next card is exposed. In each series, the number manipulated is the same. A teacher can use the same cards for different series if she writes operations and answers for 9 in pencil, for 8 in ink, and for 7 and 6 in colored pencils. The drill should be as rapid as the children can handle it. It does no harm to let them see the number on the card for an extra few seconds because they do not know what operation will be called for.

3. The teacher or the first member of each team puts a four-digit figure on the board. Then the members of each team subtract a previously chosen number. For instance, one team might make such a record as that shown to the left. Both speed and accuracy count. The same game may be played by beginning with a small number, adding a given amount to it over and over again. Each team should score some other team's work.

$$
\begin{array}{r}
5962 \\
-23 \\
\hline
5939 \\
-23 \\
\hline
5916 \\
\end{array}
$$
etc.

4. The children can combine work in arithmetic and oral English by playing "store." Each pupil prepares his own money by cutting out and label-

ing round pieces of cardboard of correct size and paper cut to the size of bills and labeled. One child of a pair is storekeeper. The customer first announces who he is, and then the conversation begins. The clerk keeps track of purchases on a card and makes change at the end of the episode. The buyer also keeps track of amounts, counts out his money and checks the change. Each pair of children should be limited to a given period of time. Otherwise, the more verbal pupils monopolize the game.

5. More of a project than a game is the calculation of amounts needed, in both money and food, for a school party or school picnic, or other joint undertaking.

6. Parchesi or any game involving dice throwing can be made into an arithmetic game by allowing a player to move forward one space if he adds the numbers on the two dice, two spaces if he subtracts the smaller from the larger, three if he multiplies, and four if he divides. If his partner challenges an answer as wrong, and it is wrong, the pupil loses three spaces, but if the challenge is wrong and the original answer right, the challenger loses the same amount.

7. After removing the king, queen, and jack from a deck of playing cards the pupils proceed as follows: The first child of a pair deals his opponent two cards. These are turned face up and added, subtracted, or multiplied, depending upon which process is being practiced. If a pupil is unsuccessful, the partner gets the cards and deals again. The deal changes hands with each correct answer. The game is won by the pupil with the most cards at the end.

8. A variation of slapjack is noisy, but the children like it. From a deck minus its face cards the dealer deals two cards. If they add up to 8, 9, 11, 12, or any other possible number agreed upon before the game is begun they are to be slapped. The child who gets his hand down first on a correct pair gets 5 points, but an incorrect slap is penalized 2 points.

9. The teacher prepares about 200 small cards, perhaps $3'' \times 2\frac{1}{2}''$, the size of half a library card, and puts a number between 0 and 9 on each. The cards are put in a box or bag. The child reaches in and selects two at random and without seeing them. He puts them down, one under the other, or one beside the other if he is to divide them. He keeps on taking cards from the box until he has a number of combinations arranged before him. Then he performs whatever operation is required, has the teacher score his work, and returns the cards to the box. Children may work in pairs, each drawing the cards for the other.

10. Children who are just learning to read numbers may get practice by the following few games. Each child is given a card with a number on it.

This is supposed to be his house number. The children "call" on each other by reading the numbers. The same game may be played with telephone numbers.[5]

11. One child is given a card with a number on it. He gets up and begins to march around the room. The others have cards with a number of dots, lines, crosses, or other small objects on them. Those whose cards contain the same number as that of the marching child get up and march with him.

12. The teacher cuts the numbers from 0 through 9 out of sandpaper. It is best to cut two series. A child is blindfolded. He draws one or more of the sandpaper numbers from a bag or box. He must tell from running his finger over it what number it is. If he draws two he puts them down beside each other on the desk and tells what each digit is and what number the two are together.

13. The class is divided into two or more teams. The teacher puts a combination on the board, erases it, waits a few seconds, and then calls on a member of one team. If he gives the right answer, his team scores one point. If he makes an error, the teacher calls on a child from another team, who can make 2 points if he corrects the error. The teacher continues to put combinations on the board, erase them, and call alternately on the two teams. The children should not be permitted to raise their hands during the game, and any child who nevertheless does so should be ignored.

14. The children form a circle with one child in the middle. Each child has been given a combination in whatever process is being studied. The child in the center has a rubber ball. He calls out a combination, such as 8 times 7, and bounces the ball. The pupil whose combination it is must answer correctly and catch the ball. If he fails in either respect, the child in the center calls a second combination, but if the second child catches it and his answer is right, he replaces the pupil in the center.

15. The children mark out a hopscotch pattern on the floor and number each area within it. Each pupil hops for as long as he can keep on adding the numbers correctly and does not touch any line with his feet. As a variation, bean bags may be thrown into the pattern, each child adding his score.

16. The teacher sits at her desk with two or three open books standing on the desk so that the children cannot see her hands. With a piece of metal or hard wood she taps on the surface of the desk. The children listen. They may call out the totals in chorus or she may call on a particular child after each series of taps. After the children are used to the game, she can tap out larger numbers than a single digit. Three taps, a pause, one tap, another pause, and eight taps would be 318.

[5] This game and the remaining ones are taken from W. S. Guiler, *Objectives and Activities in Arithmetic*, Rand McNally & Company, 1926, 122 pp.

17. The teacher draws a square on the board and then divides it into ninths with two lines running vertically and horizontally. In the nine resulting spaces she writes the nine digits in random order, a different order each time. Then she calls on the children to add the three vertical columns, the three horizontal ones, and the two diagonals.

18. The children make and fill bean bags of different colors. Values are assigned to each color and each pupil tries to throw all the bags into a wastebasket, adding the values of those he gets in. For practice in multiplication he can throw until he gets two in and then multiply their values.

When a pupil has developed concepts and is ready to begin formal drill, there are numerous sets of exercises that can be used. Not every sheet of every exercise is valuable, but a teacher can select those materials that best suit each child's needs. She should have as large a file as possible of exercises, both remedial and general.[6]

3. **Remedial Work with Problems:** The most obvious mode of attack upon defects in problem solving is an analysis of a child's technical vocabulary. He may be examined orally, or, if he reads well enough, he can take a vocabulary test.[7] In any case, the teacher should find out what concepts he lacks and help him to develop the necessary meanings.

It should be added that a failure to read adequately is often a cause of poor work in arithmetic. It often happens that a child who is being given help in remedial reading improves his work in arithmetic because of his clearer images of both words and numbers, or because he has enlarged his vocabulary, or because his eye movements are directed more accurately, or because he has learned how to attend to what he reads, or because he now looks for meaning instead of trying to memorize poorly understood words. Remedial treatment in reading sometimes produces an increase of two or three years in ability to compute and an even greater growth in problem solving. It is always wise to check a pupil's reading as a part of the diagnostic procedure in analyzing difficulties in arithmetic and to give remedial drill in reading if the child needs it.

[6] See, for instance, *Brueckner, Grossnickle, and Merton Work Books,* John C. Winston Company, Philadelphia, Grades 2–6; Buswell-John *Teaching and Practice Exercises in Arithmetic,* Wheeler Publishing Company, Chicago, Grades 3–6, one book for each grade; *Clapp Drill Books in Arithmetic,* Scott, Foresman & Company, Grades 3–8, one book per grade; Clark-Otis-Hatton, *Instructional Tests in Arithmetic for Beginners,* World Book Company, Grades 1–3; De May and McCall, *Standard Test Lessons in Fractions,* Bureau of Publications, Teachers College, Columbia University, Grades 5–8; Ruch, Knight, Greene, and Studebaker, *Economy Remedial Exercises in Fundamentals* and *Economy Remedial Exercises in Problem Solving,* Scott, Foresman & Company.

[7] See pp. 381 ff.

Training in word knowledge and reading comprehension may well be followed by study of a pupil's eye movements, using a mirror if no better equipment is available, while he reads a few verbal problems, numbers, and computational problems. He may wander up and down in a column of figures or have no pattern of movements for short division, for example. When he reads verbal problems he may bog down over each successive number, or perhaps he just skips them altogether. He can be taught to read problems once for meaning only, to disregard the numbers until he sees what the problem means, and then to go over it a second time for numbers. He may be asked to do his thinking out loud, discussing each problem with the teacher.

Once a child can read numbers reasonably well and has built up concepts for them, his best approach to problem solving is the visual representation already mentioned on page 414. At first the teacher has to help him in deciding what to draw or how to arrange the beans or the cardboard money, but soon he should begin to make his own plan. A few samples are shown below:

1. A farmer has 64 sheep in a pasture. He drives 17 of them into a special pen and puts the 9 lambs into another. How many sheep are left?

After the picture is drawn and the amounts are counted, the pupil does the computation in the usual way:

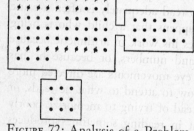

$$64$$
$$-17$$
$$47$$
$$-9$$
$$38$$

FIGURE 72: Analysis of a Problem

2. If Harry earns 75¢ each school day and $2.50 on Saturday, how much did he earn during the week?

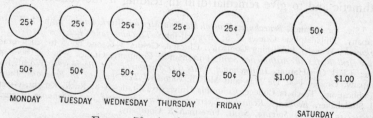

FIGURE 73: Analysis of a Problem

The pupil first draws the diagram and then counts his total. He can see, however, that five days are just alike. He therefore re-solves his problem by the short-cut method: $5 \times 75¢ = \$3.75 + \$2.50 = \$6.25$.

3. Mary's picture of her mother is 6″ x 4″. She put it into a frame that measured 10″ x 8″. How many square inches are there (a) in the picture and (b) in the border?

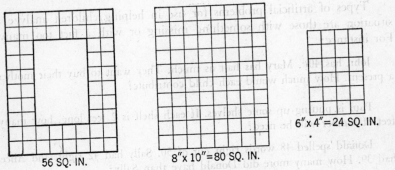

56 SQ. IN.   8″ x 10″ = 80 SQ. IN.   6″ x 4″ = 24 SQ. IN.

FIGURE 74: Analysis of a Problem

After the child has drawn and counted the squares, he can be shown how to calculate the answer:

$$8 \times 10 = 80 \text{ sq. in. in frame}$$
$$6 \times 4 = 24 \text{ sq. in. in picture}$$
$$\overline{56 \text{ sq. in. in border}}$$

This approach is primarily for the building up of concepts and confidence in attacking verbal problems. After a pupil can see through problems without visual aids he can be helped further by being given practice in reading problems without, or with, numbers and in analyzing them. If a child is so fascinated by figures that he cannot skip over them on his first reading, he can be given problems with the numbers left out, such as:

If a boy sold .... papers on Monday before school in the morning and .... papers after school at night, and if he made .... cents on each paper, how much did he earn on Monday?

After he has read a problem of this type, the pupil should be asked such questions as:

What facts does the problem tell you?
What are you supposed to find out?
What facts do you need to find the answer?
Are they all given in the problem?
Would you begin by adding, subtracting, multiplying, or dividing?
Do you get the answer after one process?
If not, which one would you use next?

Types of artificial problems for use in helping children analyze a situation are those with something missing or with a fact too many. For instance:

John has 40¢. Mary has half as much. They want to buy their mother a present. How much would each child contribute?

Paul is putting up some shelves. If each shelf is 2 feet long, how many feet of lumber will he need?

Donald spelled 48 words right out of 50. Sally had 42 right, and Alice had 39. How many more did Donald have than Sally?

After a pupil can get the essential meaning from typical problems and can see his way through at least a one-step problem and preferably through those with two steps, he may be given some help in reading numbers, in case he needs it.

The methodology is the same as that for teaching phrase reading. The best device for the purpose is a Metron-O-Scope, but a teacher can get results with cards. She prepares several "decks," each card containing a two-place number. The cards are manipulated as for phrase reading.[8] When a pupil has learned to grasp two figures at once he may go on to cards containing three-place numbers. Few people can go further, and many children cannot see a longer number than one of two digits at one fixation. Enough children can see three figures at once to make a few trials worth while, but if a pupil does not seem to learn, the drill should be abandoned. After pupils can grasp as many digits at once as their span allows, they will still need practice in reading numbers of three digits until they can proceed through them in an orderly fashion and not jump back and forth through them too many times. Finally, they should be given problems that contain numbers, reading and analyzing them in the same manner already indicated for those without figures.

[8] See p. 173.

D. RESULTS OF REMEDIAL WORK

Reports of remedial work are not numerous, but four may be quoted as illustrative of the results obtained by diagnostic treatment.[9] In one case a small group of sixth grade pupils was given remedial work for one semester. The pupils gained by an amount equal to from 5 to 19 months of normal progress during that time. Two years later 82 per cent of these pupils had made normal or above normal progress in arithmetic. The entire group showed at that time an average grade standing in arithmetic of 9.3—a half grade in advance of their actual placement. A few individual records from this study are presented in Figure 75.

The children whose scores are here presented were paired on the basis of IQ. The experimental member of each pair was given remedial work in 1937 and then returned to his regular classes, where his partner had been all the time. At the end of his training the experimental pupil in Pair A stood well above his partner and maintained this advantage throughout the next two years, during which both received only classroom instruction. In Pair B, the remedial work did not produce results in the year in which it was given, but in later years the pupil from the remedial class gained more than his partner, who, however, did not gain at all. The remedial work did not "take" on the experimental pupil in Pair C until after a year had passed, but during the second year he far outstripped his partner and the normal expectation for his grade. In Pair D, the control pupil was at all times superior to his partner. These individual records show the varying effects that remedial work may have upon children. It is no panacea, but it works oftener than it fails.

In the second experiment, the children were given careful diagnosis covering 25 operations with whole numbers, fractions, decimals, measurement, and percentage. The diagnosis was followed by completely individualized treatment. Most of the pupils responded so well that they were soon doing better work than their normally progressing classmates who had not received such attention. Those with the highest mental ages and the best initial standing improved most.

A third report concerns only eleven children who were doing unsatisfactory work in arithmetic. In computation they ranged from 50 to 80 per cent and in reasoning from 48 to 72 per cent. Most of the

[9] E. O. Bemis and W. C. Trow, "Remedial Arithmetic after Two Years," *Journal of Educational Research*, 35: 443–452, 1942; Fernald, *op. cit.;* W. S. Guiler and V. Edwards, "An Experimental Study of Method of Instruction in Computative Arithmetic," *Elementary School Journal*, 43: 353–360, 1943; and Sister Mary Jacqueline, "An Experiment in the Remedial Teaching of Arithmetic," *Elementary School Journal*, 41: 748–755, 1941.

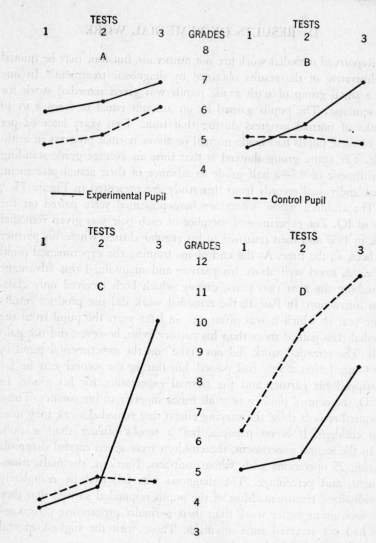

FIGURE 75: Three-Year Progress for Four Pairs of Children

special teaching was devoted to work in the fundamentals, each child studying those combinations and operations that were unfamiliar to him at the start. In six months' time the mastery of fundamentals had risen an average of 23 points, giving a total range of 76 to 100 plus one case still at 52, while the scores in reasoning had advanced 14 points to give a range from 75 to 90 plus two cases still at 50. Of the eleven children, only one did not improve at all, and one did not gain in reasoning.

The errors that children make are often remarkably specific and are therefore all the more easily remedied. For instance, one small boy wrote down correct answers to 74 of the 100 multiplication combinations but missed the following 26:[10]

$$
\begin{array}{cccccccccccccc}
9 & 0 & 4 & 8 & 0 & 9 & 9 & 0 & 7 & 0 & 9 & 0 & 6 \\
\times 7 & \times 2 & \times 6 & \times 8 & \times 7 & \times 0 & \times 4 & \times 1 & \times 9 & \times 6 & \times 0 & \times 4 & \times 0
\end{array}
$$

$$
\begin{array}{cccccccccccccc}
8 & 7 & 5 & 2 & 0 & 4 & 0 & 3 & 1 & 0 & 7 & 0 & 2 \\
\times 0 & \times 0 & \times 0 & \times 6 & \times 3 & \times 0 & \times 5 & \times 0 & \times 0 & \times 8 & \times 8 & \times 9 & \times 0
\end{array}
$$

This child missed every possible zero combination except $0 \times 0 = 0$ and a small assortment of combinations involving, 9, 8, 7, and 6. His one constant error was the multiplication of 0 as if it were a 1. A single explanation of the concept involved eliminated 20 of the 26 errors. A second child, who missed 45 out of a possible 100 addition combinations and had poor arithmetical concepts generally, worked over a period of time at building up ideas and experiences with concrete objects and at drilling himself on the combinations he did not know. At intervals he gave himself tests over the entire 100, keeping track of both his time and his mistakes. The results of his twelve successive tests appear in the table and figure below:

TABLE 78

Results of Remedial Teaching

Test	Number of Errors	Time
1	45	3′ 30″
2	25	3′ 18″
3	13	3′ 45″
4	15	2′ 30″
5	5	2′ 5″
6	6	1′ 58″
7	8	2′ 00″
8	2	2′ 5″
9	0	2′ 2″
10	0	2′ 5″
11	0	2′ 5″
12	0	2′ 6″

FIGURE 76: Graphic Record of Speed and Accuracy

[10] The two cases in this paragraph are taken from Fernald, op. cit., pp. 232 and 233. Figure 76 is used by permission of the publisher.

The last four tests were without error and the time did not appreciably decrease.

If a pupil's work is adequately analyzed, if he is given individual attention, and if he puts his efforts upon the elements that are unfamiliar to him, he is almost certain to improve and he will usually make great gains. A remedial program will not compensate for a low mentality, but it will help a child to use what ability he has to its fullest extent.

E. SUMMARY

A teacher can obtain excellent tests for making a diagnosis of children's errors in arithmetic. The objectivity of the subject matter makes many types of error relatively easy to determine. As in the case of reading, however, many children have failed so often to understand their work that they have developed a deep-seated conviction of hopelessness. More often than not, their work is so poor as to bear out their assumption of inferiority, even though their native intelligence may be good. Even the best of remedial teaching will not cure every child's arithmetical defects, but much can be done, and once in a while a teacher has the invigorating experience of working a minor miracle of remediation. Many of the drill materials, games, and exercises described in this chapter will be found useful in the regular classes for purposes of building up concepts or giving experience with this or that particular type of example.

F. REFERENCES AND PROBLEMS

1. L. J. Brueckner, *Adapting Instruction in Arithmetic to Individual Differences,* University of Minnesota, 1941.
2. L. J. Brueckner, *Diagnostic and Remedial Teaching in Arithmetic,* John C. Winston Company, Philadelphia, 1930, 341 pp.
3. G. T. Buswell and L. John, "Diagnostic Studies in Arithmetic," *Supplementary Educational Monographs,* No. 30, University of Chicago Press, 1926, 212 pp.
4. G. M. Fernald, *Remedial Techniques in the Basic School Subjects,* McGraw-Hill Book Company, 1943, 349 pp.
5. F. E. Grossnickle, *The Teaching of Arithmetic in the Elementary School,* Edwards Brothers, Ann Arbor, 1934.
6. G. Hildreth, *Learning the Three R's: a Modern Interpretation,* Educational Publishers, Inc., Minneapolis, 1936, 824 pp. (Chapters 6, 14, 19, 23.)

7. F. P. Klapper, *The Teaching of Arithmetic,* D. Appleton-Century Company, 2d ed., 1934.

8. R. L. Morton, *Teaching Arithmetic in the Elementary School,* Silver Burdett & Company, Vol. I, *The Primary Grades,* 1937, 410 pp.; Vol. II, *The Intermediate Grades,* 1938, 538 pp.

9. W. J. Osburn, *Corrective Arithmetic,* Houghton Mifflin Company, 2 vols., 1924–1926, 182 and 274 pp.

10. *Twenty-Ninth Yearbook of the National Society for the Study of Education,* Parts I and II, 1930, 749 pp.

To the Student

The following brief projects and exercises are included to give you greater insight both into the problems involved in learning and into the methods used in research. More are listed than are likely to be used in order that you may have some degree of selection.

1. Can you remember in what grade you learned (a) long division, (b) fractions, (c) column addition of several two- or three-place numbers? Does the grade-placement agree with research?

2. Get a statement of the curriculum from any school or system. How does the assignment agree with that given in Table 61?

3. If possible, examine textbooks from each decade from 1840 to 1940 as to the topics taught. What differences are there?

4. From any modern text, select a page of exercises, such as $+\dfrac{34}{19}$, $-\dfrac{431}{124}$, $\times\dfrac{371}{36}$, or $49\sqrt{1452}$ and work them all out. Then analyze the use of each combination. Is the drill given in proportion to difficulty?

5. Let each member of the class write down any 10 examples in long division with a two-place divisor and a four-place dividend. Solve your own examples and then classify them according to Table 64. Combine results from the class.

6. Analyze errors on arithmetic papers from a class of school children. What advice would you give the teacher of the class as to remedial work?

7. Write out 6 verbal problems that you consider bad for children and 6 that you think are good. State why you classify each problem as you have.

8. Read through the verbal problems in an arithmetic text and copy out any that seem to you inappropriate. Why?

9. Analyze a group of two-step problems according to process sequence as given on page 379. Are these problems arranged in order of difficulty, as far as sequence is concerned?

10. Keep a diary for three days of *all* uses you make of arithmetic, in both actual operations and concepts. Put together results for the class.

11. As you read a novel or other general book, keep a list of any arithmetical terms that appear, such as *dozen, amount, proportion, half, height, weight, acre, discount, wholesale,* and the like. To what extent is even nonmathematical matter permeated by arithmetical concepts?

12. Divide the class into pairs. Each member should write down for his partner a sum in column addition, five digits wide and 12 digits high —hard enough to make his partner work! Then each should watch the other's eye movements in a mirror. Can you tell when your partner runs off the end of his attention span?

13. Following the suggestions on pages 415 ff., fold and tear paper to represent the following fractions: 1/5, 4/5, 3/8, 5/8, 2/3, 5/6, 1/6, 7/8.

14. Make diagrams for the problems in an arithmetic text, following the suggestions on pages 422-423.

15. Using the plan on pages 415-417 solve the following examples:

$$1/2 \times 1/3 = \qquad 1/2 \div 1/3 =$$
$$2/3 \times 5/6 = \qquad 1/2 \div 3 =$$
$$1/5 \times 1/2 = \qquad 1/4 \div 1/2 =$$
$$3/4 \times 1/3 = \qquad 1/3 \div 1/4 =$$

16. Select from the class two students who have always liked arithmetic and two who have always disliked it. Can you find out why?

17. Have the instructor give a test in the division of fractions. Pick out 3 or 4 students who did poorly and analyze their difficulties.

18. Suppose you are a teacher in a city of 68,497 people. How could you give the children a concept of how large their city is?

19. Debate the use of such "crutches" as are recommended on pages 349 and 352.

20. Copy a number of examples in fractions from current textbooks. Are the rules and patterns given on pages 266 and 267 adequate for handling them?

21. Write a brief history of someone you know who disliked arithmetic and always did badly in it, giving all the information you can gather as to the reasons for the attitude and inability.

22. Assume that $1 + 1 = 2$ can be learned by a given class of children in three repetitions. How many would you expect the same children to use for $7 + 1, 2 + 3, 5 + 5, 4 + 7, 6 + 5, 8 + 7, 9 + 8$?

23. Debate the reliability of the grade-placement for the topics given on pages 327-330.

24. What counting games or other simple exercises can you suggest for building up the number concepts of first grade children?

25. Suppose you are to teach short and long multiplication to a class and that you wanted to know which pupils were ready to begin. What elements would you put into a readiness test?

17. Have the instructor give a test in the division of fractions. Pick out 3 or 4 students who did poorly and analyze their difficulties.

18. Suppose you are a teacher in a city of 68,477 people. How would you give the children a concept of how large their city is?

19. Describe the use of such "crutches" as are recommended on pages 349 and 352.

20. Copy a number of examples of fractions from current textbooks. Are the rules and patterns given on pages 266 and 267 adequate for handling them?

21. Write a brief history of someone you know who disliked arithmetic and always did badly in it, giving all the information you can gather as to the reasons for the attitude and inability.

22. Assume that $1 + 1 = 2$ can be learned by a given class of children in three repetitions. How many would you expect the same children to use for $7 + 1$, $2 + 3$, $3 + 5$, $5 + 4$, $7 + 6$, $5 + 8$, $7 + 9$, $8 + 9$?

23. Debate the reliability of the grade-placement for the topics given on pages 282-350.

24. What counting games or other simple exercises can you suggest for building up the number concepts of first grade children?

25. Suppose you are to teach short and long multiplication to a class and that you wanted to know which pupils were ready to begin. What elements would you put into a readiness test?

APPENDICES

———————————————————————————————

TERMS AND CONCEPTS DERIVED FROM
THE USE OF TESTS

PRECEPTS FOR THE TEACHER

———————————————————————————————

I · Terms and Concepts Derived from the Use of Tests

Modern research in education is based upon the results of objective tests in all subjects. Tests are used to measure either individual or group progress, to express goals and the relation of classes or children to them, to measure the results of teaching, to compare one method of instruction with another, to test intelligence, to analyze and diagnose difficulties, to measure degrees of mastery of subject matter, and generally to check upon experimental procedures. Tests have become an integral part of school life, and every teacher needs to understand their nature and to be familiar with their use. Throughout the present volume there is such constant reference to the use of tests that it seemed advisable to include a few pages about them so that the reader may be able to remedy an inadequate background of information.

Some students who read this book will quite recently have had a course on tests. Others will have had such a course but long enough ago to have forgotten a proportion of the material. A few students will take the course in the elementary school subjects before that on tests and their use in school. To help equalize these differences in preparation, this appendix has been written.

The presentation in this appendix is not intended as an exhaustive discussion of the many problems involved in the construction or use of tests. It is written expressly to supply those facts, concepts, and technical words or phrases that readers of the book will need but may not yet know.[1]

The kind of tests to be described are objective and standardized.

[1] For good general texts on tests and their use in elementary schools, see M. E. Broom, *Educational Measurements in the Elementary School,* McGraw-Hill Book Company, 1939, 345 pp.; H. A. Greene and A. N. Jorgensen, *The Use and Interpretation of Elementary School Tests,* Longmans, Green & Co., 1936, 530 pp.; A. E. Traxler, "The Use of Test Results in Diagnosis and Instruction in the Tool Subjects," *Educational Research Bulletin,* No. 18, 1936, 74 pp.

The first term refers to their form. If children are asked to answer in writing such a question as: *What is a tributary?* some of them will produce replies that are difficult to score. Some teachers would call certain of these questionable answers right, some would call them wrong, and others would give them half credit. If, however, the question reads: *What is a tributary? a small hill near a large one, a country town that sends its produce to a city, a large branch of a river, a long strip of land reaching out into the sea,* and if the children are told to select and mark the right answer, the scoring will be the same, no matter how many teachers mark it. Objective tests are those that are so arranged as to keep the scoring identical from one person to another. A test is standardized if it has been given to a wide assortment of children within the grades or ages to which it is applicable and if the scores have been averaged, so that a teacher can know what score is to be expected from pupils at a given stage of development. Thus a reading test may have norms— the name used for the average score per grade—of 18 points for Grade 3, 42 for Grade 4, 69 for Grade 5, and 92 for Grade 6. When a teacher gives such a test she can compare the results for her particular class with the norms and find out how her work compares with the average for her own or other grades.

A. METHODS OF STATING TEST RESULTS

For some tests the results are expressed in terms of grade norms, the average score per grade. For others, there are age norms, the average score per age. A few tests have both. If a number of tests in different subjects have been given, a pupil's record may read as in Table 79.

TABLE 79

Sample Norms

	Grade	Age
Arithmetic	4.6	9.3
Spelling	3.1	7.9
Handwriting	6.2	12.6
Reading	4.0	8.3
Intelligence	4.2	9.6

These results mean that this pupil's scores would place him in the upper half of the fourth grade for arithmetic, in the lower half for both reading and intelligence, in the low sixth grade in handwriting, and in the low third in spelling. His *arithmetic age* would be 9.3 years, his *spelling age* 7.9 years, and so on. By summarizing test results in this way, one can get a total picture of a child's standing. If the pupil in the above example were in the low fourth grade at the moment, he might well be excused from handwriting and allowed to put the extra time on his spelling, in which he is retarded a full year below his other subjects.

When age scores are used there may be further refinements with a wide use of abbreviations. Thus, MA stands for mental age, RA for reading age, AA for arithmetic age,[2] and so on. If one wants to compare these levels of development with the level that a pupil should have reached, in view of his chronological age, one works out a ratio. For intelligence tests, the mental age is divided by the chronological age. Three examples appear below:

TABLE 80
Derivation of IQ

John	*Mary*	*Fred*
MA $=10.2$	MA $=10.7$	MA $=10.2$
CA* $=10.2$	CA $= 7.9$	CA $=14.6$
$\frac{10.2}{10.2}=1.00$ IQ	$\frac{10.2}{7.9}=135$ IQ	$\frac{10.2}{14.6}=69$ IQ

* CA means chronological age. In some tests, notably the Binet, the ages are reduced to months instead of years and decimal fractions.

These intelligence quotients are read as 100, 135, and 69. They mean that John has exactly the mental development one would expect of a child who is 10.2 years old, that Mary is 35 per cent further developed mentally than is average for her age, and that Fred has reached only 69 per cent of the mental development that he should have at 14.6 years. The abbreviation for the intelligence quotient is IQ.

In some schools the results of reading or arithmetic tests are similarly expressed in quotients, but in this case the reading or arithmetic age is compared with the mental, not the chronological age, on the principle that a child's achievement and mental ages should be the same. This assumption is not entirely justified, but teachers sometimes need to understand what the reading and arithmetic quotients mean, regardless

[2] This abbreviation is commonly used for achievement age—a measure based upon achievement in several school subjects.

of their reliability. The three examples in Table 81 show the method of determination.

TABLE 81
Derivation of Quotients in the School Subjects

John	Mary	Fred
MA = 10.2	MA = 10.2	MA = 10.2
RA = 9.6	RA = 11.7	RA = 6.6
AA = 11.4	AA = 13.9	AA = 7.1
$\frac{9.6}{10.2} = .94$ RQ	$\frac{11.7}{10.2} = 1.14$ RQ	$\frac{6.6}{10.2} = .64$ RQ
$\frac{11.4}{10.2} = 1.11$ AQ	$\frac{13.9}{10.2} = 1.36$ AQ	$\frac{7.1}{10.2} = .69$ AQ

John has an RQ (reading quotient) of 94 and an AQ of 111. His reading is not quite as high as his mental age would lead one to expect, while his arithmetic is a little higher. Mary's RQ and AQ are 114 and 136, showing that she does even better work in both fields than her mental age would suggest she could do. Fred is not only slow intellectually (his IQ was 69) but he does not learn even up to what mental capacity he has.

Another method of expressing standing on a test is to use percentiles. In this case, one conceives of the test scores as being distributed from high to low in 100 equal steps, or percentiles, as indicated in Figure 77.

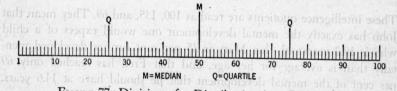

FIGURE 77: Division of a Distribution into Percentiles

The fiftieth percentile is the median, or the middle score when all scores are arranged in order of magnitude. Percentiles have meanings as follows:

If a child scores at the 10th percentile, 10 per cent of other children his age (or grade) score below him and 90 per cent score above him.

If he scores at the 47th percentile, 47 per cent score below him and 53 per cent above.

If he scores at the 99th percentile, 99 per cent score below him and only 1 per cent above.

And so on for all percentiles from 1—below which no one scores—to 100—the highest score. The 10th, 20th, 30th, 40th, 50th, 60th, 70th, 80th, and 90th percentiles are called deciles; the 25th and 50th are quartiles. Each percentile contains 1 per cent of all the scores, each decile 10 per cent, and each quartile 25 per cent.

A teacher needs to be familiar with these various ways of expressing test scores because experimental results are presented in these and similar terms. Indeed, it is only since the development of the testing movement that there have been experiments in the modern sense, so that it is only natural that experimenters in teaching methods, for instance, should use the special vocabulary of testing in describing their results.

B. TYPES OF TEST

Tests may be divided into those that are general and those that are diagnostic. The former measure progress in such a general way that the results are useful mainly to compare the standing of groups with each other or with the norms. They are often not reliable for individual scores, and they do not tell why a class is either good or poor—merely that it is. General tests are, therefore, of relatively little value to a teacher. Diagnostic tests, while not all equally diagnostic, do tell a teacher in more or less detail what error is being made by which child. This exactness of result is possible because of the way a diagnostic test is made. Suppose, for instance, that an investigator wants to test skills in decimal fractions. He first analyzes the papers of several thousand children in the division of decimal fractions and perhaps finds that they have made eleven different kinds of error. He then makes a test that has eleven subdivisions, one for each type of mistake. When Miss X gives this test, the scores on the different parts tell her that Alfred makes Mistakes 4 and 6 but no others, that Ellen makes Mistake 8, and that Christine fails on Parts 5, 9, and 11. With this information at hand, Miss X is ready to show each child exactly what to do to remedy his or her particular misunderstandings. Because of the relatively low value of the general test for a teacher and the high value of a good diagnostic test, teachers are urged to use the latter whenever a matter of teaching is involved. Because of its usefulness, the diagnostic test has been called the "teacher's test."

C. USE OF TESTS IN CONTROLLED EXPERIMENTS

The modern science of education is based essentially upon research into what should be taught and when, upon analysis of what errors children make and why, and upon controlled experiments of what teaching methods are most effective. Educators study the needs of children and adults for each item of subject matter in each school subject to find out what should be included in the curriculum and what is not needed. Psychologists study children to discover what is hard or easy for them, what interests them, what errors they commonly make, why they make them, what mental age they need for mastering this or that item or skill, and so on. Teachers often contribute to both these types of investigation, and sometimes committees of teachers carry out whole programs of research. Most information about methods of teaching are derived from controlled experiments carried on by teachers. These experiments are called "controlled" because the investigator keeps under control any irrelevant factors that might distort the significance of his results. It is by no means enough to show that a group of children who could spell 22 per cent of a given list of words in October can, as a presumed result of some special type of work, spell 94 per cent the next June, because such an experiment does not "control" the factor of growth. If the children had been given no teaching at all they would have improved their spelling somewhat merely because they had had eight months more of living and experiencing. In order to find out what effect the teaching had, one must compare the results with those obtained from children who merely grew. It may turn out that Nature did a great deal more than the teacher!

Since one group of pupils cannot simultaneously be subjected to a given type of teaching and to no teaching, and since because they grow too fast, the same children cannot be used in successive semesters, first without and then with teaching, one has to have a "control" group that is as similar to the experimental group as possible. The usual procedure is to pair each child in the experimental classes with a pupil in the control classes, so selected as to be of the same mental age, the same chronological age, the same sex, and the same standing in each school subject that has any relevancy to the experiment. The control group is then either given no training in the skill under consideration, or else it is given only the usual type of training, while the experimental group receives whatever treatment forms the basis of the experiment. The gain made by the control pupils must be subtracted from that of the experimental pupils, before one can know how much more gain there is under experimental conditions than would have been made anyway by a group of children of the same age, sex, ability, and previous training. If the control group gained 22 words per minute in their rate of reading under ordinary teaching conditions in six months' time, while a group of closely paired children gained 68 words per minute during the same period and with the same amount of time per day for practice, then the extra 46 words must be the result of the method. This type of experiment is quoted so often that its nature should be understood.

Tests are therefore essential in the modern school, and the controlled experiment—using tests as the measures of its success or failure—is the basic procedure for finding out what methods in teaching or learning in one or more school subjects are most productive of desirable results.

II · Precepts for the Teacher

The earlier form of this text contained, at the end of each chapter, a series of precepts for the teacher. Some users of the book liked this section, and some did not. Instead of including the suggestions in each chapter, therefore, the precepts have been gathered together and put into an appendix that may be used or not, at the discretion of the instructor or at the desire of the student. Since the imperative mood is supposed to produce action, the maxims have been put into the form of commands.

Perhaps the first, most important, and most useful of the principles may be expressed in the following "rule":

1. **Teach so as to avoid as many errors as possible, but if errors appear, analyze them at once and teach correctively until they are eliminated.**

The various studies of error tell teachers what mistakes are common and hence which ones to help children avoid. A good teacher can prevent many mistakes from appearing at all. For instance, a left-handed child will never form the habit of hooking his arm across the top of his desk if his teacher teaches him the correct position and grip on his pencil from the first day of school. With even the best of teaching, however, children are going to make some errors. One essential thing for the teacher to remember is that more practice of the kind already used is not as likely to cure the error as to grind it in by repetition. For instance, if a child of 10 reads by using an average of 18 fixations and 7 regressions per line, he will not be likely to improve by more reading of equally difficult material without analysis and remedial instruction, because every page he reads helps to fix his incorrect habits a little more deeply. General practice gives experience in using more and more easily what the pupil has at the moment. If what he has is correct but too slow, then general practice is all he needs; but if what he has is wrong, then further practice of the same kind is the last thing that will help him.

2. Do not try to teach a child any subject—or any section of any subject—until you know he is ready to begin.

In the chapters dealing with readiness to read, to do arithmetic, to spell, to write, and to compose, tests have been described by means of which readiness may be measured. Even if a teacher cannot obtain the necessary tests, she can use her own observation to note which children show too great immaturity, especially during the initial phases of a new subject. Readiness is an outstanding problem for primary teachers, but it continues to be important in the upper grades. Children who are immature reveal their condition by their behavior. Once a teacher has become aware of the problem, she soon begins to evaluate such behavior correctly. There is no better way to prevent errors and thus to avoid the need of remedial teaching than to make sure that children are ready to begin a subject before they are allowed to start.

3. Arrange the work so that each child knows what he is supposed to do, spends his drill periods exclusively upon what he does not yet know, and can tell when he is done with each unit of work.

The teacher of a class knows that a given type of work or drill will continue only for a predetermined length of time, but the pupils often have no way of knowing that it will not go on forever. The teacher knows also what the objective is and where the class stands in relation to it. The pupils may know none of these things, and they may become understandably discouraged. They are easily reduced to the condition of the pupil who said to the writer about his work in English, "When Teacher wants 500 words I give her 500—if she says 700, OK, she gets 700." This boy had no idea of where he stood, what the assignments were for, how long they might go on, or what he did that was either right or wrong. Compare this situation with a group of seventeen children in a small room, all studying spelling, but each working on a more or less different list of words, because each was studying only those words he did not know out of a given fifty for that week. At the beginning of the week the class average had been 39. At the end, eleven children made perfect scores, four missed one word, one missed two, and one missed four. These children knew just what they had to do, they knew where they stood, and they knew when they were done.

4. Individualize work in the drill subjects and make the children responsible for their own progress.

In the lower grades the teacher has to do the individualizing and take the responsibility, but as soon as possible the children should learn how to find their own weaknesses—with some help from the teacher—and should take over the responsibility for their own remedial drill. It is not likely that any two children in a room need to study exactly the same spelling words, exactly the same number combinations, exactly the same uses of punctuation, exactly the same vocabulary, the formation of exactly the same letters, or the solution of exactly the same problems. A teacher cannot keep forty individual programs in her mind at once, and even if she could, she could not carry them all out simultaneously. It is essential for the children to understand that each is to practice what he needs. They require some help in locating their weaknesses and in finding out what to use for practice materials, but they can and should learn to give themselves the kind and amount of drill that they need.

5. Examine the subject matter to be taught to see if it is based upon the results of research, and consider the size of the daily or weekly "dosage."

A teacher is advised to study the list of spelling words for her grade, the words in the reading vocabulary, the operations and problems in arithmetic, the books to be read, the writing skills to be mastered, and the subjects for composition, for the purpose of comparing each with the results of research. To be sure, a teacher is not usually at liberty to deviate much from the course of study, but she can know what the facts are and can be ready with suggestions for changes in the curriculum should they be needed. In the meantime she can underemphasize such elements as have been shown by research to be unimportant. It is hard to compare the actual with the proper dosage, because there is so little information as to how much children at different ages can manage, and a teacher has to rely largely upon her own judgment as to whether or not the assignments are too long for adequate mastery.

6. Teach pupils the special words and the special skills they will need to read the materials in each subject.

Learning to read is a process not confined to the daily reading class. Children have to learn how to read history, how to read geography, how to read hygiene, how to read arithmetic. They cannot simply transfer with slight modifications the skills acquired by narrative reading. Hand in hand with the early assignments in the content subjects should go instruction in reading the material.

Ignorance of technical vocabulary is the most persistent single cause of difficulty in reading specialized subject matter. Teachers are urged to determine for themselves the central core of necessary words or to acquire a good published list, and then to concentrate upon mastery of those terms needed in each section of the text before the section is begun. Children will learn the words quite readily if the teacher puts adequate stress upon them.

7. Relieve strain both physical and emotional by using short drill periods and by keeping a child's work within his capacity.

Children should never be pushed beyond their capacity to withstand pressure. If arithmetic problems are too hard, if handwriting drill lasts too long, if a teacher demands generalizations too soon, if the load of different things to do in long division requires a longer attention span than a child has, or if an assignment asks for skills a pupil does not possess or thinks he does not possess, the result is likely to be a disorganization of whatever mastery has already taken place. Ability to stand pressure varies greatly from one child to another. A teacher should be so alert to the first symptoms of overstrain that she notices them in individual pupils and stops each before he has time to become overtired. Fatigue produces errors and sets up emotional attitudes that prevent future learning and may, if extreme, operate to cause confusion of what the child learned before he became exhausted.

8. Utilize children's interests for all they are worth.

Interest is a powerful motive for getting work done. Intrinsic interest in the work itself is the best type, but any interest that can be attached to schoolwork will furnish more or less drive. The boy who wants to make a bookshelf can develop knowledge of measurement that he might never acquire through drill and practice that did not touch his interests. The little girl who collects stamps and the small boy who collects bottle caps can acquire many concepts by counting and grouping their treasures. The boy who is thrilled by football games will read avidly stories of athletic heroes, even though English classics leave him unmoved. A pupil may learn to spell more words in a day than he has in the previous month if he writes a letter that is important to him. And so on, for all subjects.

Lack of interest is a powerful force in preventing children from learning. Healthy, normal children will not read many books they do not like or write on topics that do not appeal to them. They will not be docile under unmotivated drill in spelling and penmanship. They see no great value in solving arithmetic problems that do not touch their daily lives. The teacher has numerous motives for wanting the children to learn, and some teachers are able to carry the class along on their enthusiasm, but it is better if children are urged forward by their own interests rather than by the teacher's. The most powerful motive is a genuine liking for the work, but nearly as strong is an appreciation of its usefulness in one's daily life in or out of school.

9. Relate work in school to life outside school and relate the work of every subject to that of all other subjects.

The best way to connect life in and out of school is to derive the materials of instruction from children's activities by teaching them to spell the words they spontaneously use in writing letters, to compute the answers to such problems as they meet, to read about the matters that interest them, to write well enough to meet the practical needs of their daily lives. Transfer from inside the school to outside it is vital to the unified development of the pupils. Transfer from one subject to another is also important because of its influence on learning. A teacher can get better transfer than usual if she shows pupils how to apply the measurements taught in arithmetic to the construction work of the art class, or if she uses review spelling lessons as drill material in handwriting, or if she derives topics for written work from the books the children have read, or if she asks pupils to write—as practice materials in sentence structure—single-sentence answers to geography questions. The more transfer one gets, the better, because the fewer things have to be learned over again in a new situation.

One of the results from psychological and educational research is the proof that transfer does not take place to more than a fraction of its possible extent unless teachers make the possibilities perfectly clear to the learners. It is not enough that a chance to make a transfer should exist. A high school pupil who knows that the Latin verb *paro* is a first conjugation verb and can give its forms correctly may spell *separate* as *seperate* because he does not see the common element between the two words. Even college students have been known to inquire if the cranial nerves discussed in psychology were the same cranial nerves that they had already learned in physiology! Elementary school children are even less able to transfer skills and items of knowledge from one field to another.

10. Concentrate upon accuracy and do not stimulate a child to perform a task rapidly until he can perform it well.

A letter that is inaccurately formed, an addition combination with a wrong answer, an incorrectly spelled word, an inaccurately read sentence are of no use in themselves and may act as handicaps to subsequent learning. In the world outside the schoolroom, the need for accuracy is equally great. If a child can perform a simple task both accurately and rapidly, so much the better, but if one quality or the other has to be sacrificed, it must be speed. In the interests of making accuracy paramount it is well to penalize guessing, so that a child will learn to omit answers he is not sure of. On the other hand, if a pupil is, for instance, forming his letters correctly, he should speed up his reactions until he reaches the normal rate for his age; aside from the waste of time from writing more slowly than necessary, the presumable degeneration that will take place when the pressure for adult writing speed descends upon him will be greater than it would have been had he developed a greater speed in school. Children do not need to dawdle, but even that is preferable to great speed without accuracy.

11. Give rewards to those who do well.

Various phychologists have proved the truth of the old saying that nothing succeeds as well as success. Children learn faster if they know there is a reward of some sort waiting for them. The reward may be a few words of praise from the teacher, or a gold star, or one's name on a list, or a little free time, or a half hour in the school library, or a chance to run errands, or a posting of one's work on the bulletin board for all to see. These immaterial rewards are worth more than material ones in driving power. It is a good idea to let one's standard of what is worth rewarding vary from child to child and to praise whatever any pupil does that shows effort and is above his usual level. Thus the dullard who usually misses six out of six arithmetic problems should be praised on the day he misses only five, while the bright child should receive similar recognition only when he does something worthy of his ability.

448

12. Use all possible aids to comprehension—models, pictures, examples, objects, collections, or dramatizations—to give meaning to subject matter.

If children can build a model of an Indian village, examine many pictures of Indians, study collections of objects in a museum, and dramatize a story about Indians, they are more likely to understand the beginnings of American history than if they merely read what is in a book. Physical features of the landscape can be portrayed in a small-scale model, by means of which children can see the difference between a river, a sound, an inlet, a bay, and a gulf, or between an arroyo, a gulch or coulee, a ravine, a canyon, a gorge, and a valley. Pictures of a foreign country are especially helpful in arousing interest in it, and moving pictures are even better. In the first grade, pupils learn words more easily if the corresponding objects or pictures of them are to be seen, and they build up number concepts or other abstract ideas sooner if they have objects to manipulate.

The central core of ideas in this book is concentrated into the dozen general principles above enumerated and discussed. These ideas are certainly not unique. They are, rather, the same suggestions for guidance in teaching that have been current in the educational world at one time or another since the days of ancient Greece. Their worth has been presented, discussed, and more or less proven at intervals of about 400 years ever since. Within the past three decades the progressive movement has discovered them all over again. The main thing is to get them used by every teacher. It is to be hoped that these principles, well established by tradition and well proven by modern educational experiment, will be adopted by more and more teachers in each subsequent generation, so that the average teaching of tomorrow may at least equal and perhaps surpass the best teaching of today.

Index

accelerated children, difficulties in handwriting, 298, 299
accuracy, 338, 344, 446
activities in English, 106, 258, 272, 287
addition combinations, 331
  both forms, 332
  hard and easy, 334
addition facts needed for multiplication, 353
addition of fractions, illustrated, 416
adult handwriting, 221
adult readers, 20, 21
alphabet
  errors per letter, 294, 295
  for sinistrals, 214
analysis of error, see diagnosis and errors
analysis of problems, 391 ff.
analysis of single letter, 218
arithmetic age, 146, 439
arithmetic fundamentals
  basic skills, 326
  concepts, 333
  "crutches," 349, 352, 353
  grade placement, 327 ff.
  long division, 357 ff.
  long multiplication, 354, 355
  mental age needed, 327 ff.
  skills, 326
  theories of, 324
arithmetic quotient, 438
arm movement, 208
artificial problems, 424
astigmatism, 6
attention span in column addition, 348
auditory maturity, 141
avoidance of error, 351, 442
Ayres Scale, 306

barbarisms, see pseudo errors and grammar
beginning arithmetic, see readiness
blackboard reading, 18
blending sounds, 52

book lists, 155 ff.
  for slow readers, 117

canceling 363, 365
capitalization, 262, 268, 274
carrying
  in addition, 345 ff.
    errors in, 346
  in multiplication, 353
case studies, 7, 9, 30, 33, 56, 62, 63, 82,
    104, 147, 181 ff., 217, 279
characteristics of problems, 375 ff.
checking work, 100, 360, 361
children's interests, see interest
children's uses of arithmetic, 395 ff.
  amounts, 397
  types of problem, 396
chorea, see nervous children
choric speaking, 259
clearness of impression, 242
colloquialisms, see pseudo errors
column additions, 345 ff.
  combining numbers in, 350
  up or down, 350
combining of numbers in adding, 350
comics, 120, 121
compensation, 13, 15, 16, 163
complexity
  in reading, 3
  in verbal problems, 378
  in written work, 252
complex sentences, see sentence structure
composition, see written English
comprehension, general
  depth of, 91
  errors in, 92
  factors influencing, 89 ff.
  improvement of, 95 ff.
    exercises, 98 ff.
    lessons in, 97
  reading needs, 87 ff.

449